THEORIES OF CHILD ABUSE AND NEGLECT

THEORIES OF CHILD ABUSE AND NEGLECT

Differential Perspectives, Summaries, and Evaluations

Oliver C. S. Tzeng,
Jay W. Jackson, and
Henry C. Karlson

PRAEGER

New York
Westport, Connecticut
London

Copyright Acknowledgment

The authors and publisher gratefully acknowledge permission to quote from the following:

Reprinted with permission from *Child Abuse and Neglect, 6,* Max Lesnick-Oberstein, Leo Cohen, and Arend J. Koers, Research in the Netherlands on a theory of child abuse: A preliminary report, Copyright 1982, Pergamon Press plc.

Library of Congress Cataloging-in-Publication Data

Tzeng, Oliver C. S.
    Theories of child abuse and neglect : differential perspectives,
  summaries, and evaluations / by Oliver C. S. Tzeng, Jay W. Jackson,
  and Henry C. Karlson.
     p. cm.
  Includes bibliographical references and index.
  ISBN 0–275–93832–8
  1. Child abuse. 2. Child molesting. I. Jackson, Jay W.
II. Karlson, Henry C. III. Title.
HV713.T94 1991
362.7′6—dc20   90–46516

British Library Cataloguing in Publication Data is available.

Library of Congress Catalog Card Number: 90–46516
ISBN: 0–275–93832–8

First published in 1991

Praeger Publishers, One Madison Avenue, New York, NY   10010
An imprint of Greenwood Publishing Group, Inc.

Printed in the United States of America

The paper used in this book complies with the
Permanent Paper Standard issued by the National
Information Standards Organization (Z39.48–1984).

10 9 8 7 6 5 4 3 2 1

Contents

Figures and Tables   xi

Preface   xv

Part I: Introduction   **1**

1. Child Abuse and Neglect: Epidemiology and Theorizations   3

   Historical Overview   3

   Prevalence   4

   Impact   6

   Defining Child Abuse and Neglect   7

   Theoretical Conceptions   8

   Compilation of Theories   10

   Development of Paradigms   10

2. Summary Description of Paradigms   13

   Individual Determinants Paradigm   14

   Sociocultural Determinants Paradigm   17

   Individual-Environment Interaction Paradigm   19

   Offender Typologies Paradigm   20

   Family Systems Paradigm   22

   Parent-Child Interaction Paradigm   23

   Sociobiological Paradigm   24

   Learning/Situational Paradigm   26

   Ecological Determinants Paradigm   28

Part II: Theorizations of Physical Abuse   **31**

3. Theories of Child Physical Abuse   33

   Individual Determinants Paradigm   33
      Psychiatric Theory of Physical Abuse   33
      Intrapsychic Theory of Physical Abuse   37
   Sociocultural Determinants Paradigm   41
      Social Systems Theory of Physical Abuse   41
   Individual-Environment Interaction Paradigm   46
      Resource Theory of Physical Abuse   46
      Three-Component Theory of Physical Abuse   48
      Social Psychological Theory of Physical Abuse   51
      Symbiosis Theory of Physical Abuse   53
      Social Interaction Theory of Physical Abuse   56
      Three-Factor Theory of Physical Abuse   58
      Exchange/Control Theory of Physical Abuse   62
      General Stress Theory of Physical Abuse   66
   Offender Typologies Paradigm   69
      Physical Abuse Typology   70
   Family Systems Paradigm   72
      Family Systems Theory of Physical Abuse   72
   Parent-Child Interaction Paradigm   76
      Attachment Theory of Physical Abuse   76
      Parental Acceptance-Rejection Theory of Physical Abuse 79
      Transactional Theory of Physical Abuse   81
      Encounter Theory of Physical Abuse   84
      Cognitive/Behavioral/Developmental Theory of Physical Abuse   87
   Sociobiological Paradigm   90
      Sociobiological Theory of Physical Abuse   90
   Learning/Situational Paradigm   94
      Social Learning Theory of Physical Abuse   94
      Situational Theory of Physical Abuse   98
      Coercion Theory of Physical Abuse   100
   Ecological Paradigm   103
      Ecological Theory of Physical Abuse   103

Choice Theory of Physical Abuse   106

Multilevel Theory of Physical Abuse   108

Part III: Theorizations of Incest and Sexual Abuse   113

4. Theories of the Incest Taboo   115

   Individual Determinants Paradigm   115

   Biological Theory of the Incest Taboo   116

   Sociocultural Determinants Paradigm   118

   Normative/Structural Theory of the Incest Taboo   118

   Individual-Environment Interaction Paradigm   121

   Biosocial Theory of the Incest Taboo   121

5. Theories of Incestuous Abuse   125

   Individual Determinants Paradigm   125

   Humanistic Theory of Family Sexual Abuse   125

   Sociocultural Paradigm   127

   Patriarchal Theory of Father-Daughter Incest   128

   Individual-Environment Interaction Paradigm   131

   Biosocial/Attachment Theory of Incest   131

   Family Systems Paradigm   133

   Family Survival Theory of Incest   134

   The Endogamous Incestuous Family Theory   140

   Ecological Determinants Paradigm   143

   Grounded Theory   143

6. Theories of Sexual Abuse   151

   Individual Determinants Paradigm   151

   Psychoanalytic Theory of Child Sexual Abuse   151

   Psychiatric Theory of Child Sexual Abuse   154

   Sociocultural Determinants Paradigm   156

   Socialization Theory of Sexual Abuse   156

   Individual-Environment Interaction Paradigm   160

   Four Preconditions Theory of Sexual Abuse   161

   Offender Typologies Paradigm   164

   The Male Sexual Offender Typology   164

   Typology of Female Sexual Offenders   167

Part IV: Theorizations of Psychological Maltreatment   171

7. Theories of Psychological Maltreatment   173

   Ecological Paradigm   173

   Ecological Context Theory of Psychological Maltreatment   173

   Family Breakup Theory of Psychological Maltreatment   177

   Ecological/Deficiency Needs Theory of Psychological Maltreatment 180

Part V: Theorizations of Neglect   187

8. Theories of Neglect   189

   Individual Determinants Paradigm   189

   Personalistic View of Child Neglect   190

   Individual-Environment Interaction Paradigm   193

   Social Interaction Model of Child Neglect   194

   Three-Factor Model of Child Neglect   197

**Part VI: Content and Process Evaluations
and Summaries   201**

9. Introduction to the Psychosemantic Process Model of Human
   Behavior   203

   Subjective and Objective Cultures   203

   Psychosemantic Process and Evaluation Systems   204

   Five Ecological Levels of Human Life Experiences   205

   Culture Ecology Units   205

   Process Model and Functional Steps   207

   Nature and Dynamics of Individual Components   208

   Relationships among Components   215

10. Summary and Evaluation of Theories via the Psychosemantic
    Process Model   217

    Evaluation of Major Topical Issues in Terms of the Ten
    Culture-Ecology Units   218

    Summary of Topical Issues   218

    Nature of Topical Issues in Each Culture-Ecology Unit   219

Evaluation of Topical Issues in Terms of Ten Psychosemantic
Model Components   224

   Summary of Topical Issues   224

   Conclusions   225

Physical Abuse   225

Incest Taboo   229

Incestuous Abuse   230

Sexual Abuse   231

Psychological Maltreatment   231

Neglect   232

Functional Qualities of the Psychosemantic Process Model   233

11. Perspectives from the Psychosemantic Process Model   235

  General Topical Structure of Content Issues   236

   Who: Offenders   236

   What: Types of Offenses   237

   Whom: Victimizations   238

  Psychosemantic Approach to Service Network   239

   Seven Comprehensive Service Domains   242

12. The Nature of Scientific Knowledge and Theories   247

  Knowledge Acquisition and the Scientific Method   247

  The Philosophy of Science   247

  Formal Theorization in the Social Sciences   248

  Forms of Theories   248

  The Components of a Theory   248

  The Functions of a Theory   250

  Scientific Self-Regulation Mechanisms   250

  Theory Construction   251

  Theory Evaluation   252

  The Fallacies and Pitfalls of Theories   252

  Issues and Limitations in Theoretical Analyses   253

  Conclusions   253

13. Evaluation of Theoretical Paradigms from Science   255

  Method and Procedure   255

x   Contents

Physical Abuse   265

Incest Taboo   271

Incestuous Abuse   272

Sexual Abuse   275

Psychological Maltreatment   278

Neglect   280

Summary and Discussion   281

Conclusion   287

Part VII: Cameo Application and Conclusions   **291**

14. Impact of Differential Theories on the Legal Profession:
    A Cameo Evaluation of Expert Witnesses   293

    Definitions and Characteristics of Expert Witnesses   293

    Responsibilities of Legal Professionals in Using Expert
    Witnesses   294

15. Summary and Conclusions   297

    Definition and Typology Issues   298

    Empirical Research Limitations   300

    Specific Research Deficiencies   301

    Specific Focuses for Communitywide Services   303

    Status of Contemporary Theorizations   310

    Prospects for Developing Integrated Theories   312

References   315

Index   339

Figures and Tables

FIGURES

Description of Paradigms

2.1   Three Paradigmatic Continua of Child Abuse and Neglect
Theorizations   14

Physical Abuse Theories

3.1   Schematic Representation of Psychiatric Theory   34

3.2   Schematic Representation of Intrapsychic Theory   39

3.3   Schematic Representation of Social Systems Theory   41

3.4   Schematic Representation of Resource Theory   46

3.5   Schematic Representation of Three-Component Theory   49

3.6   Schematic Representation of Social Psychological Theory   51

3.7   Schematic Representation of Symbiosis Theory   54

3.8   Schematic Representation of Social Interaction Theory   56

3.9   Schematic Representation of Three-Factor Theory   59

3.10 Schematic Representation of Types of Child Abuse   60

3.11 Schematic Representation of Exchange/Control Theory   62

3.12 Schematic Representation of General Stress Theory   67

3.13 Schematic Representation of Offender Typology Theory of
Physical Abuse   71

3.14 Schematic Representation of Family Systems Theory   73

3.15 Schematic Representation of Attachment Theory   77

3.16 Schematic Representation of Parental Acceptance-Rejection
      Theory   80
3.17 Schematic Representation of Transactional Theory   82
3.18 Schematic Representation of Encounter Theory   84
3.19 Schematic Representation of
      Cognitive/Behavioral/Developmental Theory   87
3.20 Schematic Representation of Sociobiological Theory   91
3.21 Schematic Representation of Social Learning Theory   95
3.22 Schematic Representation of Situational Theory   98
3.23 Schematic Representation of Coercion Theory   101
3.24 Schematic Representation of Ecological Theory   104
3.25 Schematic Representation of Choice Theory   106
3.26 Schematic Representation of Multilevel Theory   109

Incest Taboo Theories

4.1   Schematic Representation of Biological Theory   116
4.2   Schematic Representation of Normative/Structural Theory   119
4.3   Schematic Representation of Biosocial Theory   122

Father-Daughter Incest Theories

5.1   Schematic Representation of Humanistic Theory   126
5.2   Schematic Representation of Patriarchal Theory   128
5.3   Schematic Representation of Biosocial/Attachment Theory   131
5.4   Schematic Representation of Family Survival Theory   135
5.5   Schematic Representation of Endogamous Theory   141
5.6   Schematic Representation of Grounded Theory   143

Sexual Abuse Theories

6.1   Schematic Representation of Psychoanalytic Theory   152
6.2   Schematic Representation of Psychiatric Theory   154
6.3   Schematic Representation of Socialization Theory   157
6.4   Schematic Representation of Four Preconditions Theory   162
6.5   Schematic Representation of Male Sexual Offender Typology 165
6.6   Schematic Representation of Typology of Female Sexual
      Offenders   168

Psychological Abuse Theories

7.1   Schematic Representation of Ecological Context Theory
      (Microview)   175
7.2   Schematic Representation of Ecological Context Theory
      (Macroview)   175
7.3   Schematic Representation of Family Breakup Theory   178
7.4   Schematic Representation of Ecological/Deficiency Needs
      Theory   182

Neglect Theories

8.1   Schematic Representation of Personalistic View   190
8.2   Schematic Representation of Social Interaction Model   194
8.3   Schematic Representation of Three-Factor Model   198

Content and Process Evaluations

9.1   Ten Model Components of the Psychosemantic Process Model   207
11.1 Conceptual Inquiries about Child Abuse and Neglect   236
11.2 Seven Service Domains of Child Maltreatment   243
12.1 Components of a Scientific Theory   249
12.2 Functions of a Scientific Theory   251

TABLES

1.1   National Incidence Report on Child Abuse and Neglect for
      1986   5
1.2   Paradigms of Child Maltreatment and Their Member Theories   11
3.1   Intervention Strategies of the Intrapsychic Theory   40
3.2   Variables Significantly Associated with Child Abuse Potential
      Scores   102
4.1   Biological Characteristics of Children of Incest versus Control
      Group   117
9.1   Examples of Human Life Experiences in Ten Culture-Ecology
      Units   206
10.1 Summary of Topic Issues in Ten Culture-Ecology Units   220
10.2 Summary of Topic Issues in Ten Model Components   226
11.1 Relations between Behavioral Dispositions and Emotions   241

13.1   Process Evaluation Domains and Content Criteria for
       Scientific Theory Construction   256

13.2   Evaluation of Paradigms in Terms of Theoretical Form   260

13.3   Evaluation of Paradigms in Terms of Theoretical Components   261

13.4   Evaluation of Paradigms in Terms of Scientific Theory
       Functions   262

13.5   Evaluation of Paradigms in Terms of Scientific Self-Regulation
       Factors   263

13.6   Evaluation of Paradigms in Terms of Evaluative Criteria   264

13.7   Total Rank Scoring of Paradigms in Each Maltreatment Type
       for Each Evaluative Domain   265

13.8   Achievement Levels of Child Abuse and Neglect Theoretical
       Paradigms on 23 Evaluative Criteria   283

13.9   Overall Achievement of Nine Theoretical Paradigms on Four
       Evaluative Domains   285

13.10 Achievement Levels of Six Maltreatment Types on Four
       Evaluative Domains for Theory Development   286

14.1   Criteria for Evaluating Background Orientations of Expert
       Witnesses   295

15.1   Approaches of Theoretical Paradigms to Seven Service
       Domains in Child Abuse and Neglect   306

Preface

This book was prepared under the impetus of desperate need, in academic institutions and clinical and social services, for a comprehensive introduction to diverse theorizations of child abuse and neglect etiologies. History documents that child maltreatment has existed since the beginning of human civilization. However, the formal recognition of the problem of child maltreatment has a relatively short history. It was not until the 1960s that the gravity and scope of child abuse and neglect became a topic of serious study by professionals. During the past three decades, professionals in different occupational fields, especially medicine, psychiatry, social work, law, sociology, and psychology, have been actively involved in the identification, intervention, treatment, and prevention of child victimization and its detrimental consequences. Specifically, in studying the etiology of child maltreatment, many theoretical viewpoints have been proposed in the literature and used for clinical practice as well as academic research.

Based on different disciplinary orientations, these proposed viewpoints are rather diverse in conceptualization of basic human nature, child maltreatment causalities, and intervention strategies. Theoretical differences have also resulted in diverse empirical research programs on the cognitive, affective, linguistic, social, and behavioral sequelae of child maltreatment. Therefore, during the past two decades, child abuse and neglect has become a rapidly blooming field in both theoretical development and empirical evaluation.

Despite the existence of many theorizations, availability of empirical research findings, and implementation of various service programs, the prevalence of child abuse and neglect has not decreased, but rather has significantly increased in recent years. Economic and human costs of maltreatment are astronomical. The continuing detrimental impact on victimized children, at-risk families, and various societal institutions calls for a complete reevaluation of child victimization etiologies and societal approaches to combating the problem.

Based on an in-depth evaluation of various issues and resources involved, we have identified that current efforts of academic and service professionals have frequently been limited by (1) narrow focuses on some specific content issues, (2) single disciplinary orientations, (3) separate or disjointed efforts in designing services, (4) partial and frequently biased knowledge and skills in implementing programs, and (5) fragmental program evaluation. These limitations have severely undercut the efficiency and efficacy of human and monetary resources.

Recognizing the severity of child abuse and neglect problems, and also the responsibilities of applied research professionals, we have developed a research and service organization in Indiana—the Consortium of Child Abuse and Neglect Resources and Information Services. The Consortium has two major functions: (1) evaluation of theoretical and empirical issues about child victimization at the community, state, national, and international level and (2) education of professionals and college students (at both undergraduate and graduate levels) regarding theories, principles, and strategies in combating child abuse and neglect.

To realize the first function, we have analyzed over 140,000 child abuse and neglect cases that were substantiated or indicated for maltreatment in Indiana, and we have also compiled numerous relevant publications and educational materials. For the second function, we developed and implemented many education and training programs on prevention, intervention, and treatment of child victimization for professionals and the general public.

These activities were directed under the principles of (1) comprehensiveness in all disciplinary orientations, (2) integration of diverse theoretical approaches, (3) coordination among all available services, (4) community-based development of service systems and programs, and (5) multidisciplinary considerations of all issues pertaining to the seven Ws of child abuse and neglect—*who* did *what* to *whom* and *when, where, how,* and *why?*

Our efforts are consistent with the new service and educational recommendations advocated by the National Center for Child Abuse and Neglect. Through a three-year grant, we have established a multidisciplinary graduate training program on child abuse and neglect at Indiana University–Purdue University at Indianapolis as one of the ten model programs in the nation. As a central core of educational and research activities, an effort was made to conduct a comprehensive evaluation and integration of diverse theorizations concerning child abuse and neglect. This resulted in the compilation of over 40 different theories, models, and perspectives from the literature dealing with etiologies of child maltreatment.

As the subtitle suggests, this book contains three major products of our efforts—*description of individual theories, summaries across different theoretical views,* and *an evaluation of the current status of theorizations.* Under the first objective, all theories are organized, in accordance with their emphasis on maltreatment issues, into six "types" of child maltreatment—physical abuse, incest taboo, incestuous abuse, sexual abuse, neglect, and psychological maltreatment. In accordance with their different disciplinary orientations, these theories were further organized under nine theoretical paradigms. Etiologies of each type of maltreatment were then explained in terms of individual theories within different paradigms.

For description of individual theories (and paradigms), a common format was used that includes six sections: (1) *key concepts* used by each theory, (2) a schematic *graphic representation* of each theoretical account, (3) *theoretical foundations* concerning human nature and its development process, (4) *basic principles* of the causalities, correlates, and dynamics of child maltreatment, (5) *empirical evidence* in support, or dispute, of each theoretical account, and (6) *general evaluation* of each theorization.

In completing these six topical sections for each theory, the description of basic principles and key concepts was relatively easy because most materials could be summarized directly from the literature. The sections on theoretical foundations and empirical evidence become a bit more difficult because they usually required additional literature searches for pertinent information and, in many cases, required subjective evaluation and inferences. The most difficult part was the development of schematic graphic representations and general evaluation of individual theorizations because both tasks required comprehensive knowledge of each theory and its application to empirical situations. Furthermore, the evaluation section needed background information from many disciplinary orientations, including contemporary, as well as historical, perspectives. Henry C. Karlson, a coauthor of this book, was a formally trained historian prior to his career as a professor of criminal law and evidence. His knowledge and experiences in both history and criminal law significantly facilitated the completion of the evaluation section.

Under the second objective of this book—summarization of content issues across different theorizations, a substantive evaluation of the content issues of all individual theories and paradigms was performed in reference to the two theoretical frameworks of the psychosemantic model of human behaviors: (1) *ten culture by ecology units* defined by two (subjective and objective) cultures and five ecological levels (idiosystem of individuals, microsystem of families, exosystem of communities, macrosystem of society, and geopolitical system of international relations) and (2) *ten model components* (background characteristics, long-term stressors, short-term stressors, trend-coping mechanisms, cognitive evaluation system, affective evaluation system, behavioral disposition, habits, overt behaviors, and social/institutional consequences). These two summaries of the contemporary theoretical accounts of child victimization represent perhaps the first systematic organization of current knowledge, principles, and strategies dealing with child abuse and neglect etiologies. They can be used not only for further evaluating and/or improving individual theories, but also for integrating some new theoretical viewpoints.

In meeting the third objective, a process evaluation was conducted to assess the quality of all theories in reference to five requirement domains of theory construction in science: (1) form of theory construction, (2) decomposition of theoretical components, (3) functions of scientific theories, (4) scientific theory self-regulation mechanisms, and (5) general evaluation criteria. Within each domain, separate content criteria were generated to characterize each theory in terms of three levels of sufficiency in theory construction.

To illustrate the utilities and differential influences of various theorizations on professional practice, a cameo analysis of theoretical and empirical issues was conducted on the topic of expert witness in legal proceedings. Finally, as the final conclusions from evaluating all theorizations and their empirical evidence, six major topics were discussed in Chapter 15: issues on definitions and typologies of child maltreatment, empirical research limitations, specific research deficiencies, major focuses for communitywide services, status of contemporary theorizations, and prospects for developing integrated theories.

Overall, in writing this book, fifteen chapters were generated and organized in seven major parts for presentation: (1) introduction, (2) theorizations of physical abuse, (3) theorizations of incest and sexual abuse, (4) theorizations of psychological maltreatment, (5) theorizations of neglect, (6) content and process evaluations and summaries, and (7) cameo application and conclusions.

In time perspective, of 46 theorizations reviewed, 24 were from publications in the 1980s. The development of these theories can generally be characterized in terms of four increasing directions toward

1. *diversity* in theorizing causalities from individual conditions (stress or personality defect) to social and situational circumstances;

2. *complexity* in postulating relations from simple cause-effect linkage to multiple covariations;

3. *systemization* in compiling information from simple aggregation to hierarchical organization; and

4. *subjective cultural emphasis* in focusing content issues from tertiary intervention (medical, legal, and sociological) modes to primary and secondary preventions.

This book is prepared for three audiences: practitioners, researchers, and the general public. For clinical practitioners, the materials compiled in this book represent different theoretical orientations and strategies that are targeted for clinical application in dealing with child abuse and neglect problems. That is, for clinical practices and social services, professionals from different disciplinary orientations and occupational assignments can not only systematize knowledge and skills currently used in their own fields, but can also understand those used by other professions. Comparisons of theorizations from their own disciplines with others can improve the competency of clinical services from a multi-disciplinary approach.

For the purpose of primary prevention of child maltreatment in the general public, and also secondary prevention in at-risk groups, the materials presented in this book can serve as theoretical foundations for both formal education and information acquisition regarding the topics of who (perpetrator) did what (maltreatment behaviors) to whom (victims) and why, when, where, and how. With such information, the general public can conduct self-evaluation of certain circumstances and conditions that might put children in vulnerable positions for victimization.

For research purposes, this book seems especially important because in the past, particularly before the late 1970s, the vast majority of research on the causalities and consequences of child maltreatment has been criticized as being nontheoretically conceived, methodologically inadequate, and unscientifically executed and interpreted. It is encouraging to note that to alleviate this problem of the 1970s, theory and research on the cause-effect relationships in child victimization processes have improved significantly in the 1980s. Professionals have stressed both the importance of normal scientific development of theorizations and the need for considering the multifaceted nature of maltreatment and intervention.

As reviewed and summarized in this book, efforts have generated a large number of topic issues and theoretical inferences, but unfortunately they also reflect diversity, complexity, and inconsistency among the existing theorizations regarding the etiologies of child abuse and neglect and associated recommendations for clinical practices.

Therefore, despite the significant "diversities" of the 1980s in theory development, clinical and academic researchers are now facing the critical problems of uncertainty and controversy. In the absence of comprehensive, multidisciplinary theory development, future researchers have to work toward the refinement of existing theories through integration with other theoretical perspectives. Such pursuit of refinement and integration will lead to a new wave of evolution in theory development. Therefore, the decade of the 1990s will naturally become the "multidisciplinary integration" period of child abuse and neglect theorization.

In this evolutionary process, Parts VI and VII of this book—particularly the summaries of results from both content evaluation of theoretical topic issues and process evaluation of theory construction requirements in "normal science"—appear to represent an excellent repertoire of basic knowledge about child maltreatment etiologies. It provides an in-depth evaluation of the complexity, strengths, and weaknesses of current theorizations.

Overall, the analysis of current theories and their perspectives about clinical strategies suggests that the history of child abuse and neglect theorizations has passed through three general stages of progression—the "speculations" of the 1960s, the "introspective explorations" of the 1970s, and the various diversities of the 1980s. For the "multidisciplinary integration" of the 1990s, the future success in a rigorous, continuing development of child abuse and neglect theorization as a mature science may rely on the application of compiled materials presented in this book and also on the full adoption of summarative-inductive and functional-deductive forms of theory construction. Toward this overall goal, the materials organized and presented in this book should be considered as only the interim results of our initial compilations, evaluations, and integrations. As the evolution process increases in depth and in scope, we will continue to keep up with its progress by updating the descriptions, summaries, and evaluations of future theories and their empirical supports. Some of our present compilations and categorizations of theories into different paradigms may be considered incomplete, or even inaccurate, from various disciplinary perspectives. Such weaknesses will be evaluated and improved along with the future updating endeavor.

The initiation and completion of this book is credited to four sources of energies: *inspiration, encouragement, support,* and *assistance.* I have been a teacher all my adult life, from teaching school children at elementary, middle, and high school levels in Taiwan, to teaching adult students at undergraduate and graduate levels at the University of Illinois and at Purdue University School of Science for the past 18 years. As my own two children were model students growing up in the United States (now in college), I would never have dreamed, 5 years ago, of being involved in the field of child abuse and neglect. However, since the president of a local child abuse and neglect crisis center (Jack Sourwine) made an unusual request for my assistance, I have become deeply involved in the field: in fact, the past 4 years saw over 80 percent of my professional activities dedicated to child abuse and neglect. Since then, news reports about abused and neglected children and their families repeatedly intensify my conviction and dedication to be part of the societal "loving and rescuing force." I deeply believe that it is the call of almighty God for all capable professionals and society at large to help those helpless children.

The initial development of the Consortium and the subsequent implementation of all planned activities have received numerous encouragement from students, friends, community service professionals, and university colleagues. Special acknowledgments are extended to Lois Drake (Director, Marion County Welfare Department), James M. Miller (President, Family Service Association, Indianapolis), Ken Phelps (Executive Director, Children's Bureau, Indianapolis), Don Hamilton (Chief, Bureau of Community Health Services of Marion County Health Department, Indianapolis), Sara Meadows (former president, Child Abuse Council of Marion County), Peggy Eagen (Executive Director, Indiana Chapter of the National Committee on the Prevention of Child Abuse), Tom Rodgers (Chief, Sex Offense Branch, Indianapolis Police Department), Irv Katz (Executive Director, Community Service Council of Central Indiana), and Dr. William M. Plater (Executive Vice Chancellor and Dean of the Faculties, Indiana University-Purdue University at Indianapolis).

The initial planning and completion of this task is a part of the curriculum development for the Multidisciplinary Graduate Training Program on Child Abuse and Neglect. This development and other related tasks, such as compilation of community resources and generation of profiles of statewide victimization records, have received financial support from many sources, including the U.S. Department of Human Services, the Indiana Department of Human Services, the

Indianapolis Foundation, the Health Foundation of Greater Indianapolis, and the Lilly Endowment. Without such financial support, it would have been impossible to develop the Consortium and subsequently to implement the various activities that led to the development of multidisciplinary graduate training programs from the federal fund. Therefore, we are indebted to these public and private agencies that make this publication possible. I personally wish to express special thanks to Susan Weber (Director, National Center on Child Abuse and Neglect), Jean Merritt (former director, Indiana Department of Human Services), Kenneth Chapman (Executive Director, Indianapolis Foundation), Betty Wilson (Executive Director, Health Foundation of Greater Indianapolis), and Willis K. Bright, Jr. (Program Director, Community Development of Lilly Endowment, Inc.).

Preparation and completion of this book has been assisted by many scholars and students related to the Consortium and the Multidisciplinary Training Program. In particular, I would like first to thank Deborah L. Clark for her loyalty, dedication, and competency in editing, transcription, and manuscript preparation. I would also like to extend my appreciation to three assistants: Brandt T. Steele, who contributed to the evaluation of the child neglect theories; Miguel Gandarillas, who conducted a thorough reference check for the manuscript, and Lynn Pratt Keiser, who made a thorough critique of an early version of the manuscript and the final proofs. Finally, I am appreciative of the students from one of the training classes (Pro-Seminar II: Multidisciplinary Graduate Perspectives on Clinical/ Treatment Aspects of Child Abuse and Neglect) who participated in reviewing portions of the manuscript: Deborah L. Clark, Dorothy K. Clark, Sabrina L. Haake, Lynn P. Keiser, Elizabeth Kerr, Alice L. Loveday, Mary Ann Marvin, Stephen T. Serino, Robon M. Vanek, Cynthia A. Wagner, and Joni Schwartz.

Part I

Introduction

Chapter One

Child Abuse and Neglect: Epidemiology and Theorizations

HISTORICAL OVERVIEW

Throughout history, children have been the victims of various forms of serious maltreatment (DeMause, 1974; Holland, 1988). In fact, some archaeological evidence suggests that child abuse and neglect has been ongoing since prehistoric times (Harcourt, 1986). For centuries, prevailing norms in many cultures have considered severe physical punishment as necessary for maintaining discipline; transmitting educational, cultural, moral, and religious ideas; pleasing gods; and for expelling evil spirits (Radbill, 1974).

It has been documented that rituals of the ancient Greeks and Romans included the sacrificial killing of children (Vallois, 1961) and that fathers, according to the Patria Protestas of 700 b.c., once had the legal right to sell, mutilate, or kill their children (Holland, 1988). The ancient Greeks favored killing retarded or deformed children in order to strengthen their society (Radbill, 1974). They reasoned that children were property and that "there can be no injustice to one's own property" (Aristotle quoted in Russell, 1945).

DeMause (1974) concluded that the prevailing child disciplinary technique prior to the eighteenth century was the application of severe beatings and that nearly half of the European population perished in infancy by improper management or neglect.

Throughout history, Judeo-Christian influences have had a tremendous impact on many child-rearing practices. The Bible has been used as a rationale and justification for harsh punishment of children (cf. Holland, 1988; Harcourt, 1986; Aries, 1962). The basic belief that aggression is necessary for proper moral training is reflected in biblical passages such as: "Thou shalt beat him with the rod, and shalt deliver his soul from hell" (Proverbs 23: 14) and "He that spareth the rod, hateth his son, but he that loveth him chasteneth him betimes" (Proverbs 13: 24) (Holland, 1988).

There are many examples. In analysis of references in the Bible about children, two major themes become apparent: (1) the concept of obeying and honoring one's parents and (2) the necessity of using strong, even extreme disciplinary measures. However, this does not mean that Christians have condoned or do condone child abuse. In fact, religious organizations have been one of the most reliable sources of child protection and advocation throughout the United States and other countries. All religions have a tremendous impact on the way people conduct their lives. In terms of the rights of children, Christianity has been a significant force in shaping our cultural norms and individual behaviors, including the widespread acceptance of the physical punishment of children.

Only recently has the victimization of children been internationally recognized as a significant social problem that requires direct and immediate attention from society (French, 1984; Holland, 1988). In fact, an association to prevent animal cruelty was in force before any similar association existed to protect children: The Society for the Protection of Cruelty to Children was established in New York City out of an effort by the Society for the Protection of Cruelty to Animals in 1875 (Kempe & Helfer, 1972).

The first White House Conference on Children was held in 1909. By 1912, legislation was commenced to create a Federal Children's Bureau to deal with issues regarding the welfare of children in all classes of people (Holland, 1988). Eventually, children became recognized as a special class of people, not just "little adults." In the 1940s and 1950s the fields of child psychology and social work emerged, and more advanced social programs for children were established. Television started to bring about a heightened public awareness of the child abuse and neglect problem in the 1960s. In 1962, amendments to the Social Security Act required each state "to develop a plan to extend child welfare services, including protective services, to every political subdivision" (Thomas, 1972). Also in 1962 "The Battered Child Syndrome" (Kempe et al., 1962) was published, marking the point at which the study of child abuse and neglect became a distinct academic subject.

Since then, the extent of child maltreatment has become increasingly recognized as a significant and devastating social problem. Efforts to understand, treat, and prevent child maltreatment are progressing at many levels. Numerous academic journals routinely publish articles on the subject. There also have been many books published on various aspects of child abuse and neglect, ranging from clinical case evaluations to empirical research studies. However, despite increased awareness and efforts, studies suggest that the extent and seriousness of the problem has not wavered. For illustration, issues on the prevalence and impact of child victimization are briefly summarized as follows.

PREVALENCE

Child abuse and neglect is a widespread social problem that affects all types of family structure and all segments of the population, regardless of individual

Table 1.1
National Incidence Report on Child Abuse and Neglect for 1986

Category of Maltreatment		Number of cases	Percentage of population
Abuse	Physical	358,300	.57
	Sexual	155,900	.25
	Emotional	211,100	.34
	Total	675,000	1.07
Neglect	Physical	571,600	.91
	Emotional	223,100	.35
	Educational	292,100	.46
	Total	1,003,600	1.59
All Types		1,584,700	2.52

Note: Figures were based on 1986 revised definitions.

Source: U.S. Department of Health and Human Services (1986).

differences in cultural background, geographic location, or economic status. (However, as discussed in later sections, some groups are at greater risk of child abuse and neglect than others. For example, the poor, uneducated, and young have been considered most vulnerable). Based on some conservative estimates, one to six million children are abused and neglected each year in the United States (American Humane Society, 1986; Kempe & Helfer, 1972; Wolfe, 1985). According to the National Incidence Study (U.S. Department of Health and Human Service [DHHS], 1988), the overall rate of countable reported maltreatment cases in 1986 was 25.2 children per 1,000, representing 1,584,700 total countable cases. A summary of the findings are presented in Table 1.1.

In 1986 more than one and one-half million children were reported as victims of some type of maltreatment. Most of these were cases of neglect (63%), and nearly half (43%) were cases of abuse. The most frequent type of neglect was physical, followed by educational neglect and then emotional neglect (DHHS, 1988). The most frequent type of abuse was physical; the second most common was emotional; and the third was sexual.

In terms of severity, 60 percent of the reported cases of maltreatment resulted in moderate injuries, 19 percent in endangerment, 11 percent in probable injuries, 10 percent in serious injuries, and .1 percent in fatalities. Reports of maltreatment increased by 66 percent in comparison with the 1980 incident rate. Physical abuse reports more than doubled and sexual abuse reports more than tripled since 1980. Neither emotional abuse nor any form of neglect showed significant changes in incidence rates since 1980. Some researchers believe these figures may not be indicative of actual increases, but may simply reflect improved reporting procedures. Whether or not the incident is actually rising, the prevalence of child abuse and neglect remains excessive and the impact severe.

IMPACT

The devastating impact of child maltreatment on individuals, families, and society at large is well documented in empirical and clinical studies. Many serious long-term effects have been linked to child maltreatment, including mental retardation, intellectual and intelligence handicaps, impaired aggressive impulse control, diminished ego competency, reduced reality testing, and poor interpersonal relationships (Alfaro, 1981). Significant behavioral effects have also been traced to child maltreatment. These include uncontrollable severe temper tantrums, extreme withdrawal, rebelliousness, hostility, and overt violence. Every year, between 1,000 and 4,000 children in the United States die as a result of abuse (Alfaro, 1984).

While the overt effects of abuse, such as scarring, broken bones, mutilation, and loss of sensory function, are extremely serious, the most intense and enduring damage is usually psychological (Garbarino, Guttmann & Seeley, 1986; Hart, Brassard & Germain, 1987). Since psychological maltreatment is the most difficult type of abuse to define and study, it is also very difficult to assess its effects. One common measure of psychological maltreatment is parental rejection. A 40-year longitudinal study by McCord (1983) has indicated that of 232 "abused," "neglected," "rejected," and "loved" males, rejected children had the highest rates of juvenile delinquency and were more likely to remember their parents as being harsh. However, these observations do not reveal whether the children were "rejected" because of their high rate of delinquency or if the high rate of delinquency led to the rejection by or harshness of the parents.

In addition, child abuse and neglect has a serious impact on the structure and dynamics of society. In the longitudinal study, McCord (1983) also found that among the 97 neglected and abused children, 44 (45%) had later become criminal, alcoholic, and/or mentally ill, or had died prior to age 35, possibly as a consequence of the abuse. Another study of nearly 7,000 children found a positive relationship between child abuse and juvenile delinquency or ungovernability (Alfaro, 1984).

In summary, it appears that child maltreatment results in increased antisocial activities. Maltreated children have more serious personal problems and engage in more antisocial activities and violence toward themselves and others. When older, they end up in juvenile and adult correctional facilities at higher rates than children from the general population (Alfaro, 1984). It is evident that child abuse and neglect is a problem that affects not only the individuals and families directly involved, but all sectors of society. Therefore, in order to deal with this problem, it is necessary for all professionals from all aspects of human ecology (individual, family, community, society, world) to become involved. Hence, some basic issues such as definitions, etiological dynamics, and theories about child abuse and neglect should be well delineated and understood by all professionals.

DEFINING CHILD ABUSE AND NEGLECT

Estimates of the prevalence and impact of child maltreatment vary across different professions and service institutions. The major reason for such discrepancies is that different professions have used different definitions of child abuse and neglect.

The Federal Child Abuse Prevention and Treatment Act of 1974 defined maltreatment as "the physical or mental injury, sexual abuse, negligent treatment, or maltreatment of a child under the age of 18." The definition used by the National Incidence Study, conducted by the U.S. Department of Health and Human Services (1988), includes only children under the age of 18 who were noninstitutionalized and dependent on parent(s)/substitute(s) at the time of the maltreatment. In both definitions, children were counted as maltreated only if harm to the child was objectively demonstrated. This relatively strict definition was later revised to include an *endangerment standard* in which cases are counted if a child's health or safety is endangered through abusive or neglectful treatment.

In addition to the definition provided by the federal government, each state has its own definitions as working guidelines for public and private agencies. However, because it is difficult to define terms such as *chronic* and *severe,* child abuse and neglect terminology remains complex and ambiguous. Inability to agree on definitions leads to problems in cross-study analyses, in cross-state comparisons, and in the integration of empirical findings with theoretical considerations.

Many other definitions of *abuse and neglect* are reported by clinicians and researchers in the child maltreatment literature. None are accepted by all professionals and none are free of ambiguity. Often definitions are not comparable or reliable, and they lack operational standards.

For example, some researchers have characterized maltreatment by acts of commission (abuse) and omission (neglect) (Halperin, 1979; Watkins & Bradbard, 1982). Under this approach, child maltreatment is defined in terms of four broad types: (1) physical, sexual, and emotional abuse; (2) physical, medical, emotional, and educational neglect; (3) abandonment; and (4) multiple maltreatments that involve more than one type. Even within each type of maltreatment, many definitions are still debatable concepts across different professions.

In addition, physical abuse has been defined using three different approaches (Keller & Erne, 1983): The first approach defines abuse in terms of *actual behaviors and outcomes.* Straus (1979), for example, defined abuse as "an attack by a parent involving punching, kicking, biting, hitting with an object, or using a knife or gun." This approach has the advantage of being objective and minimizing inference about the underlying rationale for the attack (Keller & Erne, 1983).

The second approach defines abuse in terms of the perpetrator's *intention* (Burgess, 1979; Gelles, 1980). For example, Smith (1984) defines abuse as "any nonaccidental physical injury to a child inflicted by a caretaker." This definition is more accurate in reflecting the meaning of "abuse" because it takes into account intentions and acknowledges the possibility of accidents. However, this approach is less objective and invites all kinds of subjective interpretations. As a result, any evaluation attempt using this approach will inevitably run into measurement and validity difficulties.

The third approach defines abuse with a consideration of *cultural norms*. Parke and Collmer (1975), proponents of this view, define abuse as "any child who receives non-accidental physical injury (or injuries) as a result of acts (or omissions) on the part of his parents or guardians that violate the community standards concerning the treatment of children." Definitions of sexual abuse have also been approached with cultural norms in mind.

Problems are even more severe in defining other forms of maltreatment such as psychological maltreatment and neglect. For example, Lourie and Stefano (1978) have set forth a two-level definition of psychological maltreatment that consists of a broad definition for mental health professionals and a more exact definition for those involved in legal actions. Garbarino, Guttmann, and Seeley (1986) define psychological maltreatment as a concerted attack by an adult on a child's development of self and social competence. They consider maltreatment as a *pattern* of psychologically destructive behaviors in five forms: the rejecting, isolating, terrorizing, ignoring, and corrupting of a child. At least one of the five forms, corrupting of a child, cannot be defined without reference to cultural norms. The other forms may, in some instances, also reflect cultural norms (e.g., no intent to harm the child). Since problems of definition are linked to basic assumptions of child abuse and neglect, this book has special significance because it delineates numerous assumptions of separate theories and integrates them into a common framework.

THEORETICAL CONCEPTIONS

Recognition of the seriousness of child maltreatment has resulted in part from changing concepts of childhood and children's rights and in part from the activities and influence of various pressure groups. Since its initial recognition in the early 1960s, child maltreatment has been defined and analyzed from many perspectives, including those of the legal, medical, nursing, psychological, psychiatric, educational, social work, developmental, sociological, political, anthropological, and feminist perspectives. There remain a lack of agreement *among* these various disciplines and also fractions *within* each discipline. As a result, different theoretical perspectives and empirical strategies have been created among professionals concerning the definition, etiology, and development of child abuse and neglect, as well as the different methods to prevent, intervene, and treat the problem.

Specifically, theories concerning the etiology of child abuse and neglect are badly fragmented in the literature (Keller & Erne, 1983; Martin & Walters, 1982; Mathias, 1986). As stated by Martin and Walters:

The theorizing that characterizes the literature in child abuse is heterogeneous in nature. There is no parsimonious set of principles, no model, no paradigm which provides a basis for integrating all the findings which have been mentioned. Although theorizing concerning the determinants of child abuse exists, considerable effort is yet to be undertaken to provide order to the findings.

This lack of consistency and integration has resulted in an overall failure to effectively reduce the problem of child abuse and neglect (French, 1984).

To remedy these problems, an interdisciplinary approach to child maltreatment has been emphasized in the 1980s. This approach strongly focuses on cooperation and coordination of different professionals in handling child abuse and neglect cases regarding such issues as assessment, treatment plans, and data sharing. Unfortunately, under this approach, professionals still maintain their own theoretical disciplinary orientations, working routines, and preferred evaluation criteria. The various disciplines are interested in their own missions and roles. Therefore, even within a framework of coordination, different disciplines remain separate and independent with conflicting goals and conflicting interests.

Specifically, in the area of theoretical disciplinary orientation, over 40 theories, models, and/or perspectives have been proposed to address etiological issues of child abuse and neglect. From this conglomerate of theorizations, a large number of strategies for intervention, treatment, and evaluation have been proposed because the theoretical foundations of these theories, models, and/or perspectives are not all consistent and in fact are frequently conflicting. (Note: For the sake of convenience, we will use the terms "theories," "theoretical perspectives," and "theorizations" interchangeably in this book for addressing the issues of different theoretical foundations.)

In the literature of child abuse and neglect, few systematic reviews of these theories and their empirical or supporting evidence have been done. Meanwhile, the prevalence of child abuse and neglect and the severity of its impact have not decreased. In fact, some report a steady increase during the past decade (Russell, 1986; Tzeng, Jacobsen & Ware, 1988).

Academic researchers, as well as service professionals, are equally frustrated with the *inability* of current service systems to effectively combat child abuse and neglect. There is a clear need for a new national effort to address child maltreatment in terms of a comprehensive reevaluation of all related issues, including theoretical conceptualization, intervention strategies, educational programs, treatment approaches, and longitudinal impact evaluation.

To meet such national needs and also to alleviate the fragmental nature of the current service delivery system, the most important component appears to be the assessment and integration of the diverse theories advanced by researchers to explain child abuse and neglect. It is our hope that through this effort a comprehensive theoretical framework can be developed that will (1) provide a comprehensive common foundation within and among various disciplines, (2) facilitate the analysis and integration of information from all disciplines, and (3) erode the definition and conceptual problems that impede progress in the field.

For this reason, this book is designed for four major purposes: (1) compilation and description of 46 reported theories, models, and perspectives about child abuse and neglect etiologies, (2) substantive evaluation of major content issues of these theories, models, and/or perspectives in terms of the common theoretical framework of the "Psychosemantic Process Model of Child Abuse and Neglect" by Tzeng, Hanner, and Fortier (1988), (3) process evaluation of the properties of these theorizations in terms of theory construction requirements in science, and (4) integration and summarative evaluation regarding the status of existing theories, their strengths and weaknesses, major similarities and conflicts, and quality and efficiency under the scrutiny of a rigorous scientific theory construction. The needs and prospects for developing integrated theories will also be assessed. For these purposes, the methodologies used for compiling different theoretical perspectives under nine global paradigms are first introduced in this chapter.

COMPILATION OF THEORIES

In 1986, the Osgood Laboratory for Cross-Cultural Research established a Consortium for Child Abuse and Neglect Resources and Information Services. The Consortium has since amassed a diverse collection of child abuse and neglect literature that consists of publications, documents, and statistics at community, state, national, and international levels. For the present evaluation, a comprehensive search of theoretical perspectives existing in the literature available in our laboratory was initially conducted. A search was also made of psychological abstracts from the publications of the last 15 years. This effort resulted in the analysis of several hundred references. These two efforts yielded a compilation of 46 theoretical perspectives as the targets of the present evaluation.

These theoretical perspectives address four general types of child maltreatment: physical abuse, sexual abuse, psychological (emotional) maltreatment, and neglect. Theories of sexual abuse are further organized into three separate categories for evaluation: the incest taboo, incestuous abuse, and extrafamilial sexual abuse.

DEVELOPMENT OF PARADIGMS

Based on the common, as well as unique, characteristics of individual theoretical perspectives, nine paradigms of child maltreatment were developed: (1) individual determinants, (2) offender typology, (3) family systems, (4) individual-environment interaction, (5) parent-child interaction, (6) sociocultural, (7) sociobiological, (8) learning/situational, and (9) ecological.

More specifically, these nine paradigms were developed as a result of the following five-step procedure: (1) each theoretical perspective was evaluated for identification of its primary content topics; (2) from these characterizations, 19 common content topics were identified across all theoretical perspectives (e.g., socioeconomic status, family stressors, and parent-child interactions); (3) each

Table 1.2
Paradigms of Child Maltreatment and Their Member Theories

Theory	Individual Determinants	Sociocult. Determinants	Individual/ Environment	Offender Typology	Family Systems	Parent-Child	Socio-biological	Learning/ Situational	Ecological Determinants
(A) Twenty-Five Physical Abuse Theories									
(1) Psychiatric	X								
(2) Intrapsychic	X								
(3) Social Systems		X							
(4) Resource			X						
(5) Three-Component			X						
(6) Social Psych.			X						
(7) Symbiosis			X						
(8) Social Interaction			X						
(9) Three-Factor			X						
(10) Exchange/Control			X						
(11) General Stress			X						
(12) Phys. Typology				X					
(13) Family Systems					X				
(14) Attachment						X			
(15) Parental Accept.-Rej.						X			
(16) Transactional						X			
(17) Encounter						X			
(18) Cog./Beh./Developmental						X			
(19) Socibiological							X		
(20) Social Learning								X	
(21) Situational								X	
(22) Coercion								X	
(23) Ecological									X
(24) Choice									X
(25) Multilevel									X
(B) Three Incest Taboo Theories									
(1) Biological	X								
(2) Normative/Structural		X							
(3) Biosocial			X						
(C) Six Incestuous Abuse Theories									
(1) Humanistic	X								
(2) Patriarchial		X							
(3) Biosocial/Attachment			X						
(4) Family Survival					X				
(5) Endogamous					X				
(6) Grounded Theoretical									X
(D) Six Sexual Abuse Theories									
(1) Psychoanalytic	X								
(2) Psychiatric	X								
(3) Socialization		X							
(4) Four Preconditions			X						
(5) Sex Offender Types				X					
(6) Female Abusers				X					
(E) Three Psychological Maltreatment Theories									
(1) Ecological Context									X
(2) Family Breakup									X
(3) Ecological/Def. Needs									X
(F) Three Neglect Theories									
(1) Personalistic	X								
(2) Social Interaction			X						
(3) Three-Factor			X						
Total	7	4	13	3	3	5	1	3	7

theory was characterized in terms of 19 primary content topics; (4) the 19 primary content topics were then reduced to nine clusters and the nine clusters given names representing the nine paradigms; and (5) theories most heavily loaded on each paradigm were identified as *member theories/perspectives* for that paradigm. The nine paradigms and their member theories are presented in Table 1.2.

Many theories/perspectives actually overlap because our classification system is used only for identification of *general patterns* or *similarities* across different theoretical perspectives. Within each paradigm, only the general characteristics of its member theoretical perspectives are described to depict their primary focuses.

In the next chapter, each paradigm will be presented and discussed in terms of four areas of importance: *theoretical foundations; basic principles; empirical evidence;* and *evaluation of strengths and weaknesses of the paradigm.*

The first section, *theoretical foundations,* represents the general descriptions of each theoretical perspective about its position regarding the nature of human characteristics and relationships that lay the foundation for addressing issues on child maltreatment. The second section, *basic principles,* summarizes the content issues, theoretical conceptions, dynamics, and/or operational strategies of each theoretical perspective that are directly related to child maltreatment. The third section, *empirical evidence,* presents relevant materials from the literature that support (or dispute) the positions of each theoretical perspective regarding the etiology of child maltreatment. The last section, *evaluation,* contains general comments and critiques about each theoretical perspective.

In addition, in order to facilitate the presentation of an overall view of each theoretical perspective, two additional research outcomes are included in the text: (1) a schematic diagram to represent the basic principles of each theory and (2) a list of key words incorporated in the schematic diagram for describing the major topic issues of each theorization. The diagrams are derived in one of two ways: (1) the conceptualization of the authors of this book about individual theories or (2) revisions of the original figures of individual theoretical perspectives by the present authors. Of all theoretical perspectives presented in this book, the majority of the diagrams fall in the first category.

Chapter Two

Summary Description of Paradigms

The 46 theoretical perspectives reviewed in this book represent theoretical accounts of various etiological issues of child abuse and neglect problems by professionals with different disciplinary orientations. Due to the complexity of child abuse/neglect problems and the diversities of professional disciplinary orientations, these theoretical perspectives have different emphases on the situations, individuals, environments, and/or temporal circumstances that are directly, as well as indirectly, related to the causalities and epidemiology of child abuse and neglect. They pose different explanations of child victimization processes and causalities, and thus offer different prevention and treatment strategies.

However, there exist some commonalities among different theories/models in their theoretical foundations and basic principles addressing various core issues of child victimization. Such commonalities have been identified and used to organize these theories for all forms of abuses and neglect into nine general *theoretical paradigms*. These paradigms are further characterized in terms of *three bipolar continua*. As shown in Figure 2.1, the first, the *individual-cultural continuum*, places the *individual determinant paradigm* on one pole and the *sociocultural determinant paradigm* on the other pole, with the *individual-environment interaction paradigm* as the combination mode on this continuum.

The second, the *individual-family continuum*, portrays the *offender typologies paradigm* on one pole and the *parent-child interactions paradigm* on the other pole, with the *family systems paradigm* as an integration of both paradigms on this continuum. The third, the *sociobiological-sociopsychological continuum*, consists of the *sociobiological paradigm* on one pole and the *learning/situational paradigm* on the other pole, with the *ecological paradigm* as the aggregation mode of all social, biological, and psychological factors on the continuum.

For each paradigm, the common characteristics of its member theories/models will be described in terms of theoretical foundations, basic principles, and evaluation.

Figure 2.1
Three Paradigmatic Continua of Child Abuse and Neglect Theorizations

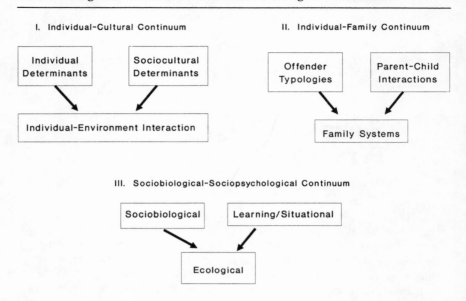

Therefore, as an overview of the general characteristics of the nine paradigms, this chapter will present only those key (and maximally representative) concepts of each paradigm in order to highlight the commonalities of its member theories/models. Such summary presentations will serve as a guide for readers to become acquainted with the essence of the existing theories in the literature. Interested readers can then proceed to further detailed evaluations of specific paradigms and their member theoretical perspectives in six subsequent chapters of this book (chapters three through eight).

INDIVIDUAL DETERMINANTS PARADIGM

The individual determinants paradigm focuses on characteristics of the individual perpetrator as opposed to characteristics of the family, community, or society. This paradigm includes the earliest attempts to explain child abuse and neglect professionally. Medical doctors and psychiatrists were the first professionals to come in contact with multiple cases of child maltreatment. Their initial attempts to explain its etiology focused on the abnormal characteristics of the perpetrator (Burgess, 1979; Newberger & Newberger, 1981; Finkelhor, 1979). This focus may have resulted from the legal system forcing perpetrators into treatment programs where they were clinically analyzed and diagnosed. The legal system, until quite recently, did not require or seek treatment for the victim or other members of the family. Therefore, other related factors such as family dynamics and social norms were not well scrutinized. This paradigm consists of four major theories—the psychiatric, psychoanalytic, intrapsychic, and humanistic theories.

Theoretical Foundations Across All Types of Maltreatment

The early theories of child abuse and neglect were dominated by psychoanalytic concepts and the psychiatric orientation. Psychiatry does not have a unified concept of human nature. Therefore, many psychiatrists have differed significantly in their theoretical orientations, which range from psychoanalytic to behavioral and to existential perspectives.

The psychiatric perspective assumes that child maltreatment is caused by abnormalities in the personality structure or functioning of the offending adult. Perpetrators are considered mentally ill to some degree, with disorders ranging from full-blown psychoses to mere fantasies of harming the child. It is frequently stated that the offender has a character disorder that allows the uninhibited expression of aggressive impulses. The list of other traits is quite long and includes immaturity, egocentrism, hypersensitivity, substance abuse, and instability in interpersonal relations. It is generally assumed that these problems are rooted in the disturbed adult's childhood. However, generally speaking, psychiatry has been most influenced in this area by psychoanalysis.

Psychoanalytic theory maintains that human nature has an instinctual base and that all behavior, thought, and emotion are greatly influenced by unconscious processes. Furthermore, early childhood experiences are considered critical to personality development because unresolved conflicts or trauma during this period may be expressed in adulthood as neurotic symptoms.

This paradigm also includes humanistic theories and theoretical concepts of ego development. Basically, human beings are considered good in nature and active in pursuing goals in life (Anderson & Mayes, 1982). In the process of personality development, there are certain stages of needs and behavioral motivators (e.g., impulses, behavioral consequences, and group norms [cf. Salter, Richardson & Martin, 1985]).

Basic Principles

Physical Abuse. The individual determinants paradigm focuses on the following factors when addressing child physical abuse causality: (1) *traumatic experiences of the perpetrator in early childhood,* such as being the victim or witness of abuse, (2) *abnormal characteristics* of the perpetrator, including psychopathology, personality defects, poor impulse control, and substance abuse, (3) *affective processes* of the perpetrator, including inappropriate or blunt emotions, and negative affect toward the child and poor self-esteem, (4) *distorted cognitive processes* of the perpetrator, including rationalizations for the abusive behavior, inaccurate beliefs about the child, and inaccurate beliefs concerning child discipline, and (5) *reinforcement* for the abuse, including being relieved of intrapsychic tension and the quieting of the child.

Sexual Abuse. Concerning sexual abuse, the individual determinants paradigm focuses on six general characteristics: (1) *trauma of the perpetrator in early childhood,* such as being abused or neglected or having an overly seductive mother; (2) *abnormal characteristics* of the perpetrator, including excessive hostility, anxiety, mental illness, alcoholism, and psychosexual disorders; (3) *lack of personal resources by the perpetrator,* including poor self-esteem, inadequate social skills, and an unbalanced personality; (4) *short-term stressors affecting the perpetrator* (which are said to trigger displacement mechanisms), including fights, work-related problems, and substance abuse; (5) *the perpetrator's cognitive processes,* such as rationalizations and irresponsibility in decision and choice making; and (6) *the perpetrator's affective processes,* including a fear of mature sexuality, a regressed ego state, and emotional transfer.

Evaluation

Due to its emphasis on subjective (personality and emotional) characteristics of perpetrators, this paradigm has been criticized as too narrow-minded, too limited in resources, and too meager in supporting evidence. Generally speaking, the difficulties of this paradigm can be summarized in the following six categories:

1. *Limited explanatory power.* This paradigm fails to adequately consider variables outside the individual perpetrator and thus is restricted to a narrow range of explanations.
2. *Focus on dysfunction.* The paradigm's exclusive focus on the "sick" individual may cause therapists and others to overlook the importance of keeping families and communities healthy.
3. *Poor methodology.* Supportive evidence for the paradigm is mostly derived from clinical evaluations of therapeutic clients, with very weak empirical considerations such as nonrandom case studies, post hoc analyses, small samples, and noncontrol group comparisons.
4. *No replication of findings.* Due to methodological difficulties and clinical focus, the empirical findings of this paradigm have rarely been objectively replicated for inferences.
5. *Relies too much on labels.* Labeling an abuser, as is the general procedure for this paradigm, fails to establish explanatory and predictive relationships about the etiology of child victimization (Newberger & Newberger, 1981).
6. *Limited applicability.* Because of its narrow focus on psychiatric causalities, this paradigm fails to account for the total population of abusers: Less than 10 percent of abusers are psychologically disturbed (Kempe & Kempe, 1976; Jacobsen, 1986).

In addition, it also may fail to distinguish between the impact of the legal system on the perpetrator and a factor leading to child abuse (e.g., depression caused by the legal system may be construed as a factor leading to abuse). Many of the empirical findings may only reflect the psychological impact of the legal system on child abusers to the extent that the paradigm concentrates upon events in the perpetrator's life that cause him to become a child abuser, and possibly also to minimize his culpability.

However, this paradigm is helpful in profiling some of the characteristics of individuals likely to become abusive. When combined with other modalities, it can provide helpful treatment, intervention and prevention strategies (Keller & Erne, 1983). This paradigm also is valuable because it initiated the child abuse and neglect field and has stimulated constructive research, debate, and progress.

Although grouped under the same paradigm because of a common emphasis on the individual, psychoanalytic and humanistic theories differ in important ways. Psychoanalytic theory tends to be deterministic in nature, regarding behavior as being determined by unconscious dynamics. Humanistic theory, on the other hand, stresses free will and responsible choice making.

SOCIOCULTURAL DETERMINANTS PARADIGM

The sociocultural determinants paradigm focuses on social and cultural factors that determine the etiology, prevalence, and continuation of child abuse and neglect. Two major theories are included in this paradigm: social systems theory of physical abuse and socialization theory of sexual abuse.

The sociocultural determinants paradigm conflicts with the individual determinants paradigm, because it asserts that variables *outside* the individual are primarily responsible for child maltreatment, whereas the individual determinants paradigm considers factors *within* the individual as causing child abuse.

Theoretical Foundations Across All Types of Maltreatment

This paradigm is founded in sociology and evolved as a force in the child abuse and neglect field shortly after the psychiatric model was introduced. The common thesis of this paradigm is that sociocultural influences have a tremendous impact upon behaviors, attitudes, and emotions, including those prosocial (e.g., helping, cooperating, and donating) as well as antisocial (e.g., hating, abusing, and discriminating) in nature.

Basic Principles

Physical Abuse. The sociocultural theory of child physical abuse, as advocated by Gil (1970, 1971, 1987), Giovannoni (1971), and Giovannoni and Bellingsley (1970), focuses on social, cultural, economic, and political factors. The major argument is that human society is based on and perpetuates a system of inequality. This inequality leads to poverty and other stressors that frustrate basic human needs. These frustrations are often violently redirected onto children.

Six basic social factors have been considered as important variables associated with child victimization: (1) *social stressors,* such as unemployment, low income, large family size, poor education, social isolation, and low social class; (2) *the mismanagement of national resources* by a minority elite insensitive to the needs of the majority; (3) *the high degree of competition for jobs,* which promotes intergroup conflict; (4) *formal and informal socialization factors* and *social ideologies* that teach selfishness and disconcern for others and thus promote violence; (5) *an established inegalitarian and abusive social order;* and (6) symbolic *social violence* against poor families.

Sexual Abuse. Finkelhor (1982) and Russell (1986) assert that sexual abuse results from socialization pressures especially in regard to masculinity. Cultural norms promote the transference of male sexuality into violence, rape, sexual harassment, and sexual abuse. Men are socialized to consider sex only as a means of gratification, to view sex partners as objects, to seek partners inferior in size and age, and to be dominant in sexual relations. Other important sociocultural variables that also influence the etiology of child sexual abuse, according to this perspective, include (1) social isolation, (2) patriarchal family norms, (3) divorce and remarriage rates, and (4) the escalation of child pornography.

These variables may also be retroactive in nature. For example, not only can social isolation influence the etiology of child abuse and neglect, but child abuse and neglect can also create the isolation. Likewise, patriarchy and child pornography may also feed on each other and in combination contribute to increased divorce and remarriage rates, which again may lead to further isolation.

Evaluation

The link between low socioeconomic status and all types of child maltreatment has been discovered by researchers at a relatively consistent rate. However, some researchers caution that the findings may be influenced by sampling errors and that such conclusions have been based largely on correlational data. Since these studies have frequently employed data from welfare statistics or other *socially reported* documents, it has been suggested that families at the lower end of the socioeconomic hierarchy are more likely to be reported and less likely to have the resources that would enable them to hide or to keep child abuse out of the public record.

It may also merely reflect that the life-style that leads to child abuse also leads to a low socioeconomic status, poor impulse control, substance abuse, and short-term goal orientation. All factors related to low achievement and low socioeconomic status may also be factors that increase the probability of child abuse. The higher rate of child abuse among families with low socioeconomic status may merely reflect this relationship, that is, common roots of poverty and child abuse. Therefore, the poor may be overrepresented in the *reported* cases of abuse and neglect, and hence, findings that link low socioeconomic status with abuse may be inaccurate. This argument has, however, been challenged by Pelton (1978) and others who insist that low socioeconomic status is directly associated with child abuse.

Although this paradigm has been criticized for deemphasizing the role of individual responsibility and choice as a factor in human behavior, overall it has provided a great deal of important information, constructed a foundation onto which to work, and widened the scope and understanding of child abuse and neglect problems considerably. However, this paradigm alone cannot offer a complete explanation of child abuse behavior.

INDIVIDUAL-ENVIRONMENT INTERACTION PARADIGM

The individual-environment interaction paradigm represents a synthesis of the individual determinants paradigm and the sociocultural determinants paradigm. The member theories of this paradigm are in essence a reaction against the traditional dualism of perceiving child abuse as the result *either* of psychological variables within the individual *or* of sociological variables outside the individual.

By taking a more complex approach, this paradigm, representing a progression in the field, comprises eight theories of child physical abuse—resource, three-component, social psychological, symbiosis, social interaction, three-factor, exchange/control, and general stress. It also comprises two theories of child sexual abuse—four-preconditions and biosocial/attachment.

Theoretical Foundations Across All Types of Maltreatment

The theories presented under this paradigm are not joined by a common theoretical foundation, but do share a common vision of child abuse and neglect as a product of multiple variables within and outside of the individual, and each attempts to link these variables in a meaningful way.

Basic Principles

Physical Abuse. This paradigm attempts to link the following variables in a general conceptualization of child maltreatment: (1) *the perpetrator's personality traits* (e.g., authoritarianism, dependency needs, impulsiveness, and psychopathology), (2) *the perpetrator's personal resources* (e.g., self-esteem, parenting skills, and stress-coping mechanisms), (3) *personal stressors* (e.g., family conflicts, illness, and disruptive child behavior), (4) *cognitive processes* (e.g., perceiving the child as being difficult, having a negative attitude toward the child, and a preconventional cognitive development level of moral reasoning), (5) *characteristics of the family* (e.g., adversive marital relationship, norms for punishment, and family dynamics), (6) *community values and norms* (e.g., subcultural acceptance of violence, childrearing practices, and community isolation), (7) *sociocultural variables* (e.g., socioeconomic status, cultural scriptings, and social controls of behavior), and (8) *characteristics of the child* (e.g., prematurity, hyperactivity, and low birth weight).

Sexual Abuse. Finkelhor (1984) asserts that there are four preconditions that must be met before child sexual abuse can occur: (1) the perpetrator must be *motivated* to abuse from some internal reason (this may involve projected emotional needs of the child victim and the perpetrator's deprivation of sexual gratification), (2) *internal inhibitors* must be lacking or weakened (this may involve alcohol, stress, learned rationalizations, culturally weakened taboos, or personality disorders that will give the perpetrator "support" for abusive action), (3) *external inhibitors* must be lacking or weakened (this may involve poor supervision, isolation, or crowded housing conditions), and (4) the *child's resistance* must be overcome (the child may be tricked or manipulated, may be emotionally unstable, or may lack sexual knowledge or greatly trust the offender).

Evaluation

This paradigm has succeeded in compiling data and organizing pertinent theoretical constructs showing that both individual and social factors are influential in the cause and perpetuation of sexual and physical child mistreatment. Unfortunately, this paradigm has yet to develop models into fully testable theories of child abuse. Some of the empirical evidence produced to support this paradigm may in fact not do so.

For example, low birth weight and prematurity have been indicated as a cause of child abuse and neglect. It is possible that other factors, such as substance abuse, poor diet, and a lack of concern for the child in the form of poor prenatal habits are the primary causes of child abuse and also happen to lead to premature and low birth weight children. Studies need to be conducted that include the control for such confounding variables.

As a result, this paradigm lacks empirical evidence that will directly test significant theoretical postulations. On the other hand, this paradigm does have the potential to undergo testing with operationalized definitions and the direct formulation of specific and unique hypotheses.

OFFENDER TYPOLOGIES PARADIGM

The offender typologies paradigm contains theories that attempt to categorize perpetrators of child maltreatment. Two member theoretical perspectives are included in this paradigm: Walters's (1975) tenfold typology of physical abusers and Groth's (1982) dichotomic schema for classifying child sexual abusers.

Groth's typology is addressed in nearly all major books of sexual abuse (e.g., Finkelhor, 1979, 1984; Russell, 1986; Jacobsen, 1986; Schetky & Green, 1988; Vander Mey & Neff, 1986) and has been frequently cited in journal articles about sexual abuse. Walters's typology, however, is not mentioned in any of the references (except his own) reviewed for this book.

Theoretical Foundations Across All Types of Maltreatment

The two member theories in this paradigm—a typology of child physical abusers and a typology of child sexual abusers—are derived from the clinical point of view. It is assumed that by classifying an abuser as a certain type, the most beneficial treatment program may be applied. These two typologies are based primarily on psychoanalytic conceptions (e.g., issues of fixation, repression, and ego development), but they also consider the influence of social norms, situational variables, and characteristics of the child.

Basic Principles

Physical Abuse. Walters (1975) classifies physical abusers into ten offender types. These ten types are based on major etiological factors involved in the victimization, which may be primarily *individual, situational,* or *cultural.* At the individual level, most offenders are: (1) socially or parentally *incompetent,* (2) acting out of *frustration* or *displacement,* (3) generally *neglectful,* (4) limited in *cognitive abilities,* such as having low intelligence and/or poor judgment, (5) *mentally ill,* or (6) *aware* of their abusive tendencies.

At the situational level, two types of abuse are defined: (1) stress induced and (2) child induced.

At the cultural level, Walters's (1975) typology considers (1) subcultural influences (e.g., subculture of violence) and (2) institutional cases of abuse (e.g., abuse in schools or day-care centers).

Sexual Abuse. According to Groth (1978, 1982), sexual offenders are either *regressed* or *fixated. Regressed offenders* are normally satisfied with sexual relations among their age-mates and molest children only in times of stress. When significantly stressed, these individuals regress to an earlier stage of development and thus a child becomes a more desirable sex partner. This sexual attraction to children is temporary and occasional. Most sexual offenders, according to Groth, are of this type.

Fixated offenders are primarily sexually attracted to children, rather than to their age-mates. This is due to a mostly permanent fixation at an earlier stage of development, which resulted from unresolved childhood conflicts. Sexual abuse here is a chronic, persistent condition not associated with stress. According to this theory, fixated male offenders prefer to abuse boys, whereas regressed male offenders prefer to abuse girls.

Evaluation

The typologies under this paradigm appear to have high face validity and relevance to the clinical setting. Classification schemes can function to facilitate research and derive more successful treatment programs. From an ecological viewpoint, this paradigm fails to sufficiently consider factors outside of the individual. Walters's typology fails to consider the interactive nature of the various etiological factors addressed and does not allow a perpetrator to fit into more than one category, which in reality may often be the case.

Groth's assertion that most abusers are regressed is not upheld by the quantitative study that found little difference (83 versus 92) between the types. This finding, however, was based on convicted perpetrators and may therefore be misleading, as the sample may not represent the general population of molesters.

FAMILY SYSTEMS PARADIGM

The family systems paradigm assumes that understanding child maltreatment requires analysis of (1) the family as a unit (or system) in and of itself and (2) how the family system fits and interacts with other systems, including individual, community, and cultural systems. This paradigm has a primary focus on child physical abuse (Straus, 1973; Gelles & Maynard, 1987) and father-daughter incest (Kuffman, Peck & Tagiuri, 1954; Lustig et al., 1966; Cohen, 1983).

Theoretical Foundations Across All Types of Maltreatment

This paradigm is rooted in modern systems theory, which conceives of social systems, such as the family, as adaptive interacting units, rather than as a collection of static parts. Child abuse is considered to be the result of influence by all individual members (units) of the system. Therefore, the theories contained in this paradigm are united by this common conceptualization of the family as a system. While the systems theory of physical abuse is more firmly attached to systems theory proper (e.g., emphasis on feedback processes, flowcharts, and system loops), the theories of incest under this paradigm (i.e., family survival and endogamous theories) merge traditional systems concepts with those of the psychoanalytical approach (e.g., an emphasis on intra- and interpsychic dynamics, unconscious ego defense mechanisms, and childhood correlates).

Basic Principles

Physical Abuse. Family systems theory considers child physical abuse as the product of the entire family unit. The family unit is influenced by individual members and surrounding social systems. Therefore, individual and sociocultural variables are considered important components as they relate to and interact with the family unit.

Considerations at the individual level include *personality characteristics* of each family member (e.g., psychopathological traits and occupational roles), *personal stressors* (precipitating factors and frustration), and *cognitive processes* (beliefs concerning the use of punishment and an internalization of a violent self-image).

At the family level, this paradigm addresses *family structure* (e.g., number of parents and size of family), *family values* (e.g., goals and level of acceptance of violence), *family dynamics* (e.g., feedback mechanisms and interactions among family members), and *interaction between the family system and other systems* (e.g., formal community organizations and neighbors).

Sociocultural level variables include *social stress, community structure,* level of *societal violence, community tolerance* of violence, and *social consequences* of violent behaviors.

Incestuous Abuse. The theories under the family systems paradigm focus on the interactions among and contributions of all family members in determining the etiology of incest. Theoretically, the family strives to maintain homeostasis. Characteristics of the incestuous *father* include desertion anxiety, regressed ego state, unwillingness to act sexually outside the family, and a loss of masculine identity. Characteristics of the nonparticipating *mother* include great dependency needs and unconscious sanctioning of the incest. Characteristics of the victimized *daughter* include pseudomaturity, poor impulse control, and underdeveloped ego functioning.

Structurally, the incestuous family experiences mother-daughter role reversal, isolation, and extreme patriarchy, and often includes parents from culturally isolated or deviant backgrounds. Dynamically, incestuous families experience role confusion, conflict, impairment of sexual relations between parents, and a fear of family breakup shared by all members. The values of an incestuous family rotate around the need to maintain family unity, family balance, and a positive social image at any cost.

Evaluation

Although family systems theory is one of the most widely used perspectives in the field of family therapy and social work, it is without much empirical support.

This paradigm is criticized for taking full blame off the perpetrator and dispersing it among all family members. However, systems theory has been regarded as a *conceptually* important perspective: Conceiving the family as a system influenced by multiple forces from within and outside has considerable merit and potential. Yet, empirical evidence suggests that the connection between family characteristics and sexual abuse is nonexistent or weak at best (Conte, 1986). Therefore, the potential of family systems approach to child abuse and neglect can be realized only if the conflicts between its conceptualizations and empirical evidence are resolved.

PARENT-CHILD INTERACTION PARADIGM

Interest in the parent-child relationship was boosted by the works of Bowlby (1969, 1973) and Harlow (1966, 1969, 1974) on the importance of parent-child attachment and by the work of Rohner (1980) on parental acceptance/rejection theory.

This paradigm consists of three major theories of child physical abuse: (1) transactional (Sameroff & Chandler, 1975; Vietze et al., 1982), (2) encounter (Zimrin, 1984), and (3) cognitive, behavioral, and developmental (Azar, 1986).

Theoretical Foundations Across All Types of Maltreatment

This paradigm was influenced by the theories of Bowlby (1969, 1970), Harlow (1974), and Rohner (1980). These individuals were among the first to stress the importance of the parent-child relationship and its impact on later life development. The binding foundation of the theories in this paradigm is the emphasis on the parent-child relationship and how it relates to the etiology of child physical abuse.

Basic Principles

Physical Abuse. There are four major assumptions to this paradigm: (1) child maltreatment is rooted in the *early life* of the child, often in the form of a *disturbed parent-child relationship,* (2) *characteristics of the perpetrator* (e.g., disturbances in impulse control, cognitive dysfunctions, and emotional needs) may lead to abusive behaviors, (3) *characteristics of the child* (e.g., resemblance to a disliked person, hyperactivity, too much or too little self-confidence, refusal to accept authority, and deviance) have a definite role in the abusive process, and (4) *environmental factors* (e.g., family/social stressors, social help networks, and contextual situations) contribute to the occurrence of child abuse.

Evaluation

Zimrin (1984) has noted the problems involved in attributing the characteristics of the parent and child and their interactions to the etiology of child abuse. It is often concluded that certain characteristics of the victim (e.g., low self-esteem, anxiety, and withdrawal) are a *result* of maltreatment, when in fact, they could be a *cause.*

In looking at parent-child interactions, this paradigm focuses on the mother-child relationship and, in general, fails to address other important factors for their contribution to the occurrence of child maltreatment. These factors include other family members; community support systems; cultural/community values, norms, and structures; socioeconomic stressors; and social isolation.

This paradigm offers valid and important insights about various dynamic relationships between husband, wife, and children. It has conducted sound empirical research. However, the issue of the role of the child as contributing to the causality of maltreatment must be handled carefully to avoid placing blame on the child, since victims often are burdened with guilt and already feel they are to blame for family disruption.

SOCIOBIOLOGICAL PARADIGM

The basic thesis of the sociobiological paradigm is that phylogenetic factors (those originating in the species's evolutionary past) and basic laws of natural selection play a substantial role in contemporary social behaviors. The insights gained by this perspective have been adapted to the problem of physical abuse and neglect of children by Daly and Wilson (1980) and Burgess and Garbarino (1983).

Theoretical Foundations Across All Types of Maltreatment

This paradigm is rooted in the field of sociobiology (e.g., Wilson, 1975; Barash, 1979; Ardrey, 1966), which emphasizes the role of genetic factors in the determination of human social behavior, such as aggression and altruism. This perspective asserts that many social behaviors are directly traceable to survival motivations, including (1) an inborn drive to pass on genetic makeup, and (2) the tendency for individuals to favor those closest to them genetically. These traits have developed because they were important to survival in humankind's evolutionary past.

Basic Principles

Physical Abuse. This paradigm emphasizes three major theoretical constructs: (1) inclusive fitness, (2) parental investment, and (3) discriminative parenting.

Inclusive fitness refers to the transmission of genetic material to future generations. This may be accomplished by an individual in two ways: (1) by directly producing offspring and helping that offspring survive and reproduce, and (2) by protecting and helping those who share genetic material survive and reproduce (Burgess & Garbarino, 1983; Daly & Wilson, 1980).

Parental investment refers to parental behaviors toward an offspring that increases that offspring's chance of survival at the cost of the parent's own ability to invest in other offspring or other genetically related individuals (Burgess & Garbarino, 1983; Daly & Wilson, 1980).

Discriminative parenting postulates that parental care is calculated, although not necessarily consciously, in terms of inclusive fitness and parental investment. If there is a probability that a child will not pay off (i.e., pass on genetic material), then the parent is less likely to contribute a great deal of energy to facilitate that child's well-being. According to this theory, then, stepparents are expected to minimize their paternal energies because of the low genetic payoff.

Three factors are likely to increase a child's risk of being abused because of the associated reduced inclusive fitness payoffs: (1) weak parent-child bonding, (2) an inadequate resource base (e.g., poverty, large family size, single parenthood), and (3) premature or defective children (Burgess & Garbarino, 1983; Daly & Wilson, 1980).

Evaluation

Burgess and Garbarino (1983) and Daly and Wilson (1980) do not stipulate that a sociobiological perspective alone can fully explain child abuse and neglect.

They stress the need to address multiple levels of analysis, such as sociological and psychological factors, in addition to evolutionary considerations. Therefore, an evolutionary perspective can provide a basic foundation by which the occurrence of child maltreatment across cultures, time, and species is explainable. But this perspective cannot, in isolation, explain, predict, or control the problem of violence at all levels.

This paradigm may explain why handicapped children are at an increased risk of victimization. Investment seems to be less predominant if the child is viewed as "unfit" or unlikely to effectively pass on genetic material. It cannot be disputed that consideration of a child's potential worth has historically played an important role in child abuse. Both Greek and Roman law encouraged, and in some cases required, killing of unfit children. Similar requirements can be found in many other cultures.

These theorists note that many animals kill their unfit offspring, and they assert that some aspects of child maltreatment may reflect similar biological motives. Many empirical studies used research results from nonhuman animals to support this paradigm. However, generalizations from bird or lion behavior, for example, to human aggression have been criticized for underestimating the role of culture and the plasticity of human behavior (Alland, 1972; Montageau, 1976).

The empirical finding that stepchildren are at a greater risk of maltreatment is based on studies of reconstituted families. This hypothesis can be confirmed only if children adopted as infants are also found to be at a greater risk of maltreatment. If not, then the important variable may not be genetic relationship, but rather parent-child attachment.

This theory cannot account for the abuse of naturally born offspring except in situations of scarce resources or where the offspring are either genetically or otherwise inferior (Giles-Sims & Finkelhor, 1984).

LEARNING/SITUATIONAL PARADIGM

The learning/situational paradigm applies social psychological studies of interpersonal aggression to the field of child maltreatment. Bandura's (1973) *Social Learning Theory* has been very influential. Likewise, *Frustration-Aggression (F-A) Theory* (Dollard et al., 1939), the F-A revision (Berkowitz, 1981), and studies that have linked aggressive behavior to specific *situations* (e.g., crowds, heat, obedience, dominance, stress) have also had significant influence. This paradigm is represented by three member theories: social learning (Bandura, 1973), situational analysis (Wiggins, 1983) and coercion (Patterson, 1982, 1986).

Theoretical Foundations Across All Types of Maltreatment

This paradigm, in addition to traditional behavioral principles such as classical and operant conditioning, emphasizes modeling, cognitive expectations, frustration, and situational factors. The intergenerational cycle of child abuse is explained in terms of exposure to *aggressive models*. Modeling may be particularly influential if the actor is rewarded. However, even if not rewarded, the observed actions are still incorporated and become a part of the observer's behavioral potential.

Basic Principles

Physical Abuse. This paradigm focuses on four behavioral principles in social learning: (1) the role of *frustration* (e.g., a child's interference with a parent's need for tranquillity by crying) in eliciting aggressive responses, (2) *aggressive cues* (environmental stimuli that have previously been associated with aggression, such as a weapon, an individual, or a place) that may act as triggering instruments in abusive situations, and (3 and 4) aggression-produced *rewards* (e.g., the quieting of a child or release of tension) and *punishments* (e.g., guilt and social consequences) that can affect the probability of future aggressive acts. These factors may operate independently, but the risk of child abuse is said to be greatest when they interact.

In addition to these four factors, an *external locus of control* and *child behavioral problems* greatly increase the risk of abuse. A *coercive cycle* of parent-child interactions may develop in the following steps: (1) a child refuses to comply to parental demands, (2) the parent enacts a disciplinary tactic, (3) the child refuses to give in, (4) the parent withdraws the tactic, thus rewarding the child's noncompliance, (5) the child persists when future demands are made, and (6) a coercion process is set in motion by which disciplinary tactics by the parent and noncompliance by the child escalate with each confrontation, eventually cumulating in abuse.

Evaluation

This paradigm generally employs sound empirical research and applies established principles of interpersonal aggression to cases of child abuse. The theories under this paradigm offer some intriguing insights and compelling analyses. However, Gelles and Straus (1979) have argued that the family is such a unique institution that theories of interpersonal aggression cannot fully account for family violence.

In addition, Wiggins (1983) has suggested that situational analyses may be limited to factors present only during episodes of interpersonal violence and that other theoretical approaches may better explain family violence. Social exchange theory, for example, may better explain variations in reactions to rewards and punishments. This paradigm fails to fully integrate different roles of stress, parenting skills, and other family members into the analysis of child abuse. Sociocultural variables and community standards are likewise not given appropriate attention.

ECOLOGICAL DETERMINANTS PARADIGM

Bronfenbrenner (1977, 1979) originated the ecological approach in studies of human development. Subsequently this perspective was applied to child abuse and neglect by Garbarino (1977). The Ecological Determinants Paradigm embraces two major theories of child physical abuse—ecological (Garbarino, 1977; Belsky, 1980; Newberger & Newberger, 1981; Nye, 1979a) and multilevel (Parke, 1982)—and two major theories of psychological maltreatment—ecological context (Garbarino, Guttmann & Seeley, 1986) and family breakup (Preston, 1986).

Theoretical Foundations Across All Types of Maltreatment

In addition to individual factors, this theory looks at three major layers of social systems, which become increasingly complex. The *family* is the basic social system, which belongs to the *community* social system, which, in turn, belongs to the *sociocultural* social system. Ecological theory analyzes both intra- and intersystem processes. Alterations or changes in one layer of the ecology will affect the family's function and structure and thus affect the relationships and behaviors of family members (Bronfenbrenner, 1979).

Basic Principles

Physical Abuse. This paradigm conceives of child maltreatment as being influenced by four different ecological levels: (1) individual, (2) family, (3) community, and (4) society. Factors at each level are analyzed and meaningful relationships are then drawn from this analysis.

At the individual level, *socialization* factors, such as being the victim of or witnessing abrasive behaviors in the family, are stressed. Abusive individuals are believed to be the product of family, community, and cultural influences. The *cognitive/perceptual* processes of abusive individuals also are stressed. For example, Newberger and Newberger (1981) differentiate four stages of parental thinking, which progress from concrete and physicalistic conceptions of the child and parental role only in terms of the parent's needs and desires to the conception of the child as an independent, complex psychological being, with the parental role including a progressive and interactive relationship with the child.

At the family level, *family values* and *child rearing practices* are deemed important variables, as are associated *stressors* (e.g., size, conflict, and status) and *interactions* among family members.

The most vital factor at the community level is the role of *support systems,* which may be formal (i.e., those available to all members of the community, such as health care, welfare, hotlines, and child-care education programs) or informal (e.g., extended family members, neighbors, and friends). *Social isolation* is another important variable, because of its inverse relationship with support systems. *Stressors* at the community level include recent moving, neighborhood levels of crime, and deviant subcultural norms.

At the sociocultural level, major determining factors include (1) the *cultural sanctioning of violence* as a means of discipline, solving problems, and expressing manliness; (2) *cultural attitudes* that historically consider children as property; and (3) *cultural beliefs* that assume children are unable to understand and be responsive to nonphysical disciplinary and control tactics. Other sociocultural *stressors* include low social class, economic status, employment, and income level.

Psychological Maltreatment. Psychological maltreatment has been defined as "the result of the child inhabiting a situation or ecology characterized by patterns of interpersonal and intersystem relationships which have influential and detrimental effect on the child's emotional development" (Preston, 1986). Psychological maltreatment is inherent in all types of abuse and neglect. Therefore, the factors noted at the various levels for physical abuse may be applied to understanding psychological abuse as well.

Garbarino, Guttman, and Seeley (1986) place parental perceptions of children on a bipolar continuum. At one pole, parents are totally unaware of their children's needs and view them as able to get along without assistance. At the other pole, children are perceived as being totally dependent, very bad, very demanding, provocative, and a problem.

Self-perceptions and perceptions of others are central to this analysis. The perceptions that children have of themselves and others are influenced by parental behaviors. These perceptions influence the child's behaviors, which in turn, influence parental perceptions of the child, as well as their own behavioral and attitudinal characteristics. Behaviors and perceptions are thus considered important variables that interact in a cyclical manner.

The child may contribute to maltreatment through excessive activity, natural shyness, or handicap. The risk of abuse is increased when the child or parent is constrained by developmental problems or is under stress or suffering from a psychiatric disorder. Risks are heightened when interactions between family members are conflictual and the availability of community support is low.

Within family ecology, Preston (1986) identified the characteristics of four types of marital separation families that involve different levels of emotional abuse: (1) *the nonabusive family* is characterized by small size, a clear functional organization, cooperation among family members, and children not being exposed to parental conflicts; (2) *the mildly abusive family* is characterized by an infrequent use of violence, intrusive feelings among parents, some parental conflict occurring in front of children, and parents being preoccupied with feelings of loss or grief from the separation, insensitive to their children's problems, and involved in litigation with their spouse or former spouse; (3) *the moderately abusive family* experiences one or more incohesive home environments with higher parental conflict, conflict being a normative part of the family life, dysfunctional cross-generational coalitions, and intrusion by members of one or both extended families; and (4) *the severely abusive family* experiences intense, chronic escalating conflict between the parents, a split between the siblings, one parent being slandered by the other in front of the children, inability to cooperate, and/or a member suffering from a serious psychiatric disorder.

Evaluation

This paradigm takes into account a wide range of pertinent factors at different ecological levels, including individual, family, community, and cultural ones. It addresses objective and subjective variables at each level. Empirical evidence has been well organized to support this paradigm. However, this paradigm often lacks specific statements and hypotheses about child abuse and neglect causality. A comprehensive range of factors have been considered, but their conceptual linkage is often inadequate. Frequently, a number of "minitheories" emerge due to the complexity of the phenomena and breadth of analysis undertaken by this paradigm.

Some of the characteristics found to be associated with abuse, low birth rate, unwanted pregnancy, and hyperactivity could indicate a larger problem. Low birth rate, for example, may be caused by poor diet, drug and alcohol abuse by the mother, and poor prenatal care. A lack of future orientation (e.g., poor prenatal care) and drug abuse may also lead to poverty, or vice versa. This would mean that poverty does not cause child abuse, but that both poverty and child abuse would be caused by the same factors. More research is needed to determine the linkages between various factors. At present, much of the empirical evidence may equally well support conflicting theories.

Many of the concepts used by this paradigm have not been operationally defined to allow empirical validation. While this is a problem in the general field of child abuse and neglect, the subfield of psychological maltreatment especially suffers from definition problems. Therefore, empirical testing of psychological abuse theories has been limited in the literature. To overcome this deficiency, some researchers, for example, Hart and others, have been working on the typologies and definitions of various psychologically abusive behaviors.

Part II

Theorizations of Physical Abuse

Chapter Three

Theories of Child Physical Abuse

INDIVIDUAL DETERMINANTS PARADIGM

The individual determinants paradigm includes two member theories of child physical abuse: (1) psychiatric and (2) intrapsychic. Both are primarily concerned with characteristics of the perpetrator.

Psychiatric Theory of Physical Abuse

In 1962, Kempe, a pathologist, and his associates (Silverman, Steele, Droegemueller, and Silver) published a paper entitled "The Battered Child Syndrome" in which the clinical conditions of child physical abuse were described. This paper propelled the problem of child abuse to national attention and established the psychiatric/medical model of causation (Lynch, 1985). This theory represents the earliest attempt to explain the occurrence of child abuse and neglect professionally (Burgess, 1979; French, 1984). The psychiatric model (see Figure 3.1), although not as dominant as it once was, continues to have significant impact on the child abuse and neglect field.

Theoretical Foundations. This theory is primarily concerned with the analysis of personality variables and their relationship to social behaviors. It is assumed that a range of normal as well as abnormal personality characteristics among individuals exists. Certain *abnormal* characteristics are said to be the *cause* of socially deviant behaviors, such as child abuse and neglect. These abnormal personalities may develop out of (1) *organic brain dysfunction,* having a direct physical etiology, or (2) *emotional dysfunction,* having a psychological etiology usually said to be rooted in the early childhood experiences of the individual. The psychiatric theory of child abuse is principally concerned with the emotionally dysfunctional adult.

Basic Principles. The basic assumption of the psychiatric theory of child maltreatment is that offenders have certain abnormal personality characteristics

Figure 3.1
Schematic Representation of Psychiatric Theory

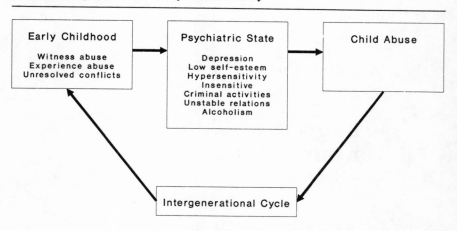

that are either absent in or significantly different from those of the general population. These characteristics, being pathological in nature, are assumed to be the major underlying cause of abusive and neglectful behaviors.

While perpetrators may range in their mental aberration from psychosis to fantasies of hurting the child, the majority are said to suffer from a *character disorder* that allows aggressive impulses to be expressed too freely. Perpetrators of this type are described as being immature, impulsive, self-centered, and hypersensitive. In addition, alcoholism, sexual promiscuity, marital instability, and minor criminal activity are said to reflect this character disorder and to be correlated with abusive behaviors (Kempe et al., 1962; Wooley & Evans, 1955).

According to the psychiatric theory, psychopathic states associated with child abuse and neglect are usually rooted in the perpetrator's early childhood. This theory suggests the intergenerational cycle of abuse as a root cause of the problem, because patterns of child rearing are regularly passed on from one generation to the next. The intergenerational cycle hypothesis states that the adult perpetrator experienced or witnessed maltreatment and thus learned his or her abusive manners. An alternative psychiatric hypothesis poses that some childhood experience, other than abuse, resulted in the perpetrator developing traits that resulted in a predisposition to act abusively (e.g., impulsiveness, lack of empathy, and/or immaturity).

Empirical Evidence. In support of this theory, some studies have linked parental mental illness with child abuse (Mrazek, 1983; Dubanoski, 1982; Maroulis, 1979), and others have identified a limited number of characteristics common to child abusers such as (1) a deprived or abusive childhood, (2) unrealistic expectations of their children, (3) lack of parenting skills and developmental knowledge, (4) an inability to empathize with their children, (5) low frustration tolerance, (6) unmet dependency needs, (7) power-authoritarianism problems, (8) low self-esteem, (9) depressed emotions, and (10) learned helplessness (Elmer, 1967; Newberger & Newberger, 1981; Smith, 1984; Spinetta & Rigler, 1972).

Two supportive studies of the psychiatric theory have been conducted by Kokkevi and Agathonos (1987) and Kluft (1987). Kokkevi and Agathonos examined the relationship between intelligence and personality profiles of child battering parents in Greece. The study included 20 cases of physical abuse and 10 cases of neglect. The major comparative results included (1) battering mothers had significantly lower I.Q. scores than mothers in the control group, (2) battering fathers and their matched counterparts *did not* show a difference in I.Q. scores, (3) battering mothers were more shy, threat-sensitive, undisciplined, self-conflicted, and likely to follow their urges than control mothers, and (4) battering fathers were more controlled and compulsive than their matched counterparts.

Kluft (1987) analyzed the parental behaviors of 75 women diagnosed by DSM III criteria as having Multiple Personality Disorder (MPD). It was found that 16 percent of these mothers were grossly abusive (their behaviors resulted in serious bodily injury to their children); 45.3 percent were classified as compromised/ impaired (they lacked the capacity, authority, and responsibility to determine what was good for their children and family); and 38.7 percent showed no parental pathology (29.3 percent were classified as competent and 9.3 percent as exceptional parents).

Psychological maltreatment was the most common form of abuse with this population (34.7%); sexual seduction the least common form (1.3%); and physical abuse accounted for 16 percent of the total of abusive cases. Although no control groups were used and no statistical comparisons were made, Kluft concluded that while MPD mothers are a group at high risk, an automatic assumption that they will maltreat their children is unfounded.

While these studies apparently support the psychiatric theory, many other empirical studies do not (DeChesnay, 1985; Lester, 1972; Oliver, 1982). For example, while substance abuse has been found to be a major factor in all types of maltreatment, Gelles and Cornell's (1985) cross-cultural analysis indicates that alcohol abuse alone is not a causal factor of child abuse. They concluded that alcohol itself does not lead to violence, but rather provides individuals with a socially acceptable excuse for their violent behavior. Therefore, alcohol functions less as a cause of abuse than as a rationalization for abuse.

In addition, no single personality profile has been singled out for all child abusers (Gelles, 1973; Spinetta & Rigler, 1972). Specifically, Gelles, for example, found that among various authors' attempts to delineate pathological profiles of abusers, there was very little agreement as to *specific* personality traits that contribute to child abuse and neglect.

Evaluation. The psychiatric theory represents the earliest attempt to systematically study the problem of child abuse and neglect, and as such has stimulated much constructive research, debate, and progress in the field. As evidenced by the empirical findings and many theoretical critiques, however, this model is limited in its range and scope. A major theoretical weakness of the psychiatric model is its *unidimensionality:* It fails to substantially acknowledge the influence of important factors (such as contexual, sociological, and familial variables) beyond the personality characteristics of the abusive adult. This model is conceptually limited because it assumes acts of violence are valid indexes of mental illness, when in fact, this assumption has no empirical basis (Keller & Erne, 1983).

Another major problem with this model is that its major support is derived from methodologically weak sources (Keller & Erne, 1983; Kinard, 1982). Most studies under this paradigm have been conducted in post hoc fashion (Spinetta & Rigler, 1972) and thus contribute little to the understanding of the etiology and prediction of child abuse and neglect.

Furthermore, much of the empirical evidence for the psychiatric model has been derived from *nonrandom case studies* of *clinical populations,* has generally focused on a *small number* of subjects, and has *rarely utilized control groups* (Burgess, 1979; Cicchetti & Carlson, 1989; Isaacs, 1981; Lystad, 1975; Spinetta & Rigler, 1972). Because of these methodological weaknesses, it has been difficult to replicate the effects of psychiatric and/or personality variables (Burgess, 1979). Even when control groups are used (as they rarely are), measurement flaws and sample inconsistencies make cross-study comparisons extremely difficult (Keller & Erne, 1983).

In addition, many of these studies fall into the *"explaining by naming"* trap in which physical abuse, for example, is explained in terms of poor impulse control. It is generally agreed, however, that labeling a behavior does not explain or predict it (Newberger & Newberger, 1981; Szasz, 1961; Myers, 1983) and may even have negative consequences as well for the individual (Szasz, 1961). Wright (1976) has suggested that abusing parents are "sick but slick": mentally ill but able to present themselves as healthy. This notion suggests that all child abusers are mentally ill, regardless of how they respond (Keller & Erne, 1983).

Given the above-mentioned limitations, it is not surprising to find that this paradigm has not received much empirical support in the academic research community (Finkelhor, 1979; Keller & Erne, 1973; Oliver, 1982). Recent estimates indicate that less than 10 percent of all child abuse and neglect cases can be attributed to a psychiatric mental disorder (Kempe & Kempe, 1976; Spinetta & Rigler, 1972; Steele, 1978; Tzeng, Hanner, & Fortier, 1988).

The psychiatric model of child abuse often notes depression or symptoms of depression (e.g., low self-esteem, poor self-concept, and feeling helpless/worthless) as the determining factors in the perpetrator that contribute to the occurrence of child abuse (e.g., Bell, 1973; Browning & Boatman, 1977; Burland, Andrews & Headsten, 1973; Evans, Reinhart & Succop, 1972; Libet & Lewinsohn, 1973). However, the empirical evidence for making such links between depression (or depression symptoms) and other psychiatric variables has been based more often on clinical speculations than on systematic research. In addition, the few systematic studies of depression in abusing parents have produced conflicting results (Kinard, 1982). Furthermore, as Newberger and New-berger (1981) have noted, a model based on individual psychopathology may overlook the important questions of what keeps people and families healthy and also may constrain issues of prevention.

In the face of opposing evidence, why do many people still use the psychiatric model to explain child maltreatment? Perhaps clinicians, who work with child abusers and witness horrifying symptoms of maltreatment, tend to conclude that individuals who perform abusive acts are (must be) "sick" and need therapeutic intervention. The psychiatric theory thus serves, for them, as a theoretical, guidelining framework for clinical evaluation and therapeutic planning.

Richard Gelles, a noted scientific researcher in the field of child maltreatment who has largely discredited the psychopathological model in scholarly publica-tions, found himself concluding that abusers were "nuts" when he spent a year in a clinical setting away from research (Gelles, 1982). He later speculated that the psychiatric model has persisted in the face of opposing evidence because we, as members of society, do not want to accept that violence is an extensive pattern in family relations in our society (Gelles, 1985). If we attribute abuse to mental aberrations or sickness and consider ourselves healthy, then we need not consider ourselves as potential abusers or some of the acts we commit (e.g., slapping a child) as abusive. Thus, the psychiatric theory serves to blind us from consider-ing other factors that cause family violence.

Although limited in explanatory and predictive power, most experts in the field agree that personality/psychiatric factors do need to be considered in order to come to a comprehensive understanding of the phenomenon of child abuse and neglect (e.g., Finkelhor, 1984; Russell, 1986; Burgess & Garbarino, 1983). Experts also agree, however, that these variables cannot in and of themselves adequately explain the etiology and dynamics of child abuse and neglect. Thus, most professionals in the field today tend to incorporate or focus on other factors such as family dynamics, community influences, and social stressors. Psychiatric and personality variables are generally only a part of their total analysis of the child abuse and neglect problem.

Intrapsychic Theory of Physical Abuse

Theoretical Foundations. Salter, Richardson, and Martin (1985) adopt the stages of ego development set forth by Loevinger (1976) to elaborate on the dynamics of child abuse. According to Loevinger, there are ten levels of ego development through which individuals will normally progress from birth to old age. These levels, considered to be on a continuum, are *presocial, symbiotic, impulsive, self-protective, conformist, self-aware, conscientious, individualistic, autonomous,* and *integrated.* The early levels are normally found only in child-hood and the latter ones are attainable only in adulthood. There are no clear-cut divisions, as these stages are general and flexible to individuals. Salter, Richard-son, and Martin (1985) believe that abusive parents frequently operate at *im-*

pulsive, self-protective, or *conformist* stages of development, and thus these three "lower" ego developmental stages are used to develop the intrapsychic theory of child abuse.

In the *impulsive stage,* individuals are motivated by impulses and the immediate consequences of behavior. In the *self-protective stage,* motivation is derived from anticipation of the short-term consequences of behavior, and in the *conformist stage,* motivation is derived from group norms. According to the intrapsychic model, knowledge of these stages are relevant only to issues concerning the *treatment* of adult child abusers and are not relevant to explaining the *etiology* of child abuse. This is because, although many adults become fixated at early developmental stages, not all become child abusers.

Basic Principles. The intrapsychic theory of child physical abuse suggests that four related components lead to physically abusive behaviors: (1) a negative affect toward the child ("accelerator"), (2) a world view that rationalizes the abuse ("mediator"), (3) an inability to control impulses ("brakes"), and (4) a payoff of abusive behavior ("reinforcer"). See Figure 3.2.

The *accelerator* component of this theory refers to the negative affect the perpetrator must have toward the child in order for maltreatment to occur. This negative affect may be the result of a number of factors, including (1) *anger* or *frustration* caused by one source being displaced onto the child (e.g., the child may look/act like a former spouse, may be blamed for the breakup of the family, or may be viewed as a competitor for attention from other adults), (2) *genuine characteristics of the child* (e.g., hyperactivity, difficult temperament) that are stressful to the parent, and (3) the *developmental incapacity to experience ambivalence* on the part of the adult caretaker, so that the child is viewed as either all good or all bad. The *accelerator* supplies the *energy* for the abuse. It is a necessary component of abuse, but not a sufficient one. In theory, for abuse to occur, the other model components must be activated.

The *mediator* component of child abuse/neglect refers to a world view held by the perpetrator that rationalizes the maltreating behavior. This may include the use of biblical quotations, for example, "spare the rod and spoil the child," clichés such as "give them an inch and they'll take a mile," or reference to group norms that condone the use of child abuse.

The *brakes* component in this theory refers to impulse control. Many authors have asserted that child maltreatment is largely the result of poor impulse control on the part of the perpetrator (e.g., Dubanoski, 1982). Salter, Richardson, and Martin (1985) distinguish between those perpetrators who are unable to control their actions because of difficulty in impulse control and those who do have good impulse control, but choose not to apply the brakes because they perceive their actions as reasonable and justified.

The *reinforcer* component of this theory consists of some type of payoff perpetrators receive from their actions. This may include (1) catharsis of emotions or impulse discharge, (2) sense of temporary power for an offender who feels powerless or is "power hungry," (3) the warding off of depression by

Figure 3.2
Schematic Representation of Intrapsychic Theory

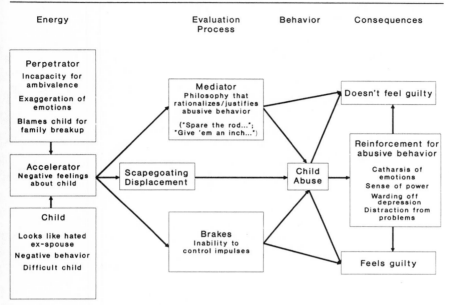

turning self-anger outward onto the child, (4) distractions from feelings of emptiness, as in cases of borderline personality disorder, and (5) distractions from interpersonal problems, such as marital discord.

According to this theory, abusive parents tend to function at relatively low ego development levels. Abusive parents may operate in one of the three developmental stages—impulsive, self-protective, and/or conformist. Five types of perpetrators may emerge from the model components: the *accelerator*, who displaces anger onto the child; the *moderator*, who rationalizes abusive behavior; the *braker*, who is unable to control impulses; the *reinforcer*, who sees abuse as a payoff, and the *displacement person*, who displaces personal problems onto the child.

Clinical intervention strategies have been developed for each component of the theory. They are presented in Table 3.1. Generally speaking, at the earlier stage of intervention, the client is encouraged to gain new, positive attitudes and behavioral dispositions toward the child; and at the later stage of intervention, the client is to learn new coping mechanisms and to develop new reinforcement habits. For some cases, however, clinical work may be applied at different phases of the model, or the clinician may attempt to intervene simultaneously at several phases along the intrapsychic pathway to child abuse.

In their schematic theory (Figure 3.2), Salter, Richardson, and Martin (1985)

Table 3.1
Intervention Strategies of the Intrapsychic Theory

Accelerator Phase	Mediator Phase	Brakes Phase	Reinforcer Phase
Help client recognize and change dislike of a child	Help client get over rationalization of the abusive behavior	Continual monitoring of client's behavior	Find alternative ways to achieve same payoff
Help client locate real source of anger	Set limits for client	Immediate application of negative consequences (e.g., removal of child)	Interfere with the reinforcing ability of the abusive behavior
Insight into scapegoating			
Help client to become and feel more effective in child management		Teach impulse management strategies	
		Arrange negative evaluation by chosen peers	

Note: Constructed from the report by Salter, Richardson, and Martin (1985).

show the successive linkage between these four model components. As the affective component, the *accelerator* functions to evaluate the child. A negative appraisal of the child fused with a world view that rationalizes abusive treatment and an inability to manage aggressive impulses may result in abusive behavior.

Empirical Evidence. This theory is derived from the authors' clinical experiences. No empirical evidence is presented to support their model, and no hypotheses are suggested in order to carry out future research in the framework presented.

Evaluation. This theory generally focuses on the behavioral dynamics of the individual that lead to child abuse. Emotional processes involved in child abuse and neglect are also analyzed from the viewpoint of an individual perpetrator. Other factors are considered briefly, such as characteristics of the child and the possibility of subcultural norms that rationalize abuse. Family, community, cultural, and international factors are generally not discussed, nor are the effects of their interactions on abuse etiology. The reason for this is that the model is designed especially for use in clinically treating abusive parents. Therefore, preventive measures are not outlined, sociological factors are not well incorporated, and the distinction between objective and subjective determinants for abusive behaviors are not delineated.

In addition, this theory is mainly a one-directional perspective with four member components. Successive linkage from negative affect to other components is not well delineated. The causal relationship for the attainment of a reinforcer through a one-directional linkage across three prerequisite components has never been empirically demonstrated. The author conceived the existence of five different types of "abusers" (i.e., "accelerator," "braker," "mediator," "reinforcer," and "displacer"), and this typology itself seems to contradict the one-directional continuous linkage among the four components.

SOCIOCULTURAL DETERMINANTS PARADIGM

The theories under the sociocultural determinants paradigm are primarily concerned with the impact of sociocultural factors on child maltreatment. Social systems theory by Gil (1970, 1971, 1987), Giovannoni and Billingsley (1970), and Giovannoni (1971) represents this paradigm.

Social Systems Theory of Physical Abuse

Theoretical Foundations. In contrast to the traditional emphasis on intraindividual factors, sociological analyses stress the influences of variables *outside* the individual. Social systems theory (see Figure 3.3) addresses the importance of human needs and social systems. The current social-economic-political system is considered a primary source of maltreatment because it thwarts basic human needs. The disparity between the system and human needs across different societal strata evoke the inequalities that become constant sources of abuse and violence.

According to Gil (1987), there are five basic human needs: (1) regular access

Figure 3.3
Schematic Representation of Social Systems Theory

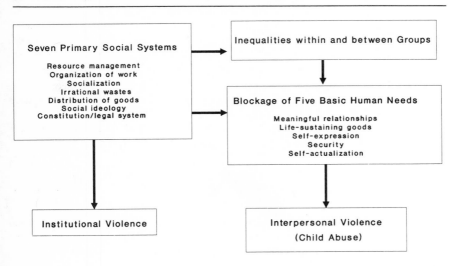

to life-sustaining and -enhancing goods and services, (2) meaningful social relations, (3) expression of creativity and production, (4) a sense of security, and (5) self-actualization. Humans are neither inherently negative (e.g., violent, domineering, exploiting, and oppressive) nor positive (nonviolent, cooperative, supportive, and loving), but have the capacity for both types of behavior. Which type emerges as the dominating tendency depends on characteristics of the surrounding social and cultural environment.

Basic Principles. According to the social systems theory, child abuse is said to be rooted in environmental and structural factors such as socioeconomic status, cultural values, situational stressors, social isolation, and lack of community supports (Gelardo & Sanford, 1987).

This theory investigates two major causes of physical abuse: (1) *structural stress,* such as inadequate financial resources, unemployment, low education, and illness, and (2) *cultural norms* concerning the use of force and violence, such as the belief that corporal punishment is a necessary part of child rearing. Stressors are unevenly distributed in society. If the use of violence is culturally approved, those under structural stress are likely to react violently in response to stress (Gelles, 1985).

Gil's (1987) theory asserts that human abuse is the result of interpersonal and cultural relations, processes, and conditions that interfere with people's fulfillment of their inherent biological, psychological, and social needs. Under such circumstances, natural physical, intellectual, and emotional potentials are blocked, and drives toward growth, development, and self-actualization are frustrated. This frustration leads to various forms of aggression, including child abuse. According to Gil, the degree to which basic human needs are fulfilled rather than frustrated depends upon factors in *seven primary social systems:*

Resource management: This theory assumes that national resources, capital, and means of production are controlled by a profit- and power-hungry "propertied" minority. This minority is less interested in meeting the actual needs of the general population and in improving the quality of life than in increasing profits and power. This causes the "propertyless" majority to become competitive among themselves, which leads to intergroup conflict based on ethnicity, religion, sex, age, education, skills, and attitudes.

Organization of work and production: The "propertied" classes encourage competition for jobs in order to decrease wage rates and thus increase profits. This increases intergroup conflicts and decreases the amount of close, meaningful relationships in the workplace and throughout society. As a result, loneliness, frustration, and alienation arise. This leads to depression, substance abuse, domestic violence, crime, and suicide in the general population.

Socialization factors: Children are raised to fit into various patterns of social structure to conform to the prevailing conditions of work production. As a result, they are required to exhibit little or no initiative, creativity, or intellectual effort.

Irrationality and wastefulness of production: It is assumed that individual businesses and the economy as a whole are not designed for the overall welfare of all the people, but rather to maximize the profits and power of the producers. This results not only in severely undermining the fulfillment of basic human needs, but also in the wasteful overproduction of unneeded goods and services. This contributes to the inflationary process, which in turn has a powerful, negative impact on individuals, families, and communities through, for example, loss of jobs and buying power.

Distribution of goods, services, and rights: Gil (1987) points out that in theory all U.S. citizens are entitled to equal civil and political rights. In reality, however, these rights are distributed unequally in terms of economic wealth, sex, age, ethnicity, occupation, education, and social class.

Social ideology: Some of the *underlying* ideologies of American culture that block the fulfillment of basic human needs include the following: (1) people are intrinsically unequal in worth and do not deserve an equal share of the resources, (2) the lives and individuality of all are not valued, (3) selfishness is a positive attribute, (4) material acquisition and competition are better than sharing and cooperation, and (5) it is justifiable to dominate and exploit others to meet our needs.

U.S. Constitution and the legal system: Gil (1987) argues that the United States is a political, but not an economic, democracy. The established inegalitarian and abusive social order is maintained and promoted by the Constitution and the legal system.

Two types of violence may evolve from the inequalities propagated by the seven social systems: *institutional violence,* which is the direct result of societal conditions, and *personal violence,* which results from conflict between an individual and prevailing social norms. Both types of violence are considered dysfunctional outcomes of underlying social realities, cultural values, mentality, institutional order, and dynamics.

Giovannoni (1971) proposes that parental mistreatment of children is the result of noxious societal forces being thrust onto families. Thus, viewing physical child abuse and neglect as a family or individual problem is misleading and invalid because child maltreatment results from broader societal violence. Two historical trends show the linkage between social forces and child abuse:

1. *Symbolic social violence* has occurred through the removal of children from their families simply because the family was poor and could not care for them. According to Giovannoni (1971), this constitutes an assault on the very structure and fabric of family life.

2. *Socially sanctioned forms of child abuse,* especially of poor children, have declined. For example, child labor, indenturing slavery, and other means of enlisting children as cheap sources of labor have been outlawed. Concurrently, societal concern over child abuse and neglect has increased.

Both Gil (1971) and Giovannoni (1971) maintain that to substantially decrease child abuse and neglect, significant changes in the social-economic-political system are necessary. Therefore, any primary prevention activity aimed only at individuals or families will fail.

To promote a more egalitarian system, and thus prevent child abuse, Gil (1987) suggests that Congress establish the following: (1) an unconditional, legal right to produce meaningful social necessities at a decent standard of living (e.g., redefining the concept of work to include childcare by parents and care of the sick and handicapped individuals by relatives); (2) an unconditional income guarantee for those individuals whose right to work is negated because of age, illness, or handicap; (3) a comprehensive health maintenance system; and (4) a tax reform that would allow a tax-free basic income at the level of an adequate standard of living, but would progressively increase with incomes above that amount.

Empirical Evidence. Studies of the sociological paradigm have related child abuse to high incidences of social dysfunctions, such as marital discord, divorce, separation, unwanted pregnancies, unemployment, poverty, social isolation, and other indicators of social and economic stress.

In a survey of 1,380 cases of child abuse reported between 1967 and 1968, Gil (1970) found that maltreatment was heavily concentrated among the lower socioeconomic classes. Sixty percent of the abuse cases were from welfare families, while only 3 percent were from families that had an annual income of over $10,000. This study also found that unemployment was highly related to child abuse. Only 52 percent of the fathers had been employed during the year preceding the abusive incident. Based on these and other research findings, Gil concluded that the basic causes of child abuse were (1) the culturally sanctioned use of force in child rearing, (2) environmental stress, and (3) a broad range of deviance in the social, physical, intellectual, and emotional functioning of perpetrators.

Three other major sociologically based studies were conducted by Giovannoni et al. (1969), Giovannoni (1971), and Griswold & Billingsley (1967). The general conclusions from these studies include the following: (1) *Abusive families had greater socioeconomic status (SES)* (measured by greater and independent sources of income, higher status positions, and more education; it is interesting to note the disparity between the SES findings of Gil and Giovannoni). (2) *Neglectful families had lower SES* than abusive or control groups. (3) Compared with control groups, *both abusive and neglectful families were significantly more socially disorganized* in relation to community behavior. (4) *Both abusive and neglectful families were more likely to suffer from interpersonal or intrapsychic disorders* (e.g., marital discord, drinking problems, or mental illness of family members) than the control group. (5) *Abusive families had significantly more interpersonal/intrapsychic disorder* than the neglectful families. The results of these three studies indicated that neglect was more closely related to poverty and abuse was more related to interpersonal/intrapsychic stress. Abuse was more randomly distributed across all socioeconomic groups.

Evaluation. This theory presents a core foundation to which all types of human abuse, regardless of form or context, may be traced. This is a unique contribution, because most theories concentrate on one major type of child maltreatment, implying that each type has a unique etiology. This theory asserts that all types of maltreatment are caused directly or indirectly by inegalitarian processes and structures of various social systems.

Although many researchers have linked child abuse with lower socioeconomic status (e.g., Gil, 1970; Kadushin & Martin, 1981; Straus, Gelles & Steinmetz, 1980), some believe low socioeconomic status groups are overrepresented because of an increased likelihood of being officially reported (Elmer, 1966; Gelardo & Sanford, 1987; Newberger et al., 1986; Pelton, 1978).

Newberger and Bourne (1978) have suggested that as the social distance between an individual and a professional increases, the likelihood of the individual being labeled abusive likewise increases. Therefore the label "abuser" is more likely to be attached to those of lower socioeconomic status. Pelton (1978) has maintained that child abuse *is* associated with lower socioeconomic status and that the "classlessness" of child abuse is a myth that has been perpetuated by professionals in order to retain the medical model.

Feminists have long charged that because of reluctance to become involved in cases of domestic violence, the police and the legal system, in effect, sanction family violence (Mathias, 1986). Two sets of conflicting social norms in the United States are relevant to this theory: (1) concern over child abuse versus the coexisting support of violent behavior, and (2) parental rights and family privacy versus the need to adequately protect children.

Gil's (1987) claims that abuse is the product of social forces over which the individual perpetrator has no control is in direct conflict with Gelles's (1983) exchange/control theory of child abuse and neglect. Gil presumes little, if any, free will of the individual in the circumstances leading to child abuse. Gelles, on the other hand, presumes child abuse to be the product of a voluntary and rational series of choices. Both models cannot be entirely correct. If the sociocultural view is correct, therapists need to understand the larger context of violence instead of thinking in terms of victims and victimizers. If therapists realize that both parties are in a cultural context that historically has said that violence is an acceptable way to keep order in the family, then therapists need not pathologize their clients or get lost in their unique pattern of interaction (Walters, interviewed in Mathias, 1986).

In terms of Gil's social systems analysis, solving child abuse and neglect and violence in general will require the "redesigning and reconstructing of social, economic, political, and cultural institutions in accordance with egalitarian, cooperative, and genuinely democratic values" (Gil, 1987, p. 169). Most researchers agree that efforts to prevent maltreatment will be limited until there are substantial sociocultural changes. Most, however, do not go as far as Gil in proposing that the *only* cure for child abuse is complete reorganization of the basic socioeconomic and political system.

In addition, one may argue that if Gil's assertion that an inegalitarian system creates child abuse, one would expect to find extremely high levels of abuse in many underdeveloped places (e.g., South Africa and Latin America) where the levels of inequality are generally higher than in the United States. Yet, no statistics or other evidence were cited by Gil to support the inegalitarian system theory. In addition, historically, income distribution has become more equitable since the formulation of labor unions in the United States. Therefore, if inequality in income is an important factor in child abuse, one would expect that levels of abuse should change as income is more equitably distributed and the size of the middle class increases in the United States. Such a causal inference from a historical perspective deserves further evaluation.

INDIVIDUAL-ENVIRONMENT INTERACTION PARADIGM

The individual-environment paradigm developed out of dissatisfaction with one-dimensional theories based solely on individual or sociological variables. It links individual characteristics with environmental forces and attempts to establish causal patterns between the two. This paradigm comprises eight theories: (1) resource, (2) three-component, (3) social psychological, (4) symbiosis, (5) social interaction, (6) three-factor, (7) exchange/control, and (8) general stress.

Resource Theory of Physical Abuse

Theoretical Foundations. The basic theoretical foundation of the resource theory (see Figure 3.4) is that when individuals want something but do not have the resources to earn it, they often resort to violence to gain it or maintain control (Goode, 1971). This theory assumes that the more resources people have (e.g., power, money, supports, parenting skills, intelligence, and self-esteem) the better they will be able to operate a social system (e.g., a family) without resorting to violence to get their way (Goode, 1971). If an individual fails to contribute needed resources to the social unit, his or her authority is resisted. As a result,

Figure 3.4
Schematic Representation of Resource Theory

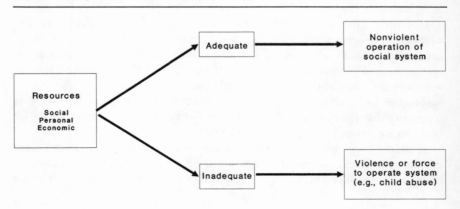

physical force is more likely to be used as a regulatory measure and to gain desired needs. This is especially true when the individual believes that authority is a right but possesses insufficient resources to gain authority voluntarily (Gelles & Straus, 1979).

Basic Principles. Resource theory, initially advocated in the child abuse and neglect field by Goode (1971), assumes that all social systems, including the family, operate to some degree on the use of, or threat of, force. The degree of force or power an individual has is positively correlated with the amount of social, personal, and economic resources held. As resources dwindle, the probability of force being used increases. Thus, a father who strives to be the dominant family leader but has little education, prestige, income, and social skills is likely to utilize violence in order to gain or maintain his dominant position in the family. Family members may also use violence as a means of addressing a grievance when they have few alternative resources available.

Empirical Evidence. Although for the past two decades the study of conjugal power relations has been dominated by various versions of resource theory, empirical evidence for the theory remains ambiguous (Katz & Peres, 1985). Scanzoni (1979) has, based on a comprehensive analytical review, concluded that most research in the United States and Europe support the theory's most basic proposition that a husband's power is positively correlated with various socioeconomic status indicators, such as income, occupation, and education. However, a number of studies have failed to support the theory (e.g., Buric & Zecevic, 1967; Burr, Ahem & Knowles, 1977; Cromwell & Olson, 1975; Fox, 1973; Kandel & Lesser, 1972), and others have been criticized for relying on data only from wives (Haukes & Taylor, 1975; Oppong, 1970).

Katz and Peres (1985) tested this theory to see if it was valid for both genders. It was found that husbands and wives differ not only in areas of family authority, but also in the very bases from which they derive their power. For the wife, more resources resulted in a greater degree of marital decision making. For husbands, however, resources apparently had little cumulative impact. Indeed, some resources (e.g., schooling) were actually negatively correlated with the husband's power. Other data support this finding (e.g., Fox, 1973; Cromwell & Olson, 1975).

Evaluation. A number of theories of child abuse and neglect emphasize the association between resources and maltreatment, for example, stress theory, resource theory, and the sociobiological theory. However, stress theory and resource theory do not require the assumption of a biologically based cause. In contrast, sociobiological theory argues that child abuse is ultimately caused by an evolutionary process that favors expending resources on children more likely to transmit the parents' genetic material. Stress theory and resource theory emphasize that the link between resources and child abuse can be found among a variety of family types.

This theory may be applied to the problem of increased risk of child abuse in stepfamilies (Giles-Sims & Finkelhor, 1984). It predicts that stepparents who bring greater resources to the new family, such as greater financial support, kindness, generosity, or love, are less likely candidates for child abuse because they would be granted authority and would not have to resort to violence.

On the other hand, a stepparent who does not bring in better resources would less likely be granted a position of authority. This may be particularly frustrating for stepfathers, because of the cultural expectation that fathers should be the head of the household (Giles-Sims & Finkelhor, 1984). Therefore, the stepfathers who fail to provide resources are at high risk in using violence to gain power in the family. Also, even though a stepparent may bring greater resources to a family unit, he or she may be refused a position of authority for other reasons (Keshet, 1980).

Giles-Sims and Finkelhor have pointed out that this theory may have constructive implications for intervention. For example, if conflicts over authority play a part in child abuse in stepfamilies, then stepparents can be counseled to avoid the frustrations involved in wanting a position of authority too soon and to alleviate the negative feeling being blocked by other family members.

Resource theory has been subjected to various conjectural and methodological criticisms: (1) self-reported sharing in decision making is questioned as a valid operationalization of power; (2) the link between resource and power base has not been delineated; (3) most studies employ only a limited number of resources, such as income, education, and occupation, and therefore fail to acknowledge the great variety of attributes that may affect conjugal power; (4) resources such as capacity for love and sex, competence in housekeeping, and being a companion and host to guests are mostly excluded (Katz & Peres, 1985); and (5) most studies rely almost completely on parametric statistics (Pearson correlations and multiple regressions) to analyze associations between ordinal variables.

The frustration-aggression hypothesis considers that displacement, in which frustration evoked by one source is redirected onto another (e.g., the child), is the primary reason for child abuse. The frustration-aggression hypothesis (Dollard et al., 1939) has been integrated with resource theory by Lobb and Strain (1984) to explain the "payday" effect of child abuse. This refers to the statistical indication that physical abuse escalates at the month's end as the payday approaches and the family is unable to buy entertainment, necessities, or stress-coping diversions. Lobb and Strain suggest this factor is more pronounced with alcoholics because there may not be enough money to satisfy their cravings during the last few days before payday.

Resource theory appears to have some relevance at a general level of analysis, but has failed to develop specific definitions of its central components. Resource theory may be more useful when combined with other theoretical conceptualizations.

Three-Component Theory of Physical Abuse

Theoretical Foundations. The three-component theory emphasizes characteristics of the perpetrator, such as low self-esteem, distorted perceptions, im-

Figure 3.5
Schematic Representation of Three-Component Theory

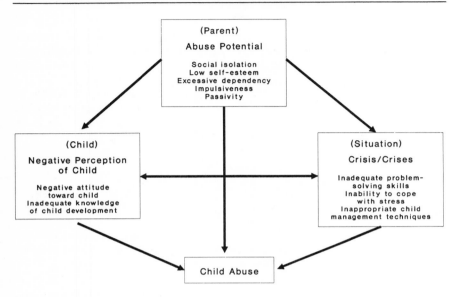

pulsiveness, and poor coping strategies, but goes beyond the traditional psychiatric approach by considering characteristics of the victim and by linking external determinants (e.g., social stressors) with internal ones (e.g., impulsiveness). See Figure 3.5.

Basic Principles. Schneider, Pollock & Helfer (1972) propose three components leading to child physical abuse: (1) the *parent:* the parent's abuse potential; (2) the *child:* the negative perception of the child as being special or difficult; and (3) the *situation:* the existence of some crisis or series of crises. Each of these three major components is further delineated into such categories.

1. *Component One: abuse potential.* The category of abuse potential includes: (1) how the parents themselves were reared, (2) a pattern of isolation, (3) the interrelationship between the parents, and (4) how the parents perceive child.

   Abuse potential is heightened when the parent's own childhood was marked by disruptive parent-child relationship. A disruptive childhood can result in *excessive dependency needs, impulsiveness,* and *passivity in adulthood.* Excessive dependency needs of the adult results in parent-child role reversal. In establishing this role reversal, abusive parents attempt to have their nurturing and approval needs met through the child (Hunka, O'Toole & O'Toole, 1985). Impulsiveness causes adults to act without prior consideration of the consequences of their behavior (Schneider, Pollock & Helfer, 1972). Passive thinking is said to underlie passive behavior, which in turn may result in either incapacitation or violence (Hunka, O'Toole & O'Toole, 1985).

   Social isolation of a family increases abuse potential because the isolated family is less likely to obtain outside help. Abuse potential also increases if the parents have low self-esteem and experienced abusive childhoods. Finally, abuse potential is expanded when parents have unrealistic expectations. Parents may, for example, feel their children should provide them with emotional support.

2. *Component Two: the child.* According to this theory, even when all the potentially abusive factors about the parent are realized, maltreatment will not occur unless two conditions are present: The child possesses special characteristics and some type of crisis is encountered.

Characteristics of the child that may influence abusive behaviors are divided by Schneider, Pollock and Helfer (1972) into two categories: (1) being a "problem" (e.g., fussy, sickly, needing special attention) and (2) reminding the parent of someone disliked. Under this categorization, two types of children are at special risk for abuse: (1) the fussy or difficult child in a family of moderate to high abuse potential and (2) an older child who is taking on new responsibilities in the family (e.g., role reversal).

3. *Component Three: the crisis.* Categories in the crisis component include (1) inadequate problem solving ability, (2) inability to cope with stress, and (3) inappropriate child management techniques. Theoretically, child abuse is always preceded by some crisis or series of crises. The crisis may be the loss of someone, either temporarily or permanently, who has in the past helped the parent deal with child problems. This crisis factor is a particularly troublesome component, because stress for one family or individual may not be stress for another.

Empirical Evidence. Evidence for each of the three components and their subcategories has been established to varying degrees. Convincing support has been established for social isolation (Parke & Collmer, 1975; Gelles, 1980), impulsiveness (Passman & Mulhern, 1977), special attributes of the child (Parke & Collmer, 1975; Elmer, 1977; Maden, 1977), and various stressors (Gelles, 1980) as being strongly related to abuse potential. Supportive evidence for the other factors has not been as strong or consistent.

Hunka, O'Toole, and O'Toole (1985) present data from two Parents Anonymous groups in support of three-component theory. However, no control groups were utilized and the number of subjects was small (N = 18). Therefore, the validity and reliability of the results are questionable.

Evaluation. Schneider, Pollock, and Helfer (1972) have brought together factors shown to be associated with child abuse and organized them under three major component headings. This serves a number of useful purposes, but fails to make any concrete causal inferences. Cause and effect variables are not explicitly delineated. Correlations are established, but do not generate causal relationships. Linkage between the components and their subcomponents needs to be clarified and predictive relationships established.

Furthermore, according to this theory, the abusive parents usually have low self-esteem, are isolated, have unmet dependency needs, are impulsive, and one of the parents is usually passive. However, this theory does not expand upon the issue of dominance between the parents as a significant interaction variable in dealing with crises.

Figure 3.6
Schematic Representation of Social Psychological Theory

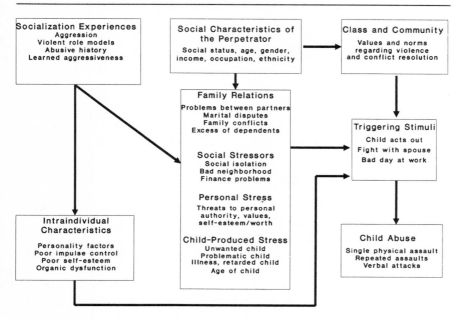

Social Psychological Theory of Physical Abuse

Theoretical Foundations. Gelles (1973) stresses six basic determinants of human behavior: (1) socialization experiences, (2) personality characteristics and mental states, (3) socioeconomic status, (4) community norms, (5) stress, and (6) antecedent conditions. This approach emphasizes social learning processes and stress-related factors, as opposed to innate or psychodynamic variables.

Basic Principles. The social psychological theory (see Figure 3.6) delineates the causes of child abuse into six interrelated components:

1. *Socialization experience of the perpetrator.* This component states that children raised by parents who used violence to cope with family problems often adopt the same problem-solving methods as the parent did.

2. *Psychopathic states of the perpetrator.* Personality traits, such as poor impulse control and actual psychiatric disorders, are considered as possible, but not necessary, intervening variables in child maltreatment etiology.

3. *Social position of the parent.* The caretaker's age, gender, and socioeconomic status are considered significant intervening variables in child abuse etiology.

4. *Situational stress.* This component emphasizes parental relations (intermarriages and marital disputes), structural stress (many children, unemployment, social isolation, and threats to parental authority, values, and self-esteem), and child-produced stress.

Three-month-old to three-year-old children are especially vulnerable to child abuse because (1) they *lack strength* and thus are easily abused, (2) they lack the capability to engage in much *meaningful interaction,* which may be *frustrating* for the parent, and (3) as new children, they may pose a substantial economic, professional, or educational stress on the family.

5. *Class and community values and norms.* This model component considers a possible subculture of violence where community values and norms regarding violence may sanction or even encourage the use of violence against children.

6. *Immediate precipitating situations.* This component includes variables such as the child's misbehaving, arguing, or acting in ways that are considered stressful by the caretaker. Whether or not these variables result in child abuse depends on psychopathic states of the parents, situational stress, and class and community values and norms.

Empirical Evidence. Gelles (1973) presents evidence for the six components assumed to be causally linked to child physical abuse. Sociological factors empirically associated with child victimization include low social class, status, education, occupation, and employment (Gil, 1971). Gil (1971) found, for example, that 12 percent of abusing fathers were unemployed at the time of the abuse and 50 percent were unemployed at some time during the year preceding the abuse.

Gelles (1973) presented evidence that children under age three are more susceptible to abuse (e.g., Resnick & Sclare, 1969; Bennie & Sclare, 1969; Galdston, 1965), but conceded that the data could possibly be misleading because similar abuse of older children may not require as much attention and thus would not be as often reported.

Gelles's assertion that many abused children are the result of an unwanted pregnancy is supported by a study by Zalba (1971), who found about half of 115 abusive families had children premaritally conceived.

Gelles (1978) surveyed a representative sample of 2,143 U.S. families to study physical abuse. The results showed that (1) 68 percent of the mothers and 58 percent of the fathers reported at least one violent act toward their child during the survey year, and 76 percent of the mothers and 71 percent of the fathers indicated at least one violent episode in the course of rearing their child; (2) boys were slightly more likely to be victims of physical abuse than were girls—66 percent versus 61 percent for the survey year and 76 percent versus 71 percent over time (no time limitations imposed); and (3) younger children were more vulnerable to some form of physical abuse than were older ones (86% for 3- to 4-year-olds, 82% for ages 5 to 9, 54% for ages 10 to 14, and 33% for the 15- to 17-year-olds).

Gelles's (1973) social psychological theory was expanded by Engfer & Schneewind (1982) to include antecedent conditions that result in more stringent assertion of parent-child power relations and more personality problems of the child observable as consequences of harsh parental punishment. This expanded model was tested in a study involving 570 West German families. The parents and one child (aged 8 to 14 years) for each family were interviewed about all aspects of family life, socialization, punishment, and child personality. The results indicated that the following conditions in rank order predicted the severity of parental punishment: (1) the child's being perceived as difficult to handle, (2) parental anger, (3) the rigid assertion of parental power, and (4) intrafamilial problems and conflicts. Harsh parental punishment and parental rejection as perceived by the child often resulted in the child's developing a conduct disorder and/or personality problems such as anxiety and helplessness.

Evaluation. Gelles (1973) asserts that psychological variables cannot generally explain child maltreatment. For a complete understanding of the phenomena, it is necessary to take into account sociological and situational variables.

The finding that the lower class is more susceptible to intrafamily violence may be interpreted in various ways. Lower-class families may be overrepresented in the statistical literature because they lack resources to help them evade official classification. Middle- and upper-class families may be overrepresented in the case literature because they are more able to afford needed therapeutic attention (Gelles, 1973).

This theory considers frustration and stress as particularly important variables. Characteristics of the parent, child, community, parental relations, and situation were also considered important, but not as an absolutely necessary factor to initiate abuse. An immediate precipitating stressor in *interaction* with the other variables is necessary.

This theory goes beyond the psychiatric theory by introducing various social factors to account for child abuse etiology. If sociological factors are significant causes of child abuse, then treating and studying individual perpetrators alone will never cure the problem entirely.

Gelles (1973) suggested societal interventions to *prevent* child abuse: (1) alleviate the disastrous effects of being poor in an affluent society, (2) encourage planned parenthood and birth control education, (3) remove the legal and social stigma of abortion so fewer unwanted children are born, and (4) provide greater education in child-rearing practices for parents.

Overall, this theory recognizes the importance of situational factors beyond the characteristics of the perpetrator and the victim. Such expansion clearly treats the child abuse and neglect etiology as a complex social psychological issue that involves multiple factors. This is a positive movement in the child abuse and neglect research community, where scientific research methods and strategies can be applied to delineate interrelationships among all variables involved.

Symbiosis Theory of Physical Abuse

Theoretical Foundations. Justice and Justice (1976) see child development as depending on a system of interactions among spouses, parent and child, child and environment, parent and environment, and parent and society. The psychosocial theory developed by them is primarily concerned with two systems: the family system and the larger system of family, environment, and culture. Specifically, within the theory, four important variables are delineated: (1) characteristics of the parent(s), (2) characteristics of the child, (3) characteristics of the family, and (4) cultural scriptings that govern parent-child interactions.

Justice and Justice assert that abuse is the product of many interacting factors in society, including mental illness, situational stress, personality, psychodynamics, family dynamics, and ecocultural systems. They place special emphasis on the "abusing family," since the family is the major system in which all of the interactions take place. They assume that the family must be considered as a total unit, rather than a collection of static individual parts, and that "child abuse is a family affair."

Basic Principles. Justice and Justice integrate a psychosocial system model with a theory of symbiosis (see Figure 3.7). The *psychosocial system model* consists of a triad of interactions among (1) *host* (parents), (2) *environment* (physical and social influences and stressors), and (3) *agent* (the child and his or her behavior). The triad is linked by a vector of *"cultural scriptings"* that regulate parent-child interactions. These scripts refer to *the accepted and expected patterns of interactions between individuals in a given society.* For exam-

Figure 3.7
Schematic Representation of Symbiosis Theory

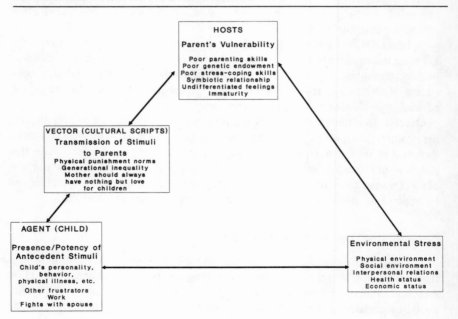

ple, the notion that physical punishment is a necessary ingredient of child management is a common cultural script in the United States.

This theory considers both parents (the host) in explaining the child abuse etiology, not just the actual perpetrator. The child is considered the antecedent agent that triggers the abuse. Justice and Justice consider abuse a consequence more of outside forces than of internal ones.

In *symbiosis theory,* symbiosis refers to the fusion of individuals to the point that one is not complete without the other. According to Justice and Justice (1976), natural fusion occurs between infants and mothers, because infants have a natural need to be nurtured and mothers to nurture. Infants are dependent on mothers, and mothers respond to children through verbal and nonverbal communications. This type of symbiosis is healthy and necessary.

However, some families perpetuate this emotional "stuck-togetherness" far beyond infancy and sometimes throughout life. Individuals in this position grow up looking for a symbiotic relationship. These individuals are "feeling" rather than "thinking" types, evaluating situations strictly on the basis of what feels right. They are said to be undifferentiated—lacking a separate self.

The less there is differentiation, the more likely it is that problems will occur during periods of stress, problems such as (1) marital conflict; (2) physical, emotional, or social dysfunction in one of the spouses; and (3) violent behavior of a spouse directed at the child. Lack of differentiation generates tension and latent anger, because of the existence of conflict between the following two opposing forces within the individual: (1) to become incorporated with another to meet the primitive needs to belong and be cared for and (2) to have a separate self and identity.

The abusing family system is therefore characterized by great intensity, force, and fusion (symbiosis). Family tension is absorbed through conflict, personal dysfunction, or violence, which may be directed at the child. In the abusing family, the root of the problem lies in the competition within the family system over which of the parents will be taken care of by the other.

Empirical Evidence. Justice and Justice do not present any direct empirical evidence for their theory of child maltreatment. Inherent in this model is the process of transmitting aggression and violence from generation to generation. This notion has been established by a number of studies, and Justice and Justice (1976) cite empirical data that link family violence to societal deviance. Furthermore, their concept of the symbiotic relationship between mother and child is very similar to the attachment and bonding processes studied by Bowlby (1973), Harlow and Harlow (1970), Ainsworth (1967), and others. Other evidence provided for their model is in the form of clinical experience and observation.

Evaluation. This theory offers a relatively comprehensive analysis of child physical abuse. It joins together a number of perspectives, including child development, family therapy, transactional analysis, biology, and systems theory. Cultural, as well as individual and family, factors are examined. They are shown as interacting variables that constantly affect one another. The model is thus useful in providing intervention strategies such as the alteration of detrimental cultural scripts at the cultural level and transactional family analysis at the clinical level.

Since the abusing family, rather than the abusing individual, is the focus of analysis, this theory may be criticized, as systems theories have been, for taking the full blame off the acting perpetrator and dispersing it among all family members. The child and the stressful behavior or condition he embodies are considered the agent that precipitates abuse. This especially may be criticized as blaming the victim for being victimized.

However, the three dyad interaction relationships between child, parent, and environment are not clearly explained. The role of the vector in these relationships is not clear either. This theory also fails to integrate the symbiosis theory of interindividual fusion with the psychosocial model, which has not been characterized in terms of three separate triad interaction vectors.

Empirical analyses have not been carried out to validate the psychosocial system and shifting symbiosis theory. Some supporting empirical studies are cited, but the primary support for this theory is from casework studies and examples.

Social Interaction Theory of Physical Abuse

Theoretical Foundations. The social interaction theory (see Figure 3.8) focuses on two causal agents: (1) characteristics of individuals and (2) social

Figure 3.8
Schematic Representation of Social Interaction Theory

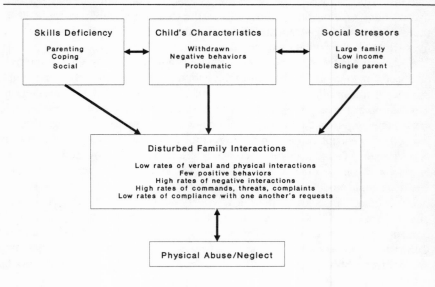

stressors. It sees stress as generating aggressive responses that are derived from sociological foundations (e.g., socioeconomic status, social support mechanisms, and family size) and also from psychological characteristics of individuals (e.g., abnormal characteristics of the parent, abnormal characteristics of the child, and parent-child interactions).

Basic Principles. According to Burgess's (1979) social interaction theory, four factors are primarily responsible for physical abuse and neglect by parents:

1. *A deficiency of parenting, social, and coping skills.* Abusing parents often lack certain fundamental social and parenting skills, as well as coping skills for dealing with daily stress.

2. *Characteristics of the child.* Certain characteristics of the child contribute to abusive parental behavior. For example, a problematic child is more likely to be abused than a nonproblematic child, especially if the adult lacks the skills necessary for handling such a child. Thus the interaction of parenting skills with a problem child is significant.

3. *Psychological and sociological stressors.* Psychological and sociological variables interact and jointly affect the parent-child relationship. Because of the nature of their *multidimensional interactions,* they cannot be validly analyzed in isolation.

4. *Disturbed family interaction patterns.* To understand child abuse and neglect, interaction patterns within the entire family must be considered, including the roles of the victim, both parents, and other members of the family.

Empirical Evidence. To generate empirical evidence, Burgess (1979) developed a research program (identified as Project Interact) based on the four basic assumptions of the theory. Observations were recorded by trained observers who spent an average of six hours a week in a family's home. The sample consisted of three types of families: (1) those where authenticated instances of abuse occurred (N = 25), (2) those where authenticated instances of neglect occurred (N = 26), and (3) those who had no record of child maltreatment (N = 29). These groups, all from a rural region in Pennsylvania, were matched on socioeconomic status and number of children.

Six major findings were reported from this study: (1) abusive and neglectful families displayed fewer interactions, especially those of a positive nature, than did their matched counterparts; (2) mothers in abuse families exhibited negative behavior (e.g., threats and complaints) toward their children over 60 percent more than control mothers; (3) in neglect families, mothers displayed negative behaviors over twice as often and fathers 75 percent more often than the control families; (4) one-parent families exhibited fewer parent-to-child verbal and physical contacts than did the two-parent families; (5) single-parent families exchanged negative verbal and physical behaviors twice as much as did the two-parent families; and (6) there was a significant and positive correlation between family size and the frequency of negative exchange among family members, and a significant negative relationship between family size and the frequency of positive interaction.

In summary, this study found abusive and neglectful families to be deficient in overall interaction levels, especially those of a positive nature. When interactions did occur, they were often negative. Single-parent and large families were especially susceptible to low levels of positive and/or high levels of negative interactions.

Burgess's findings are also supported by other studies that have associated large, overcrowded families with child maltreatment (Herman & Hirschman, 1981; Vander Mey & Neff, 1982; Finkelhor, 1978; White & Cornely, 1981; Burgess, 1979; Conte & Schuerman, 1987). The single-parent family factor is apparently not limited to physical abuse and neglect, as Conte & Schuerman (1987) found child sexual abuse to be significantly associated with separated or divorced marital status.

Evaluation. This theory is backed by specific empirical evidence and sound methodology, both of which are often lacking in child abuse and neglect studies. This model was one of the earliest attempts to emphasize simultaneously (1) parenting skills, (2) nonpathological characteristics of the perpetrator, (3) characteristics of the child, and (4) a combination of both psychological and sociological factors.

The empirical findings presented by Burgess are explainable in some valid ways, but important constructs of the model (e.g., disturbed family interactions) were not assessed in terms of already existing data. In addition, the validity of Project Interact may be questioned on the grounds that the presence of the observer in the family home may have influenced the family's interactive behavior. Another weakness is that the sample consisted of a small number of subjects—all from a rural area in an eastern state. Therefore, Burgess's (1979) otherwise enlightening study may be limited in its power for inference to the general population. In addition, this study, while claiming to be interactional, relied primarily on sociological explanations and did not seem to consider many psychological factors. It was asserted that social and psychological factors cannot be evaluated in isolation. However, the study did not attempt to measure any psychological variables, such as locus of control, impulsiveness, or authoritarianism. Empirical studies for measuring these variables seem desirable.

Three-Factor Theory of Physical Abuse

Theoretical Foundations. The three-factor theory examines intraindividual factors that lead to a high degree of aggression propensity and stress factors that cause aggression to be expressed. Lesnik-Oberstein, Cohen, and Koers (1982) utilize Kohlberg's stages of moral reasoning to help explain low general parental inhibition of overt aggression.

Basic Principles. Lesnik-Oberstein, Cohen, and Koers's three-factor theory states that physical abuse is the outcome of (1) a high level of general parental aggression, (2) a low level of parental inhibition of overt aggression, and (3) the focusing of parental aggression on the child (see Figure 3.9).

Figure 3.9
Schematic Representation of Three-Factor Theory

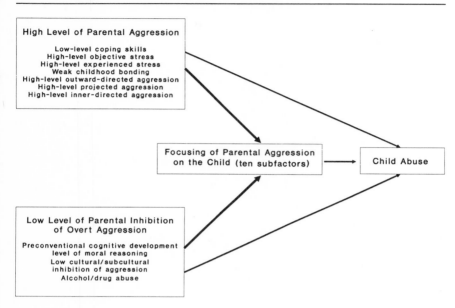

The first factor, *high level of parental aggression,* is the result of a combination of the following seven subfactors: (1) low level of coping skills, (2) high level of objective stress, (3) high level of experienced stress, (4) weak bonding in childhood (harsh upbringing), (5) high level of outward aggression, (6) high level of projected aggression, and (7) high level of inner-directed aggression.

The second factor, *low parental inhibition of overt aggression,* results from the combination of three major conditions: (1) preconventional cognitive-developmental level of moral reasoning (taken from Kohlberg [1976], it refers to a developmental stage where social and moral rules are experienced as "external to the self"), (2) low cultural/subcultural inhibition of overt aggression, and (3) substance abuse.

The third factor, the *focusing of parental aggression on the child,* refers to two general circumstances: (1) aggression from other sources displaced on the child, and (2) aggression brought on by the child itself, when, for example, the parent's expectation of the child is frustrated. More specifically, the authors propose ten subfactors to account for the two general circumstances: pre- and post-natal experience with the child, too high developmental expectations of the child, role reversal, dissatisfactory experience (including disappointment, negative events, and/or frustration) with the child, specific aggression or displacement of general aggression toward the child, and finally, low specific inhibition of aggression toward the child.

Figure 3.10
Schematic Representation of Types of Child Abuse

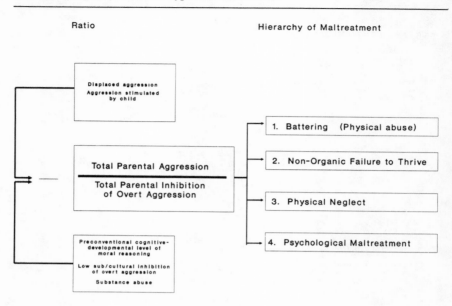

The theory posits that the degree of child abuse severity is determined by the *ratio* of total parental aggression feeling to total parental inhibition of overt aggression. High numerical values of the ratio result in battering, while lower numerical values result in nonorganic failure to thrive, physical neglect, and emotional abuse (Lesnik-Oberstein, Cohen & Koers, 1982). This aspect of the theory is shown in Figure 3.10.

Empirical Evidence. This model is currently being subjected to empirical testing (personal communication from Lesnik-Oberstein to Tzeng, April 9, 1990). Fifty hypotheses derived from the theory have been proposed by the authors. Examples of the hypotheses, categorized by Lesnik-Oberstein, Cohen, and Koers (1982) into seven measurement domains, are as follows:

1. *Social hypotheses*
    "Compared to families in which child abuse does not occur, families in which child abuse does occur will have less living space per person."
2. *Marital hypotheses*
    "Compared to parents of children who are not abused, one or both parents of a child who is abused will (1) show lower marital adjustment and (2) show greater negative feelings towards the partner."
3. *Personality and psychopathology of the parents*
    "Compared to nonabusing parents, abusing parents (one or both) will show (1) greater depression and (2) greater hostility."

4. *Medical history of the parents*

"Compared to nonabusing parents, abusing parents (one or both) will show a greater amount of physical illness in the year prior to the child's hospitalization."

5. *The child*

   a. Mother's pregnancy: "Compared to nonabusing mothers, abusing mothers will show (1) greater incidence of having experienced the pregnancy as unpleasant and (2) greater incidence of physical illness during the pregnancy."

   b. Prematurity: "Compared to nonabused children, abused children will show greater incidence of premature birth."

   c. Illness of child: "Compared to nonabused children, abused children will show a greater incidence of illness in the first year of life and a greater incidence of illness in the year prior to hospitalization."

   d. Postnatal separation: "Compared to nonabused children, abused children will show a greater incidence of early (24 hours/48 hours/72 hours/72+ hours) separation from the mother after birth."

   e. Conception: "Compared to nonabused children, abused children will show a greater incidence of having been unplanned, and a greater incidence of having been undesired prior to birth."

   f. Legitimacy: "Compared to nonabused children, abused children will show a greater incidence of illegitimate birth."

   g. Delivery: "Compared to nonabusing mothers, abusing mothers will show a greater incidence of delivery complications."

6. *Parent attitude toward the child*

"Compared to nonabusing parents, abusing parents (one or both) will show (1) more autocratic child-rearing attitudes, and (2) more rejecting child-rearing attitudes."

7. *Upbringing of parents*

"Compared to nonabusing parents, abusing parents (one or both) will show (1) a more punitive upbringing and (2) a greater incidence of having felt unloved by one or both parents."

In the proposed research program, a battery of tests will be given to parents and a single test to children over three years old. Results from the hypotheses testing will provide an empirical evaluation of this theory. (Note: As of the date of this evaluation, January 1990, a literature search was done and no reports of such research were found in the child abuse and neglect literature in the United States).

Evaluation. This theory provides a relatively comprehensive approach to discussing the etiology of child physical abuse. It has three major strengths: (1) It takes into account a number of relevant subfactors at the macro (cultural) and micro (family) level (e.g., parental and cultural influences); (2) it provides a schematic model to delineate the causal relationships among various subfactors; and (3) it derives fifty hypotheses for empirical testing.

This theory has the following weaknesses: (1) Interactions between the three major factors are not clearly delineated; (2) the model and its assumptions are not yet empirically supported; (3) very few external or concurrent works are presented to support the theory; (4) the strategies and procedures for measuring all of the subfactors have not been elaborated on; and (5) practical applications of the theory are not discussed.

Exchange/Control Theory of Physical Abuse

Theoretical Foundations. Gelles's (1982, 1983, 1985, 1987) exchange/social control theory of family violence (see Figure 3.11) is rooted in social exchange theory (e.g., Homans, 1958; Blau, 1964), which assumes that human social behavior is naturally guided by the "minimax" strategy—to minimize costs and maximize rewards. Family interactions are dependent on the *reciprocal exchange* of rewards among members. Behaviors are based on the net balance of actual or perceived rewards and costs, which may be *internal* (e.g., induction or reduction of anxiety and guilt) or *external* (e.g., economic gains or losses, friendship, and good or bad self-image).

The basic premise of the exchange/control theory is that humans strive to obtain the most *profitable outcome* and maintain *distributive justice*. According to the principle of distributive justice, humans prefer equal relationships. If relationships are perceived unequal, then individuals suffer psychological discomfort and attempt to restore balance to the relationship. The *reciprocal norm* dictates that normal interpersonal interactions should remain balanced, with each party involved receiving and giving equally. When relationships become unequal, there will be a tendency for them to become unstable. The involved individuals will be motivated to leave the relationship. Unequal *interfamily* in-

Figure 3.11
Schematic Representation of Exchange/Control Theory

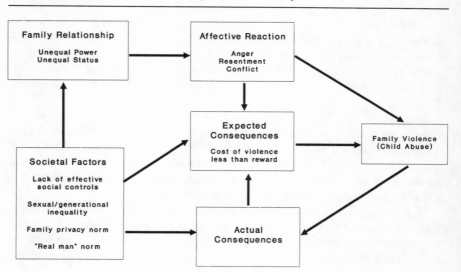

teractions are not as easily terminated as other types of interpersonal interactions (e.g., between salesperson and buyer, friends, or employee and employer) and thus may result in increased anger, resentment, conflict, and violence.

Basic Principles. Gelles's (1983, 1985) central postulation is that people use violence in the home "because they can." This general assumption is delineated into three subpostulations:

1. Family members are more likely to use violence in the home when they expect the costs of being violent to be less than the rewards.

2. The absence of effective social controls (e.g., police intervention) over family relations decreases the costs of one family member's being violent toward another.

3. Certain social and family structures reduce social control in family relations and, therefore, reduce the costs and increase the rewards of being violent (Gelles, 1983, 1985).

These three subpostulates are directly derived from three social norms that are said to contribute to all types of family violence: (1) sexual and generational inequality norms, (2) family privacy norms, and (3) "real man" norms.

The sexual/generational inequality norm allows adults to use violence against children without fearing retaliation. This could explain why child abuse decreases as children grow older and stronger and thus are more able to fight back.

The *family privacy norm* dictates that families deserve exceptional privacy and noninterference by others, including neighbors and outside agencies. This norm therefore reduces the probability of outside intervention. People are reluctant to intervene in cases of suspected family violence, and the police, prosecutors, and courts are likewise often hesitant to take strong action in such cases. The legal system is often put in the bind of deciding either to break up the family or to protect its individual member(s). The former is viewed as a drastic step and thus, except in extreme cases, the family is usually kept together (Gelles, 1983).

The *"real man" norm* refers to the disposition to view aggressive behavior as a positive "manly" attribute (Toby, 1966). Hence, instead of resulting in a loss of status, acts of family violence may actually be reinforced through status gain. Even if status is lost, individuals may attribute abusive behaviors to a loss of control or the influence of alcohol or other drugs (Gelles, 1983a).

According to this theory, certain social controls would commit people to the social order and punish family members for acts of violence. However, weak or absent social controls will result in family violence. Social controls designed to *prevent* violence between family members may include (1) the victim's potential to fight back (e.g., the victim's strength in comparison with the perpetrator's), (2) institutional consequences, such as imprisonment, and (3) social consequences, such as the loss of status (Gelles, 1983a, 1985).

Empirical Evidence. Gelles and Hargreaves (1981) found that abusive mothers decrease abusive behaviors as their children grow older. This may be due to the greater risk of retaliation by a bigger and stronger child. This interpretation supports Gelles's postulation that generational inequality contributes to child abuse.

It may be, however, that the reduction in child abuse by mothers as their children grow older results from the children's spending less time with their mothers and more of their time with friends or in school. In addition, as children grow older they may demand less help from their mothers as they develop the ability to care for themselves. This would result in fewer demands and less stress on the mother. If these factors indeed contribute to the reduction in abuse, Gelles's emphasis on generational inequality is not supported.

On the other hand, Straus, Gelles, and Steinmetz (1980) found children aged 3 to 5 and 15 to 17 were most likely to be physically abused. Such findings are explainable by the exchange/control theory in terms of investment return: Younger children may be abused because their parents perceive them as costing much and giving little in actual return, and older children may be abused because their parents view their child-rearing energies and investments as yielding disappointing results (Gelles, 1983a). This study also found that isolated families that have very unbalanced power relations are at special risk of child abuse.

Research has furthermore shown that children with special characteristics, such as being handicapped, premature, ugly, or extra demanding, are at greater risk of being abused (Friedrich & Boriskin, 1976). The parents of these children may perceive the parenting costs as outweighing the rewards (Gelles, 1983a).

Evaluation. Exchange/control theory explains many findings of child physical abuse. By emphasizing the importance of cultural norms (e.g., reciprocation, sexual and generational inequality, family privacy, and "real man" norms) in determining violent behaviors, this theory has validity and utility in explaining child maltreatment. The family privacy norm has, for example, been considered a fundamental value of American family life that may be abrogated only in the face of a compelling state interest (Melton & Davidson, 1987).

According to Gelles (1983a), the greater the disparity between *perceived investment* in a family relationship, such as parenting, and the *perceived returns* on such investment, the greater the likelihood of violence. Violence is viewed as a last resort to a lack of reciprocity in the family. Gelles asserts that violence may become a primary alternative when it is culturally approved and brings immediate gratification. Spanking, for example, is culturally sanctioned and often results in immediate emotional reward and cessation of the unwanted behavior of the child.

Exchange/control theory also has important implications for treatment. Gelles (1982, 1983, 1985) stresses the need for greater social control over family relations and costs of family violence. Therefore, clinicians should (1) stress behavioral responsibility by not accepting rationalizations for abusive behaviors, (2) reject cultural norms that permit violence, (3) help reduce family isolation, and (4) promote more democratically run households.

If exchange/control theory is correct, implementation of the following social policies could help reduce and prevent family violence: (1) Eliminate abusive cultural norms that accept and promote violence, such as reducing media violence and prohibiting the use of physical punishment by teachers and parents; (2) reduce economic, generational, and sexual inequalities; and (3) increase the response capacity and resources of the criminal justice and child welfare systems.

Family violence and child abuse occur, according to this model, because the rewards of violence outweigh the costs. In order for this model to accurately describe the *causes* of child abuse, however, it must explain why child abuse is viewed as rewarding by the perpetrator. This issue was not clearly delineated by Gelles.

Some empirical data conflict with the social norms used to explain the rewards gained by child abuse. If sexual inequality and the "real man" norms are important components of child abuse, one would expect that men would be violent toward their children more often than women would and that female children would be victims of physical abuse more often than male children would. Empirical data, however, show that there is no clear sexual difference in child victimization.

In fact, two of the social norms—family privacy and generational/sexual inequality—noted by Gelles are often found in Oriental households, and the reported rate of child abuse in Oriental households is relatively low. Observational reports, for example, indicate that China has relatively low rates of parental child abuse and of aggression among children (Sidel, 1972).

Cross-cultural comparison studies between Taiwan and the United States indicate that physical punishment is used less than half as frequently and spankings only one-fourth as frequently in Taiwanese families (Niem & Collard, 1971; Freedman & Freedman, 1969). Goode (1971) reported that in Japan physical punishment is not a common disciplinary measure and child abuse is infrequent. Therefore, Gelles's model may explain some forms of family violence in the Western culture, but it appears unable to explain all forms of child abuse.

This theory advocates the liberal use of societal punishment as a deterrent to family violence and has noted benefits derived from such actions. However, psychological and criminal justice literature points to various negative aspects of punishment. Psychological research has disclosed that punishment of an undesirable behavior is less effective than the replacement and rewarding of desirable behaviors (Goldstein, 1983). Punishment has also shown to have negative side effects, including the escalation of aggression (Munroe & Munroe, 1975). Studies of the criminal justice system have found that punishment (e.g., through incarceration) does not deter undesired behaviors.

Swift intervention with relatively minor punishment may, however, be effective in deterring some forms of family violence. When a report of wife beating leads to an arrest—even if prosecution is subsequently dropped—studies have noted a marked reduction in family violence. This may indicate that with an increased probability of punishment, the punishment itself need not be severe to deter antisocial conduct. Overall, the exchange/control theory ascribes to what is basically an economic model. The key elements of cost (inequality) and benefits (rewards) have been defined in terms of subjective perception and social norms.

The intervening psychological variables associated with the behavioral action-inaction continuum have not been addressed. Nor do they account for the impact of overt child maltreatment behavior on the subjective characteristics of the perpetrator (e.g., guilt and depression).

Gelles has apparently made no attempt to directly test the basic postulations of exchange/control theory through systematic and empirical studies. The theory, as it is applied to family violence, evidently has not been tested or improved in any manner since its original conception by Gelles.

General Stress Theory of Physical Abuse

Theoretical Foundations. According to Farrington (1980, 1986), stress underlies the occurrence of violence in the modern family. Stress consists of seven components:

1. *stressor stimulus,* or series of stressor stimuli—the occurrences, chronic or acute, that tend to add stress to our daily lives;
2. *objective demand*—the objective reality of a particular stressor that is independent of any cognitive process of perception or definition on the part of the individual or social system;
3. *subjective demand*—how the affected person or the social system defines the situation;
4. *response capabilities*—skills and abilities possessed by the individual or social system with which the stressor stimulus can be responded to;
5. *coping behavior*—overt behavior that is actually utilized by the individual or social system in response to the stress;
6. *stress level change*—changes in the stress level of the individual or social system as a result of stressful experiences; and
7. *consequences*—the possible results of the stress experience.

An individual or social system, such as the family, is said to be stressed if the response to a stressor stimulus is insufficient in adequately minimizing or otherwise negating the demand generated by the stimulus (Farrington, 1986).

It is assumed that most individuals can withstand some stress throughout their lives and high levels of stress on occasion (Kratcoski, 1982), but experiencing high levels of stress for an extended period, especially in childhood or adolescence, can have severe consequences (Strasburg, 1978).

Basic Principles. According to Farrington (1986), the etiology of family violence can be reduced to three primary principles (see Figure 3.12): (1) Families experience much stress; (2) families are not adequately equipped to handle stress; and (3) family violence is both an intuitively reasonable and socially acceptable response to stress and/or frustration in American society.

Families experience much stress: This proposition states that the modern family operates under considerable stress, because stress-inducing factors are

Figure 3.12
Schematic Representation of General Stress Theory

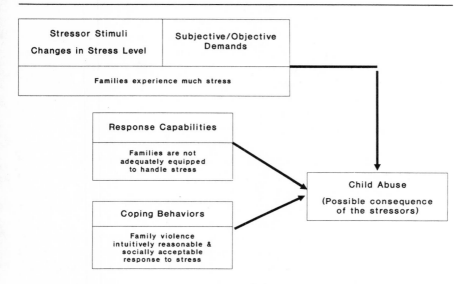

inherent in the structure, functions, and position of the modern family in the larger society.

Elements likely to present important stressor stimuli include the maintenance of economic self-sufficiency, the successful socialization of children, and the sexual satisfaction of marital partners. These stress factors also impact on families because individuals may react to personal stressors in the family context. Stressors need not be dramatic or catastrophic, but may be relatively routine and even mundane matters.

Families are not adequately equipped to handle stress: Each individual and family has various skills, attributes, and resources for dealing with stress. At the individual level, response capabilities include intelligence, resourcefulness, and prior experience with similar stress stimuli. At the familial level, response capabilities include (1) *internal resources* such as family cohesiveness, viable and legitimate power structures, and communication skills; (2) the *social support* among the extended family members and the larger community; and (3) the combined *personal resources* of individual family members.

Family structural characteristics that may impede their ability to resolve stressful situations include a relatively small size, the inability to pick and choose an optimally efficient membership, and a high level of emotional involvement among the members.

Family violence is both an intuitively reasonable and a socially acceptable response to stress and/or frustration in American society: There are a number of possible responses to stress other than violence. They include positive goal-directed behavior, the avoidance or denial of the stressor, and the internalization of pathological psychological states. There are many personal and social factors that interact to determine which particular response to stress is chosen.

Social norms encourage and reinforce the use of violence as a response to stress and frustration in U.S. society. These norms exist at societal, subcultural, and family levels. As a result, violence can be perceived as an appropriate and effective way to achieve desires and as an acceptable means of responding to frustration. Social norms also legitimize violence even—and perhaps especially—within the context of the family.

In determining stress vulnerability, two factors are considered: (1) how the family defines and evaluates the stressor stimuli and (2) the nature of the particular response capabilities the family and its individual members possess. Different families define situations differently, and thus certain situations produce stress in some families but not in others. Likewise, families with different skills and resources are inclined to use violence as a stress-coping method at different times for different reasons.

Farrington predicts there will be (1) an increase of stress experienced by families, such as inflation, employment instability, and/or shortage of affordable housing; (2) continued conflict and tension between and within traditional sex roles; and (3) an increase in the legitimization of violence in American society in general and specifically within the context of the family, including increases in violent crime, media and sports violence, and the frequency with which children are involved in acts of aggression in a variety of contexts. Furthermore, Farrington maintains that (1) many situational factors associated with stress-induced violence, such as substance abuse and family crowding, will continue, and (2) support for family research and family support services will decrease, because of the political position that the government should stay out of family affairs. Therefore, Farrington (1986) predicts that all incidents of family violence are likely to rise in the future.

Empirical Evidence. Stress theory in general has been used to explain the increased risk of abuse in stepfamilies and has received empirical and theoretical support (Justice & Justice, 1976; Straus, Gelles & Steinmetz, 1980). It has been well documented that stepfamilies experience stress and that stress is related to child abuse (Giles-Sims & Finkelhor, 1984).

The seven basic components of Farrington's model were developed by "utilizing and integrating schemes developed by a number of stress theorists" (Farrington, 1986). Empirical evidence for the model was not presented. Supportive evidence is cited for the three propositions that families experience much stress, that they are not adequately equipped to handle stress, and that violence is an intuitively reasonable and socially acceptable response to stress.

Evaluation. Farrington's general stress model assumes that stress is a multilevel phenomenon and, therefore, the model can account for stress at the individual and social systems (e.g., family) levels of analysis. A general model of stress applicable to individuals and systems is relevant to the analysis of family stress, because it allows parallel discussion of stress as it affects individual family members, particular family units, and entire family institutions (Farrington, 1986).

This theory explains *instrumental* and *expressive* aggression. Instrumental aggression, used to obtain an objective, such as to quiet a child or settle a dispute, is considered a coping behavior, selected from the reservoir of response capabilities. Expressive aggression, which has no rational purpose or goal, is conceptualized as frustration-based violence, that is, a "second-order" consequence of an unresolved stress situation (Farrington, 1986).

This theory synthesizes stress theory generally, family stress theory per se, the life events and life stress literature, and frustration-aggression theory. However, Farrington notes that the specific processes within these various theoretical interpretations have not been sufficiently articulated and synthesized into a clear and convincing social psychology of violent behavior.

Stress theory appears to explain more correlates of child abuse than either sociobiological or normative theories. It offers sound explanations of associations between child abuse and socioeconomic status, large family size, and family disruption and has implications for intervention efforts. For example, if stress from conflicting expectations causes child abuse, then counseling to help family members redefine their expectations and act consistently with these expectations may reduce overall stress levels (Giles-Sims & Finkelhor, 1984).

The linkage between Farrington's model and family violence is completely derived from a post hoc analysis. Empirical studies need to be considered in order to adequately assess its validity. Furthermore, the notion of relative deprivation, an important theoretical concept in the frustration-aggression literature, was not integrated into the general stress model.

In providing support for the general stress theory, Farrington at one point claims that a structural characteristic of families that may impede their ability to resolve stressful situations is a "relatively small size." This is in direct conflict with empirical evidence that has found large-sized families more vulnerable to child abuse and neglect, and Farrington himself acknowledges that family density is a factor related to risk for family violence.

Farrington acknowledges that stress is neither a necessary nor a sufficient condition for family violence to occur. However, other factors that may explain why violence is not associated with stress are not included in the theory. Therefore, as a theory of family violence, it lacks comprehensiveness because it relies on stress as the only cause of family violence.

OFFENDER TYPOLOGIES PARADIGM

The offender typologies paradigm includes theories that classify perpetrators according to a set of criteria. Walters's (1975) typology of physical abusers, consisting of ten categories, is the prototype of this paradigm.

Physical Abuse Typology

Theoretical Foundations. Walters (1975) asserts that abusive behavior may be delineated into ten categories for clinical analysis depending on the major etiological factor, which may be individual, situational, or cultural in nature. All abuse is not elicited from the same stimulus and all abusers cannot be treated with the same method. Therefore, the classification scheme evaluates abusive behavior in terms of individual competence, social norms, and situational appropriateness.

Walters, in his attempt to differentiate different types of abusers, hopes that the results might offer the basis for the construction of a theory and the development of treatment models that are unique to the perpetrator.

Basic Principles. Walters categorizes physical abusers into ten types. These types are based on the characteristics of abusers evaluated in the clinical setting.

1. *Socially and parentally incompetent abusers* are considered the result of a learned intergenerational pattern of discipline.
2. *Frustrated and displaced abusers* redirect their anger from one source to the child.
3. *Situational abusers* are generally nonabusive, but become so under a particularly stressful situation.
4. *Neglectful abusers* subject their children's lives to various dangerous situations due to neglect.
5. *Accidental or unknowing abusers* suffer from extremely poor parental judgment, limited intelligence, or mental retardation.
6. *Victim-precipitated abuse* occurs when the child elicits, for example, through nagging, an aggressive response from the parent.
7. *Subcultural abusers* are found in cultures that especially condone the use of violence for discipline.
8. *Mentally ill abusers* suffer from an actual behavioral or mental disorder.
9. *Institutionally prescribed abuse* refers to those cases of abuse which occur in institutions, such as schools, day-care centers, and detention homes.
10. *Self-identified abusers* are aware that their own child-rearing practices are deviant. These individuals are socially successful and are usually highly motivated to solve the problem.

As shown in Figure 3.13 these ten categories may be placed under four major headings. The first, *personality,* consists of emotional displacement and frustration, mental illness, and poor judgment; the second, *parenting behavior,* consists of parenting incompetency and deviant child-rearing practices; the third, *situations,* consists of stress and situational neglect; and the fourth, *social forces,* consists of subcultural norms and institutional environments.

This outlook asserts that perpetrators can be helped and child victimization can be stopped. It proposes that any abusive behavior that has been learned can be unlearned.

Figure 3.13
Schematic Representation of Offender Typology Theory of Physical Abuse

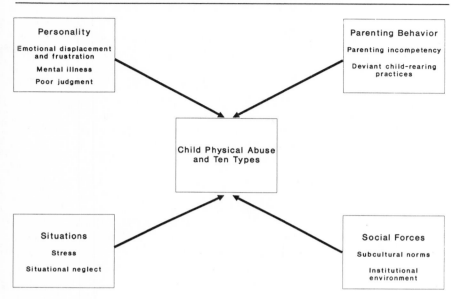

Empirical Evidence. Being a clinically derived classification scheme, evidence for this typology is solely in the form of case examples and illustrations. No empirical studies are presented to substantiate the validity or reliability of the types.

Evaluation. This ten-level analysis of physical abusers appears comprehensive and addresses a number of relevant issues. A lack of parenting skills has been found by Tzeng et al. (1988) to be a major stressor associated with child maltreatment. This finding may support Walters's assertion that the majority of abusers fall into type one, socially and parentally incompetent adults.

This analysis incorporates relevant theoretical issues, such as intergenerational learning, frustration-aggression, situational influences, and the subculture of violence. A number of ecological levels are addressed: individual, family, community (subculture), and cultural (institutions). This analysis also considers characteristics of the child (type six, victim-precipitated abuse), a consideration often lacking in theories of child abuse.

Walters's (1975) analysis may be suited for clinical assessment and treatment, but provides little in the area of directly predicting or preventing child maltreatment. The types presented by Walters fall into the "explaining by naming" trap. Labeling a behavior does not explain it and may actually be detrimental in some cases. Type four, neglect, is not appropriately placed in this scheme. Neglect is a higher-order classification type (like physical and sexual abuse) under which the other causal types (e.g., parental incompetence, situation, and accidental) should logically fall.

Walters fails to adequately consider the interactions and overlap between various causal types. Frustrated abusers, for example, may displace anger onto a child (type 3) only during an unusually stressful situation (type 4), which may be propagated by characteristics of the child (type 6) and parental incompetence (type 1) coupled with poor judgment (type 5). In light of the anecdotal nature of this approach, (mostly clinical speculations with very little or no empirical evidence and no validity or reliability data), this typology needs to be considered at a preliminary stage. With empirical testing, it may be found to be accurate, reliable, valid, and thus helpful to future researchers and service providers, but until then it must be taken with caution.

FAMILY SYSTEMS PARADIGM

Systems theory links different social systems and explains their interdependence and interactions. The concepts derived from the systems approach have been important and highly influential in the field of child abuse and neglect, especially in the areas of intervention and counseling. This paradigm has had a strong impact across all types of maltreatment. The theory reviewed under physical abuse is family systems theory of physical abuse.

Family Systems Theory of Physical Abuse

Theoretical Foundations. The systems theory of physical abuse (see Figure 3.14) is rooted in modern systems theory, which considers social systems as interrelated, dynamic, and multivariate phenomena that operate as adaptive units rather than as a collection of static parts (Buckley, 1967). This theory seeks to discover the interrelations between the parts of the total social structure and to trace how characteristics of each part affect one another and interact. As a general model, systems theory has as its primary purpose to describe the functioning of various systems, such as the family. Therefore, it is not a causal theory.

Basic Principles. Family is considered a goal-seeking adaptive unit. Therefore, child maltreatment as a form of family violence is an output of the total family system. It is not simply the product of chance aberration, inadequate socialization, or individual psychopathology (Steinmetz & Straus, 1973). Actions by any family member or other system impinges on the family and reverberates throughout, creating emotional and/or behavioral changes in each member (Glick & Kessler, 1974; Post, 1982).

Eight propositions are set forth by Straus (1973) concerning family violence:

1. Family violence has *diverse causes,* for example, unreasonable normative expectations, dysfunctional personality traits, frustrations, and marital conflicts.

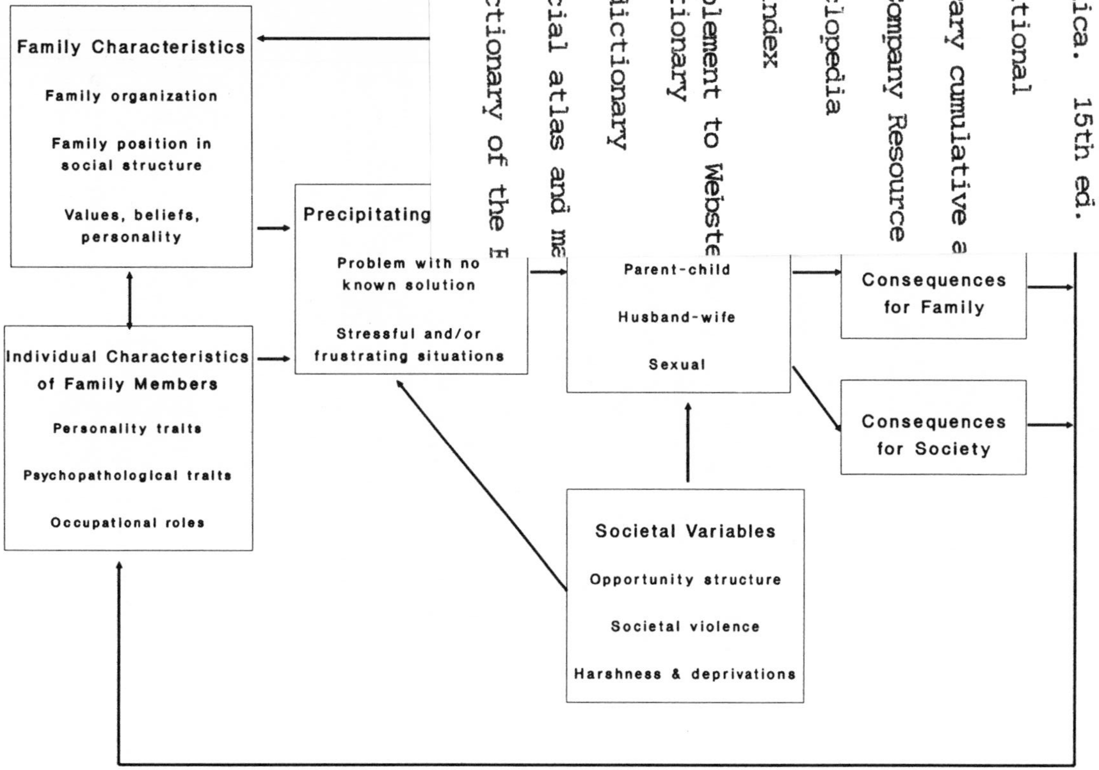

ry school library collec

edia Americana

Britannica.　[14th ed.]

Britannica.　15th ed.

Britannica.　15th ed.

international

ty Library cumulative a

ccess Company Resource

s encyclopedia

times index

a supplement to Webste
al dictionary

glish dictionary

commercial atlas and ma

se dictionary of the E

Figure 3.14
Schematic Representation of Family Syste

Consequences for Family

Consequences for Society

Parent-child
Husband-wife
Sexual

Societal Variables
Opportunity structure
Societal violence
Harshness & deprivations

Precipitating
Problem with no known solution
Stressful and/or frustrating situations

Family Characteristics
Family organization
Family position in social structure
Values, beliefs, personality

Individual Characteristics of Family Members
Personality traits
Psychopathological traits
Occupational roles

2. Family violence *occurs at extremely high rates,* relative to the rate of publicly known cases.

3. Most violence is either *denied or not labeled deviant* by societal or family norms, for example, the use of physical punishment.

4. Stereotyped imagery of family violence is *learned in early childhood* from parents, siblings, and other children through the powerful mechanisms of modeling and imitation.

5. The stereotypes of family violence are *continually reinforced* for adults and children through *ordinary social interactions* (for example, high value on the tough male image).

6. Violent persons are often *reinforced for violent acts* and thus the probability of their using violence again is increased.

7. When the use of violence to settle a conflict goes against family norms, a *secondary conflict* is likely to occur that tends to produce additional violence.

8. Family violence is more likely when the perpetrator's *role expectation* or self-concept is one of being violent or "tough."

A *discursive format* of these propositions stresses the systems aspect. The family as a social system is stressed through the everyday interactions of its members, which may result in violence or conflict. The likelihood of violence as a systems product is increased when *positive feedback* processes, such as labeling, conflict over the use of violence, reinforcement of violent behavior, and "tough" or violent roles, are in operation (Straus, 1973).

Other factors that perpetuate family violence include *congruent relations* between the abusive act and four other factors: (1) the goals of the offender and family system; (2) the abuser's self-concept as a violent person; (3) the victim's role expectancies and low degree of power; and (4) high community tolerance of the abuse.

Straus (1973) structures the process relationships among various factors under different circumstances in a computerized flowchart. It specifies alternative causal flows possible and feedback loops that maintain the system's operation or start deviation sequences. If violence becomes an element of the system, the system may stabilize at that level through negative feedback or dampening processes. It may also proceed on an upward spiral, escalating until the family unit is destroyed by an event such as divorce, desertion, or murder. Changes that can halt the upward spiral include the dropping or avoiding of violence-producing roles and the development of nonviolent means to deal with conflicts.

Empirical Evidence. Evidence for family systems theory has often been in the form of clinical case examples, as it is a perspective utilized by many therapists and social workers.

Straus (1973) offers no direct empirical evidence for the general systems theory of family violence. Evidence for the proposition exists, but does not necessarily support systems theory specifically. For example, proposition number one—violence between family members arising from diverse causes—is easily supported, but is so general that it cannot really qualify as a theoretical statement about causality.

Evaluation. Systems theories of family violence focus on describing a relationship pattern of the family that functions to maintain the family unit in a balanced state. This theory has served to investigate a wide range of family problems, including child physical (Straus, 1973; Gelles & Maynard, 1987) and sexual abuse (Cohen, 1983), spouse abuse, and adolescent parricide in abusive families (Post, 1982). A positive attribute of Straus's (1973) systems model is its applicability and emphasis on empirical research. Unfortunately, this emphasis has not been capitalized to a significant degree. The potential utility of all family systems approaches can only be realized if they are based more firmly on consistency between conceptual frameworks and empirical findings (Conte, 1985).

Straus (1973) indicates four areas in which systems theory needs elaboration: (1) elements delineated (e.g., inputs, outputs, operations, and decisions) need to be expanded to fully account for family violence; (2) the decision and operation factors need to be subdivided and broken down in greater detail; (3) interactions between the nuclear family and surrounding systems, such as neighbors, extended relations, and formal social control agencies, need to be specified; and (4) the operations and decisions specified need not be under conscious deliberate control.

By considering all parts of the system as complementary, reciprocally interacting and influencing one another, pure systemic theory regards violent relationships as complementary—the victim is considered to be as responsible as the perpetrator. It is assumed that the family "needs" violence to sustain homeostasis. In this respect, systemic theories are similar to some psychodynamic notions that assert that some abused children "need" abuse to gratify unconscious conflicts.

However, the assumption that abusive families need violence does not explain why abuse often leads to the breakup of the family. Although some abusive families continue, many others do not. Systems theory needs to examine the reasons for these conflicting results.

Some criticize family systems theory for spreading the blame of child abuse among all family members (including the victim), thereby relieving the perpetrator of full responsibility. However, others have argued that a true systemic analysis does not necessarily blame the victim or relieve offenders of responsibility. Instead, its purpose is to increase understanding through greater analytic complexity by investigating the family as a whole unit with its intrafamilial interactions and processes.

Overall, this theory is positive in that it looks beyond individual characteristics of the perpetrator to the victim and it treats the act of family violence as interrelated and counterbalanced within a normal system of family. The components of this theory, organized in a computerized operational flowchart, could lead to therapeutic intervention at various dysfunctional points within the family. However, the elements of the flowchart, especially regarding individual characteristics, need to be expanded and detailed and the interrelationships among the elements need to be redefined and modified such that the complex nature of clinical intervention for both mild and severe cases can be accounted for.

PARENT-CHILD INTERACTION PARADIGM

Bowlby's (1973) studies of mother-child bonding (or attachment) have been quite influential in the area of parent-child relations. The importance of parent-child interactions is represented by five member theories of this paradigm: (1) attachment theory, (2) parental acceptance-rejection theory, (3) transactional theory, (4) encounter theory, and (5) cognitive/behavioral/developmental theory.

Attachment Theory of Physical Abuse

Theoretical Foundations. The attachment theory is rooted in studies on mother-child bonding and is especially grounded in the work of Bowlby (1980) and Ainsworth (1978, 1979). It is assumed that early experiences are important for later development and that human infants have an innate disposition to form intimate relationships that are essential for survival. Personality and mental health are dependent upon a secure childhood, which results from continuous and positive interaction between caretaker and child (Bowlby, 1951).

Basic Principles. The basic principle of attachment theory is that sensitive, responsive, and accepting parenting during the first year of an infant's life results in a secure attachment relationship between the child and parent, and parental behaviors that are insensitive, unresponsive, and rejecting result in an anxious or insecure attachment between the parent and child (cf. Aber & Allen, 1987; Ainsworth et al., 1978; Belsky, Rovine & Taylor, 1984).

Attachment is not automatically formed after birth. It develops over the first year of an infant's life, following many healthy parent-child interactions. Such interactions result in proximity and, ultimately, security, trust, and affection between the parent and the child (Egeland & Erickson, 1987).

Bowlby (1973) suggested that initial cognitive expectancies set up a process of defensive exclusion or selective perception that filters incoming information in accordance with these expectations. Parent-child attachments may be either secure or anxious. *Secure attachments* are likely when the parent is sensitive, responsive, and predictable in meeting the child's needs, whereas *anxious attachments* are the result of opposite behaviors, such as being insensitive and unresponsive in meeting the child's needs (see Figure 3.15). The caregiver should also provide the infant with comfort when distressed and should act as a secure base from which the infant may explore.

Egeland and Erickson (1987) utilize Sroufe's (1979) developmental-organizational theory in conjunction with attachment theory. According to this perspective, development is considered to be a series of issues and a sequence of adaptations. Each developmental phase contains specific issues that present spe-

Figure 3.15
Schematic Representation of Attachment Theory

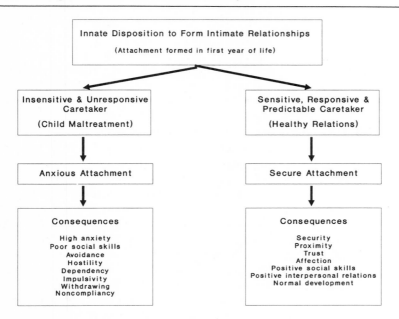

cial challenges to the individual's ability to integrate behavior in adaptive ways. Individual differences arise with respect to the differential quality in adapting to these challenges. Each level of development requires integration and differentiation of former accomplishments. Thus, successful integration will determine subsequent developmental adaptation (Egeland & Erickson, 1987).

Four *childhood developmental stages* and their corresponding issues are discussed by Egeland and Erickson. At age one, a major issue is to establish a sense of *trust* and *security* by forming a secure relationship with the caregiver. At age two, a major issue is the child's emerging *autonomy*. Around age three, socialization factors such as *self-control* and *self-esteem* become the salient issues. Around ages four and five, *social and emotional competence,* as demonstrated in positive interaction with peers, acceptance of adult guidance, and a confident assertive approach to classroom activities, become primary issues for the child.

In the study of child abuse and neglect, the focus is not on individual behaviors, but rather on patterns of behaviors and how children organize their behaviors around salient developmental issues. Developmental factors must be considered because of the differential meanings at different ages (Egeland & Erickson, 1987).

Heinicke (1984) has stressed the role of prebirth parental personality and marital characteristics in the subsequent development of quality parent-child bonding and family relations. Four factors are considered relevant to postnatal development: (1) the personality variable of maternal anxiety, (2) the social interaction variable of husband-wife adaptation, (3) the role variable of the mother's occupational commitment, and (4) the ecological variable of available and adequate substitute child care.

Empirical Evidence. Egeland, Sroufe, and Erickson (1983) found that children who had been classified as anxious/avoidant in infancy were highly dependent on preschool teachers, were noncompliant, and had poor social skills. These children were frequently described by their teachers as hostile, impulsive, giving up easily, and withdrawn.

Aber and Allen (1987) studied three domains concerning the effects of maltreatment on early childhood development: (1) relationships with novel adults, (2) efficacious motivation (to produce a desired effect), and (3) cognitive maturity. Subjects were 190 children four to eight years old. Ninety-three were maltreated, 67 demographically matched nonmaltreated from families receiving welfare, and 30 nonmaltreated middle-class families. On the measure of "secure readiness to learn in the company of novel adults," maltreated children scored significantly lower than welfare children, who scored lower than middle-class children. On the measure of "outer directedness," maltreated children and welfare children scored higher than middle-class children, but did not significantly differ from each other.

Thus, unlike its effect on secure readiness to learn, child abuse does not appear to have an effect on young children's outer-directedness over and above the effects attributable to their lower socioeconomic status. There are several possible explanations for this finding.

First, although previous studies indicate that maltreated preschool children are more compulsively compliant with parental demands than nonmaltreated children, it may be that such compliance has not yet been generalized beyond this particular relationship to relationships involving other adults.

Second, perhaps outer-directedness in early childhood cannot be incrementally affected by maltreatment because the poverty and sources of failure associated with low socioeconomic status have already done all possible damages.

Another position suggests that whether maltreatment has an effect on children over and above the effects of low socioeconomic status appears to depend on the areas of development under investigation. From both the attachment and ecological perspectives, this position makes sense. Neither theory predicts blanket impairments in development due to maltreatment but, rather, impairments in specific domains at particular stages of development.

Heinicke (1984) found that prebirth personality and marital characteristics influence early family development. Two prebirth factors significantly related to the parent-child relationship were the mother's adaptive competence and her trust in the relationship with the child. In a two-year follow-up study, Heinicke concluded that weakness in these two factors contributes to feelings of maternal ambivalence toward the infant, which results in lower self-esteem and greater aggression by the child.

Evaluation. Attachment theory has had considerable impact on the child care field. Bowlby (1951) asserted that children thrive better in bad homes than in good institutions, and thus supported the view that children should be kept with their families at almost all costs and that removal into foster care should be regarded as a last resort (French, 1984).

Recently, however, this view has been challenged. Howells (1974), for example, has maintained that this view places many children at risk in their own homes. Bowlby stated that the natural mother is not exclusively the most important caretaker for the child. Different groups now hold various and often conflicting views on this subject (French, 1984).

Rather than explaining child maltreatment etiology, this theory focuses on the differential impact that various types of attachment (anxious or secure) have on the development of a child's personality, behavior, and cognitions. This theory also focuses on what constitutes abuse and has special implications for the area of psychological abuse and neglect. Aber (1987), for example, suggests that during early childhood, maltreatment will inevitably disrupt a dynamic balance between two behavioral dispositions: (1) the motivation to establish close, safe, and secure relationships with adults and (2) the motivation to venture out to explore the world in a competency-promoting fashion.

Attachment theory has provided strong theoretical bases for a number of therapeutic programs. For example, *the holding environment* program was designed to break the cycle of abuse (Dougherty, 1983). It is based on the concepts of the attachment theory and humanistic theory and attempts to replicate the warm, accepting atmosphere of a healthy parent-child relationship. This program assumes that parents who abuse or neglect their children were frequently deprived of caring, consistent, and encouraging parenting themselves (Dougherty, 1983).

However, this theory is too narrow in focusing on the developmental relationships between the parent and the child. It has three major weaknesses: (1) It ignores the importance of continued developmental requirements for all children (e.g., morality, values, and perceptions); (2) it downplays the significance of early childhood interactions with other persons and institutions (e.g., siblings, media, and childcare institutions); and (3) it overemphasizes the role of lack of love in anxious attachment on the development of undesirable personality characteristics (e.g., high anxiety, avoidance, dependency, noncompliancy). Finally, empirical and longitudinal evaluation of various conditions, as they are stipulated in this theory, is needed to delineate more detailed dynamics and the nature of the *process* involved in developing intimate attachment and associated requirements.

Parental Acceptance-Rejection Theory of Physical Abuse

Theoretical Foundations. Parental acceptance-rejection theory, advocated by Rohner (1980, 1986), assumes that (1) early childhood experiences are central to adult personality development and behavior, (2) the most vital childhood experiences are those associated with the parent-child relationship, (3) the parent-child relationship may be positive or negative, (4) children perceive their parents as accepting or rejecting them, (5) perceptions of acceptance lead to healthy development and positive characteristics, and (6) perceptions of rejection lead to unhealthy development and negative characteristics.

Basic Principles. Parental acceptance-rejection theory (see Figure 3.16) may be conceived as a one-dimensional continuum with parental rejection and parental acceptance anchoring the two opposing poles (Kitahara, 1987). At the *rejecting pole* (lacking warmth and affection), child maltreatment may be displayed in terms of physical abuse (e.g., hitting or slapping), psychological abuse (e.g., disapproval or verbal hostilities), or neglect (e.g., being indifferent, resentful, ignoring, unresponsive, or remote). At the *accepting pole,* parental accepting behavior may also be displayed physically (e.g., hugs and kisses) and psychologically (warmth, acceptance, and praise).

The child's perception of parental behavior ultimately defines where the parent-child relationship lies on the acceptance-rejection continuum (Kitahara, 1987). Theoretically, rejected children are likely to be aggressive, hostile, and dependent adults. These individuals usually have low self-esteem, are emotionally unresponsive and unstable, and have a negative world view. Furthermore, rejection is often transmitted from generation to generation. This rejection

Figure 3.16
Schematic Representation of Parental Acceptance-Rejection Theory

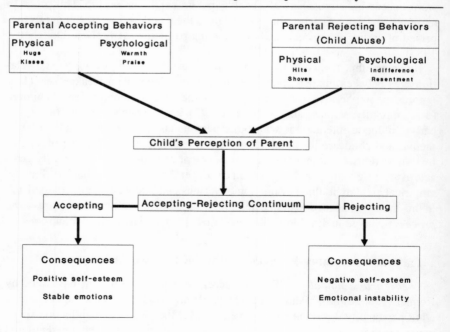

cycle results in rejected children rejecting their own children (Rohner, 1980; Kitahara, 1987).

Empirical Evidence. To test this theory, Kitahara analyzed the responses of 71 Swedish college students (20 males and 51 females) to the *Parental Acceptance-Rejection Questionnaire* (PARQ) and the *Personality Assessment Questionnaire* (PAQ). The PARQ measures four precepts of parental behavior: (1) perceived warmth and affection, (2) perceived hostility and aggression, (3) perceived indifference and neglect, and (4) perceived undifferentiated rejection (i.e., unrelated to the first three).

The PAQ measures self-perception along seven dimensions: (1) hostility, aggression, passive aggression, and problems with the management of hostility and aggression, (2) dependence, (3) self-esteem, (4) self-adequacy, (5) emotional responsiveness, (6) emotional stability, and (7) world view. Kitahara (1987) found parental rejection scores predicted negative perceptions of the self. Total PARQ scores were significantly correlated with total PAQ scores in a manner suggesting that rejection perception leads to a negative assessment of the self. Perception of low warmth was strongly associated with a person's negative self-esteem and emotional instability. All aspects of personality assessment, except dependency, were about equally associated with the specific aspects of parental rejection. Dependence was not associated with any aspect of parental rejection.

Evaluation. From the scientific empirical research point of view, parental acceptance-rejection theory has the following strengths: (1) It systematizes a large number of findings; (2) it has led to the development of a number of psychometrically adequate questionnaires; (3) it has been tested cross-culturally; and (4) it may be considered to be an important concept for understanding the parent-child relationship (Kitahara, 1987).

However, this theory narrowly explains the complex phenomenon of child abuse and neglect in terms of a single parental acceptance-rejection dimension. Other variables in family and environmental contexts are not dealt with (e.g., parental personality characteristics and social norms and values). These variables may be long-term or acute stressors that may cause or facilitate parental acceptance and rejection dispositions. The present theory is therefore too simple to account for multidimensional characteristics of child abuse and neglect etiology.

Transactional Theory of Physical Abuse

Theoretical Foundations. The transactional theory is developed from the considerations of other theoretical perspectives that include stress theory, parental acceptance and rejection theory, and parent-child attachment theory. Therefore, this theory emphasizes four central components (see Figure 3.17): (1) characteristics of the parent, (2) characteristics of the child, (3) the parent-child relationship, and (4) external stressors (Sameroft & Chandler, 1975). This theory is concerned with three forms of child maltreatment: neglect, nonorganic failure to thrive, and physical abuse.

Figure 3.17
Schematic Representation of Transactional Theory

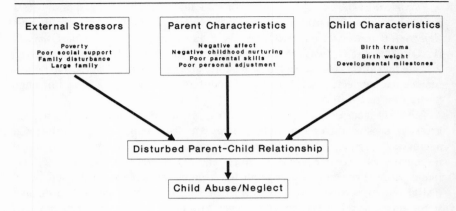

Basic Principles. This theory has three basic principles: (1) Child maltreatment is rooted in the early life of the child, often in the form of a disturbance in the parent-child relationship; (2) certain characteristics of the offender influence the occurrence of child maltreatment, and (3) environmental stressors on the family contribute to the etiology of child maltreatment (Vietze et al., 1982). According to transactional theory, interactions between developmental characteristics of the child (e.g., birth trauma) and external stress (e.g., poverty) significantly influence the occurrence of developmental risk in children.

Empirical Evidence. In order to operationalize this theory, Vietze et al. (1982) interviewed mothers in terms of seven basic factors: (1) feelings about pregnancy, (2) social support systems, (3) mother's own nurturing during childhood, (4) family stress events, (5) parenting skills, (6) personal adjustment, and (7) developmental milestones (e.g., when babies first smile, when a baby can understand right from wrong, etc.). Families were classified as either high or low in risk of future child maltreatment. Of the 1,401 expecting mothers interviewed, 273 (19.9%) were classified as high-risk mothers, and 225 subjects were placed in the low-risk comparison group.

The high- and low-risk groups were compared on five measures: newborn behavioral assessment, infant-mother interactions, maternal perception of infant temperament, developmental assessment, and child maltreatment.

The high-risk and low-risk groups did not differ significantly in terms of age (mean of 20.9), ethnicity, marital status, or education. High- and low-risk newborns did not differ significantly on measures of birthweight, gestational age, Apgar scores (routine battery of tests given to newborns that includes breathing, color, heart rate, etc.), or gender. The high-risk group had a significantly lower proportion of women with first pregnancies than did the low-risk comparison group.

Of the 498 families studied, 70 (14%) experienced child maltreatment. Fifty-three (76%) of these 70 families had been identified as at high risk for maltreatment (significant at the .001 level). Differences between the high- and low-risk groups were statistically significant in terms of neglect (24 vs. 7 cases) and nonorganic failure to thrive (28 vs. 9 cases), but not in terms of physical abuse (9 vs. 3 cases).

Newborn follow-up observations revealed that (1) there was no significant difference between the groups in newborn behavior, except that high-risk infants smiled less than their low-risk counterparts; and (2) high-risk mothers spent less time cradling or providing any type of caregiving to their infants than did low-risk mothers.

One-month follow-up observations revealed that (1) high-risk infants cried more than twice as long as low-risk infants; and (2) high-risk mothers spent more time in the room with their infants but beyond arms' reach; they spent less time looking at their infants while feeding them; and they spent significantly less total time interacting with their infants than did the low-risk mothers (Vietze et al., 1982). Three-month observations revealed that low-risk mothers and infants spent significantly more time in positive vocalizations.

Six-, twelve-, and eighteen-month follow-up observations revealed no significant differences between the two groups in terms of mother-infant interactions or maternal perception of infant temperament.

Evaluation. This theory has three basic strengths: empirical orientation, multifaceted structure, and focus on prevention.

Empirical orientation: This theory emphasizes scientific empiricism. Vietze et al. (1982) used matched control groups and reliable behavioral measures at various stages of the experiment.

Multifaceted structure: This theory maintains that child abuse and neglect is a complex problem. Characteristics of the child, the parent, parent-child interactions, and stressors were all considered.

Focus on prevention: Since this theory is primarily concerned with predicting child maltreatment, it has special relevance for prevention. The work done under this theory (Vietze et al., 1980, 1982; Altemeier et al., 1979) supports the notion that at-risk families may be identified via prenatal maternal interviews.

As pointed out by Vietze and associates (1982), a program using this method could not be 100 percent accurate and would inevitably yield some false positives and false negatives. Such a program would have to be careful with labeling individuals as potential child abusers. Vietze suggests offering the at-risk group a variety of services on a voluntary basis without labeling them in any way, or, ideally, offering services to all families who obtain their prenatal care through hospitals.

This theory has three primary weaknesses in relation to specific hypothesis, model, and macrosystem factors.

Specific hypotheses: Although overall cases of child maltreatment were predicted, the only hypothesis tested (and confirmed) was that high-risk families would be reported for child maltreatment more than would low-risk families. Vietze and associates did not generate any hypotheses from transactional theory concerning the specific measured variables (e.g., interaction observations, newborn behavior, and maternal perception of infant temperament).

Model: This theory lacks a theoretical model showing detailed components, causal linkage, and interactions.

Lack of considering macrosystem factors: Transactional theory emphasizes mother-child interactions and considers community and familial factors to a degree (e.g., the role of stress and poverty). However, cultural/societal factors are not addressed, and the role of other family members (e.g., father, siblings) are minimized.

Overall, this theory emphasizes empirical evaluation of child abuse and neglect and the impact of longitudinal interactions between stress and behavior. This theory offers a considerably significant step toward the development of child abuse evaluation and preventive strategies.

Encounter Theory of Physical Abuse

Theoretical Foundations. Encounter theory, as described by Zimrin (1984), assumes that characteristics of the child and characteristics of the parent interact and affect one another. Child abuse occurs when these two sets of characteristics clash (see Figure 3.18). Personality traits and behavioral attributes are said to develop within a dynamic process of exchange between individuals. Therefore, just as children are influenced by parental behaviors and attitudes, they also influence and elicit new modes of behavior from their parents.

Basic Principles. This theory has three basic principles: (1) A parent's abusive behavior has a negative impact on a child; (2) a child's attributes influence the parent's abusive behavior; and (3) the encounter of traits and needs is a risk factor

Figure 3.18
Schematic Representation of Encounter Theory

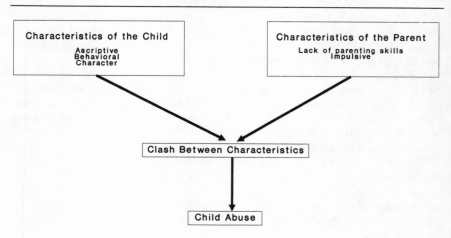

with regard to abusive behavior. This theory holds that an abusive situation will be a result of the encounter between character traits and needs of both the parent and the child in interaction (Zimrin, 1984).

The impact of child abuse and neglect: The negative impact of child maltreatment on physical, behavioral, and emotional development has been examined in detail in the literature by researchers. Traits of the abused child most often affected include self-image, the expression of emotion, relations with others, and aggression. These traits may develop as a direct consequence of the parent's abusive behavior, with the child being an innocent victim. According to Zimrin, most of the literature considers the perpetrator fully responsible for the abusive behavior, while the child's contribution is minimized. Zimrin asserts that this analysis is unrealistic because it portrays the child as a "tabula rasa" whose personality is formed as a result of child abuse. Therefore, characteristics of the child that may cause parental abusive behaviors are examined in this theory.

Parent's abusive behavior as a result of the child's attributes: Characteristics of children that may elicit abusive behaviors are delineated into four categories by Zimrin (1984):

1. *Ascriptive characteristics* over which the child has absolutely no control, such as gender or resemblance to a certain member of the family.
2. *Behavioral characteristics* such as hyperactivity or other behavioral problems.
3. *Character traits* such as excessive self-confidence or a lack of it, obedience or refusal to accept authority.
4. *Deviance* such as prematurity or physical handicap.

These characteristics can contribute to abusive behaviors in several ways: *Direct links* to abuse may involve physical handicaps that put extra stress on the parent. *Symbolic links* may include ascriptive characteristics that have symbolic value for the parent, such as resemblance to a disliked husband. Another symbolic link may be the use of *projection,* whereby parents attribute their own undesirable characteristics to a child and then abuse the child because of them. In these cases, the symbol mediates between the trait and the abusive behavior (Zimrin, 1984).

The encounter of traits and needs as a risk factor with regard to abusive behavior: According to this model, the particular encounter due to different personalities and needs of the parent and the child creates and enhances all abusive behavior (Zimrin, 1984). Zimrin maintains that theories that hold abusers exclusively responsible for their behaviors are not sufficient to explain the majority of the child abuse cases. As individuals react to one another and change, it is possible that at one point the encounter between the personalities of a parent and child may not result in abuse, while at another point, when one of the participants has undergone change, the nature of the encounter changes too, and abuse may occur.

Empirical Evidence. It has not been adequately determined if the correlation between being abused and certain characteristics, such as aggression, low self-esteem, and difficulties in showing and receiving affection, reflects causation or impact.

No empirically based evidence for the proposition that characteristics of the child may cause the abuse was presented by Zimrin. However, other supportive arguments (e.g., Delsardo, 1974; Belsky, 1978) and clinical examples regarding the characteristics of the child were provided. Similar evidence was provided for the proposition that examines the interactive effect of the child's and parent's personalities and how they can change each other's traits and behaviors.

Evaluation. Zimrin (1984) considers the importance of characteristics of both the child and the parent and their interactive effect in child abuse. Characteristics of the child have been shown to be associated with abusive behavioral patterns. Martin and Walters (1982) have presented data showing that emotional problems of the child significantly correlated to emotional abuse; physical defect or illness of the child significantly correlated to neglect; and sex, age, and emotional problems of the child significantly correlated with sexual abuse. Many studies, as has been noted in previous theories, have also noted characteristics of parents that can be related to abusive behavior.

The relationship of cause and effect in these correlates, however, has not been fully examined. Neglect is more likely to occur when a child has greater needs due to defect or illness. In some circumstances, neglect may in fact have caused the defect or illness. In sexual abuse, emotional problems of the child may be the effect and not the cause. Until the relationship of cause and effect is determined, the support for the encounter theory cannot be found in the raw data.

The parent-child interaction aspect of the encounter theory has also received empirical support. Martin and Walters, for example, found parent-child conflicts significantly associated with abandonment, physical abuse, and sexual abuse.

The inclusion of factors outside the individual perpetrator to explain the etiology and continuation of child maltreatment is now widely accepted and advocated by most researchers in the field. However, the degree to which other factors are considered varies. The real advantage of this theory lies in its emphasis on the parent-child interactions.

While characteristics of the child and parent and their interactions are important variables to be investigated, they cannot fully explain child abuse. Other factors that have been shown to play an important role in child maltreatment include (1) other family members, (2) community support systems, (3) cultural and subcultural values, (4) socioeconomic stressors, (5) social isolation of the family, and (6) family privacy norms. Unfortunately, these factors are not found in encounter theory, and their exclusions are not explained by Zimrin.

This theory comes close to blaming the child for the perpetrator's behavior: In some cases, "the child's traits and characteristics have caused him or her to become an abused child . . . thus the child is the cause of the parent's abusive behavior insofar as the parent reacts to his or her characteristics" (Zimrin, 1984). Although it is true that the child's behavior or trait may be the trigger of an abusive act, this stance reduces the perpetrator's responsibility for the abusive behavior and its consequence. Characteristics of the child can influence parental behavior. This should not, however, be regarded as a sole cause of maltreatment. The child should not be further burdened with guilt that he or she "caused" the family violence. Apparently, this model focuses exclusively on the situational variables that are directly involved in the parent-child interaction and abuse behavior. Since similar situations and similar personality characteristics of the child may not necessarily elicit abusive behavior patterns from average parents, the encounter theory is really too simple and too narrow in addressing the complex issues involved in child physical abuse.

Furthermore, it should be noted that because of personality differences, parents and children do not always naturally get along. This does not mean that all such relationships are or will be abusive. However, helping one party cope with negative *(perceived* or *real)* characteristics of the other party can only help improve parent-child interactions. Recognizing background characteristics of each person and the *trigger* situations for their confrontation could lead to understanding, acceptance, and/or adjustment and thus less irritation and better communication.

Cognitive/Behavioral/Developmental Theory of Physical Abuse

Theoretical Foundations. Cognitive/behavioral/developmental theory (see Figure 3.19), advocated by Azar (Azar, Fantuzzo & Twentyman, 1984; Azar, 1986), is based on five primary concepts: (1) parent-child interactions, (2) parental impulse control, (3) parental cognitive factors (attitudes and beliefs), (4) family stress, and (5) availability of social support.

This framework is based primarily on social psychological literature concern-

Figure 3.19
Schematic Representation of Cognitive/Behavioral/Developmental Theory

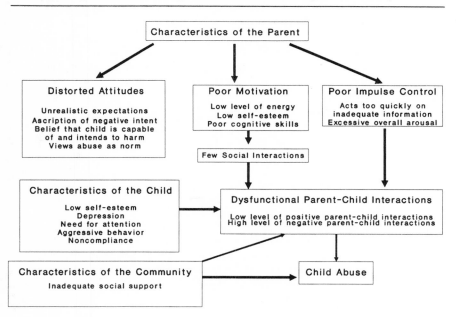

ing the role that cognitive and developmental factors play in the causation and impact of aggression in general and child physical abuse in particular.

Basic Principles. Azar's (1986) framework of five primary concepts has special relevance to the etiology and impact of child maltreatment. The first three— parent-child interaction disturbances, parental disturbances in impulse control, and parental cognitive dysfunctions—appear to be at the core of maltreating behavior and may also explain developmental disturbances suffered by victimized children. The last two—high levels of family stress and low levels of social support—are situations in which maltreatment and developmental disturbances are more likely to occur. These five factors are said to overlap and interact. The three core areas are discussed separately for clarity.

Parent-child interaction disturbances: High levels of negative interaction occur in maltreating families. This may not alone explain abuse, but clearly would have a negative impact on the socialization experience of the child and could explain subsequent aggressive behavior and the low self-esteem often exhibited by victims of child abuse. The child may be so desperate for attention that even aversive attention may become reinforcing. Through experience, the child learns to elicit abusive contacts with the parent. This type of interaction is susceptible to cyclic escalation. As the parent habituates to the child's aversive behavior, the child increases the level of behavior to attract the desired attention.

Decreased levels of overall and positive interaction may be due to (1) characteristics of the child that lessen his or her ability to reinforce interactions with the parent (e.g., low birth weight and preterm deliveries), (2) distorted attitudes regarding the developmental needs of infants, (3) low parental levels of energy and general sense of adequacy, and (4) teenage parents, who are less active, less verbal, and less contingently responsive to their infants (Field, 1980).

Impulse control problems: Based on empirical data, Azar (1986) suggests maltreating parents may, when confronted with a problem requiring careful consideration, act too quickly on inadequate information. These individuals may have an excessive overall arousal level to environmental stimuli. Since a high level of arousal is aversive, such parents may need to withdraw. If withdrawal is not possible, then aggression, in the form of child abuse, may erupt.

Cognitive disturbances: Many child maltreaters are deficient in cognitive skills (Schilling et al., 1982). Cognitively low functioning individuals are less likely to engage in social behavior. Azar (1986) suggests that cognitive limitations could help explain the lower levels of parent-child interactions found in some maltreating families.

According to this theory, five cognitive appraisals by parents may trigger maltreatment: (1) being in a state of relative deprivation, (2) believing that children are capable of and are purposefully acting in a manner intended to harm them, (3) having unrealistic expectations of their children, (4) ascribing negative intentionality to their children's behavior, and (5) viewing maltreating behavior as culturally sanctioned.

Unrealistic expectations may explain why most child maltreatment occurs in response to the child's noncompliance (Herrenkohl, Herrenkohl & Egolf, 1983). Such expectations also would result in the child's continuously getting a message of inadequacy, and thus may explain the onset of lowered self-esteem and depression found among abused children (Kazdin et al., 1985).

Maltreating behaviors are more likely to occur when they result in low probability of negative consequences or in greater positive ones. Aggression is more persistent when it is reinforced intermittently, which is usually the case in child-rearing situations. Cultural views of child rearing are also considered important in child abuse etiology. Physical punishment is often sanctioned by societal norms and thus some maltreating parents may consider their behaviors consistent with social norms despite their extremity.

Empirical Evidence. High levels of negative interactions in maltreating families have been reported by a number of studies. However, such behaviors have not been shown to be *unique* to maltreating families (Azar, 1986). More support exists for the hypothesis that maltreating parents interact significantly less with their children and less positively than do nonmaltreating parents in matched control groups (e.g., Burgess & Conger, 1978; Bousha & Twentyman, 1984; Dietrich, Starr & Kaplan, 1980).

Both low-birth-weight and preterm children have been shown to be overrepresented by the abused population of children. Depressed mothers have been shown to interact less with their children and to perceive them more negatively (Ovaschel, 1983). Feelings of inadequacy have been linked to the use of physical punishment (Welch, 1985), and maltreating parents have been found to have poor problem-solving abilities (Azar et al., 1984).

Some researchers have found that maltreating parents perceive themselves to be less able to cope with stress (Conger, Burgess & Barrett, 1979; Mash, Johnston & Kovitz, 1983; Rosenbeg & Respucci, 1983). Azar and colleagues (1984) found that abusing and neglectful mothers had significantly higher unrealistic expectations, particularly in the area of children's assuming adult role responsibilities. Other empirical studies have found that maltreating mothers tend to ascribe more negative intentionality to children's behavior than do nonmaltreating mothers (Plotkin & Twentyman, 1983; Larrance & Twentyman, 1983).

Evaluation. Azar (1986) suggests that parent-child interaction disturbances, parental disturbances in impulse control, and parental cognitive dysfunctions can explain the etiology and impact of physical child abuse. The integration of cognitive, behavioral, and developmental perspectives offers explanations for both etiological and impact findings. Thus, this theory could potentially explain both the occurrence of parental aggression and the negative sequelae observed among maltreated children. Because of this dual explanatory power, this framework can foster theory development and could improve treatment and prevention efforts. This framework emphasizes empirical research and empirical data to formulate its various theoretical constructs.

Behavior, cognition, and development need to be considered in the intervention and prevention of child maltreatment. Consideration of only one area will have limited results (Azar, 1986). For example, improving parenting skills may promote a parent's sense of efficacy and reduce the potential for abuse, but will not directly help improve lowered levels of stimulation provided to the child. Unless stimulation is enhanced, the prognosis for the child's overall development is still poor. Cognitive factors addressed by Azar (1986) suggest that behavioral changes alone will be insufficient to produce lasting changes in dysfunctional families. Attitudinal and cognitive disturbances also need to be considered.

A hypothesis presented by Howells (1981) is consistent with this theory. Howells has speculated that the process of *attribution error* may be involved in some cases of child sexual abuse. Children elicit strong emotional reactions in many individuals. These reactions are usually appropriately labeled as parental or affectionate feelings toward the child. However, some individuals may label their physiological reactions as sexual and thus act toward children in a cognitively consistent manner.

Like the other theories under this paradigm, the major weakness of this analysis is its limited focus on mother-child interactions. Other factors, including other family members and socioeconomic status, are not given a significant role in the etiology and dynamics of maltreatment.

SOCIOBIOLOGICAL PARADIGM

The sociobiological paradigm has been influenced by cultural anthropology, sociobiology, physical anthropology, and ethological studies. Theorists working in this paradigm are primarily interested in how phylogenetic factors influence social behaviors. This paradigm is represented by the sociobiological theory of child physical abuse.

Sociobiological Theory of Physical Abuse

Theoretical Foundations. The sociobiological theory is rooted in general sociobiological theory (e.g., Wilson, 1975; Barash, 1979). It emphasizes the role that genetic factors play in determining human social behaviors, such as conflict, aggression, and altruism. According to this view, many social behaviors may ultimately be traced to *survival motivations* that have their origins in humankind's evolutionary past.

Daly and Wilson (1980) and Burgess and Garbarino (1983) assert that to come to full understanding of the phenomenon of child abuse and neglect, phylogenetic factors (those originating in the evolutionary past) must be considered *in conjunction with* social and psychological ones (Daly & Wilson, 1980; Burgess & Garbarino, 1983).

Evolutionary biologists generally define human nature in physical evolutionary terms. Consequently, this paradigm emphasizes the genetic bases and adaptive values of behavior according to the laws of natural selection or differential reproduction (Daly & Wilson, 1980; Burgess & Garbarino 1983; Wilson, 1975; Barash, 1979).

Basic Principles. This theory is concerned with three basic principles and how they relate to child maltreatment: (1) inclusive fitness, (2) parental investment, and (3) discriminative parenting.

Inclusive fitness refers to the transmission of parental genes to succeeding generations. According to this analysis, many human behaviors can ultimately be explained in terms of their contributions to inclusive fitness. Under this principle, the parent's natural children are less vulnerable than adopted children for maltreatment. *Parental investment* is defined as any investment by the parent in an individual offspring that increases the offspring's chance of surviving (and hence reproductive success) at the cost of the parent's ability to invest in other offsprings (Trivers, 1971). Therefore, the handicapped child is more vulnerable than the healthy child for abuse. *Discriminative parenting* refers to the concept that parental maltreatment is directly and negatively associated with the degree of genetic kinship and true biological parenthood. Therefore, the parental abuse is discriminative. So stepfathers will minimize their paternal energies because of the low genetic payoff (Burgess & Garbarino, 1983; Daly & Wilson, 1980; Wilson, Daly & Weghorst, 1980).

Three factors may reduce *inclusive fitness payoffs* and thus increase chances of child maltreatment (see Figure 3.20): (1) weak parent-child bonding; (2) an inadequate resource base such as low socioeconomic status, large family size, births too rapid in succession, and single parenthood; and (3) premature and defective children (Daly & Wilson, 1980; Burgess & Garbarino, 1983).

Two related theoretical postulations have been proposed by ethologists in the Lorenz-Tinbergen school of thought: First, the features and proportions of an infant convey a sense of cuteness that in turn releases an adult human's *instinct of*

Figure 3.20
Schematic Representation of Sociobiological Theory

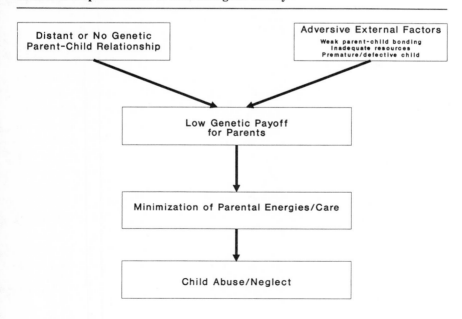

protectiveness (Kuttner, 1983); and second, violent crimes and war may be explained by the existence of a human's *aggressive instinct*. These two instincts play an important role in an adult's treatment of children with whom the adult has a different biological relationship.

Empirical Evidence. The sociobiological theory seems to be supported by a number of findings related to the relative occurrence of child abuse and neglect in stepfamilies. Daly and Wilson (1980) report that children living with one natural and one stepparent are 2.2 to 6.9 times as likely to be abused as those living with two biological parents, and 1.1 to 4.1 times as likely to be neglected. Burgess (1979) found that in 69 percent of 27 sampled families, the stepparent was the official perpetrator. It was found that when the stepparent was also a natural parent (in nine of the families), the abuse victim, in all but one case, was a stepchild rather than a natural child. These findings are consistent with the report by Duberman (1975) that only about half (53 percent) of stepfathers and a quarter of the stepmothers admitted having parental feelings toward their stepchildren.

This paradigm considers the importance of parent-child attachment and resource adequacy. Studies have found parent-child bonding to be an important factor in positive parent-child relationships (Daly & Wilson, 1980; Parker & Parker, 1986; Ayoub & Milner, 1985; Heinicke, 1984) and in the prediction of families at risk for maltreatment (Vietze et al., 1982). Furthermore, studies have found that an inadequate resource base, such as poverty, crowded living quarters, or other stressors, contributes significantly to the etiology of child maltreatment (Daly & Wilson, 1980; Burgess & Garbarino, 1983).

The sociobiological hypotheses about the protectiveness instinct of parents were further examined by Berman (1980). In reviewing the literature documenting the response of parents, college students, and young adults of either sex to films, photographs, or live children, Berman found that there lacked conclusive evidence for a protective reaction or for any awareness of anatomical cuteness.

Evaluation. The sociobiological approach in general does have some useful qualities, especially when kept in perspective with other levels of analysis, such as social and psychological ones, as is proposed by Burgess and Garbarino (1983) and Daly and Wilson (1980). It can, for example, help to reaffirm the continuity between humans and other organisms and has produced stimulating research, debate, and theory.

An evolutionary perspective can help explain why child maltreatment occurs across cultures, across time (Daly & Wilson, 1980; Burgess & Garbarino, 1983; Korbin, 1977), and across species as well (Schaller, 1972; Hrdy, 1974).

However, this theory has a number of limitations. For example, Giles-Sims and Finkelhor (1984) have pointed out two difficulties with this theory: (1) It cannot account for parental abuse of natural children except in situations of scarce resources where certain children in the family are genetically or in other ways inferior, and (2) the parental investment hypothesis is internally contradictory. Unless resulting in the death of the child, abuse is likely to result in an increased demand on parental resources.

Some empirical findings seem to run contrary to the assumptions of the sociobiological paradigm. For example, in their study of child sexual abuse, Parker and Parker (1986) found (1) that the nonbiological status of father was not significantly associated with abuse among those who were with their stepdaughters during the early socialization period, and (2) that there was no significant association between involvement in early child care and the biological status of fathers.

Much of the empirical evidence for this theory rests on findings that child abuse in stepfamilies is more prevalent than child abuse in families without stepparents. However, the exact nature of the relationship between child abuse and the stepfamily structure has not been adequately determined (Giles-Sims & Finkelhor, 1984). It is possible that the association between child abuse and stepfamilies is spurious and that each is actually caused by a common set of other variables. For example, individuals with certain personality characteristics or poor social/communication skills may be at risk of both divorce and child abuse.

Regarding the two postulates of the Lorenz-Tinbergen ethological school that humans have (1) a *protective instinct* that may be triggered by the physical appearance of infants and juveniles and (2) an *aggressive instinct* that may account for criminal violence and war, Kuttner (1983) studied their contradiction in terms of comparing data on child abuse and neglect with data on violent crimes. The results indicate that child abuse or potentially hazardous child neglect occurs with twice the frequency of violence toward adults.

Therefore, Kuttner argues that if aggressive drives are "proved" by 500 acts of violence per 100,000 citizens, then more than 1,000 acts of violence or neglect cannot be used to "prove" the existence of an opposite biological urge to shield children from injury. Thus, the theory is internally inconsistent. If theoretical consistency is to be retained, then the higher rates of violence against children must be said to be evidence for a stronger instinct to harm the weak and defenseless members of society than to harm mature adults.

In addition, the theory fails to explain why the majority of families do not engage in physical abuse that causes severe injury. Nonabusive families would appear to, in some way, overcome the natural aggressive drive instinct. There is an inconsistency involved in describing human nature based upon such analysis of behavior rewarded by society. One needs to ask why violent acts are only reported at a rate of 500 per 100,000 (0.5 percent) and not at a far higher rate, if a natural aggressive drive instinct exists.

Furthermore, Kuttner (1983) suggests that, in light of internal consistencies, instinct theory should be abandoned in favor of theories that emphasize the plasticity of human behavior. This would mean emphasizing prevention in the educational and training domains, rather than finding ways to circumvent built-in drives.

Any behavior, including child abuse, should be considered as the result of the interaction between nature (unlearned traits and genetic endowment) and nurture (learned patterns) (Montageau, 1976; Alland, 1972). The implications of the sociobiological theory for the elimination of child abuse among stepparents is not optimistic. If the ultimate cause of child abuse lies in the genetic endowment of the participants, then to affect change by altering present conditions would be most difficult. Furthermore, hypotheses derived from such a theory would be less amenable to empirical investigation and less fruitful for further speculation into the problems of child maltreatment. Stress theory, resource theory, and sociobiological theory are not necessarily contradictory, and therefore the former perspectives may be more constructive for identifying goals in intervention (Giles-Sims & Finkelhor, 1984).

LEARNING/SITUATIONAL PARADIGM

The learning/situational paradigm is primarily concerned with analyzing child maltreatment from the perspective of empirically derived principles of behavior based on general and social learning theories. Under this paradigm, three theories of child physical abuse are identified: social learning, situational, and coercive processes.

Social Learning Theory of Physical Abuse

Theoretical Foundations. Bandura (1973) asserts that learning principles are sufficient to explain the development and maintenance of human behavior. In addition to classical and operant conditioning, the social context and observational learning are considered crucial to understanding behavior.

Bandura applied the social learning principle to the "learning" of aggressive behavior and its subsequent application to parent-child aggressiveness. (See Figure 3.21.) Other people, starting with one's own parents, serve as important models that provide valuable learning experiences. These models provide at least four types of learning context for the acquisition and maintenance of aggressive behavior: (1) aggression as an option to our already learned behavior; (2) how to be aggressive; (3) when and where aggression is appropriate or not appropriate according to social norms; and (4) the consequences of aggression. If the model is successful or rewarded in some way, the behavior is more likely to be imitated by the observer (Sherod, 1982).

To achieve "successful" observational learning, the observer must (1) be attentive to the model, (2) retain in memory what was observed, (3) produce motor reproduction, and (4) have a motivation to perform the behavior (Penrod, 1986:75). The most influential models are the family, the subculture, and mass media. Contrary to instinct and drive theories of aggression, social learning theory predicts that successful (rewarded) aggressive behavior is more likely to recur, not less likely, and that watching aggression will often result in imitation, not catharsis.

According to social learning theory, human nature is a vast potentiality influenced by direct and vicarious experience, and it takes on a variety of forms

Figure 3.21
Schematic Representation of Social Learning Theory

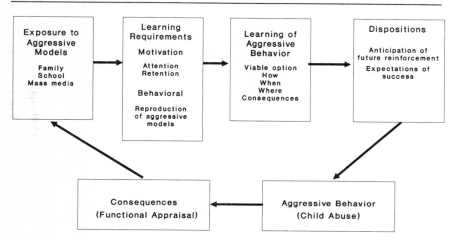

within biological limits (Bandura, 1973). Motivation is considered a cognitive construct with two primary sources: (1) the anticipation of future reinforcement and (2) the expectation of success based on experience in setting and reaching successive subgoals (Hall & Lindzey, 1985). There are no human developmental stages, according to Bandura. Rather, development is a continuous process of learning, as well as relearning, via direct experience or observation (Penrod, 1986).

Basic Principles. Although learning theory has not been advanced formally in the child abuse and neglect literature (Gelardo & Sanford, 1987), many of its basic principles have been applied to the problem.

This theory emphasizes the parent-child relationship and modeling and observational behaviors. Children who observe their parents using violence or aggression to solve family problems are likely to incorporate this behavior pattern into their own behavioral repertoire. Such behavior by a parent may teach the child that the proper way to respond to frustration is aggression and that "get-tough" force is the way to achieve results (Kratcoski, 1982).

Furthermore, children who witness interparental violence may be at risk for developing dysfunctional coping and interpersonal problem strategies that may directly affect their interpersonal relationships and academic performances (Goodman & Rosenberg, 1987).

Early childhood experiences are linked to established adult behavior patterns (Bandura, 1973). These experiences largely determine how an individual's personality develops, how an individual will interact with his or her own children, and how these experiences are transmitted to the next generation (Kratcoski, 1982). Therefore, children raised in a kind and loving way are likely to raise their own offspring in a similar manner, while children who are disliked and abused often treat their children in the same way.

Empirical Evidence. Many reports from laboratory and natural settings studies have show that learning factors, such as reinforcing a behavior, play a significant role in increasing levels of aggression (Munroe & Munroe, 1975). Bandura's social learning theory has enjoyed widespread support from many sources, including laboratory experiments (e.g., Sherrod, 1982), naturalistic observations (e.g., Myers, 1983; Biaggio, 1983), statistical analysis of social records (Myers, 1983), and ethnographic studies (e.g., Chagnon, 1977, Dentan, 1979, Munroe & Munroe, 1975).

Kratcoski (1982) compared 281 abused and 714 nonabused youths on violent acts directed toward significant others. It was found that 26 percent of the subjects abused in childhood had eventually attacked, beaten, kicked, or directed some other form of violence toward significant others, while only 14 percent of the nonabused subjects ever exhibited such behavior. This different was statistically significant.

Among those who did engage in violence, 45 percent of the abused and 18 percent of the nonabused directed such violence toward members of their immediate family, with the mother, stepmother, or siblings being the most frequent victims. There was little difference between the two groups in violence toward institutional staff (27 percent of the abused versus 32 percent of the nonabused).

Physical punishment was the major form of discipline used by parents of the violent youths. The violent youths also had lower frustration tolerance and fewer coping skills to deal with people and situations. They were often immature, were not very verbal, had difficulty in understanding cause and effect relationships, and were self-serving (Kratcoski, 1982).

Ethnographic studies of the socialization process are in congruence with Bandura's theory. The Yanomamo of North Brazil and South Venezuela, for example, are described as a very aggressive, male-oriented culture where many children are victimized in childhood (Chagnon, 1977; Harris, 1974). Little girls are punished for hitting, even in defense of a mean brother. Boys, however, are never punished for hitting, and fathers are delighted when their young sons hit them in the face. They are raised to be suspicious, hot-tempered, and quick to take violent action against the slightest offense (Chagnon, 1977).

Dentan (1979) studied the Semai of Malaya and found that violence is perceived as terrifying and is met with passivity or flight. There is no institutionalized way of preventing violence—no social controls, courts, or police. Since external controls are weak, they have developed internal ones, which are passed down by the process of socialization (Dentan, 1979). In discussion of Semai socialization, Dentan explains how children are taught to fear the "violence" of nature (e.g., thundersqualls) and then to equate this violence with the expression of human violence. Thus, children are taught to fear their own aggressive impulses through games and nature. A popular game with Semai children is "a sort of symbolic rehearsal for refraining from violence."

In a Polish-Finnish comparative study, Fraczek (1985) concluded that social and moral approval (or disapproval) of aggression are the main sources of enhancement (or reduction) of violence and brutality in social life, and that these attitudes are the direct result of socialization experiences and serve as mechanisms regulating interpersonal aggression.

An interesting case study in this context would be the Pilaga, who, according to Henry (1940), think of their villages and households as peaceful and harmonious, although they are actually filled with tension and hostilities.

In regard to the impact of televised violence, the evidence from both correlational and experimental studies indicates that it leads to a modest increase in aggressive behavior and desensitization to violence (Myers, 1983; Eron, 1987).

Evaluation. The social learning theory exemplifies the significant impact of modeling behavior on society and especially on children. The social learning theory has maintained an overall scientific orientation by utilizing controlled studies and careful data analysis.

Numerous studies on the socialization process support the theory's basic foundations. It is further supported by real-life observations and has gained wide acceptance from other fields, such as sociology and anthropology. Its implications for promoting altruism are also supported by much data (Segall, 1983). In addition, the theory has remained flexible and responsive to new data. In recent years, it has shifted to a much greater emphasis on cognitive aspects of learning (e.g., on how to act in a more appropriate and acceptable manner) (Hall & Lindzey, 1985).

This theory has highly significant implications for the prevention of child abuse and the promotion of altruism. It promotes a general belief that if parents and/or members of society decrease children's exposure to aggression and increase their exposure to prosocial behaviors, such as cooperation, the children should turn out to be less aggressive and more altruistic in their interactions. Also, just as children are taught to obey and respect adults in our society, they can be taught to recognize inappropriate adult behaviors and to say "no" to an adult (Horowitz, 1985).

This theory also has significant implications for intervention and treatment aspects of child abuse and neglect. This theory can be applied to "reeducate" at-risk parents and adults about concepts of socialization elements (e.g., gender equality, norms, values, and culture). Parents can also be taught "new," better stress-coping skills and communication methods.

A limitation of this theory is that it does not account for individual genetic or biological influences that would also shape decision processes and behavior. In addition, this theory generally fails to account for the child's developmental stages and characteristics (e.g., age, intelligence, and support of peers) in determining the extent to which the child's personality is impacted by witnessing aggressive acts (Rosenberg, 1987).

Finally, exposing a child to witnessing interpersonal violence and destruction of property may be considered a form of psychological abuse (Rosenberg, 1987).

Therefore, this theory should be expanded to address many issues on emotional (psychological) abuse, including its definitions, etiology, prevention, and evaluation.

Situational Theory of Physical Abuse

Theoretical Foundations. The situational theory analyzes child maltreatment from a social psychological perspective, especially in terms of research findings on interpersonal aggression (Patterson, 1975, 1977). Certain factors are assumed to be present whenever human aggression is expressed. (See Figure 3.22.) Wiggins (1983) asserts that three consistent factors cause human aggression across various situations: (1) *frustration* or *interference,* defined as the blockage of a goal response; (2) *aggressive cues* (e.g., models of behavior), defined as environmental stimuli previously associated with aggressive behaviors; and (3) *aggression-produced rewards and punishments,* defined as past reinforcing consequences of aggressive behavior. These three factors can operate independently, but aggression is more likely when they interact with one another.

Family violence is considered a special case of interpersonal aggression subject to all relevant abstract principles. Therefore, Wiggins generalized the findings from studies of the three consistent causal factors to a theory of interpersonal aggression in the context of family violence.

Figure 3.22
Schematic Representation of Situational Theory

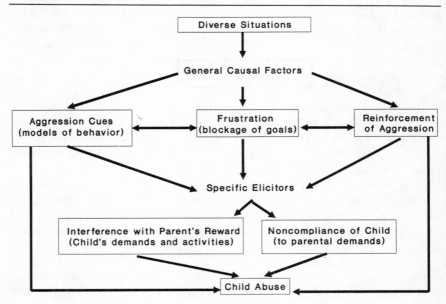

Basic Principles. Wiggins (1983) examines two general elicitors of parental violence against children: *interference* with the parent's rewards and *noncompliance* of the child with demands.

Interference refers to any block or delay in the parent's receiving a gratification or reward (e.g., crying child, dirty diapers, or spilled food). It is grouped into three categories: (1) the many services or needs children demand because of their dependence on others, coupled with unrealistic parental expectations (especially when the child is premature or handicapped); (2) activities of the child that interfere with the husband-wife relationship (e.g., the husband spending too much time coaching their son's baseball team), and (3) activities that interfere with a parent's tranquillity (e.g., excessive crying).

Noncompliance refers to the noncompliance of the child with the parent's demand. Wiggins suggests that the child's noncompliance with the parent's specific demand may trigger the issue of general control, power, or authority of the parent. Therefore, the abusive act occurs not for the fulfillment of specific demands, but rather for the restoration of parental control, power, or authority. For example, facing a child's rebellious attitude, a parent may say, "I had to teach him who is the boss." This control of the parent over the child is role related. Furthermore, the parental control is frequently facilitated by social norms of parental dominance over children. In fact, in response to the child's noncompliance, the parent's violent behavior against the child is frequently "rewarded" (encouraged or praised) by other adults. In addition, family isolation and community attitudes toward supporting the *extreme privacy* of the family also contributes to child maltreatment.

Empirical Evidence. The factors delineated by Wiggins are derived mainly from empirical social psychological research. There is ample supportive evidence for the three general causal factors of aggression (frustration, aggression cues, and reinforcement) in social situations. The two specific elicitors of parental violence against children (interference and noncompliance) were derived from two studies of situational factors associated with child physical abuse (Young, 1964; Elmer, 1977).

Unrealistic parental demands (expectations) of the child's abilities as a major causal factor in child abuse has been supported by a number of empirical studies (e.g., Parke, 1982; Garbarino, Guttmann & Seeley, 1986; Martin, 1981; Newberger & Newberger, 1981).

Preterm and/or handicapped children have also been reported to present major interference factors that put these children at greater risk of abuse and neglect (Ellerstein, 1981; Martin, 1981; Gray, 1981). Some theorists contend that prematurity itself is not directly related to child maltreatment, but rather mediates a disruption of the normal mother-child bonding process, a disruption that often occurs when a baby is premature or of low birth weight (Klein & Stern, 1971; Martin, 1982).

Evaluation. The situational theory appears to represent the reality-based consideration of day-to-day living situations that most families encounter at times. It addresses specific causal elicitors of parental violence; therefore, this theory can be used to develop effective programs for reducing family violence, for example, stress management, parenting skill training, organization of family time, prioritizing needs, and the utilization of humor and communication skills.

However, the situational theory is limited to factors present during *episodes* of interpersonal aggression. More stable variables of the environment and persons involved (personality characteristics of parents and children and their interactions) are not considered as an integral part of the theoretical foundations. For example, it fails to consider factors such as the child's looking like or reminding the parent of a disliked former spouse, or the child's reminding the parent of an earlier mistake or failure.

In addition, this theory fails to delineate the methods needed to relieve frustrations and redirect aggression cues. In this regard, different theoretical approaches may be better suited for the analysis of other family violence types. Social exchange theory, for example, has great potential in explaining variations in reactions to rewards and punishments (Wiggins, 1983). To the extent that treatment of low-birth-weight, preterm, and handicapped children appears to be consistent with this theory, it should be considered that some negative behaviors (e.g., prenatal drug or alcohol abuse, improper diet) which may lead to those conditions may also contribute to child abuse and neglect.

Coercion Theory of Physical Abuse

Theoretical Foundations. Stringer and La Greca's (1985) coercion theory (see Figure 3.23) incorporates social and traditional learning principles in an attempt to examine the mother's role in child management and how her behaviors and perceptions may induce and resolve a dysfunctional coercive cycle of aggressive parent-child interactions.

Basic Principles. The basic premise of the coercion theory is that if a mother lacks *effective child management skills* or if the family experiences some type of *stress* (e.g., divorce and financial problems), a *coercive cycle* of parent-child interactions may evolve (Stringer & La Greca, 1985).

An example of how a coercive cycle may develop follows: (1) the mother makes a request or demand from the child; (2) the child refuses to cooperate or comply; (3) the mother withdraws request or demand to stop the child's negative reaction (e.g., screaming or throwing a tantrum); (4) the mother receives short-term relief, but the child is "rewarded" for undesirable behavior (e.g., whining); (5) therefore, future requests from the mother will most likely be met with noncompliance from the child; and (6) this initiates a coercion process through which both the mother and the child escalate these behaviors in attempts to gain control over the other (e.g., spanking by the mother). Consequently, the child learns aggressive behaviors in interpersonal relationships both inside and outside the home. This learning leads to poor circumstances in parent-child and peer relations, academic performance, and self-concept (Brassard & Gelardo, 1987).

Stringer and La Greca (1985) hypothesize that a mother's *potential for abuse* is

Figure 3.23
Schematic Representation of Coercion Theory

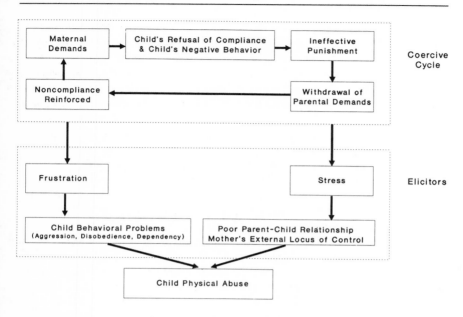

perpetuated by two major factors: (1) the severity of the child's behavior problems, and (2) the mother's having an *external* locus of control. Thus, both factors are related to the coercive cycle and the abusive potential of a mother.

Child behavior problems associated with the coercive process include *aggressiveness, disobedience,* and *dependency.*

External locus of control of the mother may be one of two types: (1) belief in control by powerful others, and (2) belief in control by chance (Levenson, 1981). Parental inconsistency in child rearing has been linked to the chance subscale, whereas authoritarian child rearing has been linked to the powerful others subscale. Both inconsistency and authoritarianism have significant associations with the coercive process (Stringer & La Greca, 1985).

Empirical Evidence. Some observational studies have described aggressive, coercive behaviors in abused children (Burgess & Conger, 1978; Conger, 1981) but others have found no behavioral differences between abused and nonabused children (Mash, Johnston & Kovitz, 1983).

Stringer and La Greca (1985) conducted a study to test the hypothesis of the coercion theory: Mothers' reports of child behavior problems and their external locus of control would be related to potentials to commit child abuse. In this study, 95 mother/child pairs in a low-income population were interviewed and compared on three measures: Milner's (1980) Child Abuse Potential Inventory, Levenson's (1981) Locus of Control Scales, and the Revised Behavior Problem

Checklist (RBPC) by Quay (1983). The RBPC included measures of conduct disorder, socialized anxiety, anxiety withdrawal, attention problems/immaturity, and motor excess.

The major results of this study include the following: (1) For mothers of both boys and girls, perceptions of control by powerful others and perceptions of control by chance were related to abuse potential; (2) mothers' reports of their sons' anxiety-withdrawal and conduct-disorder behavior problems were related to potential to abuse; (3) there was a significant association among lie scores, internality, and abuse potential for mothers of girls; (4) mothers with high abuse potential reported significantly more behavioral problems in their children; and (5) the coercive cycle may escalate after a significant family stressor, such as divorce. (See Table 3.2.)

In the same study, the 47 mothers who scored above the median (in the high group) on the child abuse potential measure were compared with the 48 mothers who scored below the median (in the low group). Overall, the high group mothers rated their children significantly higher in (1) conduct disorder, (2) socialized anxiety, (3) anxiety withdrawal, (4) attention problems/immaturity, and (5) excess motor movement. Additional analysis indicated that male children scored higher on all five behavioral problems and that there were no significant differences between single-parent and two-parent families.

Evaluation. This theory offers valuable insights by linking the coercion process between a mother and a child to the continuum approach that considers that the potential for child maltreatment exists to some extent in all families (Reid, Patterson & Loeber, 1981; Stringer & La Greca, 1985). This emphasis may lead to the resolution of a negative interaction style such that a treatment method may be initiated to intervene (e.g., working with the mother regarding coping skills, stress management, and self-esteem).

However, since the coercive cycle may involve different constellations of

Table 3.2
Variables Significantly Associated with Child Abuse Potential Scores

Mothers with Sons	Mothers with Daughters
External locus of control/ perception of powerful others controlling events	External locus of control/ perception of powerful others controlling events
External locus of control/ perception of chance controlling events	External locus of control/ perception of chance controlling events
Perceiving child as having conduct problems	Internal locus of control
	Lie scores
Perceiving child as being anxious and withdrawn	

Note: Constructed from the report by Stringer and La Greca (1985).

perceptions for mothers with daughters rather than sons (Stringer & La Greca, 1985), coercion theory may not be as applicable to mother-daughter interactions. This theory is also limited because it does not consider family members outside the mother-child relationship and it fails to integrate the role of stress and parenting skills in the family analysis.

This approach has methodological problems in empirical research. It involves many uncontrollable confounding variables, and the problems with using forced choice questionnaires in data collection (e.g., the Child Abuse Potential Inventory). In addition, it relied on partial correlation in data analyses of the three central variables (child abuse potential, behavioral problems, and locus of control). These methodological issues fail to address all concerned and related topics simultaneously and thus limit a rigorous evaluation and empirical testing of this theory.

ECOLOGICAL PARADIGM

Bronfenbrenner (1979) initiated the ecological paradigm in the field of child development. Garbarino (1982) and others subsequently adopted it to the field of child maltreatment. The multidimensional nature of child maltreatment is stressed, and variables at individual, family, community, and societal levels are examined. This paradigm includes three member theories: (1) ecological, (2) choice, and (3) multilevel.

Ecological Theory of Physical Abuse

Theoretical Foundations. Ecological theory (see Figure 3.24) considers the family as a social system surrounded by and in interaction with other social systems. Social systems are conceived as existing in layers, ranging from the family and the community to the broader sociocultural system (Bronfenbrenner, 1977). To understand the family, according to the ecological perspective, both intra- and inter-system analyses must be evaluated (Preston, 1986). Any alteration or change in any of the systems can affect the family's function and can subsequently produce transformations in its structure. Therefore, behavior and interpersonal relations within the family unit are influenced by larger community and sociocultural fluctuations.

Basic Principles. This theory assumes that consideration of interrelationships among individuals (both the caretaker and child), families, and outside environment (community and society) is necessary to completely understand child abuse and neglect. The etiology of child maltreatment is viewed as *circular,* rather than *linear.* Abusive behaviors are the result of specific sequences of interactions among family members and between the family and community.

Child abuse results from the combination of three major factors: (1) an individual's developmental history (some may be predisposed to abuse), (2) stress-

Figure 3.24
Schematic Representation of Ecological Theory

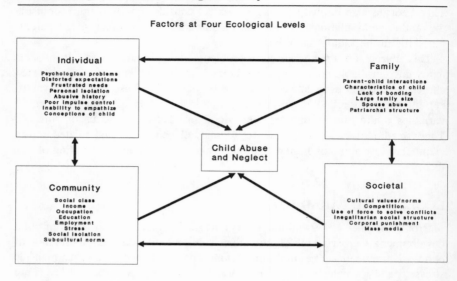

Factors at Four Ecological Levels

producing forces within and beyond the immediate family, and (3) the values and child-rearing practices that characterize the society or subculture in which the individual, family, and community are embedded (Belsky, 1980).

To have a complete understanding of child abuse and neglect, Newberger and Newberger (1981), working within an ecological framework, identify *four levels of parental thinking* about children and the parental role in the family: (1) concrete and physicalistic conceptions of the child, (2) an understanding of the parental role only in terms of the parent's own needs and desires, (3) an awareness of the child as a complex psychological being, and (4) the parental role as embedded in an ongoing and reciprocal relationship between parent and child. Inconsistence among these four levels will eventually force the family to become a highly conflictual environment. Child physical abuse may thus become a stress-coping mechanism for the parent.

Two systems play an important role in abuse through influence on the community: (1) *The world of work,* which includes unemployment and poverty, induces frustration, a sense of powerlessness, and parent-child conflict at home. As a result, unemployment and poverty are highly associated with domestic violence and child abuse. What needs to be determined, however, is whether poverty and unemployment create a risk of abuse and if they are related to abuse at a higher level than are other factors. (2) *Neighborhoods* where child-abusing families are isolated from formal and informal support systems do not provide parents with role models in the community or with social networks; parents thus lack interpersonal skills necessary for social relationships.

At the societal level, cultural attitudes toward violence, corporal punishment, and children have a significant impact on child-rearing practices. For example, in the United States, society generally accepts physical punishment as a means of controlling children's behavior. Also, children are considered to be property to be handled as parents choose. Such cultural values and belief systems interact with factors from other ecological levels (individual, family, and community) to foster the abuse and neglect of children (Newberger & Newberger, 1981).

Belsky (1984) focuses on the interaction among parental psychological resources, characteristics of the child, and the contexual factors of stress and support. For example, unskilled parents will experience more stress than skilled parents when dealing with a child's developmental characteristics. Furthermore, when families suffer from various stressors (e.g., financial, occupational, educational, or marital), lack personal coping skills, and/or have little support from others, they have a higher tendency to react in an abusing fashion.

Empirical Evidence. Newberger and Newberger (1981) conducted a comparative study in parental awareness of children's cognitive development with abusive and nonabusive parent groups. It was found that abusive parents scored significantly lower on measures of parental awareness toward their children than did their matched counterparts. In addition, child abusive families were found to have a significantly lower income level than the nonabusive families. Empirical evidence for supporting the relationships between child maltreatment and different ecological factors is also available.

For example, at the individual level, abused children (toddlers) show more negative behavior than the control sample. What is not known is whether the negative behavior caused the abuse or the abuse caused the negative behavior. The Social Interaction Model, for example, considers the characteristics of the child as important causative factors in abuse.

At the family level, such problems as role reversal, household disorganization, and marital conflict were found to cause the children to become targets of family violence. Furthermore, the following three conclusions were obtained from empirical studies: (1) physical abuse in households was high where husbands and wives had observed their abusive parents hit one another, (2) observations of parents hitting each other will definitely increase the rate of violence toward family members, and (3) abuse increases where there is a power dominance by one parent.

Evaluation. This perspective maintains that researchers of child abuse should investigate the relations among the variables from different ecological levels rather than focus on single factors or multiple factors at one level. This theory has two major advantages over many other theories: (1) it acknowledges that child abuse and neglect is a complex phenomenon, and (2) it is successful in organizing all pertinent data from four ecological levels.

This theory seems to have three weaknesses: (1) it fails to make direct statements of causality, (2) specific hypotheses are not generated or tested, and (3) the four levels of analysis are not sufficiently linked either in theory or in empirical evaluation.

Choice Theory of Physical Abuse

Theoretical Foundation. According to Nye's (1978, 1979) "maximum profit" theory, human beings make an infinite number of choices in ecological contexts of daily life, to reduce *costs* and to maximize the *rewards* for the most *profits* (or least losses). (See Figure 3.25.) *Costs* represent any status, relationship, interaction, milieu, or feeling disliked by an individual. A cost can be manifested in two forms: (1) *punishment*—dislikable things happen to the individual, and (2) *rewards forgone*—rewarding conditions or objects (e.g., relationships, positions, and feelings) are forgone because a competing alternative is chosen.

Rewards, on the other hand, represent any pleasure, satisfaction, and/or gratification the person enjoys. The choice theory emphasizes the individual's evaluation between rewards and costs involved in any contemplated sequence of action. In general, humans seek the most profitable long-term outcomes (given that short-term outcomes are constant) and the most profitable short-term outcomes (given that long-term outcomes are constant). Therefore, people choose outcomes in all circumstances that provide the most rewards when costs are constant, and also choose outcomes that lead to the fewest costs when rewards are constant.

The choice selection process may involve exchanges of alternatives in different ecological conditions (e.g., in exchanges with other individuals, institutions, or society as a whole). While exchanges usually involve choices, choices may not necessarily involve exchanges (Nye, 1978).

This theory is based on the following propositions about the nature of human

Figure 3.25
Schematic Representation of Choice Theory

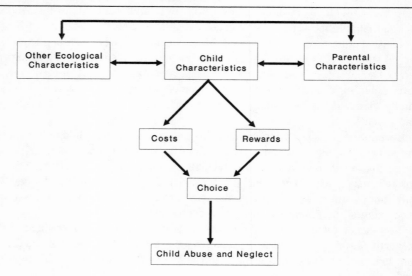

beings (Nye, 1980): (1) people are basically rational beings; (2) people are actors (decision makers) as well as reactors; (3) social life requires reciprocity; (4) the more one has something, the less additional units are worth; (5) humans are born asocial rather than prosocial or antisocial; (6) all behavior involves costs and rewards; and (7) people can continue long-term investments with the expectations of achieving more favorable outcomes.

Nye applies the theory of choice to several areas of family interaction and specifically to the explanation of family behavior (Nye & McDonald, 1979). For example, parental behavior is considered as the choice of the parent to accept lesser costs of child care and socialization than to incur larger costs from neglecting those "duties" imposed by the society.

Basic Principles. The choice theory proposes that violence in the family is a viable alternative to other actions for obtaining rewards and avoiding costs because rewards for underlying violence are immediate and costs can also be immediately identified. In addition, since society requires that parents provide adequate care and socialization for their children, Nye made two propositions about the role of violence in relation to legal and cultural norms: (1) violence, as a disciplinary alternative, becomes more frequent in families where there are no legal or cultural norms proscribing it; and (2) in societies that proscribe violence against some (e.g., wives) but permit it against others (e.g., children), violence becomes less frequent toward those protected individuals than toward those unprotected individuals.

These two propositions further explain the effect of normative structure and social control over illegitimate violence against children. Generally speaking, violence that violates legal or other norms is usually hidden and occurs more frequently in the absence of family members (isolation circumstances). Its detection is more likely to be followed by sanctions (costs) either from formal social institutions (e.g., police and courts) or informal community resources (neighbors, relatives, and friends). Therefore, Nye hypothesizes that child abuse is less frequent in families with relatives and/or friends living nearby and is more frequent in single-parent than two-parent families.

The other major contributing cause of child abuse and neglect is the overestimation of young children's capabilities. Parents see young children as adults in small bodies. Therefore, when the child fails to react to parents intellectually or emotionally as an adult, the parents attribute this to lack of responsibility or affection on the part of the child rather than to the immaturity of the child's early development level. When the parents overestimate the child, it becomes difficult for the child to meet expectations; his or her responses usually fall below the parent's *comparison level* (standards) for evaluating the rewards and costs of the parent-child relationship. Therefore, the more parents overestimate the intellectual and social development of the child, the more likely it is that the parents will engage in child abuse and neglect.

Furthermore, because parents usually cannot leave the parental relationship with the child, the child's inability to achieve the parent's comparison level leads to frustration and anger on the part of the parent. Therefore, child abuse may become a means of modifying the child's behavior or as a means of inflicting costs on one who inflicted costs on the parent. Under this principle, Nye proposed a formal hypothesis as follows: "The more the expectations of the parent exceed the capabilities of the child, the more likely the parent will abuse the child."

Empirical Evidence. No empirical research program was conducted to directly substantiate the propositions of the choice theory. However, two general characteristics from clinical observations and empirical studies seem to support the major framework of the choice theory: (1) social isolation of the parent from the outside world and other adults increases child abuse, and (2) family stresses and poverty tend to change the evaluation process of interaction alternatives between parents and children.

Evaluations. Nye's choice theory addresses human behavior from an economic perspective. When societies have weak or absent legal or normative structures, punishment for all forms of antisocial behavior is also weak or absent. As punishment, either legal or social, is one of the major costs of family violence, the costs of family violence will be less when punishment is absent. Nye's choice theory appears similar to Gelles's exchange theory. Individuals make rational choices to achieve the greatest benefit at the lowest cost. A family that has relatives or friends nearby is one in which abuse is more likely discovered, and discovery leads to the cost of punishment. Cost in this model becomes the magnitude of punishment discounted by the probability of discovery and of punishment actually being imposed.

Overall, this theory addresses ecological *circular* impact on child maltreatment from interactions among family members, family, and the community. However, its overemphasis on rational cost-reward comparisons appears to ignore the roles and dynamics of emotional and possibly irrational behaviors in many child maltreatment incidents.

Multilevel Theory of Physical Abuse

Theoretical Foundations. The primary focus of the multilevel theory (see Figure 3.26) by Parke (1982) is on the social environment, which is analyzed from three angles:

1. *Socialization influences.* In contrast to a traditional psychiatric emphasis on abnormality of the abusive adult, this theory assumes that normal parents are socialized into abusive child care patterns through the interactive influence of cultural, community, and family factors, rather than through the sheer influence of parental personality variables.

2. *Cultural attitudes.* Cultural attitudes toward violence and the rights of children and parents are stressed, as well as the level of violence in other areas of social influence.

3. *Family norms.* At the family level, Parke considers four aspects of family norms: the

Figure 3.26
Schematic Representation of Multilevel Theory

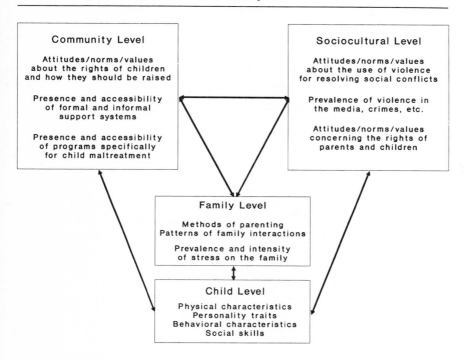

type of child-rearing practices, the amount of stress on family members, the family interaction patterns, and characteristics of the child. This theory is a macrostructural analysis in which a variety of social contexts are involved in evaluating social behavior.

Basic Principles. This model assumes that (1) normal parents are socialized into abusive child care patterns through the interactive impact of cultural, community, and familial influences; (2) the community has educational and monitoring functions for the child-rearing practices of family members, sets community standards concerning the appropriate treatment of children, and provides a series of informal and formal support systems to aid in implementing these functions and provide stress alleviation for families (Parke, 1982); and (3) family level factors, such as type of child-rearing practices, stress, family member interaction patterns, and characteristics of the child, need to be considered in the analysis of child abuse.

These three sources of influence are viewed as separate but interrelated aspects of a multifactor social interactional system (Parke, 1982). The direction of influence among the various factors involved in child abuse is bidirectional, each source being able to influence another source directly or indirectly through another source. Therefore, abuse is best understood by a detailed analysis of interaction patterns among family members and by considering the role that informal and formal community support systems play in family interaction patterns (Parke, 1982).

The role of culture in child abuse: At this level of analysis, two factors are delineated: (1) cultural sanction of violence as evidenced by the use of physical disciplinary tactics in controlling children, and (2) cultural attitudes toward the rights and abilities of children, including the historical view of children as property and the failure to appreciate the higher cognitive ability of children to understand and be responsive to nonphysical disciplinary and control tactics.

The family as the context of child abuse: The parent's own socialization experience, parent-child interactions, the role of all family members, and the level of social stress are all deemed necessary factors at the family level of analysis to fully understand any child abuse problem.

Socialization: A primary assumption at this level is that a parent's own history of disciplinary treatment predisposes his guidelines for disciplining children. These methods come to be viewed as morally right and justified (Parke, 1982). Therefore, being raised under physically punitive child-rearing methods may set the stage for child abuse.

Parent-child interactions: Parent-child interactions may be such that abusive behaviors are shaped into the behavioral repertoire of mothers who may have a history of abusive behavior. It is presumed that a mother may be rewarded by an abusive behavior because the undesired behavior of the child is stopped. This behavior then becomes more likely to be repeated and possibly escalated.

The role of all family members: To fully understand child maltreatment, Parke asserts that (a) the whole family, including parents and children, must be considered, and (b) abuse may be the result of direct, as well as indirect, family interactions.

Social stress: This aspect of the theory has four major propositions: (a) In general, abuse may erupt in otherwise normal families because of unusual or mounting stress; (b) stress is not class related, but different social classes may experience different types of stress; (c) stress is understood from a subjective angle in terms of the individual's and the family's cognitive interpretation of the stressful event and their capacity to cope with it; and (d) coping with stress is related not only to characteristics of the individual, but also to community characteristics, especially in terms of the availability of social support systems (Parke, 1978, 1982).

The role of community support systems: Two types of community support systems are delineated: (1) informal support systems (e.g., friends and neighbors) and (2) formal support systems, including both general and abuse-specific support systems (e.g., protection agencies and community shelters). These systems have been elaborated by Parke as follows:

Informal support systems: Parke argues that child abuse may be related to the relatively recent shift from extended to more nuclearized families. In extended families, child care stresses could be alleviated by the assistance of other family members, and an experienced mother could be readily available for modeling, teaching, and assisting the new mother.

General support systems: General types of the formal support system within each community include such agencies as health-care facilities, counseling services, employment agencies, educational institutions, social-work services, housing assistance, and welfare assistance. Abuse-specific types include hotlines, child-care education, and individual and group therapy. It is argued that the family must be analyzed as part of the community because community factors have been shown to play an important role in the development of family and also in the etiology of abuse.

Empirical Evidence. The view that child abuse is partially due to the cultural sanction of violence is supported by a number of cross-cultural studies that compare rates of murder, assault, battery, and media violence (Parke, 1982). For example, in comparison with Canada or England, the United States is higher in all comparison categories (Geis & Monahan, 1976; Liebert, Neale & Davidson, 1973; Steinmetz, 1974). In comparing the U.S. with Taiwan, studies have found physical punishment of any type used less than half as often by Taiwanese families and spankings only one-fourth as often (Niem & Collard, 1971; Freedman & Freedman, 1969).

Goode (1971) found physical punishment as well as child abuse to be infrequent in Japan, and data from China indicates that physical punishment, aggression among children, and incidents of child abuse are all relatively low (Sidel, 1972).

Parke (1974) demonstrated that five-year-old children can be effectively controlled by a prohibitory rationale based on property rights: Young children are able to comprehend and appropriately respond to rational forms of discipline without the use of physical punishment.

A number of other studies (e.g., Disbrow, Doerr & Caulfield, 1977; Green, Gaines & Sandgrund, 1974; Van Stolk, 1972) have indicated that abusing caretakers are deficient in parenting skills or have limited knowledge of disciplinary tactics. Other studies (e.g., Davitz, 1952) have shown that under stress, predominant behavioral dispositions are the most likely responses. Therefore, if a parent has limited knowledge of disciplinary tactics, he or she is more likely to use physical punishment when under stress.

In terms of family interactions, evidence has shown that marital conflicts and husband-wife violence may be an important factor in the etiology of child abuse. Pedersen, Anderson, and Cain (1977) found the level of negative affect between parents was positively correlated to the amount of negative affect the parents directed toward their children.

A number of findings support the theoretical notion that parent-child interactions are important in understanding child abuse. For example, abuse is often focused on one child in a multichild family (Bakan, 1971; Fontana, 1971). Abused children may have special characteristics that tax the parent-child relationship, such as hyperactivity (Morse, Sahler & Freidman, 1970), prematurity and low birth weight (Parke & Collmer, 1975; Stevens-Long, 1973; Fanaroff, Kennell & Klaus, 1972), unattractiveness (Dion, 1974), and/or being the result of an unwanted pregnancy (Birrell & Birrell, 1968; Nurse, 1964).

Much data supports the notion that abusive individuals and families often are isolated from the community and lack social relationships (e.g., Elmer, 1967; Merrill, 1962; Lenoski, 1974; Young, 1964). In an analysis of 58 New York State counties, Garbarino (1976) demonstrated that as the adequacy of social support systems and human resources increased, the degree of child maltreatment decreased and vice versa.

Evaluation. This theory takes into account a wide range of pertinent issues and factors at the individual, family, community, and cultural levels. It addresses subjective and objective issues at each ecological level. Parke (1982) furthermore provides an abundance of empirical data to support the theoretical propositions.

Although some linkage was provided between components from different ecological levels (e.g., the transmission of cultural attitudes to parental behaviors), this theory lacks a comprehensive analysis of causal relationships among individual components from all levels. In essence, what Parke (1982) has seemingly presented is a number of independent "mini-theories" that are not fully developed and tested for their interactions. This is a problem with many models of child abuse and neglect, especially with those taking an ecological approach. They tend to be very general by taking in all relevant findings, thus making it difficult to elaborate specific statements about causality.

For example, to the extent that some studies show prematurity and low birth weight as related to child abuse, more research is needed to determine whether those characteristics actually cause abuse or are direct evidence of other facts related to abuse. Both low birth weight and prematurity may be related to drug abuse, poor diet, or a lack of prenatal care. It may be that a parent who displays this behavior is also at a greater risk for child abuse, and thus low birth weight and prematurity is direct evidence of those behaviors.

In short, there are many potentially confounding variables that need to be sorted out with more rigorous empirical testing.

Part III

Theorizations of Incest and Sexual Abuse

Chapter Four

Theories of the Incest Taboo

This chapter presents three theoretical perspectives about the origin of the incest taboo—*why incest is considered wrong or antisocial.* Theories of what causes violation of the taboo (i.e., intrafamilial sexual abuse) are presented in Chapter 5. Whether or not the incest taboo is universal has been much debated. Arguing that the incest taboo is not universal, Maisch (1972) cites the Kalang tribe of Java, which considers mother-son marriages good luck, and the Bantus of East Africa, who allow intrafamilial marriages when sons are too poor to buy wives. Middleton (1962) notes that sibling marriages were encouraged in Egypt to retain family wealth and property. Mormons in the northwestern United States practiced incestuous marriage to avoid marriages outside their faith. This practice became so common that the Utah state legislature of 1892 passed a law prohibiting incest (Justice & Justice, 1979).

Yet, Murdoch (1949) asserts that exceptions to the universal incest taboo do not hold up under the scrutiny of scientific investigation. He argues that ethnocentric biases and ignorance have resulted in invalid conclusions concerning the practices and beliefs of other cultures.

In current literature, there are three major theoretical stances concerning the origin (etiology) of the incest taboo: (1) the biological theory (under the individual determinants paradigm), (2) the normative/structural theory (under the sociocultural paradigm), and (3) the biosocial theory (under the individual environment interaction paradigm).

INDIVIDUAL DETERMINANTS PARADIGM

Under the individual determinants paradigm, there is one theory evaluated for its analysis of the incest taboo: the biological theory.

Biological Theory of the Incest Taboo

Theoretical Foundations. The biological theory, rooted in the sociobiological field, asserts that human behavior is largely determined by genetic and evolutionary forces.

Basic Principles. Proponents of the biological theory believe that the incest taboo developed because of the negative effects incest has on the survival of the species (see Figure 4.1). Incest is said to result in unfit or even deformed offspring. Other theorists have held that incest was common among many cultures but that the taboo developed as negative effects of incest became prevalent (cf. Durkheim, 1963).

Other proponents of the biological theory of the incest taboo have identified the negative impacts of incest on children. These theorists rest on the assumption that incest results in a less fit species, and that the children of incest were a greater hardship on the survival of early humankind, both phylogenetically—because of the biological deficits, such as lower IQ, and malformations—and culturally—because of the simultaneous loss of productive help and the added burden on developing societies.

Empirical Evidence. In an analysis of incest myths recorded among small-scale primitive societies, Segner and Collins (1967) discovered that one-third of the myths that contained incest as a major theme described deformed offspring or infertility as a consequence of the incest.

In a comparative analysis of children of married first cousins and children of nonconsanguineous marriages, Schull and Neel (1965) found that the former group was somewhat smaller in physique, more susceptible to infections, less intelligent, and more likely to be born with congenital defects than the latter.

A number of studies compared the children conceived from incestuous relationships with those of nonincestuous relationships. Two exemplifying studies (Adams & Neel, 1967) are presented in Table 4.1. These studies indicated that the offsprings of incestuous relationships were generally afflicted with some sort of severe or moderate deficit, or died, at a much greater rate than children of nonincestuous relationships.

The Adams and Neel (1967) study compared 18 children of incestuous couples

Figure 4.1
Schematic Representation of Biological Theory

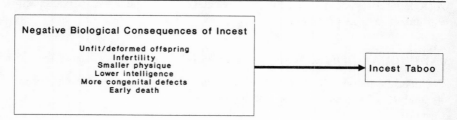

Negative Biological Consequences of Incest

Unfit/deformed offspring
Infertility
Smaller physique
Lower intelligence
More congenital defects
Early death

Incest Taboo

Table 4.1
Biological Characteristics of Children of Incest versus Control Group

(A) Adams and Neel's Study		
Variables	Children of Incest (N = 18)	Control (N = 18)
Normal at birth and 6 mos.	7	15
Congenital birth defect	0	1
Died in early infancy	5	0
Severely retarded	2	0
Borderline IQ	3	0
Retained for further IQ testing	0	2
Bilateral cleft palate	1	0
(B) Seemanova's Study		
Variables	Children of Incest (N = 161)	Control (N = 95)
Mental retardation	25%	0%
Congenital birth defects	20%	5%
Multiple congenital malformations	6%	0

Note: This table was constructed from two sources: (A) from Adams and Neel (1967) and (B) from Seemanova (1971).

with 18 matched control-group children who were conceived from nonincestuous couples. The children were examined on a number of levels, including (1) normality at birth and at the age of six months, (2) congenital birth defects, (3) death in early infancy, (4) intelligence, and (5) the existence of a bilateral cleft palate. It was found that while 15 of the 18 nonincestuous children were developing normally at birth and at six months, this could be said for only 7 of the 18 incestuously conceived children—a difference of over 50 percent.

Another striking difference was found in the domain of death in early infancy. Nearly one-third (5 of the 18) of the children conceived through incest died in their early infancy, whereas none of the other children from the nonincestuous parents died within this time span. Intelligence was also found to be substantially different in the two groups of children. IQ tests indicated that three (or one-sixth) of the incestuous children had borderline IQs, while all nonincestuous children were within a normal range of intelligence (with two of the control children retained for further testing).

Few differences were found in analysis of congenital birth defects or bilateral cleft palate. These problems were very low for both groups. None of the incestuous children showed signs of congenital birth defects, and only one of the control-group children showed such a type of disorder. One of the incestuous children had a bilateral cleft palate, but none of the other children did.

The study by Seemanova (1971) yielded similar results. Seemanova focused on the analysis of three major variables: (1) mental retardation, (2) congenital birth defects, and (3) multiple congenital malformations. This study involved 161 children of incest and a control group of 95 children from nonincestuous relationships. The most formidable finding was that a full quarter of the children of incest were diagnosed as being mentally retarded. On the other hand, none of the children in the control group was diagnosed as such. Furthermore, 20 percent of incest children suffered some type of congenital birth defect, whereas only 5 percent of the control-group children showed signs of such defects. Lastly, multiple congenital malformations were apparent in 6 percent of the incest-produced children, but none from nonincestuous relations.

More research, however, needs to be conducted in this area. Although incest may increase the harm done by recessive genes, it may also increase the benefit arising from beneficial recessive genes. Some Polynesian cultures practiced brother/sister marriages, but killed all offspring showing negative traits. Cultures such as the ancient Greeks, where because of a lack of mobility the probability of some blood relationships between spouses was very high, also killed babies showing harmful traits, thereby removing negative genes from the gene pool. In addition, inbreeding is a process used to improve both crops and livestock. Incest taboo can therefore not be explained totally by a desire to avoid damaged offspring.

Evaluation. This theory offers a seemingly valid explanation of the etiology of incest taboo. However, it fails to adequately take into account all cultural and social forces that play a tremendous role in determining social norms and expectations, including those dealing with sexual behaviors.

SOCIOCULTURAL DETERMINANTS PARADIGM

The sociocultural determinants paradigm seeks to understand human ecological phenomena by studying objective social indicators and subjective cultural norms, values, and attitudes. Many theorists have looked to these types of data in order to explain the incest taboo. Their efforts are represented by the normative/structural theory.

Normative/Structural Theory of the Incest Taboo

Theoretical Foundations. The normative/structural theory of the incest taboo rejects the biosocial hypothesis. It focuses on the structure and function of social values and norms. (see Figure 4.2.)

Basic Principles. Lévi-Strauss (1956) proposes a normative theory that views

Figure 4.2
Schematic Representation of Normative/Structural Theory

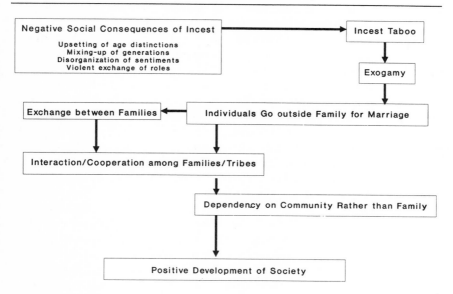

the incest taboo as a primary structural phenomenon of human society. According to this theory, the incest taboo guarantees the exchange of women, and from this fundamental exchange come all other exchanges. Because of the incest taboo, family members must look outside of the nuclear family for marriage, which leads to *exogamy*, the taboo of marriage to certain kin. The institutionalization of exogamy, in turn, leads to a shift of dependency from the family to the community. Such a shift is a requirement for the development of a society (Lévi-Strauss, 1956; Rist, 1979).

White's (1948) culturalogical theory also views the incest taboo as serving a primary social function to *encourage interactions between groups*. This theory maintains that the human species could not have survived without interfamily and intertribal cooperation, and since the incest taboo guaranteed the exchange of women between groups, it helped to ensure such cooperation and to strengthen extrafamilial bonds or "transfamilial roles" (White, 1948; Lester, 1972; Parsons, 1954). This view also suggests that the incest taboo, by defining and limiting the degree of closeness among family members, is one of society's mechanisms for encouraging appropriate individualization (Rist, 1979).

Malinowski (1927) asserted that incest resulted in the upsetting of age distinctions, the mixing up of generations, the disorganization of sentiments, and a violent exchange of roles. Therefore, the sociological view holds that if incest was widespread then there would be disintegration of the family system and of the society in which families interact.

From an economic perspective, Justice and Justice (1979) have suggested that the incest taboo developed out of a *need for economic survival*. The taboo, it is argued, forced families to join together and share their resources at a community level. Incest would disrupt the division of labor and also the cooperative relationships necessary for the smooth running of the economic unit. With greater economic stability, there was an increase in the exchange of ideas and things that were necessary for cultural evolution (White, 1948).

Empirical Evidence. This theory poses that stepfather incest is relatively more prevalent than natural father incest because stepfathers, as nonblood relatives, are subject to weaker normative taboos against incest (Giles-Sims & Finkelhor, 1984). While the normative theory of incest has face validity, there is actual little supportive evidence for it. In many U.S. jurisdictions, laws proscribing incest do not apply to steprelations (Wulkan & Bulkey, 1981), suggesting that the incest taboo is weaker or absent among this population. However, no attitude survey exists that indicates that the taboo is weaker for stepparents (Giles-Sims & Finkelhor, 1984).

The evidence for this theory of incest avoidance is mostly in the form of ethnographic descriptions of various cultures such as Egypt, Hawaii, and ancient Peru (Swan, 1985). Cultural factors have been delineated into specific units and analyzed in terms of the theory.

Evaluation. This theory holds that the incest taboo developed because of its negative effects on both family and interfamily relations. However, it has been pointed out that premarital sexual intercourse between family members would not necessarily prevent alliances between families (Lester, 1972). This theoretical approach emphasizes the influence of cultural factors on individual behaviors.

Normative theory is not inconsistent with the sociobiological or biosocial theories of incest, but does not require a biologically based foundation (Giles-Sims & Finkelhor, 1984). The incest taboo may be stronger for genetically related persons for any number of reasons.

Finkelhor and Redfield (1982) found that the strength of various incest taboos does not necessarily correlate with the frequency of their occurrence. Specifically, they consider father-daughter incest to be more taboo than mother-son incest, yet it has been much more prevalent in clinical reports.

This model has implications for intervention of sexual abuse. For example, if weak norms against sexual abuse by stepparents create a potential for violations as predicted by normative theory, then norms and their legal sanctions can be changed (Giles-Sims & Finkelhor, 1984).

Overall, this theoretical approach emphasizes the influence of social and economic factors on individual sexual behaviors. From the evolutionary perspective, it provides an excellent historical account for the development of marital institutions in human societies and provides unique insights into the macrological processes and structures that influence child sexual abuse behaviors.

INDIVIDUAL-ENVIRONMENT INTERACTION PARADIGM

The individual-environment interaction paradigm attempts to integrate the theoretical propositions of intraindividual- and sociocultural-based perspectives. By combining these two approaches, the biosocial theory represents a more complex approach to the study of incest norms and behavior.

Biosocial Theory of the Incest Taboo

Theoretical Foundations. Biosocial theories assert that intimate relationships among family members that occur early in life function to subdue, if not completely eliminate, their sexual desires (Gordon & Creighton, 1988). This sexual avoidance mechanism is activated regardless of whether the relationship involves a parent and child (Parker & Parker, 1986), brother and sister (Fox, 1980), unrelated children living in a kibbutzim (Shepher, 1983), or individuals joined in a sim-pua type marriage in some cultures (where they are brought up together as children and married as young adults).

Therefore, this theory holds that the taboo originated in the family itself, not out of sociological factors, and not because of biological abnormalities. Van Den Berghe (1983) suggests incest aversion is precultural and that it involves negative imprinting on intimate associates during a critical period of early childhood (roughly between ages 2 and 6).

The biosocial theory of incest avoidance was initiated by Westermarck (1921); revived by Fox (1962); studied by Wolf (1970), Shepher (1983), and Van den Berghe (1983); and elaborated on by Parker and Parker (1986). Parker and Parker combine biosocial theory with attachment theory to study father-daughter incest, which will be elaborated on in chapter five.

Basic Principles. The biosocial theory does not view the incest taboo as a cultural mechanism. In a so-called "Westermarck hypothesis," Westermarck (1921) hypothesized that intimate childhood associations are sufficient to preclude sexual arousal because noninstinctive mechanisms are able to produce an aversion for sexual relations among those who have shared early, prolonged, and intense interaction throughout childhood (Parker and Parker, 1986).

Incest avoidance, then, is partly due to the fact that extreme familiarity leads to habituation, which, in turn, reduces sexual arousal (see Figure 4.3). As Parker and Parker put it, "familiarity raises the threshold for sexual excitation by making potential sexual stimuli relatively dull and uninteresting." According to the biosocial theory, familiarity does not make sex aversive per se, but rather, lowers the anticipated reward value, and thus decreases its probability of occurrence. The taboo makes incest aversive and reinforces barriers.

Biosocial view runs contrary to the normative/structural views of Lévi-Strauss and White, which state that the incest taboo developed as a means to facilitate

Figure 4.3
Schematic Representation of Biosocial Theory

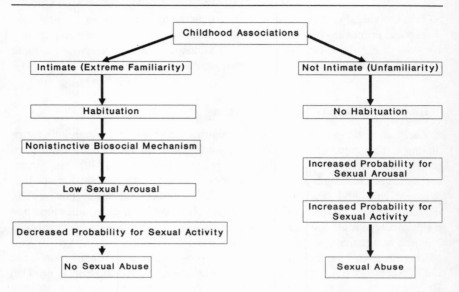

societal welfare (i.e., to achieve the advantages of establishing ties outside the family). It also runs contrary to the biological theory, which states that the incest taboo is a function of the negative genetic consequences of inbreeding (Wolf, 1970).

Empirical Evidence. Evidence for a biosocial mechanism has been evaluated by many authors. For example, Shepher (1971) studied sexual avoidance among co-reared kibbutz children; Wolf (1966) studied two types of marital practices among rural Taiwanese; and Fox (1967) and Parker and Parker (1986) studied child abuse among stepparents and natural parents. Overall, these studies provide partial support for the biosocial theory.

A cross-cultural study by Goodwin and DiVasto (1979) indicates that physical closeness between mothers and daughters is much less likely to be subject to sexual taboos than are father-daughter contacts. Indeed, in some cultures, such as the Hopi, Siriono, and the Alorese, mothers commonly fondle the genitals of their nursing infants, and in the West, mothers tend to show more emotional and physical closeness toward their daughters than toward their sons (Goodwin & DiVasto, 1979).

Physical isolation has been positively associated with the occurrence of incest cross-culturally: Studies in rural France (Lutier, 1961) and in rural Israeli collective settlements (i.e., kibbutzim) indicated that children raised together in an intimate environment ceased sexual play after puberty and did not subsequently marry, despite the fact that the incest taboo did not impose against such marriages (Parker & Parker, 1986).

Ethnological observations and laboratory studies of primate and other species point to the existence of phylogenetically based inbreeding avoidance mechanisms in sibling and mother-son relationships. However, for these populations, it appears that the most probable factors are early, sustained, and prolonged associations, rather than biological kinship relations. Data show that primates (including humans) tend to select mates who are neither too familiar nor too strange or novel (Parker & Parker, 1986).

In order to provide empirical evidence for the Westermarck hypothesis, Wolf (1970) examined two types of marriage arrangements in an area of Taiwan: (1) The major form, in which the bride and groom are joined when they are young adults, and (2) the minor form (sim-pua marriage), in which the bride is taken into her future husband's household in infancy or early childhood and is raised as a member of his family.

In support of the hypothesis, Wolf found that marriages of the minor form resulted in (1) more separations and divorces, (2) fewer births, (3) greater marital discord and dissatisfaction, and (4) more adultery. Wolf (1970) concedes that other factors could partly explain these findings, but asserts that taken as a whole, the evidence clearly supports the hypothesis. (It should be noted that the sim-pua marriage is no longer extant in Taiwan in the 1980s).

In support of biosocial theory, Parker and Parker (1986) found that (1) sexually abusive fathers (or surrogates) are more likely to have been away from home for a long period of time during the first three years of their daughters' socialization periods than fathers in a nonabusive comparison group, and (2) sexually abusive fathers (or surrogates) are less likely to have been involved in child-care and nurturing activities (e.g., diapering, feeding, playing) during the first three years of their daughters' lives than a nonabusive comparison group of fathers.

Evaluation. The mechanisms proposed by this biosocial theory could suffice to explain the infrequency of sexually abusive behavior in some societies. This theory may help explain incest to a degree, but the fact that incest or sexual relations between people intimate in childhood does occur suggests that such indifference or aversion can be overcome.

If this theory is correct, it would be expected that natal parents would be less likely than nonnatal parents to abuse their children sexually. In addition, this theory implies that natal parents who sexually abuse their children should show greater degrees of social, economic, and psychological distress than their nonnatal abusing counterparts (Gordon & Creighton, 1988). Since a stepparent is less likely to have been present during the child's critical period, the avoidance mechanism would less likely be engaged and consequently incest would more likely occur.

Giles-Sims and Finkelhor (1984) have pointed out the following problems with this theory: (1) the evidence is derived mainly from studies involving sexual avoidance among peers, not among adults and children; (2) the incest avoidance mechanism is said to be incorporated at an early age (ages 2 to 6), not when one is an adult; (3) the theory suggests that daughters would initiate fewer and resist more sexual advances by their natural fathers rather than by stepfathers.

Some research findings reject this hypothesis. Incest is almost always initiated by the parent and generally is a very negative experience for the child. An explanation of stepfather incest from the biosocial perspective needs to propose a mechanism that creates lower inhibition in the father, not the daughter.

On the other hand, Summit and Kryso (1978) have argued against this theory. They assert that the incest taboo must have originated outside the family because people who live together, who depend on each other for love and support, and who have intimate daily contact with each other will tend to develop sexual relationships with each other.

If the biosocial theory is correct, there would be no need for laws regulating incest, because incest would be naturally avoided. Laws become necessary only to prevent conduct that individuals want to engage in, but society wishes to prevent. If the biosocial theory is correct, incest (as opposed to child molesting) would rarely, if ever, take place, and no laws relating to incest would be necessary. The very existence of such laws, both statutory and religious, gives reason to question this theory's validity.

Overall, the biosocial theory offers some intriguing hypotheses concerning the nature of the incest taboo and related sexual phenomena, but has not received much empirical support for a conclusive perspective.

Chapter Five

Theories of Incestuous Abuse

INDIVIDUAL DETERMINANTS PARADIGM

The individual determinants paradigm focuses on intraindividual and personality factors associated with incest. The humanistic theory represents this paradigm.

Humanistic Theory of Family Sexual Abuse

Theoretical Foundations. Humanistic theory, developed mainly from the works of Rogers, Assagioli, Perls, and Lowen (cf. Anderson & Mayes, 1982), assumes the following concepts: (1) Humans are basically prosocial/altruistic in nature; (2) people want to feel good about themselves; (3) people have a natural inclination toward growth and self-actualization; (4) people are capable of change, and self-awareness facilitates the ability to choose and change behavior; (5) each person is unique; (6) people are personally responsible for their choices and the consequences; (7) in order to develop a positive self-image, humans need to relate to others positively; and (8) humans' past experiences are important to understanding present behavior patterns and gaining control over future directions.

There are, according to Maslow (1954), five basic needs that humans strive for in a hierarchial, progressive manner: (1) *physiological needs,* such as for food, water, and air; (2) *safety needs,* such as the need to feel secure, safe, and out of danger; (3) *love needs,* such as the need for affiliation, acceptance, and love; (4) *esteem needs,* such as the need for achievement, approval, competence, and recognition; and (5) *self-actualization needs,* such as the need for self-fulfillment and realizing one's own individual potentialities (Rubinstein, 1975).

Basic Principles. The humanistic theory (see Figure 5.1) was used to develop an integrated, community coordinated approach to case management and treatment of intrafamilial sexual abuse by Anderson and Mayes (1982). The basic

Figure 5.1
Schematic Representation of Humanistic Theory

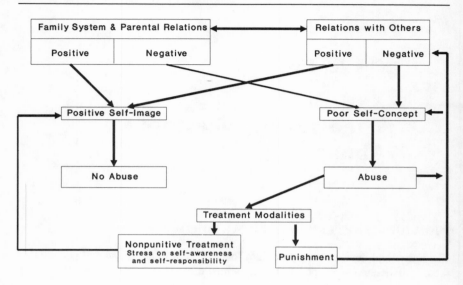

principle of this approach is that the offender has committed the sexual abuse because of his own lack of self-esteem and possession of a negative self-concept. He does not have the ability to meet his own needs in a positive way and thus has reacted by sexually abusing his child. Such "coping" behavior will further intensify his guilt feelings and serves to confirm the low opinion he holds of himself.

The humanistic treatment approach assumes that people are capable of and predisposed to growth and positive change. People can be guided in a manner that will increase their self-awareness and self-esteem, thereby increasing their ability to manage their own behavior positively.

Under this principle, this theory emphasizes the holistic development of a family system. Anderson and Mayes make five basic assumptions about the family system: (1) The family is a system in which each member strives to maintain some type of balance, and any change in one part of the system will directly or indirectly affect the other parts; (2) the family system is made up of individuals, and thus consideration must be paid to individual needs before the family as a whole is addressed; (3) disturbances in the family system may be manifested in a variety of ways (including child sexual abuse); (4) the foundation of the family system is the parents, and, therefore, the degree to which there is marital discord or harmony has great implications for the whole system; and (5) acts of abuse in the family are the direct result of the low self-concepts of the individuals involved.

Disturbance of the family system will result in many negative effects, including family violence and sexual abuse. This theory emphasizes present and future relationships within and outside the family. Insight into the past is an important key to understanding present behaviors and gaining control over the future. The striving for growth and self-actualization is considered a natural human process. The rate at which it occurs depends on each individual's unique characteristics. Therefore, each family member is approached in a humanistic manner.

The foundation of treatment is to increase self-awareness and self-concept. Punitive approaches will decrease self-concept and thus increase the likelihood of future abusive acts by the offender. Helping the perpetrator gain self-awareness and take self-responsibility are also said to be important goals for intervention in abusive patterns of behavior.

The specific treatment of family sexual abuse advocated by this approach involves individual counseling of each family member, followed by counseling of significant pairs (e.g., mother and daughter, father and abused daughter, marital couple, etc.). Social service groups that simultaneously involve detectives, social workers, prosecutors, and therapists in cooperation are coordinated in functioning to help the victim overcome the burden of guilt and damaged self-esteem and to help the family reach the eventual goal of family reconstruction.

Empirical Evidence. This approach was employed in a communitywide treatment program by Anderson and Mayes (1982) for dealing with over 50 victims and some of their families over a three-year period. The effectiveness of this program was clinically observed, and similar programs in philosophy and structure have been successfully implemented in many communities across the United States. However, as far as testing the relationship among various theoretical concepts (self-esteem, self-awareness, abuse reactions, etc.) there is still a lack of large, systematic scientific research evaluations. Thus, no empirical evidence was cited to support this clinical approach.

Evaluation. Humanistic theory does not make clear the roles of cultural and community systems. Unfortunately, the cognitive and affective domains involved in behavioral change are not clearly distinguished. The relationship between deficiency in meeting basic needs and deviant reactions of intrafamilial sexual abuse is not delineated at the empirical level.

This theory does have strength in that it emphasizes family systems and parental relationships, and at the same time it stresses the perpetrator's behavioral responsibility and self-awareness. It also has special significance for the treatment domain: Its advocation of positive, nonpunitive treatment will definitely increase the development of healthy interactions within and outside the family. Empirical research is needed to delineate the nature and dynamics of this approach.

SOCIOCULTURAL PARADIGM

The sociocultural paradigm stresses variables external to the individual that affect his or her behavioral dispositions, overt responses, and attitudes. Under the maltreatment type of incest, this paradigm is represented by the patriarchal theory.

Figure 5.2
Schematic Representation of Patriarchal Theory

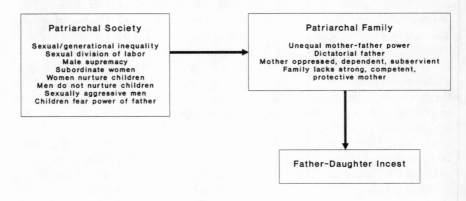

Patriarchal Theory of Father-Daughter Incest

Theoretical Foundations. The patriarchal theory assumes that various social, economic, and political processes operate directly and indirectly to support and maintain a social order and family structure of extreme patriarchy (male domination). Patriarchy is said to be the root cause of the historic pattern of subordination of women and children and the cause of systematic use of violence directed against them by men (see Figure 5.2).

Basic Principles. Herman (1981) believes father-daughter incest results from a family structure of extreme patriarchy, where the father acts as a dictator and views his children as his personal property. This family structure is derived from and maintained by the cultural attitudes of sexual predaceousness and misogyny (Rush, 1980; Herman & Hirschman, 1977; Herman, 1981).

Herman (1981) asserts that in incestuous families, the mother is usually oppressed by, and extremely dependent upon and subservient to, her husband. This may be due to an emotional or physical disability. Without a strong, competent, and protective mother, daughters are more vulnerable to incestuous abuse.

This theory maintains that even in very disturbed marriages, husbands are usually able to command sex from their wives and therefore no father is ever driven to incest for lack of sexual fulfillment. Herman (1981) asserts that patriarchal societies implicitly condone the father's right to use female members of his family, especially his daughters, as he sees fit:

Male supremacy invests fathers with immense powers over their children, especially their daughters. The sexual division of labor, in which women nurture children and men do not, produces fathers who are predisposed to use their powers exploitatively. The rearing of children by subordinate women ensures the reproduction in each generation of the psychology of male supremacy. It produces sexually aggressive men with little capacity to nurture, nurturant women with underdeveloped sexual capacities, and children of both sexes who stand in awe of the power of the father. (p. 62)

Herman (1981) proposes a direct positive relationship between the degree of male supremacy and sexual division of labor and father-daughter incest. Herman also proposes the converse: The more egalitarian cultural and family norms are and the more fathers and mothers share childrearing duties, the less likely it is that father-daughter incest will occur.

Others have stressed similar sociocultural elements. Rush (1980) and De-Mause (1974), for example, note that certain elements of the male subculture have approved of sexual interaction with children for centuries. This approval, coupled with other elements of the patriarchal culture, such as viewing children as property and the norm that children should absolutely obey their fathers, makes it easier for men to overcome inhibitors against sexually abusing children (Araji & Finkelhor, 1985).

According to Herman (1981), the only way to prevent incest is to change the power relations between mothers and fathers. This follows the premise that when fathers rule but do not nurture, and mothers nurture but do not rule, the conditions favoring the development of father-daughter incest prevail.

Empirical Evidence. Most of Herman's postulations are not empirical but clinical in nature. Many of the postulations of patriarchal theory were drawn from Herman's (1981) clinical study of 40 women who had been victims of incest. These women were all white, in their twenties or early thirties, predominantly Catholic, and mostly from Massachusetts; all were psychotherapy outpatients. There was no control group.

Incest was defined as "any sexual relationship between a child and an adult in a position of paternal authority." Thirty-one of the subjects had been victimized by their biological fathers, five by their stepfathers, and four by adoptive parents.

Support for Herman's patriarchal theory of father-daughter incest is primarily in the form of descriptions of the incest families made by the 40 victims. These women describe their fathers as "perfect patriarchs," who were for the most part very successful, highly authoritative, and tended to use force to dominate the family. The families of the incest victims adhered rigidly to the traditional sexual division of labor. None of the mothers had enough skill or experience to make survival on their own a realistic option. Male superiority in these families was unquestioned.

Other reports that have drawn similar conclusions were also presented. For example, a number of observers have described incestuous fathers as having above-average work histories (e.g., Weiner, 1962; Maisch, 1972) and therefore possibly being less nurturing and having a strong motivation to maintain a patriarchal role (Lustig et al., 1966).

Evaluation. Herman (1981) is reacting against the notions of the seductive daughter and the collusive mother found in some of the popular and clinical literature. In much of the clinical literature the father is spared responsibility for his deviant actions. He is often said to be forced into the relationship with his daughter by an unloving, cold wife and a seducing daughter.

The victim daughter has been described by other clinical reports as not being innocent, but rather as cooperating, active, initiating, and/or enjoying the incestuous relationship with the father (Henderson, 1975). The mother also has been said to play a causal role in the incestuous behavior of her husband because of her inability or refusal to satisfy her husband's sexual desires or demands.

Unlike systems theory, Herman's patriarchal theory does not blame dysfunctional families for the occurrence of incest, but rather places the blame on patriarchy as expressed in society and in the family, and on male socialization. Therefore, where systems theorists suggest whole-family treatment programs, those with a patriarchal perspective tend to favor criminal sanctions against offenders and the reinforcement of public standards about sexual contact as solutions to child sexual abuse (Finkelhor, 1982).

Herman's analysis of father-daughter incest takes blame off the mother and daughter and places it on the father. This analysis seems as much an emotional reaction *against* what others have suggested to be causal factors of incest as a rational analysis of what Herman believes causes father-daughter incest. This could lead to a loss of objectivity in clinical interpretation. Subjective clinical studies such as the one carried out by Herman are especially vulnerable to analytic biases.

All of the incestuous families in Herman's (1981) study had a traditional division of labor, and the abusers were committed to the father role in terms of being financial providers. Therefore, focusing on commitment to the care-giving dimension of the father role rather than to the economic role may help explain variations in the propensity to sexually abuse children (Gordon & Creighton, 1988).

There are no studies that have investigated the cultural norm or attitudinal theory of sexual abuse. The assertion that sexual offenders hold more patriarchal attitudes or have attitudes that give more legitimacy to having sex with children has not been tested (Araji & Finkelhor, 1985). In order to be empirically tested, patriarchy needs to be operationally defined and matched control groups utilized.

Patriarchy is not a family structure that is limited only to the United States (Finkelhor, 1980). Therefore, cross-cultural analyses may be particularly useful in testing the patriarch hypothesis. For example, Japan has been described as a highly patriarchal society and therefore should, according to Herman's basic thesis, have high rates of father-daughter incest. If this is not true, then factors other than extreme father dominance must be involved.

One major drawback of this theory is that it is reductionistic in nature, lacks complexity, and has no empirical support. It uses one factor (patriarchy) to explain incest. Not only are single-factor explanations rarely useful in social science (Gelles, 1985), but also incest has been shown to have many diverse causal factors, all of which may not be reduced to the single cause of patriarchy.

Patriarchy may have some facilitating role in cases of child sexual abuse (Finkelhor, 1982), but this has yet to be empirically established.

INDIVIDUAL-ENVIRONMENT INTERACTION PARADIGM

The individual-environment interaction paradigm is generally quite complex, as it attempts to combine numerous internal (e.g., personality and cognitions) and external (e.g., cultural norms and values) processes in order to come to a complete understanding of social phenomena and individual behaviors. The biosocial/attachment theory of incest (see Figure 5.3) represents this paradigm.

Biosocial/Attachment Theory of Incest

Theoretical Foundations. The biosocial/attachment theory integrates biosocial theory of incest avoidance, originally associated with Westermarck (1921), and attachment theory as set forth by Bowlby's (1969, 1973) investigations into the nature of early parent-child bonding and the consequences of its disruption. It is assumed that the early parent-child relationship is central to a child's normal biological and psychological development and is critical to the child's development of positive emotional, behavioral, and social characteristics.

The affective link between parent and child is said to provide the child with

Figure 5.3
Schematic Representation of Biosocial/Attachment Theory

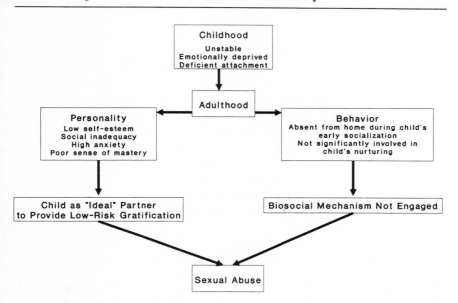

generalized trust, a secure base from which to explore the physical and social environment, as well as mastery and competence (Parker & Parker, 1986). Impairment of this bond may have significant negative effects by hindering the development of a secure base and explorer abilities and by causing chronically high levels of arousal and anxiety. These negative effects may persist and, perhaps, become irreversible (Parker & Parker, 1986; Denelsky & Denenberg, 1967; Rutter, 1972; Harlow & Harlow, 1970).

Basic Principles. Parker and Parker (1986) consider incest avoidance a conditioning process by which very familiar potential sexual mates constitute habituated stimulus objects associated with low sexual arousal. They base the following theoretical assumptions on a review of the child sexual abuse literature: (1) Offenders are overwhelmingly male and victims mainly female; (2) parental deprivation in the offender's childhood leads to his low self-esteem and massive social inadequacy; (3) offenders are not generally mentally ill; (4) incestuous abuse is not generally accompanied by physical abuse; and (5) stepfathers or other father-surrogates are overrepresented among perpetrators.

Attachment may have phylogenetic origins. A close mother-child bond facilitates survival of the young and encourages the development of subsequent interpersonal skills. Deficient attachment may be linked to child abuse and neglect in terms of symptomology or causality. Poor attachment in early life has been shown to be related to depression, an inability to establish close interpersonal relationships, and personality disorders (Parker & Parker, 1986). According to this theory, attachment appears to initiate a set of cognitive expectancies and interpersonal skills that influence the probability of specific behavioral outcomes.

Sexually abusive fathers are often described as having high levels of anxiety, poor interpersonal relations, low self-esteem, and little sense of personal mastery. These factors have also been shown to be indicative of poor and/or anxious attachment. For these individuals, the child is an "ideal" partner, providing low-risk gratification of needs for affection and sex (Parker & Parker, 1986).

Theoretically, a noninstinctive biosocial mechanism produces a repulsion for sexual relations among those who have shared early, prolonged, and intense interaction during childhood. Westermarck (1921) believed this learned aversion was incorporated universally into the conduct of human behavior as the incest taboo. Parker and Parker (1986) theorize that extreme familiarity leads to habituation, which reduces sexual arousal. This process does not necessarily make sex aversive. Rather, it lowers the anticipated reward value and thus decreases the probability of its occurrence. They argue that it is the cultural taboo against incest that actually makes it aversive.

This theory assumes that a strong parent-child bond early in the child's socialization results in the propagation of a noninstinctive biosocial mechanism in the parent that effectively inhibits sexual arousal associated with the child. Therefore, deprivation in the father-child bonding process substantially magnifies the potential for sexual abuse. Parents continuously and intimately involved in early child care will be less likely to become sexually aroused by their children and thus less likely to abuse them than those not as closely involved.

Empirical Evidence. There is considerable empirical support for the attachment perspective. Also, there exists a general consensus among developmental theorists that the bonding process is vital to a healthy parent-child relationship and is necessary for the sound psychological and biological development of a child. On the other hand, the biosocial theory has not received as much empirical support, nor has it received widespread acceptance by the field of cultural anthropology.

Parker and Parker (1986) provide empirical evidence for both of these positions. From analyzing data collected from 56 abusers and 54 matched non-abusers, Parker and Parker found that (1) sexually abusive fathers tended to experience greater instability during their early childhood than did fathers in the nonabusive comparison group (the difference approached but did not reach significance); (2) sexually abusive fathers were more likely to have felt emotionally deprived of love and affection during their early socialization than were the nonabusive comparison group; (3) sexually abusive fathers were more likely to have been absent from home for long periods during the early years of their daughters' socialization than were fathers in a nonabusive comparison group; and (4) sexually abusive fathers were less likely to have been involved in child care and nurturant activities during the first three years of their daughters' lives than were those fathers in a nonabusive comparison group.

Evaluation. This approach offers an innovative perspective by integrating research and theory in the developmental processes related to attachment theory with an anthropological analysis of the incest taboo. Further research is needed to support biosocial theory. It is possible to explain sexual abuse without considering the existence of the noninstinctive mechanism proposed by biosocial theory. For example, Finkelhor's (1984) four preconditions model provides a plausible explanation for a wider range of sexually abusive behaviors without relying on a biosocial mechanism. Social learning theory could also adequately account for the findings of biosocial theory by considering principles of learning and cognitive processes. These different perspectives may be compatible and should be integrated as a more complete theory.

Biosocial/attachment theory would benefit by including various other social and contextual factors that have been found to be important correlates of sexual abuse (e.g., characteristics of the child) and by expanding its scope to explaining sexual abuse not associated with deficient parent-child attachment.

FAMILY SYSTEMS PARADIGM

The family systems paradigm assumes that all family members have a role in the occurrence and/or maintenance of incestuous abuse. The etiology of incestual abuse has been studied through many various theoretical approaches. Specifically, the concept of family as a system has been incorporated in various theoretical perspectives to address the phenomenological characteristics of dysfunctional families that involve incest.

Among the most frequently studied is the combined use of psychodynamic and family system theories. This combination enables the theorists to postulate the underlying causal factors (e.g. personality disorder) of individual system (family) members and their relationships. In this process, various structural components of the family as a functional system have been identified for theoretical explanation of incestual etiology. Theorists thus emphasize the nature and characteristics of boundaries between individual family members and also of the interactional properties among various sub-systems. Each incestuous family as a dysfunctional system can further be differentiated in terms of various system typologies (e.g., open vs. closed system, and enmeshment vs. disengagement).

In order to fully account for the etiology of incestuous abuse, it seems necessary to assess the dysfunctional characteristics of all individuals as separate units of a family system. In this regard, psychoanalytic perspectives have frequently been used in conjunction with the family systems approach for addressing dysfunctional characteristics of family members. As the focus of this chapter, two major theoretical perspectives under the Family System Paradigm of Incest will be described: Family Survival Theory represents one of the earliest psychoanalytic analyses of incest, and Endogamous Theory represents a more recent approach to incest.

Family Survival Theory of Incest

Theoretical Foundations. The family survival theory (see Figure 5.4) mostly relies on neo-Freudian concepts of the individual and family. Both intrapsychic and intrafamily dynamics are used to explain incest. This theory goes beyond the individual intrapsychic approach, advocated by the psychoanalytic/psychiatric schools, by suggesting that the whole family unit needs to be understood to successfully understand incest. The family is considered a system that strives to maintain a delicate homeostatic balance. This balance is established through the interdependence of all family members. Any change in one part of the system affects and is accommodated by the rest of the system. Therefore, the proper way to study incest is to examine the roles that each individual member of the family plays in the etiology and continuation of the incest (de Young, 1982).

Basic Principles. According to this theory, father-daughter incest functions to reduce tension in a dysfunctional family and requires the mother's conscious or unconscious participation and/or sanction (Lustig et al., 1966). A dysfunctional family usually has two major characteristics: (1) an unstable family structure that generates continuous uncertainty about the family's ability to satisfy its members and stay together, and (2) an inability to function effectively in the pursuit of socially approved goals and in conformity with socially defined values. Therefore, dysfunctional families have to rechannel energies into forms of interactions

Figure 5.4
Schematic Representation of Family Survival Theory

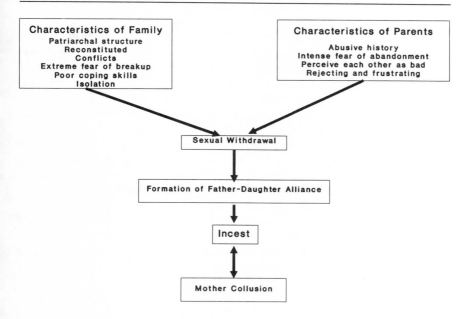

that maintain the family unit at any cost despite severe conflicts with cultural norms.

Incest is viewed as a *behavioral interaction* that functions to reduce family tension and thus maintain family unity (Kaufman, Peck & Tagiuri, 1954; Lustig et al., 1966; Cohen, 1983). Incest is also considered a *symptom of family pathology* (de Young, 1982), which may be the manifestation of a basic need for warmth and nurturance (Cohen, 1983). It is continued secretly as a structured pattern of family interaction and functions as a defense against potential family disintegration. Once this process is initiated, it tends to be self-perpetuating because of the feedback processes involved.

In explaining the etiology of father-daughter incest, this theory considers characteristics of five target groups: (1) father, (2) mother, (3) daughter victim, (4) nonparticipant siblings, and (5) the family as a whole.

The fathers: Incestuous fathers are said to have many of the following characteristics: (1) high levels of desertion anxiety (Cohen, 1983); (2) emotional, relational, or economical deprivation in their childhood (Cohen, 1983; de Young, 1982); (3) a negative or ambivalent relationship with their own parents, especially the father (de Young, 1982); (4) a regressed ego state to allow pregenital sexual acting out; (5) a need to appear the strong patriarch; (6) loss of masculine identity; (7) self-centeredness (Sgroi, 1982b); (8) lack of competent role model to follow in childhood; (9) overcompensation and reliance on early experiences (de Young, 1982); and (10) a motivation to maintain a facade of role competence (Lustig et al., 1966).

For these men incest becomes a means of projecting the hostility they feel toward their own mothers and for fulfilling the oedipal liaison denied them as children (Cavallin, 1966; Lustig et al., 1966). Fathers may justify their behaviors by rationalizing that they are protecting or legitimately teaching their daughters about sexual behaviors (Cohen, 1983). Other rationalizations include seduction by daughter victim, alcohol, mental illness, and sexual liberation from archaic and repressive sexual attitudes (de Young, 1982). These characteristics are generally attributed to childhood experiences.

Nonparticipant mothers: Nonparticipant mothers of incestuous families are characterized as the "cornerstone of the pathological family system" (Basini & Kentsmith, 1980; Brant & Tisza, 1977). De Young (1982) considers the mother's role especially critical because, as a parent, she has a great deal of intrafamilial power and thus can prevent or halt incest. Horowitz (1985) considers the mother the controlling force behind the incestuous family, because of her withdrawal and inattention to family problems.

The major characteristics of this type of mother include (1) a strong need to be mothered (Lustig et al., 1966; Kaufman et al., 1954); (2) ambivalent or negative feelings toward her own mother (de Young, 1982); (3) unconscious hostile feelings toward the victim daughter; (4) a significant dependency on the victim daughter as a substitute to her wife-mother role (Cohen, 1983); (5) fear of close sexual relationship, especially with males, and sexual rejection of their husbands; (6) the possibility of being sexually abused themselves as children (de Young, 1982); and (7) unconscious homosexual strivings (Lustig et al., 1966; Kaufman et al., 1954).

Nonparticipating mothers tend to develop certain coping strategies to deal with the abuse and their unhappiness (de Young, 1982). The major coping strategies include sexual withdrawal from husbands, physical and emotional incapacitation in role responsibilities, absence from home, and role reversal with the daughter. These strategies may also inadvertently set the stage for paternal incest. De Young does not blame the mother, but insists that her behaviors and intrapsychic dynamics are important variables to understand the etiology and continuation of incest.

Most of the mothers know about the incest or at least suspect it, but choose to do nothing about it; their collusion sets the stage for the incest to be initiated and allows it to continue over time.

Victim-daughters: There has been a good deal of controversy on the role victim-daughters play in incest. Lukianowicz (1972) has characterized the child as a willing temptress and therefore culpable for the victimization; Schultz (1980) characterized child victims as naive seducers; and Gruber (1981) considered the children as innocent victims.

Theorists have reported that child victims of incest generally have one or more of the following characteristics: (1) pseudomaturity, which facilitates role reversal with the mothers, (2) guilt over the possible dissolution of the family, (3) low tolerance for family tension, (4) limited capacities for handling impulses, (5) underdevelopment of ego functions, (6) being the oldest or a special daughter (e.g., handicapped, abandoned, or born out of wedlock), (7) viewing women's roles as deprecating and self-sacrificing, (8) looking like the mother, (9) being passive and unable to retreat or refuse her father's advances (de Young, 1982; Lustig et al., 1966; Cohen, 1983), (10) encouraging the incest if she feels that she is responsible for its initial occurrence, and (11) willing to *identify* with her aggressor so that she may share his power. These characteristics are more frequently manifested in a patriarchal family structure, which tends to produce attention- and affection-starved children.

Nonparticipant siblings: Because patriarchally structured families tend to create children who are attention- and affection-starved, siblings of the incest victim may view the victim only in terms of the attention she is receiving and thus may become highly jealous rivals for attention. This may result in discipline problems and induce socially destructive and self-destructive acts. Quite frequently, the nonparticipant siblings may imitate the seductive facade of the incest victim (de Young, 1982).

Frequently, in the incest family, the siblings of incest victims realize that the incest is taking place and actually play an unconsciously or even consciously collusive role in setting up the victim. This role may be played out of fear or a motivation to maintain the family unit (de Young, 1982).

The family unit: The general characteristics of dysfunctional families involved in father-daughter incest include (1) a heavy reliance on noninstitutionalized role relationships (e.g., the daughter's taking on the role of the mother), (2) cultural isolation or cultural deviance, (3) participation in the incest in some form by all members, (4) the incest serving to reduce tension among members by preventing confrontation with the real source of tension, (5) the incest serving to maintain family integrity only so long as its members, especially the mothers, are able to present a facade of role competence, and (6) an aura of physical violence in most incestuous families that directly contributes to many of the dynamics and effects of incest.

In summary, the family pathology theory of incest takes the following theoretical stances: (1) The problem must be considered from a multigenerational view; (2) sexual abuse is symptomatic of a dysfunctional family unit in which every member of the family (including the abused child) makes direct contributions to its development and maintenance; and (3) the problem may not itself have significance, but rather may have a not readily apparent meaning within the family. For example, sexual abuse may function as a tension-reduction mechanism or as a means of displacing feelings of isolation (Conte, 1986).

Empirical Evidence. De Young (1982) interviewed 80 (72 female and 8 male) *victims* of incest ranging in age from 4 to 53 (mean age = 23), 69 incest *offenders,* aged 13 to 69 (mean age = 35), and 12 *nonparticipant family mem-*

bers, consisting of 10 wives of incestuous fathers and 2 husbands of incestuous mothers.

Of the 60 paternal incest victims, 22 were also repeatedly abused physically, and 11 were occasionally abused physically. The remaining 27 not physically abused did report witnessing physical abuse directed against their mothers or siblings. In addition, 12 (24%) of the incestuous fathers/stepfathers in this study reported that they also frequently or occasionally beat their children or wives. These data support de Young's (1982) hypothesis that incest families are inherently violent.

The social isolation factor is supported by empirical data (cf. Russell, 1986). The childhood deprivation factor is also supported by many studies. Gebhard and others (1965), for example, found that 59 percent of incarcerated incestuous fathers came from broken homes, and Riemer (1940) discovered that a majority of incestuous fathers grew up in poverty. In de Young's (1982) clinical study, 12 (24%) of the incestuous fathers came from broken homes, 22 (43%) had been physically abused by their fathers as children, and 19 (37%) had been either sexually abused or raised in a family in which incest was occurring.

However, most empirical research rejects the assertions made by this paradigm concerning the *causal role* of the mother and daughter in the etiology and perpetuation of incest (Herman & Herman, 1981; Russell, 1986; Finkelhor, 1984; Conte, 1986). For example, Conte (1985) found that 32 percent of 66 incest cases had no indication of role reversal at all and that the number of indicators of role reversal varied greatly over the remaining cases.

The hypothesis set forth by Lustig and others (1966) that the father is unwilling to act out sexually outside the family because of a need to maintain a positive social image is rejected by de Young's (1982) clinical study that found that 38 (75%) of the incestuous fathers had had at least one extramarital affair; it is also rejected by Gebhard and associates (1965), who found this figure to be 84 percent.

Evaluation. This theory has had considerable impact on the field of child abuse and neglect. Muldoon (1979) suggests that incestuous households be labeled "character disordered families" in reference to their insidious role reversals, blurring of affectional patterns, and distortions of generational boundaries.

Much of the literature based on the family survival theory has presumed that incest is fundamentally different from other types of abuses in which children are sexually victimized. For example, it is assumed that fathers who sexually abuse their children significantly differ from other extrafamilial child sexual abusers. This assumption has not been tested. Indeed, preliminary findings indicate that incestuous and nonincestuous abusers may share more commonalities than differences (Conte, 1986).

The potential utility of family models, such as the family survival theory, to the understanding and treatment of intrafamily sexual abuse can be realized only if these models are based more firmly in conceptual frameworks and empirical evidence consistent with each other. As noted by Conte (1986), the connection between characteristics of the family and sexual abuse has not been established, and the literature suggests that such a connection is weak.

The family systems approach has been criticized for taking the blame off the perpetrator and dispersing it among all family members (including the abused child). Using systems theory as a foundation, Swan (1985) has rejected the victim- and offender-centered model. Swan emphasizes that since children may receive "rewards" (e.g., sensuous interchange, attention, power, or special favors) by engaging in sexual behavior with adults, clinical intervention of intra-familial sexual abuse should avoid blaming the parent and instead should focus on education and marital therapy.

However, Swan is not suggesting that the child is responsible for the abuse, but rather that "regardless of how seductive or provocative a child is toward a parent, the ultimate responsibility for the sexual encounter lies with the adult because of age, experience, power, maturity, and social responsibility." As evidence about incestuous behavior is gathered, it is becoming apparent that there are different types of incestuous behaviors (e.g., father-daughter; brother-sister) and different types of perpetrators (e.g., Groth's fixated vs. regressed molesters). While this orientation still maintains the victim/offender perspective, it suggests a move away from a narrow classification of the abuse on the basis of force, power, and relationship (Swan, 1985).

Studies show that children are aware of the incest taboo and feel a sense of guilt about their part in incestuous behaviors (Swan, 1985). Swan asserts that the method of blaming the parent may have therapeutic value by letting the child place his or her felt guilt onto the adult, but also polarizes the child's overall evaluation of the parent. Switching the blame as a therapeutic strategy to reduce guilt, Swan argues, will lead to a weakening of family ties and will not promote any existing positive functions of the family. Furthermore, it solidifies negative memories that are likely to have future consequences (e.g., the long-term result of blame switching may become permanent).

Justice and Justice (1979) have been criticized by Herman (1981) for portraying the mother as a major cause of the father-daughter sexual relationship. The mother is described as keeping herself tired and worn out, frigid, and wanting no sex with her husband. This is another way, according to Justice and Justice, for the mother to "bow out" of her sex role as a wife and give reason to the husband to look elsewhere for sex. Justice and Justice contend that mothers in families where father-daughter incest occurs want a role reversal with their daughters:

The mother wants to become the child and wants the child to become the mother. This basic symbiotic quality is reflected in nearly all . . . the mothers whose husbands and daughters engage in incest. It expresses the mother's struggling attempt to get the care and nurturing that she missed in her own childhood. In inviting the daughter to take over her role, she is suggesting that the daughter also become their mate's sex partner. (p. 97)

This passage is typical of family survival analysis. It is this type of analysis in which the mother and daughter are portrayed as the causal agents of child abuse and the father as the "victim," which is most strongly opposed by other theorists and feminists.

Conte (1986) suggests a five-step improvement plan for family survival theory: (1) Expand the perspective to include all forms of sexual abuse (not just incest); (2) expand the range of systems to include all individuals, dyads of individuals, and other naturally occurring groups in the family's ecological environment; (3) identify the processes associated with the development and/or the maintenance of sexual abuse (e.g., the function of sexual abuse, family myths, secrets, themes, or beliefs that family members share in common); (4) increase research efforts; and (5) emphasize treatment intervention research.

The primary weakness of the family survival theory is its lack of empirical methodology, evidence, and support. Most of the studies designed to support this perspective are methodologically weak and actually tend only to describe the pathological nature of individual family members. Factors presumed to be the cause of incest (e.g., mother-daughter role reversal) may actually be the result of incest (Conte, 1986).

The Endogamous Incestuous Family Theory

Theoretical Foundations. Will (1983) combines systems theory concepts with psychodynamic analyses and builds on family transactional theories of incest and sexual abuse. Incest represents a symptom of family dysfunction. Its often persistent and enduring nature may suggest that incest serves as a function for the family system as a whole and that powerful homeostatic mechanisms contribute to its maintenance. The power of such homeostatic mechanisms can be revealed in the way that a family may close ranks and deny existence of problems when incest is initially disclosed. Furthermore, incest, as a dysfunctional family transactional pattern, may be replicated from one generation to the next. The victim of incest usually grows up to form a family in which further incest occurs (Steele, 1978).

Because of the complex nature of incest, Will's family transactional viewpoint emphasizes the importance of evaluating different levels of etiological phenomena simultaneously (sociological, family transactional, and individual psychological).

Basic Principles. Two types of incestuous family structures are described by Will (1983): chaotic and endogamous. In "chaotic" families, there is general family disorganization, including the blurring of intergenerational boundaries and role confusion among family members. Incest appears to be but one feature of family chaos. Other significant problems in the chaotic family include the deficiency of basic instrumental functions—family members have difficulty getting up in the morning, the provision of meals is chaotic, and there is little differentiation between sibling and parental subsystems, which usually results in chaotic behavioral controls.

According to Will, incest is not confined to chaotic families alone. It occurs throughout the entire social scale. Therefore, Will's family transactional viewpoint emphasizes the fundamental issue as to what role and function incest serves for a dysfunctional family. Between the two types of families, Will is primarily concerned with endogamous family structure because incest is presumed to serve a function for the family as a whole.

In the "endogamous" family (see Figure 5.5), incest is *not* simply a feature of family chaos, but rather may develop under two general conditions: (1) The coping mechanisms of a disturbed family can no longer effectively deal with particular family conflicts, and (2) the family considers these conflicts a threat to its survival. From this perspective, incestuous behavior is seen as a means of reducing tension by helping the family avoid facing conflicts that are seen as having catastrophic consequences. Once started, incest reinforces the dysfunctional transactional patterns that engendered it and hence can be a very enduring symptom.

Will describes several important psychodynamic characteristics of incestuous families: (1) The spouses of an incestuous family often share the experience of having been abandoned or frustrated by a parent of the opposite sex, and thus each develops an intense fear of abandonment. This common experience becomes their shared unconscious bond, which is expressed through the isolation of the family. (2) Each spouse starts to perceive the other as the bad, rejecting, and

Figure 5.5
Schematic Representation of Endogamous Theory

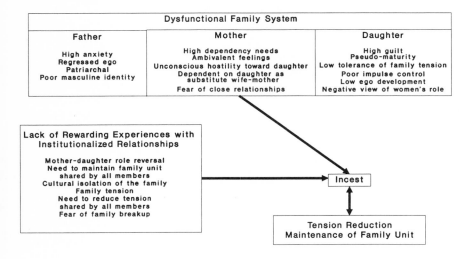

frustrating parent, which leads to sexual withdrawal and increases the fear of abandonment. (3) The breakup of the family is unthinkable for both. (4) The father turns to the daughter for sexual fulfillment because going outside the family would indicate family breakdown. (5) The wife colludes with the incest by "not seeing" it because of her fear of family breakup.

The family dynamics that activate this situation are reinforced in three main ways: (1) The incest strengthens the father-daughter alliance and hence the inappropriate intergenerational boundaries in the family; (2) it is necessary to maintain the secret of incest within the family; and (3) the necessity of maintaining the secret of the incest from the outside world eventually leads to even greater family isolation.

Noting that transactional mechanisms are themselves not sufficient to explain all incestuous cases, Will (1983) addresses other family risk factors: (1) a family structure of extreme patriarchy—fathers functioning like martinets and mothers reciprocating with submissiveness; (2) a reconstituted family in which the father is not biologically related to the children such that the incest taboo is weakened; (3) parental history of sexual abuse—the abusive cycle of incest as part of dysfunctional coping mechanisms; and (4) rigid emphasis on genital sexuality by both husbands and wives (e.g., a "coital fixation" by wives) and bizarre moral beliefs surrounding "sinful masturbation" and "nonsinful incest" by fathers.

Empirical Evidence. The transactional mechanisms presented by Will (1983) were based on clinical case studies. No scientific methods of analysis were mentioned. Of the four risk factors presented, the patriarchal factor is based on descriptions, the reconstituted family and genital-sexuality-emphasis factors are based on a survey, and one reference is cited for the parental history factor.

Evaluation. The endogamous family theory is basically a reworking and synthesis of psychodynamic theories of sexual abuse and therefore also is vulnerable to the same general criticisms, such as incomprehensiveness, poor methodology, and inability to explain. Furthermore, theories of this nature often disperse responsibility for the incest throughout the family. At times a great portion of the blame is set to rest on members other than the actual perpetrator. Frequently the mother has been labeled the "cornerstone" (Basini & Kentsmith, 1980; Brant & Tisza, 1977) or "controlling force" (Horowitz, 1985) of the incestuous family. Other writers have suggested that the mother may be relieved when the daughter assumes the sexual role in the incestuous relationship (Yorukoglu & Kemph, 1966). Incest for the daughter has been labeled an unconscious oedipal "wish come true" (Cohen, 1983), and nonparticipant siblings have been said to suffer from "incest envy" (Berry, 1975).

Will's theory is basically concerned with explaining why incest continues as a durable pattern of interaction within a family system. By utilizing various psychodynamic constructs in connection with three primary reinforcing mechanisms, Will's transactional theory does appear to offer a heuristic working model for therapists with a psychodynamic foundation.

However, as an explanatory theory to account for the etiology of child mal-treatment, this theory suffers from the same weaknesses that other clinically based theories do, namely in their lack of (1) empirical evidence, (2) stringent definitions, (3) component operationalization, (4) direct causal links, (5) control groups, and (6) significant number of subjects. These methodological limitations make it impossible to conclude that the family dynamics reported in this theory are truly unique for the incestuous family (Cohen, 1983).

ECOLOGICAL DETERMINANTS PARADIGM

The ecological determinants paradigm generally compiles data from multiple ecological levels (e.g., individual, family, community, and society) and empha-sizes the overlapping of and interactions among various ecologies. The grounded theoretical theory (see Figure 5.6) is used to represent this paradigm.

Grounded Theory

Theoretical Foundations. Vander Mey and Neff (1986), in evaluation of a substantial body of literature on incest, conclude that while contemporary social-science attention to incest as a taboo or an aversion is highly *theoretical,* the

Figure 5.6
Schematic Representation of Grounded Theory

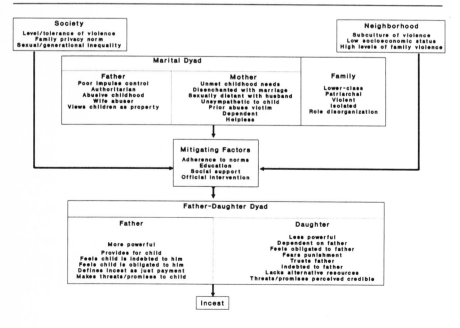

empirical research effort is conspicuously *atheoretical*. As a result, research unguided by theoretical considerations frequently becomes unwieldy and stale—a noncumulative array of answers to unrelated questions. To overcome this difficulty, Vander Mey and Neff address the need for a well-developed and empirically grounded theory. Their theory is defined as "grounded" because it is formulated inductively: First, many pieces of empirical data were observed, and second, from these specific and concrete observations abstract conceptualizations and statements are deduced. Further, most traditional incest theories are considered at a "dead end" because these theories start with the premise, implicit or explicit, that there is an incest taboo or aversion to be explained. Here, both taboo and aversion assumptions are questioned and an alternative orientation proposed.

Vander Mey and Neff hypothesize that many fathers experience an occasional sexual desire in response to their daughters. They do not act on that impulse because of certain social and psychological barriers (especially the strong concern for the daughter's welfare). However, some fathers, because of harsh, unemotional, and unsupportive environments in their own childhoods and also because of other subcultural factors (e.g., drug use) in their present life patterns, have often failed to develop the capacity for altruistic responses to their sexual desires. A second hypothesis put forth by Vander Mey and Neff is that many perpetrators redefine or rationalize what is good for their daughters in a fashion congruent with their own desires.

Based on this new theoretical orientation, Vander Mey and Neff's theory addresses three basic questions pertaining to incest: What are the effective external barriers in response to incestuous sexual desires of some fathers? How can these barriers be strengthened? How are these barriers in place throughout all segments in society? Answers to these questions are centered around the development of grounded theory.

Grounded theory is thus rooted in a synthesis of sociocultural determinants and other individual variables. Therefore, this orientation challenges the fundamental assumptions of most traditional (taboo and aversion) theories. In short, it is an eclectic resource-based model that addresses the interplay of power and resource dynamics within the social environment.

Basic Principles. The grounded theoretical model is an eclectic, research-based explanation of father-daughter incest. It depicts contributing factors to and mitigating factors against father-daughter incest.

To develop their grounded theoretical model, Vander Mey and Neff (1986) utilized *inductive* rather than *deductive* reasoning. They generated abstract statements by considering many specific observations. They reviewed the vast array of existing data on the subject of father-daughter incest and derived their theoretical conclusions.

Vander Mey and Neff (1986) consider father-daughter incest at four levels of "actors' milieus": the society, the neighborhood, the marital dyad and the family, and the father-daughter dyad. In addition to these four levels, certain mitigating variables are considered.

Social factors: At the society level, four major factors are closely linked to the etiology of father-daughter incest: (1) the society's general level of violence, (2) its general tolerance level of violence, (3) its reverence for family privacy, and (4) the ascription of inferior status to women and children.

Incest is considered an act of sexual aggression. It is asserted that the general level of societal violence, including sexual and physical aggression, is very high. This fact is evident in statistical crime reports. The acceptance of a high level of violence by the general public is reflected in the wide range of violence in popular movies, television programs, novels, and magazines.

The reverence of family privacy is considered an important social norm in incest abuse because it allows families to become relatively closed systems. If a family is not subject to outside criticisms and/or input, then the deviant behaviors of abusing parents are more likely to avoid detection.

Sexual and generational inequality is said to be important to understanding child incestuous abuse because of its impact on the rights and welfare of women and children in male-dominated societies. It is asserted that as a society becomes more egalitarian, violence toward women and children becomes less acceptable and less prevalent.

Neighborhood factors: The neighborhood is conceived as the immediate link between the family and society. Three variables at this level are considered critical in the understanding of incest: (1) subculture of violence, (2) low socioeconomic level, and (3) high levels of family violence.

Vander Mey and Neff (1986) describe two types of neighborhoods: the "good" and the "bad." In good neighborhoods, homes are well kept up, the members are ambitious, and violence is low. A bad neighborhood has poor-quality and low-maintenance housing with significant crowding. It generally is perceived by insiders and outsiders as an area of high violence.

The effects of these types of neighborhoods on families is substantial. Good neighborhoods provide social support for its members and are conducive to feelings of positive self-esteem, security, and trust in others. Bad neighborhoods, on the other hand, generally fail to supply decent social support for its members and are conducive to feelings of negative self-esteem and fatalism.

It is asserted that if a community is characterized by a subculture of violence, if it lacks sufficient neighborliness (friendliness, reciprocity, and support among inhabitants), and if it is generally low in socioeconomic status, then the probability of family violence (including incest) occurring within that community is increased.

Family situations: In terms of the marital dyad and the family, it is asserted that if a family is characterized by general family violence, patriarchy, social isolation, role disorganization, and low socioeconomic status, then the children of that family are susceptible to incestuous abuse. Other major risk factors at the family level are alcohol abuse by the father, inadequate housing, marital discord, a marriage initiated by pregnancy, several successive births, a passive mother, a father reared in a harsh and unemotional environment, and a mother with unmet childhood needs.

Father-daughter dyad: At this level, the power (resource) differential between the child and adult in the context of the other levels is stressed. In fact, Vander Mey and Neff (1986) define incest in terms of power inequality: "Incest as child abuse occurs when a person who holds a position of power in a child's intra-family life sexually victimizes that child. . . . The child is open to exploitation because of the inequality of the relationship."

The child sexual abuse perpetrator is portrayed as a man who has a great need for power. To satisfy this need, he exploits the unequal distribution of power within the family system.

It is asserted that the resource inequality between the father and daughter is significant enough that "bargaining," at least while the child is young, is minimal and, when combined with a lack of support from her mother or outsiders, the child has no option but to submit to her father's demands. This submission is not viewed as voluntary, because it is done to avoid physical punishment asserted by the father's threats and/or to fulfill a sense of obligation to the father because he is the parent and provider.

The degree of *dominance-subjugation* is considered of primary importance by the grounded theoretical model. This is defined as the probability that the father's demand will be obeyed by the child. The family is viewed as a structure of dominance, with the father at the top of the hierarchy: He has the greatest strength and commands more power in the family than anyone else. This domination is due to the fact that the father is male, the predominant breadwinner, older, larger, and stronger. The child has none of these attributes and is usually reliant on the father for food, shelter, protection, and direction. The abusive father may not adhere to the social norm dictating that he is responsible for supplying his child with these survival commodities and skills. Instead, the abusive father may have the distorted belief that the child owes him because of his resource investment (e.g., time, energy, money) in the child.

According to the grounded theoretical model, the role of threats and promises is essential in understanding why the child may comply with the sexual demands of her father. The use of threats of punishment and promises of rewards is considered further exploitation of the power differences between the child and adult male. In addition to the use of material goods (e.g., promising money, toys, or threatening withdrawal of allowance or freedom to visit friends) and threats/promises involving physical harm, powerful threats/promises may involve love, affection, positive feelings of self-worth, imprisonment, divorce, or harm to the victim's mother.

In light of the above discussion, Vander Mey and Neff (1986) assert that victims of incestuous abuse generally possess the following characteristics: (1) feeling particularly dependent on the father for love, security, food, shelter, clothing, and guidance (i.e., sexual/generational inequality and unequal power distribution); (2) feeling abnormally obligated, fearful, trusting, and indebted to the father (refers to the distorted view of family roles and responsibilities that the father has and that he has instilled in the daughter); (3) lacking alternative resources (e.g., a strong mother, ability to be independent, and lack of social support); and (4) perceiving the father's threats and promises as credible (e.g., threats of physical harm to the daughter or mother, promises of clothing or toys).

According to the grounded theoretical model, the *stratification of power resources in the family* is considered a substantial etiological factor in father-daughter incestuous abuse cases. Physical domination (size and strength) is furthered by economic domination. The daughter is thus placed in a subordinate position. In more egalitarian, less patriarchal families, where power is more evenly distributed between the mother and father, the daughter is far less vulnerable to sexual abuse. There are, according to Vander Mey and Neff, three reasons for this finding: (1) When the mother has more power she may serve as a resource for the daughter; (2) if a family is not patriarchal, power is more evenly distributed and thus children may have more power, be less dominated, feel less obligated, and be less dependent on the father; and (3) egalitarian families tend to be higher in socioeconomic status and thus are less likely to resort to family violence as a means of experiencing power.

Mitigating variables: The grounded theoretical model also considers factors that can reduce the probability of incest taking place. Such preventive conditions are called mitigating factors. These factors are found within the four-level life-milieu scheme, but are discussed separately for heuristic reasons. Four mitigating factors are considered: (1) adherence to normative proscriptions against incest, (2) education, (3) social support, and (4) official intervention.

First, *adherence to normative proscriptions* refers to the potential perpetrator's failure to abuse because of the internalization of social norms (his conscious, or superego) against such behavior. When fathers do not acknowledge and/or accept such norms and other risk factors are present, the probability of incest is significantly increased. This is an important deterrent, but can be overcome with rationalizations or rejection of cultural norms.

Second, *sex education* for children is considered the factor with the single most effective potential for preventing incestuous abuse. This must include discussions about sexual boundaries and how to react to sexual advances, and helping children become familiar with their body parts and functions.

Education of the general public through public service announcements is also necessary. These announcements should especially reveal (1) what child abuse is, (2) the severity and lasting impact of child sexual abuse, and (3) that the responsibility for incest lies entirely with the parent, regardless of any circumstances.

Media and community reporting can also educate the general public as to the prevalence and signs of incest. This may prompt suspicious mothers and/or potential and actual victims to report or take preventive measures against the perpetrator. This education can also inform and warn potential perpetrators. When informed, all adults can serve as mitigating resources.

Third, *social support networks* (e.g., abuse hotlines, shelters, community counseling centers, various agencies, extended family members) can also help mitigate against incest by (1) reinforcing the norms of the larger society, (2) serving as resources to act as buffers when a family or individual is faced with overwhelming stress, and (3) providing mothers and children a source that can lessen dependence on the father.

Fourth, *official intervention* generally includes intervention by legal sources such as the police, the child welfare department, or some other established organization. The primary function of such interventive efforts is to prevent recidivism by known or suspected abusers. The threat of official intervention, however, may also work to prevent initial abuses from occurring. In the past, the threat of official intervention was very limited. Now, however, with increased media coverage and public awareness, this factor can be a significant deterrent.

Empirical Evidence. At the societal level, Vander Mey and Neff (1986) focus on three variables: the level and tolerance of violence, family privacy norms, and social patriarchy. However, they offer little discussion of the empirical data on the influence of these variables.

In terms of the extent and tolerance of violence, it is noted that statistical reports show that American society is beset with high rates of physical and sexual aggression. A speculative review of the mass media's portrayal of such acts (Rush, 1980) is said to indicate a high degree of aggression tolerance. It is observed also that pornographic media frequently involve children and scenes of incest (Pierce, 1984). However, no serious attempts were made to discuss the linkage between observing media violence and pornography and father-daughter incest.

The high degree to which the privacy of the family is revered is considered important in this etiology of incest abuse. Again, however, little empirical data is presented to support this argument. It is simply stated that this norm accounts for the "nobody's business" response to intervention efforts (Specktor, 1979) and that it indicates that social isolation is crucial in child abuse cases.

The inferior status of women and children is discussed as a significant causative factor of father-daughter incest, but no empirical studies are discussed that could ground this assertion. They state, but do not elaborate, that "research" indicates that male dominance and female subservience are often found in incest families. Most studies cited by Vander Mey and Neff (1986) are clinical in nature and do not employ sound scientific methods, such as the use of control groups.

In addition, the status of women in American society has substantially changed. A far larger proportion of women are seeking higher education and are employed outside the house, thereby possessing some degree of economic independence. If incest is significantly related to the inferior status of women, it should have decreased in recent years as the status of women increased. Therefore, empirical evidence is needed to substantiate this causal relationship.

The importance of neighborhood variables are empirically validated by the citation of two studies. Garbarino and Sherman (1980) found that even if a neighborhood is low in socioeconomic status, it may be considered positive by its inhabitants if it is characterized by solidarity, reciprocity, and neighborliness. Ditson and Shay (1984) mapped out the occurrences of reported child abuse cases and found that 63 percent were concentrated among low-income families receiving governmental aid. Again, although the assertion is made, these findings are not empirically linked to father-daughter incest to a sufficient degree.

Regarding the family environment, many risk factors were cited through analysis of case reports (e.g., Finkelhor, 1980). These include aggressive family norms, male dominance, social isolation, disorganized family roles, and poor socioeconomic status (low income, unstable employment, and low education). However, the empirical foundations of such variables are not well delineated or used to specifically support the grounded theoretical model.

"Father-daughter dyad" factors are essentially those that revolve around the issues of unequal father-daughter power relationships. The assertions that the father and daughter are unequal in power, that the father uses illegitimate power when initiating incest, and that the daughter's submission is usually not voluntary are well established in the literature. The discussion by Vander Mey and Neff (1986) is, however, primarily at the theoretical level. They focus on reviewing the various theoretical positions concerning the roles of dominance-subjugation, threats and promises, and lower stratification in families in incest. Little empirical research about these variables are presented to support the grounded theoretical theory.

Evaluation. This theory goes beyond the traditional psychoanalytic orientation on incest taboo and aversion. It emphasizes the ecological resources and correlates. Specific risk factors are identified from compilation of various clinical case reports. It also emphasizes intervention and prevention efforts from all aspects of society. Perhaps the most important contribution of this theoretical orientation is the emphasis on the need for basic research that should involve larger samples, comparison samples, cross-cultural research, more integrated measurement of antecedents and effects, longitudinal designs, and a greater reliance on substantiated cases of incest in descriptive research. This more rigorous methodology should compensate for the subjective inferences from small and convenient samples, clinical and caseworker observations, and frequently unsubstantiated self-reports. Therefore, because of the lack of empirically sound findings in the literature, Vander Mey and Neff rely heavily on interpretations and inferences of clinical data for support of the conceptualizations of the grounded theory.

In addition, the four characteristics of victims addressed by Vander Mey and Neff (1986) tend to blame incest on the victim, whereas the four social factors of incest tend to blame the incident on society and the ecological environment. The precise causal relationships between these two inductive reasonings are not well developed to account for the dynamics of incestuous problems. The role of abusive fathers and the role of nonparticipating mothers and siblings have not been well delineated. Therefore, this theoretical perspective seems shallow and imprecise in consideration of incest causes and etiological correlates.

Furthermore, the basic principles advocated by Vander Mey and Neff are apparently not ecologically valid from a cross-cultural perspective. For example, the inferior status of women and children in Eastern cultures does not necessarily correlate with the incidence of physical or sexual abuse.

Finally, how the four levels interact is not well discussed. It is asserted that individuals are engaged in several different levels of interaction and that no level operates without influence from the others. Thus, incest is considered the result of multiple interactions among society, neighborhood, family, and father-daughter dyad variables. It is assumed that no single variable or set of variables at one level can suffice to account for father-daughter incest. However, no attempts are made to conceptually link the four levels of milieus formally. Each level is presented generally in isolation from the others for heuristic reasons, with the stated understanding that in reality each level affects and is affected by factors at every other level.

Chapter Six

Theories of Sexual Abuse

The theories presented in this chapter attempt to address the problem of child sexual abuse from a broader perspective than those of the preceding chapters. These theories have been used to explain both intra- and extra-familial child sexual abuse.

INDIVIDUAL DETERMINANTS PARADIGM

Theories of child sexual abuse under the individual determinants paradigm include two member theoretical perspectives: the psychoanalytic theory and the psychiatric theory. These theories focus on the perpetrator's intrapsychic dynamics, psychopathology, motivations, and personality traits.

Psychoanalytic Theory of Child Sexual Abuse

Theoretical Foundations. Psychoanalytic theory (see Figure 6.1) has two basic assumptions: (1) Unconscious processes greatly influence and may even determine conscious feelings, thoughts, and behavior; and (2) early childhood experiences are central to the development of adult personality (Freud, 1939).

Basic Principles. A number of child sexual abuse theories assume that perpetrators are unable to fulfill their emotional and sexual needs in adult heterosexual relationships. Psychoanalytically oriented theories link this phenomenon to intrapsychic conflicts associated with early childhood experiences of the perpetrator, such as oedipal conflicts or castration anxiety (Fenichel, 1945; Gillespie, 1964).

According to Glueck (1954), child sexual offenders often had overly seductive mothers, resulting in arousal of their incest anxiety and, as a consequence, a fear of adult women and mature sexuality. This fear leads these individuals to choose nonthreatening children as partners.

Figure 6.1
Schematic Representation of Psychoanalytic Theory

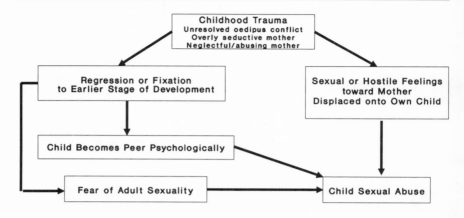

Another psychoanalytical view of sexual abuse concentrates on the perpetrator's fixation at an early stage of psychosexual development. This may be due to an unusually pleasurable experience that arouses a conditioned response to that early childhood stimuli; or it may be due to an unusually negative experience that may deter sexual maturation, or to compulsive repetition of the original situation in an effort to change the outcome (Finkelhor, 1979).

Many pedophiles are assumed to have arrested psychosexual development and as a consequence to be emotionally immature. Sexual offenders therefore prefer children because they are at the same emotional level and respond to similar childlike preoccupations (Hammer & Glueck, 1957; Groth & Birnbaum, 1979; Bell & Hall, 1976). They may also have low self-esteem and poor social skills. Relating to children, therefore, offers them a chance to feel powerful and in control (Hammer & Glueck, 1957; Loss & Glancy, 1983).

Others believe that sexual offenders were victimized in childhood and their offending behaviors are an attempt to reverse the victimization roles. By identifying with the aggressor they overcome their own sense of powerlessness by becoming the powerful victimizer (Howells, 1981; Groth, Hobson & Gary, 1982; Storr, 1965).

Incestuous desires, according to psychoanalytic theory, have the strength of an instinctual drive, and all affectional ties have a sexual origin, even though no specific sexual acts may have occurred: "The first object selection of the boy is of an incestuous nature and . . . is directed to the forbidden objects, the mother and the sister" (Freud, 1939). Contemporary psychoanalytic explanations emphasize the centrality of the incest experience in evolving neuroses and developmental fixations (e.g., Cohler, 1987; Eisnitz, 1984; Katan, 1973; Shengold, 1980).

Psychoanalytic theory stresses childhood correlates and intrapsychic dynamics. For example, a father may "date" his daughter as he did her mother when he was young or he may be searching for the mother he craved as a child in the oedipal period. Incestuous men may also have hostile feelings toward their mothers. These men may transfer these feelings to their wives and daughters and thereby fulfill the oedipal liaison denied them as children (Rist, 1979; Cavallin, 1966; Lustig et al., 1966).

Cohler asserts that some victims of incest obtain a secret satisfaction, fulfill penis envy, and reinforce feelings of grandiosity at having been chosen over a sibling. Guilt may also ensue when these unconscious wishes come true. The victim regards the relationship with extreme ambivalence, because she gains the father as a lover and replaces her mother (a deep unconscious wish), but loses a parent (Cohler, 1987).

Guttman (1986) suggests that as society moves away from participatory gerontocracy, the role of male elders as superego and "culture tenders" erodes. This leads to the weakening of the cultural regulation of social life. When culture and extended families are no longer regulated by strong elders, then unsupported, isolated nuclear families become the staging ground for various forms of child abuse. This psychoanalytic perspective is interesting because it focuses on societal/environment factors rather than on intrapsychic dynamics.

Empirical Evidence. This theory is derived from clinical speculation based on a limited number of subjects with various pathological conditions (Newberger & Newberger, 1981). Therefore, empirical evidence for the psychoanalytic perspective on child sexual abuse is very weak.

Evaluation. Although many of the studies suffer from methodological problems, sufficient evidence exists to support the hypothesis that many sexual offenders were victims of childhood sexual trauma (Araji &Finkelhor, 1985). This evidence is supported by several theories, including those based on learning processes and family interactions.

Any theory containing an intergenerational transmission component must address the issue of sex differences in victimization. Intergenerational transmission does not explain why males become primarily victimizers and women become victims (Araji & Finkelhor, 1985).

This theory fails to significantly consider factors at the family, community, social, or geopolitical level. While focusing on individual characteristics, advocates of this approach may fail to consider other factors that may be contributing to the abusive behavior. Certain characteristics of the child, for example, may serve as a significant long-term stressor (e.g., retardation, extended sickness, and economic strain) or a triggering antecedent stressor (e.g., acting out and nagging) may be present. A number of studies have found these characteristics to be significant factors of child maltreatment (cf. Reidy, 1977; Starr, 1982).

Despite these weaknesses, the psychoanalytic approach has made significant contributions in the treatment of sexual victimization. It may be especially helpful when it is used in conjunction with other modalities (Newberger & Newberger, 1981).

Psychiatric Theory of Child Sexual Abuse

Theoretical Foundations. The psychiatric theory (see Figure 6.2) is based on the early medical forensic field of psychiatry. It is assumed that child sexual abuse is basically the result of deviant personality characteristics of the perpetrator.

Basic Principles. According to the early medical theory of Krafft-Ebing (1941), child sexual abuse is "possible only to a man who is a slave to lust and morally weak, and, as is usually the case, lacking in sexual power." Individuals who commit child sexual abuse are placed into one of two categories: nonpsychopathological cases and psychopathological cases.

Nonpsychopathological offenders are said to lack courage or faith in their virility. Krafft-Ebing further characterized nonpsychopathological cases into three categories: (1) individuals who have experienced mature heterosexuality at all levels and are motivated by the craving of novel sexual experiences, (2) individuals who are afraid of mature women or are unsure about their own virility, and (3) adult females who sexually abuse boys entrusted to them (the motivations for such acts vary widely).

According to this theory, *psychopathological offenders* account for most child sexual abuse cases. Most have an acquired mental weakness (e.g., dementia, alcoholism, paralysis, or mental debility). Other causes include organic mental defects, states of morbid unconsciousness, and a morbid disposition of psychosexual perversion.

Empirical Evidence. Krafft-Ebing provided no evidence from empirical re-

Figure 6.2
Schematic Representation of Psychiatric Theory

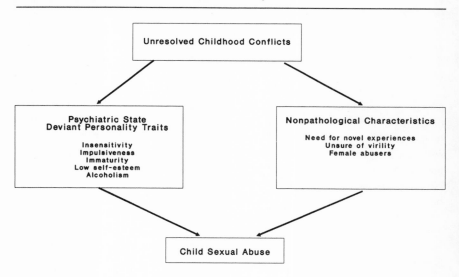

search. Some clinical descriptions were provided. However, the psychiatric model of sexual abuse is generally not supported. Lester (1972) concluded that sexual abusers do not, on the whole, differ greatly from control group subjects in terms of psychological pathology. Others have characterized sexual abusers as individuals with low impulse control, authoritarian personalities, low self-esteem, and a lack of empathy (Meiselman, 1978). However, these characteristics have not been empirically validated.

Although a number of studies have been carried out using objective measures, such as the Minnesota Multiphasic Personality Inventory (MMPI) (e.g., Atwood & Howell, 1971; McCreary, 1975; Toobert, Bartelme & Jones, 1959), the Edwards Personal Preference Schedule (Fisher, 1969; Fisher & Howell, 1970), the Kelly Repertory Grid (Howells, 1978), and the Semantic Differential (Frisbie, Vanasek & Dingman, 1967), no consistent personality-trait findings have emerged except that child sexual molesters tend to be somewhat more shy, passive, and unassertive than average individuals and that their sexual identification is not significantly feminine (Lanyon, 1986; Langevin, 1983).

Alcoholism has been consistently shown to be associated with the occurrence of child abuse (Meiselman, 1987; Vander Mey & Neff, 1982; Dubanoski, 1982; Finkelhor, 1978; Blumberg, 1974). Maisch's (1972) review indicated that about 30 percent of all sexual offenders were also chronic alcoholics. Virkkunen (1974) found this figure to be at 50 percent. These factors suggest that alcoholism is related to sexual abuse and that there is greater psychopathology in alcohol-related sexual abuse (Finkelhor, 1978). Parker and Parker (1986), however, found no difference in the use of alcohol or drugs between sexual abusers and nonabusers in their comparison study of 56 abusers and 54 control subjects.

Evaluation. The traditional views of Krafft-Ebing (1941), Freud (1953), and Ellis (1942) share two basic premises: (1) All sexually deviant behaviors are theoretically and etiologically similar, and (2) they represent a single type of psychopathology, namely, a form of character disorder (Lanyon, 1986). These premises are unidirectional and noninteractive. The inefficiency of this approach is evident from clinical and empirical analyses of cases through other theories (e.g., psychoanalytic analysis and family systems).

Many studies under this theory are based on only those adult offenders who have been caught, and therefore may not represent the general population of molesters. Therefore, from the viewpoint of early intervention, primary attention should be given to younger, rather than to adult, offenders (Lanyon, 1986). In addition, because this approach has generally not utilized any nonabusing comparison groups, many of the traits believed to cause child abuse may in fact be shared by an unknown proportion of the nonabusing population (Parke & Collmer, 1975).

Although a number of investigators agree that sexual offenders share some common personality characteristics, such as immaturity and inadequacy, proponents of this theory often make broad and unwarranted inferences from their studies that should not be advanced beyond the status of clinical inference.

Furthermore, even well-established evidence of immaturity and inadequacy on the part of sexual offenders does not necessarily fully explain their sexual interaction with children (Araji & Finkelhor, 1985).

SOCIOCULTURAL DETERMINANTS PARADIGM

The sociocultural determinants paradigm focuses on environmental factors external to individuals that have a significant impact on their behaviors. The socialization theory is one such theory that examines the phenomenon of child sexual abuse.

Socialization Theory of Sexual Abuse

Theoretical Foundations. The socialization theory considers child sexual abuse at psychological and sociological levels (see Figure 6.3). At the psychological level, this theory details clinical analyses of abuse victims and profiles of perpetrators. Psychological variables include victims' attitudes, knowledge, and beliefs about sexual abuse, fear of sexual assault, and degree of emotional upset and trauma. Sociological variables include socioeconomic status, religious background, type of work, education, ethnicity, and age.

The distinction between sexual and physical abuse is emphasized. Sexual abuse is characterized by a preponderance of male offenders. Therefore, it is stressed that the etiology of child sexual abuse is in the socialization process of the male, rather than in problems of inadequate and disaffected parenting (Finkelhor, 1982; Russell, 1986).

Basic Principles. Russell (1986) and Finkelhor (1982) emphasize the socialization of male sexuality. Cultural norms addressing masculinity issues promote the transference of male sexuality into violence, rape, sexual harassment, and sexual abuse. Altering cultural notions of masculinity should significantly reduce the prevalence of child sexual abuse.

Other sociological factors also contributing to child sexual abuse include social isolation, male dominant (patriarchal) family structure, greater divorce and remarriage rates, and the erosion of sexual norms (e.g., the escalation of child pornography). Finkelhor speculates that rises in expectations concerning sexual activity, which are fueled by the sexual revolution and thwarted by the more critical role that women are playing in sexual relationships, may also be a factor in sexual abuse etiology. The "sexual revolution" has also helped bring sexual abuse phenomenon out into the open. As divorce rates have exposed children to more stepfathers or mothers' lovers or boyfriends (and thus have increased their risk to sexual abuse), they may have also rescued many from an abusive situation (Finkelhor, 1982).

In analyzing sexual abuse, some theorists exclude the sexual issues involved, maintaining that the underlying factors in all abuse cases (including sexual) are those that concern power and control, hostile and aggressive impulses, and need

Figure 6.3
Schematic Representation of Socialization Theory

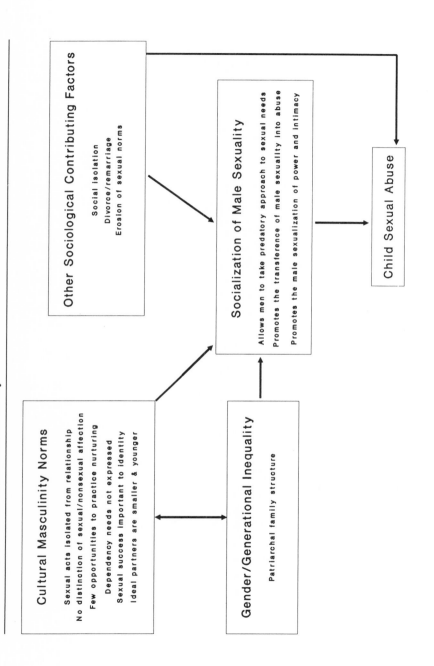

for affiliation (e.g., Sgroi, 1982; Groth & Burgess, 1977; Swan, 1985). Russell (1986) asserts that many of these analyses fail to recognize that males are socialized to sexualize power, intimacy, and affection, and sometimes hatred and contempt. Since the vast majority of sexual abuse is committed by adult males, the problem should be evaluated in the context of severe gender and generational inequality. Socialization norms tend to escalate this problem by allowing males to take a "predatory" approach to sexual gratification.

Finkelhor (1982) outlines four differences between men and women in sexual orientation that help explain higher rates of sexual abuse by men: (1) Women learn earlier and more completely to distinguish between sexual and nonsexual forms of affection, whereas men are given fewer opportunities to practice nurturing and to express dependency needs except through sex; (2) men are socialized to view heterosexual success as much more important to their gender identities than are women; (3) men are socialized to be able to focus their sexual interests around sexual acts isolated from the context of a relationship; and (4) men are socialized to view their sexual partners as persons who are younger and smaller than themselves, whereas women are socialized to see their appropriate sexual partners as older and larger than themselves.

Finkelhor suggests the following social changes to help eliminate sexual abuse: (1) providing men more opportunity to practice affection and dependency in nonsexual relations, (2) deemphasizing the accomplishment of heterosexual needs as the ultimate criterion of male adequacy, and (3) encouraging men to practice enjoying sexual relations based on equality.

Mohr, Turner, and Jerry (1964); Friedman (1959); and others also view sexual abuse as arising from cultural values. Certain themes of normal male sexualization tend to make children "appropriate" objects of sexual interest. This includes the value, emphasized in the male socialization process, of being dominant and the initiator in sexual relationships, and also the value of having youthful and subservient partners (Araji & Finkelhor, 1985).

Empirical Evidence. Russell (1986) conducted an empirical study involving a random sample of 152 adult females who had been abused by relatives before reaching the age of eighteen. In comparison with results from other empirical studies, some inconsistencies about various social ecological variables have been found in association with sexual abuse histories. For example, three major low-risk factors were identified that included (1) being raised by both biological or adoptive parents, (2) *low* (rather than high) income background, and (3) a Jewish religious upbringing. Three major high-risk social variables were (1) *high* (rather than low) income background, (2) mother with a high-school education (as opposed to some college, or eighth-grade education or less), and (3) being raised by a stepfather.

A rural background and having a mother who worked during her daughter's childhood years were not high risk factors for incestuous abuse. However, Russell indicated that *risk* of incest was positively correlated with income, whereas the degree of incest *trauma* was negatively associated with income. Incest trauma was more extreme in households with lower income. Russell's risk-income correlation data is exactly the opposite of Finkelhor's (1984) findings that incest victims were more likely to be from lower-income families. This may be due to the fact that Finkelhor's study was limited to a survey of college students. College students are themselves a special group and may not represent the general population as a whole. Finkelhor suggests that individuals who attend college are probably healthier psychologically than those who do not, and that most individuals who experienced the trauma of childhood sexual abuse may not have pursued higher education. Therefore, Finkelhor's data may actually underestimate the real risk of child sexual abuse for lower-class children. Russell argues that since her data is not limited to a particular group (e.g., students), it may be more accurate in reflecting the social class composition of an urban community.

Brother-sister incest, which has been suggested by some studies and theories to be often mutual and relatively benign, was found to be the second most traumatic form of incest, after father-daughter incest. Incest abuse was found not to be repeated in 43 percent of the cases in Russell's study, but these cases, nevertheless, were very traumatic.

In an early study of 930 women randomly sampled in San Francisco, Russell (1984) found that sexual abuse by stepfathers was much more prevalent than sexual abuse by natal fathers (17% vs. 2%) and that the impact of the abuse was greater when committed by a stepfather (47% "very serious") than by a natal father (26% "very serious"). Gorden and Creighton (1988) also found nonnatal fathers to be disproportionately represented among paternal abusers but natal fathers more likely to subject their victims to intercourse.

Russell (1975, 1986) and Finkelhor (1979, 1982) stress the importance of cultural norms that define masculinity and promote and maintain the transference of male sexuality into violence, rape, sexual harassment, and sexual abuse. Others also link male socialization with violence and sexual abuse (e.g., Scher & Stevens, 1987; Brownmiller, 1975; Watts & Courtois, 1981; Stevens & Gebhart, 1985). In an extension of Weis and Borges's (1973) social control model of sexual aggression, Berry (1979) suggests that pornography and violence against women are due primarily to a "cultural sadism" ingrained in the social structure and attitudes of individuals.

Pornography is assumed to have a direct impact on the occurrence of sexual abuse. Each month over 250 magazines depicting sexual acts between children or between children and adults are published and sold (Denson-Gerber & Hutchinson, 1979). The sexual abuse literature available in this area suggests that exposure to such pornography promotes acceptance of such material and its messages (Bowen, 1987; Zillmann & Bryant, 1984).

Evaluation. This theoretical perspective emphasizes the determining role of the cultural ecology system—both subjective (psychological) and objective (sociological)—in normal development of human beings as well as in "deviant development" of aggressive and abusive behavior. The fundamental assumptions of this approach are quite contradictory to those of the humanistic theory, where individual characteristics and differences are appreciated for their contribution to the etiology and treatment of child sexual abuse.

The link between socioeconomic status and child maltreatment has frequently been questioned for empirical and methodological reasons (e.g., Finkelhor, 1978; Russell, 1986). For example, as Russell has pointed out, most empirical studies that linked low socioeconomic status to child abuse and neglect have been based on very selective samples, have not employed control groups, and thus actually are not suited to evaluate the trends of child maltreatment across social status variables.

Furthermore, this theory argues that child sexual abuse is partly due to the cultural norm of sexual and generational inequalities. It is argued that sexual victimization is a way in which men maintain their control and power, as the use and threat of its use can keep women intimidated (Brownmiller, 1975). The process is said to start in childhood with the victimization of girls.

Unfortunately, sex has become a valuable commodity in society, and it is plausible that a dominant group (such as men) may construe things such that their access to it is maximized (Finkelhor, 1979). A number of cultural beliefs may also contribute to making women and children sexually vulnerable. For example, family members may be regarded as possessions of the man and therefore subject to unusual and generally undetected liberties with them. Also the belief that the male's sex drive is overpowering and in need of satisfaction allows men to rationalize antisocial sexual behaviors. In such a system of severe sexual and generational inequality, women and children often lack the resources that would enable them to defend themselves against sexual victimization (Finkelhor, 1979).

Although this theory is fairly effective in explaining the etiological factors at the cultural level in sexual abuse of women by men (generally male perpetrators and girl victims), it lacks full explanatory power for other ecological levels (e.g., individual characteristics and family dynamics). Furthermore, children are a subordinate group in almost every society, and both women and children probably have more power in the United States than in most other societies. This theory does not explain well why, given their universal powerlessness, children are often sexually exploited in some societies and not in others (Finkelhor, 1979). In short, the major weakness of this theory is that it ignores the important role of personality defects of perpetrators as advocated by the individual and interactive paradigms.

INDIVIDUAL-ENVIRONMENT INTERACTION PARADIGM

The basic premise of the individual-environment interaction paradigm is that both characteristics of the individual and his/her environment contribute to behavioral outcomes. Under the maltreatment of sexual abuse, Finkelhor's four preconditions theory represents this paradigm.

Four Preconditions Theory of Sexual Abuse

Theoretical Foundations. The theoretical foundations of this theory can be summarized in terms of internal (within the individual) and external (environmental) influences on behavior (see Figure 6.4). Internally, the sexual drive is considered a primary motivator. Behavioral intentions are induced by emotional needs or desires and sexual arousal, and regulated by internal inhibitors (e.g., conscience, guilt, and internal moral standards). Externally, situational factors (e.g., where and when the subject is located) function to further regulate behavioral intentions. Finally, the influence of other people's responses (including the victim's) determine the overt behavior and probability of its subsequent expression.

Basic Principles. According to Finkelhor (1984, 1986), four sequential preconditions lead to sexual abuse: (1) The perpetrator is motivated to sexually abuse a child; (2) the perpetrator overcomes internal inhibitors against the motivation; (3) the perpetrator overcomes external inhibitors against the motivation; and (4) the perpetrator, or some other factor, undermines or overcomes the child's resistance.

Precondition 1: Motivation. Motivation to sexually abuse includes the three components of emotional congruence, sexual arousal, and blockage. Not all of these motivational components are necessarily present in all abusers, but one or more of these three are found in all abusers. (1) *Emotional congruence* exists when a sexual relationship with a child fills some important emotional need or desire for the perpetrator, such as a need to feel powerful or in control of sexual relationships, or to remedy some early childhood abuse by reenacting it in the role of the abuser. (2) *Sexual arousal* exists when the perpetrator finds children unusually sexually arousing. While the source of this pattern is not well understood, in some cases it may involve biological abnormalities (cf. Berlin, 1982; Finkelhor, 1982). (3) *Blockage* exists when the perpetrator is not being sexually gratified. This may be due to personality factors, such as shyness or sexual anxiety, social skills deficits, or relationship difficulties.

Precondition 2: Internal inhibition. Internal inhibitors, such as guilt, fear of punishment, or incongruent moral standards, must be overcome before sexual abuse can occur. Factors (counterinhibitors) that may weaken inhibitors include alcohol, stress, learned rationalizations, culturally weakened sexual taboos, and/or personality traits (e.g., impulse disorder).

Precondition 3: External inhibitors. Environmental impediments or restraints exist because of the antisocial nature of child abuse. Factors that cause these inhibitors to be undermined include: (1) poor child supervision, (2) the isolation of the child, and (3) the offender having unusual opportunities for access to a child (e.g., the child is alone or housing conditions are crowded).

Precondition 4: Resistance by child. The child victim may be a significant external inhibitor by (1) having a personality that discourages abusers, (2) making it explicitly clear that he or she is not the kind to be tricked or manipulated into sexual activities or keeping secrets, and (3) declining ploys, fighting, or running away. Many things may undermine a child's resistance, including, for example, being emotionally insecure, lacking knowledge about sex, and being especially trusting of the abuser.

Figure 6.4
Schematic Representation of Four Preconditions Theory

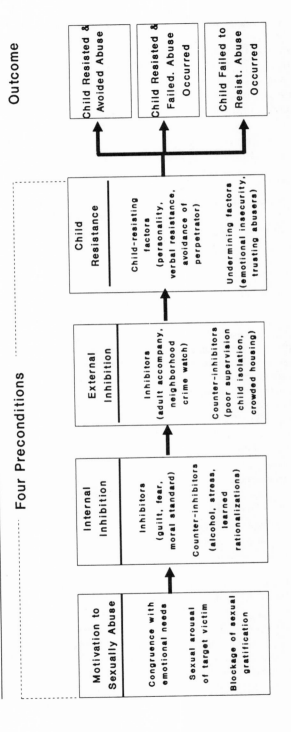

Finkelhor (1984, 1986) offers a schematic model that was revised by the present authors, as shown in Figure 6.4. This model shows how these four preconditions come into play sequentially. First of all, emotional congruence, sexual arousal, and blockage combine to produce, within potential perpetrators, a motivation to become sexually involved with children. In the next phase, some potential perpetrators overcome internal inhibition to act on their motives. Those who do act on their motives face external inhibitors. If external inhibitors are overcome, potential perpetrators arrive at stage four. At stage four there are three possibilities: (1) The child resists and avoids abuse, (2) the child resists but fails and is abused, or (3) the child fails to resist and is abused.

Empirical Evidence. Although Finkelhor has done a great deal of empirical research and comprehensive literature reviews in the field of child sexual abuse (for example, Finkelhor, 1978, 1979, 1983, 1984, 1986), direct empirical testing of this model has not been carried out. However, some supportive evidence has been presented to support general concepts of this model.

In a study of 521 parents, Finkelhor (1984) identifies the following family characteristics as being associated with the sexual victimization of girls: (1) an income under $10,000, (2) rural setting, (3) an unhappy marriage in which parents showed little mutual affection and little affection toward the child, (4) fathers who were blue-collar workers and who held conservative family values, and (5) mothers who had never finished high school and were often ill and sexually punitive. Although mother's education and father's and mother's education combined were a significant factor, father's education alone was not.

The second component of the first precondition, sexual arousal, finds support in the literature that most sexual abusers find children unusually sexually arousing to them (Freund, 1967; Quinsey, 1977).

Blockage of motivation, the component of unreleased sexual tension, may be due to shyness, sexual anxiety, or poor social skills. Social skills deficits have been indicated by others as characteristics of child molesters and pedophiles (Glueck, 1965; Goldstein, Kant & Hartman, 1973; Langevin et al., 1985).

Araji and Finkelhor (1985), in their review of pedophilia, concluded that (1) pedophiles do show an unusual pattern of sexual arousal toward children; (2) pedophiles are blocked in their social and heterosexual relationships; (3) the use of alcohol plays a disinhibiting factor in many cases of pedophile offenses; (4) children, because of their lack of dominance, may have some special meaning for pedophiles; and (5) many pedophiles were themselves victims of pedophile behavior as children. These characteristics of pedophilia and their relations in child sexual abuse appear to support the general concepts of the four preconditions.

Evaluation. This theory has the following positive attributes: (1) It is fairly general and thus applicable to all sexual abuse types; (2) it incorporates, expands, and goes beyond the family systems model, considering individual, family, and cultural traits; (3) it focuses on the emotional meaning of the sexual activity for the offender and considers a deviant pattern of sexual arousal that may play a role in sexual abuse; (4) responsibility is not placed on the mother, although it is recognized that her behavior may play a role in abuse at precondition three (e.g., poor supervision); (5) the sequence of events is ignited with the offender's motivation and then internal state inhibition; (6) it was developed by a comprehensive review and integration of all the factors proposed to contribute to sexual abuse, including those related to victims, families, and offenders; (7) it has clinical implications for working with abused children and families, indicating that evaluation and intervention can take place at four separate sites to prevent sexual abuse from recurring; and (8) it is open-ended, so that new findings and ideas can be incorporated.

However, the four preconditions theory has the following limitations: (1) It does not elaborate on the role of long-term or short-term stressors (counterinhibitors at various stages); (2) general characteristics of individuals and family are taken into account, but not elaborated; (3) its high level of generality is useful for incorporating data, but limits the theory's precision in prediction within and across different preconditions; (4) the various components of the model lack operational definition for measurement and thus fall short of empirical testing of the theory; and (5) it does not explicitly specify the interactive nature of the various components and their relationship within the family dynamics in conjunction with child maltreatment. It should also be noted that Finkelhor's (1984) identification of income under $10,000 as a characteristic of abusive families is in conflict with other studies (e.g., Weiner, 1962; Maisch, 1972; Herman, 1981) that found incestuous fathers to be highly successful with above-average working histories.

OFFENDER TYPOLOGIES PARADIGM

Theories under the offender typologies paradigm classify sexual offenders. Two major typologies of sexual abuse offenders are Groth's (1978, 1982) typology of male offenders and Mathews's (1987) typology of female sexual offenders.

The Male Sexual Offender Typology

Theoretical Foundations. The male sexual offender typology theory assumes that child sexual abuse is either a persistent fixed pattern of behavior or a regressive type of behavior that emerges when some overwhelming stress is experienced. Therefore, the psychoanalytic concepts of *fixation* and *regression* are central to this theory.

Basic Principles. Groth's (1978, 1982) typology places male offenders into two distinct categories: fixated and regressed offenders (see Figure 6.5). *Fixated child offenders* are temporarily or permanently stalled at a stage of psychological development deemed immature for their age group. This fixation, resulting from unresolved formative issues, leads these individuals to be primarily sexually

Figure 6.5
Schematic Representation of Male Sexual Offender Typology

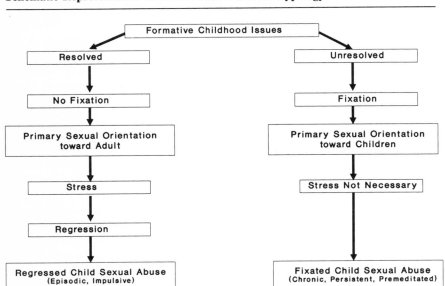

oriented toward children. Fixated offenders are assumed to have been sexually attracted to children since adolescence (Geiser, 1979). Child molestation for this group is a chronic, persistent condition not precipitated by stress. Sexual offenses tend to be premeditated, with boys often the preferred victims (Groth, 1978, 1982).

Regressed child sexual offenders do not have children as their primary sexual orientation. Instead, their sexual attraction to children reflects mostly the temporary expression of an earlier stage of development. It is usually associated with stress and/or certain situations. The vast majority of sexual offenses are generally of this type (Breese et al., 1986; Groth, 1982; Russell, 1986). Regressed offenders suffer from extremely complex, unsatisfying, or anxiety-laden relationships (Geiser, 1979).

Groth contends that sexual offenders tend to exhibit a number of pronounced traits common to both fixated and regressed offenders: (1) They are more passive and submissive rather than active and assertive; (2) they have an intrinsic feeling of isolation, self-alienation, separateness, and apartness from others; (3) they have an underlying mood state of emptiness, fearfulness, insecurity, and depression; (4) they are despondent, rigid, and fearful of being unable to function adequately in a heterosexual relationship; and (5) they tend to replace anxiety-producing adult relations with children who symbolize their own immaturity (Groth, 1982; Panton, 1979).

Although the dynamics of incest and extrafamilial sexual abuse are considered similar, Groth (1978) contends that there are some differentiating factors. In extrafamilal sexual abuse, the dynamics of the individual is the primary focus, whereas in every case of parental incest, there is some form of family dysfunction. The interrelationships of all family members must be examined, including the structure of the family network and the dynamics of the participants.

In incest families, Groth (1982) identifies two major patterns: (1) passive-dependent and (2) aggressive-dominant. In the *passive-dependent* type, the husband relates to his wife emotionally more as a dependent child than as a competent partner. As the wife turns elsewhere for emotional fulfillment and support, the father turns to his daughter to act as his companion-wife-mother. This arrangement eventually turns into a sexual relationship.

In the *aggressive-dominant* type, the husband maintains a position of power by keeping his wife and children economically dependent on him and socially isolated from extrafamily relationships (Groth, 1982). He selects a very insecure or immature spouse to maintain feelings of strength, power, and control, but this spouse is unable to provide him with much emotional support and thus he turns to his daughter to fulfill his emotional needs and sexual demands (Groth, 1982).

Empirical Evidence. Evidence for this theory is derived mainly through case examples, clinical estimations, and observations. A screening of 175 males convicted of child sexual assault was carried out by Groth (1978), with the following results: (1) 83 were classified as fixated offenders and 92 as regressed offenders; (2) fixated offenders were slightly younger (late twenties) than regressed offenders (early thirties); (3) overall, 67 percent of the offenders were known to the victims, but 83 percent of the fixated offenders were either complete strangers or only casually acquainted with their victims, whereas the victims of the regressed offenders were equally distributed among relatives, close friends, casual acquaintances, and complete strangers; (4) 49 percent of the victims were coerced through intimidation or threat, 30 percent through bribery, trickery, or pressure, and 20 percent through a brutal and violent attack in which the primary goal of the offender was to harm the victim; (5) 53 percent of the perpetrators chose female victims, 29 percent male victims, and 18 percent victims of both sexes; (6) 49 percent of the cases were confined to sexual play, 38 percent involved sexual penetration, and 13 percent involved both sexual play and penetration; (7) the victims had a mean age of 10; (8) there were more male victims (42%) than female victims (34%) in the fixated offender group, and more female victims (71%) than male victims (16%) in the regressed offender group; (9) 88 percent of the fixated offenders never married, whereas 75 percent of the regressed offenders did marry; and (10) 76 percent of the regressed offenders were exclusively heterosexual in their life-style, and 24 percent were bisexual.

Evaluation. Groth's (1982) typology is the most widely accepted distinction between types of child molesters (Russell, 1986). This theory appears to have face validity, relevance for therapeutic decision making, and usefulness in the study of child sexual abuse. Psychological characteristics, motivations, family dynamics, stress factors, sexual development, and predisposition attributes are all considered. Incest is considered a complex and multideterminants problem. This theory is best suited for therapeutic procedures, assessment, and prognosis of child sexual abusers.

Groth's analysis lacks good empirical evidence. If it is accurate, then it may be useful for research in the etiology and treatment of incest. As it stands, however, it must be considered with caution. Groth's analysis does not deal with incest committed by family members other than fathers, although uncles and brothers are often perpetrators (Finkelhor, 1979, 1984; Russell, 1986).

Clinical observations indicate that the regressed offender is the most common type. Such observations seem to be incongruent with Groth's more objective work (1978b). In Groth's study of 177 randomly sampled adult males convicted of sexual assault against children, 85 were classified as "fixated" offenders, and 92 as "regressed" offenders—a pretty even split. In contrast, Groth (1982) estimated that clinically, approximately 90 percent of incest offenders were of the regressed type. This discrepancy may be because the earlier study consisted of convicted individuals, and fixated offenders are more likely to be caught and convicted because their crimes are more likely to be repetitive in nature.

This theory is deficient in two ecological areas—community and societal variables—that may significantly influence child sexual abuse.

Typology of Female Sexual Offenders

Theoretical Foundations. The typology of female sexual offenders is based on a clinical model of child maltreatment. Psychiatric, personality, socialization, and demographic (e.g., age) variables are all emphasized. Some attention is given to family dynamics and victim characteristics.

Mathews (1987) argues that since males and females differ in terms of socialization and moral development, it is necessary to develop different sexual abuse models to explain female perpetration rather than simply extend the ones based on male sexual offenders. (See Figure 6.6.)

Basic Principles. Mathews delineates four types of female sexual offenders: (1) exploration/exploitation, (2) personality disordered, (3) male coerced, and (4) male accompanied.

Exploration/exploitation abusers: About one-half of adolescent female offenders fall into this category (Mathews, 1986). These offenders fear sexuality, have a need for being in control of their victims, and are sexually inexperienced, even with masturbation. They are described by their parents as shy, loners, active, and nervous. They are afraid to acknowledge their sexuality because they fear losing control. They are sexually rigid and repressed and tend to disassociate themselves from the arousal associated with the abuse.

They tend to be self-deprecating and socially detached or to lack social skills.

Figure 6.6
Schematic Representation of Typology of Female Sexual Offenders

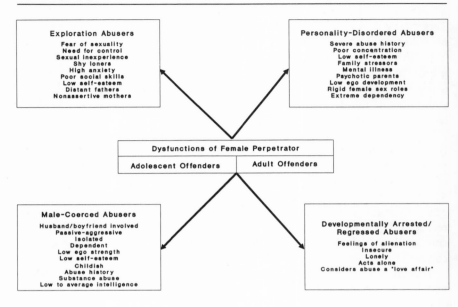

These adolescent perpetrators often have absent or distant fathers, and/or non-assertive and very shy mothers. Their families generally express some rigidity around sexual issues.

Their victims are males, age 6 or younger, and not siblings. The abuse generally involves fondling during baby-sitting situations. The offense is usually an isolated event characterized as detached, with no intimacy and low emotionality.

Personality-disordered abusers: These female perpetrators may be adolescents or adults. They are characterized by having (1) severe sexual and physical abuse histories (usually by male family perpetrators), (2) poor concentration, (3) low self-esteem, and (4) many family stressors. They often have mental illness or psychotic parents. The abusive adolescents have poor self-esteem and low ego development. The abusive adults have problems with psychopathic deviance, rigid female sex roles, dependency, and severe psychological distress. These individuals are generally diagnosed with borderline, dependent, or avoidant personality disorders. The abuse often replicates their own abuse, whereby an identification with the aggressor (their own abusers) appears to be operating.

The abuse generally occurs more than once and with the same victim. The victim is usually their own child, relative, foster sibling, or neighbor, and a female between infancy and age 10. If the victim is older (ages 7 to 10), the abuse is more severe (penetration).

Male-coerced abusers: In this category, female perpetrators are coerced into deviant sexual behavior by a husband or boyfriend upon whom they are very dependent. For the adolescent abuser, the offense is usually a one-time event. For the adult abuser, the abuse may be recurring.

Adult abusers in this category are characterized as passive-aggressive, extremely isolated, dependent, and with low ego-strength and self-esteem. Adolescent abusers show some dependent characteristics and peer-security problems. Both adult and adolescent abusers often are very childlike, and report sexual and physical abuse histories.

Husbands or boyfriends generally initiate the sexual abuse before the women's involvement. Their involvement is initially forced, but later they accept the abuse as the norm and eventually initiate it themselves. These women report that only 0 to 20 percent of their sexual experiences have been positive. The coercive husbands have a history of sexual abuse, and are diagnosed as pedophiles.

Male-accompanied abusers: In this category, there is male and female involvement in the abuse, but neither are coerced. The victims are generally older (over 14 years of age) and acquaintances of the female abuser's children. The female perpetrator may have a history of psychological disturbance or be conduct-disordered and antisocial. These abusers are also often heavy substance abusers with low-to-average intelligence. Some have experienced psychological and sexual abuse. The offenses tend to be more violent and the victims are more likely to be females.

Developmentally arrested or regressed abusers: These female perpetrators are usually in their twenties or older; are characterized as feeling needy, insecure, and lonely; and act alone. They usually have age-appropriate sexual relations. The victim is typically a male between the ages of 11 and 16. Offenders in this category usually do not consider their behaviors inappropriate and thus view the abuse as a "love affair."

Empirical Evidence. Supporting evidence for this typology comes from Mathew's clinical experience in treating female adolescent sexual abusers (N = 9) and adult female sexual abusers (N = 14). Of the nine female adolescent sexual abusers, 33 to 40 percent reported having been sexually abused, about 25 percent by females. All of the adult female offenders were sexually abused. Psychological testing of the offenders supplies some supportive evidence for each of the categorical types, except the developmentally arrested or regressed type (Mathews, 1987).

Evaluation. This typology brings to light an important differentiation between male and female perpetrators. Until recently, female sexual abusers have been placed in the same categories of male sex offenders or victims for treatment (Mathews, 1987). Most sexual abuse theories have generally not addressed differences between male and female offenders. Because the vast majority of sexual abuse cases are perpetrated by males, there has been little work conducted in the area of female sexual offenders.

However, female sexual offenses do occur. According to Finkelhor and Russell (1984), in approximately 24 percent of all male-victim and 14 percent of all female-victim cases, the perpetrators were females, either acting alone or with a partner. It might be interesting to note that most female abusers have been themselves abused, but this is not always so for male offenders. Therefore, it is important for professionals to understand differences between male and female offenders in developing theoretical frameworks for treatment purposes.

The primary limitation of this typology is that it is based on a small number of clinical cases (N = 23). Mathews's (1986) data base was limited to four previous publications (i.e., Finkelhor & Russell, 1984; Wolfe, 1985; McCarty, 1981; Marvasti, 1986).

Part IV

Theorizations of Psychological Maltreatment

Chapter Seven

Theories of Psychological Maltreatment

Only recently has psychological maltreatment been given reasonable attention. This is partly due to difficulties of defining, measuring, assessing, and intervening in cases of psychological maltreatment. Psychological maltreatment is, however, considered by many to have the most serious impact of all maltreatment types and to be inherent in all cases of maltreatment, including physical and sexual abuse, and neglect. Levesley (1984), for example, found that when the primary type of child maltreatment was physical abuse, emotional abuse was present in 45 percent and neglect in 44 percent of the cases. When neglect was the primary type of maltreatment, emotional abuse was present in 67 percent of the cases.

ECOLOGICAL PARADIGM

The ecological paradigm has been applied to the theoretical analysis of child psychological maltreatment by three theories: (1) ecological context theory, (2) family breakup theory, and (3) ecological/deficiency needs theory.

Ecological Context Theory of Psychological Maltreatment

Theoretical Foundations. Ecological context theory addresses the importance of three ecological contexts—individuals (parents and children), family, and social (community and macro) environments. These ecological contexts form three successive circles, with the individual context as the core, the family context in the middle, and the environment context containing both. Their relationships are characterized by two processes: (1) the progressive, mutual adaptation of the family and the environment, and (2) the complex interactions of many social systems that overlap with family life and influence human development. Mutual adaptation involves *social habitability,* which refers to the quality of the environment in which people and families develop. Political, economic, and social systems determine social habitability. They are important in understanding the basic causes of psychological maltreatment. Humans are assumed to be constantly developing and continually engaged in creating conceptions of who they are and in comprehending the situations they encounter. Thus, behavior is influenced by perceptions of self and others and by previously acquired and reinforced patterns of communication in social interactions (Garbarino, Guttmann & Seeley, 1986).

Parental perceptions of the child are considered to exist on a continuum. On one end, parents view the child as being able to get along without help (unaware of needs); on the other end, they perceive the child as being "very bad, very demanding, provocative, and a big problem."

Basic Principles. According to the ecological view of Garbarino, Guttmann, and Seeley (1986), child psychological maltreatment is the result of dysfunctions of one or more ecological contexts. At the family level, family communications reveal how individuals see themselves and others. Self-perception and the perception of others are necessary for understanding family communications, especially communication defects among maltreating families. Therefore, to identify and understand child maltreatment and its dynamics, perceptions of self and others, as well as the interaction of these perceptions with personality characteristics, must be understood.

A child's perceptions of self and parents are influenced by parental activities. These perceptions influence the child's behavior, which, in turn, influences parental perceptions of the child and of their own personality characteristics. These parental characteristics and perceptions will further shape their own activities, which subsequently influence the child's personality characteristics and perception of the parents. This theory, then, involves a host of perceptions, personality characteristics, and behaviors of both the parent and the child. As shown in Figure 7.1, they interact and influence each other in a cyclical fashion within the family environment.

At the *community level,* inadequate social resources and community stressors, such as isolation and unemployment, tend to create a sense of frustration and powerlessness among parents. They establish the background for child maltreatment because under these stressors parental coping skills and social support systems tend to fail. Low socioeconomic status is not the only community level stressor. Middle- and upper-class families who adopt destructive lifestyles or live in alienating neighborhoods can be maltreating as well (Garbarino, Guttmann & Seeley, 1986).

At the *macroenvironmental* level (see Figure 7.2), two major types of abusing families are reported: (1) the resourceless, impoverished family overwhelmed by the demands of life, and (2) the middle-class, alienated family engaged in a destructive life-style. The less support available to a family (e.g., available day-care centers, inexpensive stress-relieving entertainment), the greater the risk of child maltreatment. Another key element at the environmental level of analysis is

Figure 7.1
Schematic Representation of Ecological Context Theory (Microview)

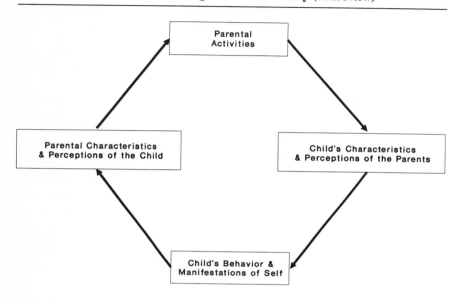

Figure 7.2
Schematic Representation of Ecological Context Theory (Macroview)

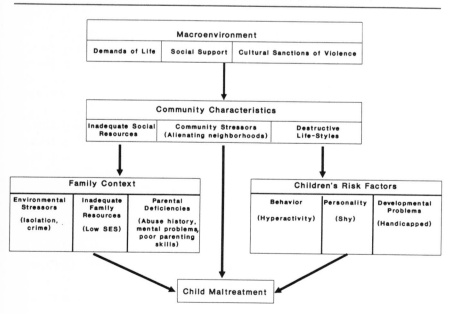

the cultural sanctioning of the use of physical force to solve problems in general, and specifically those problems involving children.

At the *individual level,* children may consciously or unconsciously trigger or even cause their own maltreatment through excessive activity, natural shyness, or some mental or physical handicap. The risk of abuse is greatest when the child or parent is limited or constrained by developmental problems. For example, children with learning disabilities, social deficits, or emotional handicaps are at increased risk for abuse, and parents under considerable stress or with personality problems are more likely to abuse their children. These risks are heightened when interactions between the spouses or parents and children are strained. The risk of abuse is further raised if the availability of community support is low.

In summary, environmental stress factors (e.g., poverty), coupled with *family context stressors* (e.g., heavy child-care responsibilities) cause families to lose whatever positive constructive coping skills have been previously acquired and thus force families to slip into an escalating pattern of child maltreatment (Garbarino, Guttmann & Seeley, 1986).

Empirical Evidence. Many components of this theory are supported by empirical findings. For example, research has shown that a number of community factors play a causal role in child maltreatment, including lack of prosocial support systems, poverty, unemployment, crime, poor housing, and unavailability of services (Garbarino, Guttmann & Seeley, 1986).

Garbarino (1977; 1984) found that the highest rate of physical child maltreatment occurs in communities with the fewest human and social service agencies. Family context factors empirically related to maltreatment include marital conflict, stress, social isolation, large families, and heavy child-care responsibilities (Garbarino, Guttmann & Seeley, 1986).

At the individual level, many researchers have found that maltreating parents have unrealistically high expectations of their children, have been maltreated themselves as children, suffer from impulsiveness, have low self-esteem, are inconsistent in their parenting style, suffer from substance abuse, have inadequate parenting skills and methods, and/or have mental or physical problems (Garbarino, Guttmann & Seeley, 1986).

Evaluation. Ecological context theory examines how community variables are related to child psychological maltreatment. Prevention efforts should include three primary targets: legal, educational, and community areas (Germain, Brassard & Hart, 1985). *Legal considerations* for prevention include the encouragement of laws that respect the rights of children, appropriate definition of maltreatment, effective prosecution of perpetrators, and effective protection for victims. At the *educational level,* courses in family planning, family life education, child development, and lifelong coping skills are advocated. At the *community level,* Garbarino and Vondra (1983) advocate neighborhood-based national health services, greater community awareness of services, and collaborative efforts among social agencies, churches, industry, and schools.

In their discussion of the perceptual factors associated with psychological maltreatment, Garbarino, Guttmann, and Seeley seem to offer conceptually constructed arguments, but fail to provide much empirical data to delineate the complexity of parental perceptions of the child, the child's perception of the parent, and the perceptual interactions of all family members. Related concepts such as mutual adaptation between the family and the environment are not operationally defined in a manner that may be empirically researched. This theory is also weak in its failure to define the types and nature of psychological maltreatment and its relationship with various abuse-precipitating factors at different ecological levels.

Family Breakup Theory of Psychological Maltreatment

Theoretical Foundations. The family breakup theory, originated by Bronfenbrenner (1977), assumes that the family is a fundamental unit of social organization around which increasingly complex levels of social organization are layered (e.g., the community and larger sociocultural environment). These various strata of social organizations are all interactive and affect one another. Therefore, characteristics or changes in one organization (e.g., the community) can have a significant impact on another (e.g., the family). In order to conduct an accurate analysis of the family system, according to the ecological perspective, both intra- and intersystems must be evaluated (Preston, 1986). Therefore, this theory considers unemployment, poverty, the isolation of the family, cultural/subcultural norms involved in conflict resolution and aggression, and the availability of social helping systems within the community as contributing factors to the occurrence of child abuse and neglect.

Basic Principles. Preston (1986) applied the ecological perspective to analyze separated families and the psychological maltreatment of children. Psychological abuse is defined as the consequence of the child's inhabiting a situation or ecology that can be characterized by dysfunctional patterns of interpersonal and intersystem relationships. Such relationships are influential and detrimental to the child's emotional development (Preston, 1986).

A primary cause of emotional abuse is family breakdown and marital separation. Children often are not informed of the separation or the reasons for it. They feel rejected by the absent parent and perceive themselves as a burden on the custodians.

Preston (1986) identifies *four types of separated families* in reference to different levels of emotional abuse of children (see Figure 7.3). *The nonabusive family* is relatively small in size and has a clear organizational structure and functional pattern of interrelationships among its members. The parents in this family are cooperative, mutually agree to separate, are not separated "under the same roof" for very long, agree on visitation arrangements, and are opposed to or very reluctant to pursue litigation. The children in this family type are nonsymptomatic, not directly involved in decisions about the separation, and not involved or exposed to parental conflicts.

Figure 7.3
Schematic Representation of Family Breakup Theory

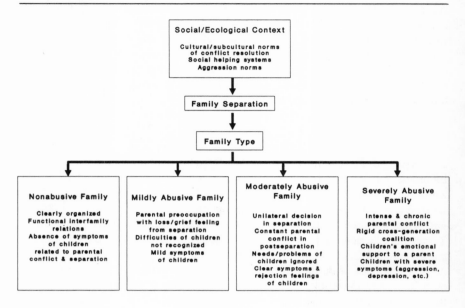

The mildly emotionally abusive family has (1) a noticeable increase in the frequency and intensity of parental conflict, (2) infrequent violence or threats of violence, (3) a custodial parent who considers the other parent intrusive, and (4) some parental conflict in front of the children. The parents in this type of family may be preoccupied with feelings of loss or grief from the separation, insensitive to the children's difficulties, and involved with litigation. The children in this type of family may begin to show mild symptoms.

In *the moderately abusive family,* the separation decision is usually unilateral. This type of family experiences (1) slightly higher parental conflict, (2) parental conflict as a normative part of the postseparation family's life, (3) the start of dysfunctional and cross-generational coalitions, and (4) intrusion by members of one or both extended families.

In this type of family, one or both parents may be (1) insensitive to the children's problems, (2) more concerned with winning the fight with the other parent, (3) more emotionally dependent on the children (this may involve a parent-child role reversal), (4) exhibiting behavior consistent with a severe personality disorder, and (5) unable to cooperate. The children are likely to be symptomatic and uncertain about their belongingness in the family and to feel rejected by one or both parents.

In the severely abusive family, there are (1) intense, chronic, and escalating conflict between the parents, (2) a rigid cross-generational coalition, (3) a split between the siblings, and (4) a degeneration of one or both parents in front of the children. Parents in these families generally are unable to cooperate and are insensitive to their children's problems and needs. Furthermore, they may have a serious psychiatric disorder, and may be involved in litigation. The children are generally excessively involved in giving emotional support to a parent and are often symptomatic—aggressive, depressive, psychosomatic, or conduct disordered.

Empirical Evidence. Preston (1986) cites some empirical evidence to support the general proposition that family breakdown is associated with emotional distress in children. Studies have found, for example, that both family breakdown (Chandler, 1981) and *concern* over family breakdown (Ochiltree & Amato, 1985) are significant stressors for children. Other studies have indicated that the impact of family disintegration on children is more related to the structure and functioning of the family after the separation than to the actual process of the separation itself (Martin et al., 1975; Wallerstein & Kelly, 1980).

Researchers have noted some similarities between the long-term symptoms, including personality characteristics, of abused children and the difficulties of children in adjusting to family breakup (Sardoff, 1985; Hepworth, Ryder & Dryer, 1984; Wallerstein & Kelly, 1980; Kurdek, Blisk & Siesky, 1981). These symptoms include wariness of relations with adults, vicarious affection, depression and withdrawal, difficulties with trust, external locus of control, pseudo-maturity, emotional-cognitive splitting, over/under school performance, poor self-esteem, difficulties in intimacy, and psychiatric symptoms (Preston, 1986).

Preston devised a checklist to assess the extent to which family environments were emotionally abusive to children. This checklist was used to survey 98 families who attended a family court for one month (65 percent for litigation cases, 35 percent for voluntary counseling). The average period of separation was 2.6 years. The results of this study indicated that (1) half of the family environments were moderately to severely emotionally abusive; (2) the duration of the separation was correlated with the presence, but not severity, of emotional abuse; (3) parental conflict was correlated with both the duration and severity of emotional abuse; (4) there was a significant relationship between the severity of emotional abuse and the parents being involved in litigation before the court; and (5) in nearly half (43 percent) of the families, there were one or more symptomatic children (e.g., aggression, defiance, regression, depression, psychosomatic symptoms, learning difficulties).

Evaluation. This theory of psychological abuse may have some merit in the preliminary establishment of a fourfold typology of family dissolution. By relating family and individual symptomatology to various forms of family separation and to treatment and prevention efforts within community and social systems, an accurate typology can provide insights and guidance for handling potential or existing abusive situations within the family context.

In order to be successful, however, a typology of this nature must be based on solid empirical measures that at least correlate the proposed types with successful treatment or preventive evidence. Discriminant validity of the types also must be established in order to show that the different categories actually represent distinctive types of separation-family dynamics. If the hypothesized types significantly overlap, the success of the corresponding treatment/prevention efforts will concurrently be less reliable.

In light of the very limited evidence for this typology, it must, therefore, be considered as a preliminary model requiring further examination, testing, and validation. It is possible that when these steps are taken, this typology will undergo significant alterations. Therefore, until validity and reliability data have been collected, this typology must be regarded in a precautionary manner.

Finally, as far as the prevention of psychological maltreatment is concerned, although improvement of family circumstances after separation is important, the prevention of family breakup is, perhaps, more important. In this regard, this theory does not address the causality and prevention of family separation.

Ecological/Deficiency Needs Theory of Psychological Maltreatment

Theoretical Foundations. Hart, Germain, and Brassard (1987) consider that humans are best understood from developmental and holistic perspectives. Each individual has some basic needs and motivations along with various psychosocial states of development. They develop the etiological theory of child psychological maltreatment around the theoretical works by Maslow (1968, 1970) and Erikson (1968).

Briefly, Maslow emphasizes basic human needs in personality development that are in hierarchical order. These needs include (1) physiological needs (e.g., food, clothing, and drink) that sustain human survival requirements; (2) safety needs (emotional security in family relationships and environmental security in living circumstances); (3) love needs (close and bonding relationship with parents, relatives, and siblings); (4) esteem needs (self-concepts and identities with respect to internal and external status of mind); and (5) self-actualization needs (philosophy and goals in life for fulfillment of human potentialities). The fulfillment of these needs requires the successive attainment of the lower and basic needs. These needs are also linked to the human developmental stages in personality, moral developments, and value systems.

Based on Maslow's conceptualization, Hart, Germain, and Brassard dichotomized human basic needs into (1) "deficiency needs" that include physiological, safety, belongingness, and love needs, and (2) "growth needs" that include self-actualization, desire to know and understand, and aspiration of aesthetic values. (These two forms of needs can be labeled as "D-needs" and "B-needs" in relation to the external world and individual beings, respectively).

Along with various developmental stages, children of all ages are actively pursuing the attainment of both types of deficiency and growth needs. Social institutions having the responsibility for child care are required to ascertain that children's needs are met in the course of their development.

Erikson (1968) advocates the importance of different stages of psychosocial development for children. Hart, Germain, and Brassard (1987) emphasize the developmental characteristics of children as they are directly relevant to the nature and impact of human ecological contacts (families, communities, schools, and society as a whole) on the development of children in physical, cognitive, affective, and behavioral conditions.

In addition, other theories have also been emphasized under the ecological and deficiency needs theory. They include the work in cognitive development by Piaget (1932), moral development by Kohlberg (1976), psychosexual development by Freud (1939), and competency development by Havighurst (1972) and White (1948).

This theory adopts the ecological conceptualizations from child developmental research. Because of the complex nature of child development, this theory stresses the importance of interactive effects on behavior and meanings of (1) the child as a dynamic system of individual; (2) the microsystems of families, schools, day-care centers, and other community agencies that the child experiences on a day-to-day basis; (3) the exosystems and macrosystems in the child's developmental environments, such as school, parent's workplace, public and private institutions in the community, and culturally institutionalized patterns of belief and behavior. The roles and functions of these systems for meeting the needs of children are evaluated in reference to the conceptualizations of psychological maltreatment.

Basic Principles. Hart, Brassard, and Germain (1987) defined maltreatment as an attack on the basic motivational and needs systems of children. More specifically, psychological maltreatment or "mental injury" is defined by Landau and associates (1980) as "an injury to the intellectual or psychological capacity of a child as evidenced by an observable and substantial impairment in the child's ability to function within a normal range of performance and behavior, with due regard to the child's culture."

This theory integrates human ecological contexts with the concepts of deficiency needs in child development. Accordingly, psychological maltreatment would then include acts of behavior *omission* and *commission* (see Figure 7.4). These acts usually deny or frustrate efforts on the part of the individual to satisfy his or her own basic psychological needs to the degree that the individual's function becomes maladaptively deviant, which in turn jeopardizes the attainment of basic deficiency needs of the children and/or jeopardizes his or her care. Therefore, acts of omission represent psychological neglect and emotional unresponsiveness.

Commissive behavioral patterns: Seven specific behavioral patterns have been

Figure 7.4
Schematic Representation of Ecological/Deficiency Needs Theory

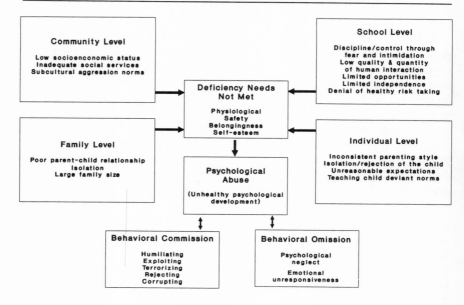

identified as commission acts that tend to injure children's psychological well-being:

1. *Rejecting* represents refusal in acknowledging, believing, receiving, or accepting of children (e.g., an adult purposively refuses to acknowledge a child's request for help).

2. *Degrading* represents behavioral patterns that deprive a child of dignity and self-respect (e.g., labeling a child as inferior or "stupid").

3. *Terrorizing* represents a situation in which a child is impressed with terror or coerced with intimidation (e.g., an adult forces a child to observe violence directed toward loved ones).

4. *Isolating* represents circumstances where the child is physically separated from all others, especially peers and loved ones (e.g., a child is locked in a closet for extended time).

5. *Corrupting* represents various acts that change the child's state of mind from justice, truth, and prosocial dispositions to injustice, deception, and antisocial behaviors (e.g., a child is taught to degrade those racially or ethnically different).

6. *Exploiting* represents an act that unfairly utilizes other individuals or conditions for one's own advantage or profit (e.g., a child is coerced to participate in the production of pornography for commercial purposes).

7. *Denying emotional responsiveness* represents a situation in which responsible individuals or institutions fail to provide sensitive, necessary caregiving for healthy so-

cial/emotional development of the child (e.g., a child is mechanistically avoided for the needs of hugs, kisses, and talk).

Maltreatment domains: Hart, Brassard, and Germain cited eight different domains of psychological maltreatment as they were proposed by the International Conference on Psychological Abuse of Children and Youth (1983):

1. *Mental Cruelty* consists of such undesirable acts as using verbal abuse and downgrading, setting unreasonably high (or low) expectations for achievement, and treating with dramatic discrimination.

2. *Sexual abuse and exploitation* represents a situation where the child is forced to engage in such behaviors as incest, rape, pornography, and prostitution.

3. *Living in dangerous and unstable environments* puts the child in situations of civil and international war, high crime and violence, or severe family instability.

4. *Drug and substance abuse* places the child in a culture where he or she participates in the use of controlled substances or drugs.

5. *Influence by negative and limiting models* represents a situation where the child is modeled with narrow, rigid, self-destructive, violent and/or antisocial behaviors.

6. *Cultural bias and prejudice* consists of a situation in which the child is placed in a culturally different minority group where unfairly limited expectations or opportunities are imposed.

7. *Emotional neglect and stimulation deprivation* represents a situation in which the child is deprived of essential love, attention, and sensory stimulation for physical and psychological needs.

8. *Institutional abuse* represents the dysfunction of child-caring institutions where the child undergoes various forms of psychological maltreatment.

These eight domains would generate various forms of abuse and neglect that have been labeled under various typologies, all related to psychological maltreatment. Based on this premise, the ecological and deficiency needs theory assumes the following: (1) Psychological maltreatment is the core component of all forms of child abuse and neglect; (2) the psychological consequences of child abuse and neglect are generally the most devastating; (3) child maltreatment consists of more than an interaction between two people; and (4) to understand child maltreatment, at least three levels need to be addressed: (a) the child, (b) the microsystems experienced by the child, such as the family, school, and church, and (c) the social and cultural systems experienced by the child less directly, such as the parent's workplace, city council, and cultural norms.

On the issues of intervention and prevention of psychological maltreatment, Hart, Germain, and Brassard (1987) address the need to work simultaneously at three ecological levels: the microsystem (family), the exosystem (community/society), and the macrosystem (culture). Specific recommendations for each ecological level are described as follows: At the *family level,* the parent-child relationship is considered most critical. Behavioral manifestations of maltreating parents usually reflect the fact that parents (1) tend to ignore, isolate, and reject their child, (2) give partial and inappropriate responses to the child's needs, (3) set unreasonably high demands for the child or, the opposite, prevent the child from realizing his or her potential, (4) teach the child values that deviate from community norms, and (5) are inconsistent in their parenting style. The best corrective intervention to reverse these harmful behaviors is in the form of the caretaker's involvement with parent aides or a parenting group in combination with caseworker services.

At the *community level,* five major undesirable schooling conditions were identified that block, distort, or reduce the fulfillment of the deficiency needs and self-actualization (growth) needs for children: (1) discipline/control through fear and intimidation, (2) low quantity and quality of human interaction, (3) limited opportunities/encouragement to develop competency and self-worth, (4) encouragement to be (or remain) dependent, and (5) denial of opportunities for healthy risk taking. These undesirable conditions can be avoided by various preventive measures, for example, eliminating corporal punishment and taking a more positive attitude toward children and their rights as human beings.

At the *cultural level,* measures for preventing psychological maltreatment of children include the reduction of the cultural level of violence, recognition of an unconditional right of all individuals to meaningful work, and elimination of negative attitudes, feelings, and behaviors aimed at racial and ethnic minorities.

Empirical Evidence. Most of the empirical studies conducted in support of this theory have focused on the community level. Factors that have been reported to be significantly correlated with psychological maltreatment include poverty; unemployment; isolation; large families; heavy child-care responsibilities; absence of adequate health care, day care, and entertainment for children; social status; education level; and subcultures of violence, as well as other stressors (Garbarino, Guttmann & Seeley, 1986; Newberger & Newberger, 1981; Vander Mey & Neff, 1986; Fagan, Stewart & Hansen, 1983; Mehta et al., 1979).

Evaluation. This theory takes into account the complexity of the child abuse and neglect phenomenon by addressing the issue at various ecological levels and also by examining the interactions that take place among the three ecological levels (family, community/school, and society). However, the precise relationships between subdomains of each ecological level and also the relationships across different levels are not operationally defined for empirical evaluation. Therefore, answers to many empirical questions are not conclusive (i.e., how different ecological factors influence one another, how each contributes to the problem, and how interventions can be established at each level and also across different levels).

The subjective meanings of maltreatment acts (e.g., humiliation and corruption) are determined simultaneously by the characteristics of individuals (both abusers and victims) and the social ecological systems involved. Since meanings of the same acts or same circumstances will vary with the individual's age, time, and situation, the norms ("standards") of developmental characteristics of the child (including cognitive, moral, psychosexual, and competency) are of funda-mental importance to the evaluation of the nature and impact of psychological maltreatment. In this regard, this theory provides an excellent general framework for identifying different types of psychologically abusive and neglectful behav-iors. However, the dynamic nature of the typologies and their causal impact on deficiency needs are not delineated. Despite this weakness, the differentiation of behavioral typologies in psychological maltreatment is a significant contribution of this theory.

Part V

Theorizations of Neglect

Chapter Eight

Theories of Neglect

The terms *abuse* and *neglect* have been routinely linked as inseparable, interrelated concepts about child maltreatment. However, the incident reports and the criteria for their identification and evaluation are quite different. Despite such differences, child neglect has not received equal attention in the professional community as a rigorous discipline by itself. Child neglect accounted for over 50 percent of incident reports of abuse and neglect at the national level, but it accounts for less than 10 percent of published and research reports in all professional journals. Child neglect by itself has not been the major focus of theoretical development. For this reason, there are really no theories or models of neglect per se that are currently being used by the service community.

However, in order to present a general view on how the etiological issues of child neglect are addressed by various professionals, an effort was made to compile existing theoretical viewpoints about child neglect. This effort resulted in the identification of three major theoretical frameworks: (1) personalistic view of child neglect, (2) social interactional model, and (3) three-factor theory of child neglect.

As these three theories (or models) are usually by-products of the study of child abuse, their presentations will be somewhat redundant to those presented in earlier chapters on abuse. However, for the purpose of maintaining self-sufficiency in the presentation of child neglect theories/models, such redundancy appears to be necessary. In fact, it proves to be helpful in an evaluation of child neglect study as a rigorous discipline.

INDIVIDUAL DETERMINANTS PARADIGM

The personalistic view of neglect is presented under the individual determinants paradigm because it asserts that the basic cause of parental neglect is a deficient personality.

Personalistic View of Child Neglect

Theoretical Foundations. Many researchers favor a personalistic view, in which the parents' neglectful behavior is seen as the result of a deficient parental personality (Polansky et al., 1981). This view is closely related to the psychiatric view, in which parental pathology is posited as the source of child physical abuse (Kempe et al., 1962), but it incorporates undesirable social conditions such as poverty and isolation as the stressful neglect-inducing factors. (See Figure 8.1.)

Basic Principles. Hally, Polansky, and Polansky (1980) stated that neglectful parents are unlike other parents of the same status in that the neglectful parents suffer from character disorders. The three most prevalent disorders are the apathy-futility syndrome (AFS), the impulse-ridden character, and infantile emotional functioning.

The *apathy-futility syndrome* represents a mixed state of personality characteristics that are often revealed among neglectful parents. These characteristics include (1) a strong belief that none of their efforts are worthwhile, (2) a lack of or greatly inhibited emotional responses, (3) superficial emotional relationships and intense loneliness, (4) inability to properly function in many important areas of living, (5) passive-aggressive expression of anger, (6) reluctance or refusal to commit to positive stands, (7) "verbal inaccessibility" to others, resulting in a reduced capacity for solving problems due to the nonexistence of internal dialogue, and (8) the ability to cause those with whom they associate to experience the same feelings of futility (Polansky, 1985).

In addition, these individuals may possess other characteristics, such as a tendency toward concreteness in thinking, all-or-none stereotyping, conversion reactions, and psychosomatic illnesses. These individuals have a limited capacity for self-observation, which can lead to a distorted self-image. The presence of

Figure 8.1
Schematic Representation of Personalistic View

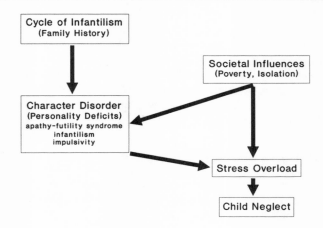

character flaws prevents the parents from effectively caring for their children. The fact that certain aspects of their lives do not seem worthwhile causes these parents to believe that the lives of their children are also somewhat unimportant.

Additional characteristics of the typical at-risk mother include limited intelligence, low education, and a history of lack of employment. This mother probably married the first or second man who showed any interest in her, and this man tended to be one who was not capable of functioning adequately due to lack of educational and vocational skills. The at-risk mother is also typically very egocentric, has little idea of how to care for a child, and comes from a family with retarded or criminally deviant parents (Polansky, Borgman & DeSaix, 1972, in Polansky et al., 1981).

The *impulse-ridden parents* are those who have great difficulty in delaying gratification of their own wants and needs. These parents are prone to leaving their children for days at a time, with only a younger child or no one at all to supervise. The inability of these parents to control impulsive behaviors leads to neglectful parenting.

Neglectful parents are also characterized by *infantilism,* which involves several characteristics that prevent parents from caring adequately for their children. The predominant indicative factor in infantilism is immaturity. The parents have not completed ego development and therefore approach problems with less competence than most adults. Further, these parents have no real capacity for self-observation and have very external views of their situations, so they are unlikely to realize their responsibilities for child care. Also, these parents are characterized by a sense of incompleteness. Tasks may be started, but the emotional state of these parents prevents them from following through on many important matters involved in the rearing of their children.

Polansky and associates (1981) suggest that the *cycle of neglect* might be said to derive from an intergenerational cycle of infantilism, begun by the current neglecter's parents. In this cycle, the current neglecter's parents were unable to properly care for their children due to their infantile behavior patterns and were therefore guilty of neglect.

In addition to personality deficits causing neglectful behavior patterns, societal influences such as poverty and isolation from support networks also play an important role in facilitating the development of child neglect. Poverty usually represents the absence of material goods in the household, which intensifies the feelings of powerlessness and self-devaluation. Social isolation intensifies the inaccessibility of both material objects and mental and emotional communications. Therefore, the social factors function as moderating variables to increase the effects of the parents' personality deficits.

Thus, the personalistic view emphasizes that the parents' personality deficits make them more susceptible to the stresses that are related to individual and social factors. While adequate parents are able to handle these stresses appropriately, neglectful parents experience a stress overload and must rely on disordered personality characteristics to cope with them.

Empirical Evidence. It is common knowledge that parents, even with the same socioeconomic and demographic characteristics, will not necessarily treat their children in the same way. While some parents raise their children well and provide everything children need to realize their potentials, other parents in the same situation may neglect their children, failing to provide them with the essentials of life.

Professionals involved with neglectful parents were questioned as to whether they recognized the apathy-futility syndrome in their clients (Polansky et al., 1981). They were very familiar with the AFS characteristics listed, indicating preliminarily that the syndrome has face validity. The quality of bringing about the same feelings of futility in others particularly struck a chord with professionals.

In addition, Polansky and colleagues (1981) claim to have validated the syndrome by devising a scale measuring the degree of apathy-futility present in mothers and finding that the degree of apathy-futility correlated negatively with the quality of care the mothers provided for their children. Further, they found in their studies of neglectful mothers that the characteristic of impulsivity correlated negatively with the quality of child care. Rohrbeck and Twentyman (1986) also found evidence of impulsivity in their study of neglectful mothers. In the same study, however, impulsivity was found to be present to a greater extent in abusive mothers, so it is doubtful that impulsivity is a characteristic unique to neglecting mothers.

Seagull (1987) suggests that neglectful mothers be viewed as located on the external side of the locus of control scale. This is consistent with the personalistic view under the area of infantilism, in which the parents have a very external view of their problems. It is also consistent with the apathy-futility syndrome, in which the parents do not feel they have any control over what happens to them.

Giovannoni and Billingsley (1970) found that neglectful mothers felt more isolated from their neighbors and relatives than nonneglectful mothers, despite the fact that they all had equal access to social support networks. This lends support to the view that isolation is a result of a personality deficit in the neglecting parent more than of other objective cultural factors (e.g., poor home environment). Polansky and associates (1985) found the situation to be much the same in an early study. Despite objective cultural similarity in neighborhoods, the neglectful mothers felt that their neighborhoods were less friendly and supportive. This, again, raises the issue of parental personality deficit as a cause of child neglect.

Boehm (1964) discovered that neglect complaints seldom involved only one type of behavior. The majority of complaints were concerned with a group of problems and were related to the behavior problems of the parents, not the children. This indicates that the behavior of the parents is consistently inadequate, a factor that, in turn, indicates a personality deficit.

In a study on the relationship between alcohol use and the occurrence of child neglect, MacMurray (1979) found that alcohol should be viewed as a contributing moderator factor, rather than a major cause for child neglect, because alcohol use can be seen as a stressor with which some neglectful parents must cope.

Polansky and others (1985) found that the proportion of neglectful mothers who had completed high school was much lower than that of the nonneglectful mothers. In addition, the neglectful mothers had more children, and a large proportion of the neglect families had no father figure present. These factors represent stressors that might affect the child-care behavior of neglectful parents.

Evaluation. The personalistic view of child neglect relies heavily on personality factors present in the parents but also takes into account other social factors influencing the occurrence of child neglect. This approach has two fundamental merits.

First, taking into account both personality and social factors (stressors), the personalistic approach covers many areas and provides a good balance of elements for consideration of the etiology of child neglect. This allows for flexibility in working with a variety of cases dealing with child neglect. Because this approach does not attempt to be too specific, it is not limited in its scope.

Second, this approach is also strongly supported by empirical evidence. The characteristics of apathy-futility, impulsivity, and infantilism have been found in many neglectful parents by various researchers. In addition, various empirical studies indicate that adverse social factors usually result in emotional stresses to parents that, in turn, tend to increase the prevalence of neglectful parenting.

The personalistic view of child neglect may be seen as a modification of the psychiatric theory. It proposes personality deficits instead of parental pathology and considers the environment and stressors affecting child-rearing practices. Ultimately, the personalistic view posits that people faced with the same situations react in different fashions. Therefore, adequate parents cope effectively, while neglectful parents do not. Because of the similarity of the two groups of parents' situations, the neglectful behavior must be the result of a personality deficit on the part of the neglecting parent.

Although the generality of the personalistic view provides flexibility in considering neglect situations, it also leads to confusion in certain matters. For example, the question of what causes the parental personality deficit in the first place is not satisfactorily answered. The intergenerational cycle of neglect is offered at this juncture, but then the issue of the origin of the cycle arises. However, given the difficult nature of this problem, this oversight is understandable and merits further study.

Overall, the personalistic view presents an excellent approach to dealing with neglectful factors. Considering the complexity of the problem of child neglect, this approach may be seen as an initial attempt in developing a theoretical framework for a comprehensive study of the child neglect problem.

INDIVIDUAL-ENVIRONMENT INTERACTION PARADIGM

Under the individual-environment interaction paradigm, two approaches of child neglect are presented: (1) the social interaction model, and (2) the three-factor model.

Social Interaction Model of Child Neglect

Theoretical Foundations. The social interaction model of child abuse (see Figure 8.2) is based firmly on Gelles's social psychological model of child abuse (Gelles, 1973). This model is also applied to child neglect, because it is frequently considered as a form of abuse. This model posits many of the same ideas as the social psychological model, but adds interaction between members of the family as another important factor (Burgess, 1979).

Briefly, the social psychological model proposes the following: (1) The socialization process of the individual is important in determining child-rearing practices in later life; (2) a certain amount of child abuse is a function of psychopathic states of individuals, but psychopathology has its social origins; (3) structural conditions of the society (e.g., family roles and unemployment) frequently create stresses for parents that are associated with abusive behavior toward children; (4) the characteristics and roles of children play an important part in producing stresses for parents and also in creating various precipitating situations that require the parent's immediate actions; and (5) subjective cultural characteristics of each community (e.g., values and norms regarding child behavior and punishment) predetermine the parent's behavior dispositions and actions in handling child disciplinary situations.

The social interaction model generates four theoretical foundations: (1) the importance of certain fundamental social and parenting skills for parents, (2) the contributory role of the child's characteristics in abusive parental behavior, (3) the importance of interactions and effects of various psychological and sociological variables on the parent-child relationship, and (4) the impact of differ-

Figure 8.2
Schematic Representation of Social Interaction Model

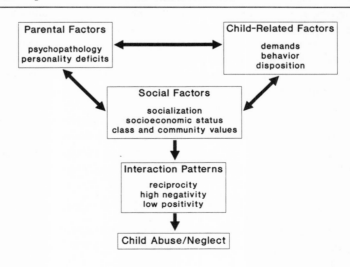

ent family interaction patterns on abusive parental behaviors. Although the above principles were not developed directly for examining neglect per se, they have been applied, to some extent, to the explanation of neglectful phenomena and dynamics.

Basic Principles. The social interaction model relies primarily on the interactions of three types of factors: parental factors, child-related factors in the family, and social factors. In addition, interaction patterns between parents and children are also considered by Burgess and Conger (1978) as important factors contributing to the occurrence of child abuse and neglect.

Gelles (1973) delineated some of the social factors that can affect parents' behavior toward their children. These include (1) socialization experience, (2) social position of the parent, (3) values of the class and community, (4) and structural stress factors.

The *childhood socialization experience* of the abusive parent involves an atmosphere of violence. Usually coming from a household in which abuse was the preferred method of discipline, this parent had a role model of violence through which to develop his parenting strategies. It is through this socialization that the parent obtains many of his/her values and norms regarding child behavior and discipline.

The *social position of the parent* also plays an important role in the occurrence of abuse, according to Gelles. Factors such as age, sex, and socioeconomic status can affect the ability of the parent to effectively cope with the difficulties of child-rearing. For example, a parent of low socioeconomic status would not be as well equipped to handle an economic catastrophe (e.g., sudden job loss) as a parent of higher status.

The *values of the class and the community* in which parents live are also important determinants of parental behavior. A community in which violence is seen as an acceptable form of discipline can facilitate the occurrence of abusive parental behavior. When violence is the community norm, there is no immediate social deterrent against using violence against one's children.

Structural stress factors, such as unemployment and isolation, are also proposed by Gelles as contributing factors in the occurrence of child abuse. These adverse conditions can create an atmosphere in which the level of stress is very high. This high level of stress, in turn, may increase the likelihood of using abusive behavior toward children as a coping mechanism.

Further, Gelles lists personality characteristics of the parents as further possible contributors to the occurrence of child abuse. Parental psychopathology can range from psychopathic or sociopathic disorders to personality deficits. The presence of parental psychopathology inhibits the parent from effectively coping with many of the stresses that face the average parent. The inability to cope with these stresses can lead to the occurrence of child abuse.

Finally, factors relating to the child, such as disposition, behavior, and demands, were also listed by Gelles as important in understanding the occurrence of child abuse. A child who is difficult (e.g., colicky, incontinent, presenting discipline problems) can put a great deal of strain on a parent by testing his or her patience constantly. In addition, a child who is retarded, physically deformed, or who was unwanted can create stresses that might lead to abuse by certain parents.

The social interaction model incorporates the factors listed by Gelles (1973) into its representation of child abuse and neglect. The main difference of the social interaction model is that it emphasizes the interactions of the members of the family and the importance of different interaction patterns in the development of abusive and neglectful behavior.

Especially important, according to Burgess and Conger (1978) is the *reciprocal nature* of the child-parent relationship. They stress that there is a give-and-take between the parent and the child in a family. The child can affect the parent through his or her actions, just as the parent affects the child through his or her actions. An interactive family relationship in which the child ignores the parent can have a strong influence on the possibility of the occurrence of child neglect and abuse. This assessment goes beyond simply considering the effect of the child's characteristics on parenting adequacy. It emphasizes the effect of the child's interactive capabilities on parenting adequacy, putting the child in a new perspective.

Empirical Evidence. Burgess and Conger (1978) studied the interactional patterns of three different types of parents in an attempt to discover differences that might provide information as to how each family functioned. The daily interactions of three different types of families (i.e., neglecting, abusing, and control families) were compared over a period of four separate six-hour sessions. Significant differences in their patterns of interaction were identified.

The neglectful parents were characterized by their extreme negativity and low rates of positive interactions. They were the most negative and the least positive of the three groups involved in this study. They were half as likely as controls to emit positive responses, and twice as likely as controls to behave negatively. Neglectful parents also made the most requests of their children and were the least compliant with their children's requests as compared with the other groups in this study.

The characteristics of neglected children were also examined in the study. Although there were no significant differences between the neglected and the control children in responding to their mothers, the neglected children did manifest significant differences in interaction with their fathers. That is, in comparison with the control children, they exhibited much fewer verbal communications, behavioral interactions, and physical contacts with their fathers.

In comparisons between neglectful and control mothers' ratings of their children's behavior, Rohrbeck and Twentyman (1986) found that neglectful mothers rated their children as having more conduct problems. The neglectful mothers did not differ from the abusing mothers on their perceptions of the behavioral problems of their children. However, neglected children were rated as more dysfunctional than either the abused or the comparison children. These results seem to support the view that an unsatisfactory interactive pattern between the parent and the child may contribute to child abuse and neglect.

Bauer and Twentyman (1985) measured annoyance data in abusing, neglectful, and control mothers with regard to their children's behavior in different situations. It was found that neglectful mothers were less likely than abusive mothers to perceive that their children acted to annoy them in such situations as (1) child misbehaving with others present, (2) child angry with parent (e.g., because of parental failure to fulfill child's desires), and (3) idiosyncratic stressful situations faced by each mother.

Neglectful mothers were also less likely than abusive mothers to become annoyed in stressful situations. In comparison with the control mothers, the neglectful mothers did not differ on any of the annoyance measures. These results lend support to the idea that negative interactions might contribute to abusive patterns of behavior but not to the development of neglectful patterns of behavior.

Evaluation. The social interaction model adopts a comprehensive view of child abuse and neglect, encompassing both social and individual factors. This model takes into account factors similar to those utilized by the personalistic view (Polansky et al., 1981), but stresses the social aspects, as opposed to the personality aspects.

The consideration of societal, family, and individual factors lends flexibility to this model. In addition, the emphasis on interactions among these patterns provides further insight into the phenomenon of child abuse and neglect. The observation of interactional patterns is a useful method of evaluating firsthand the behaviors and situations that may be linked to neglectful and abusive parenting.

Empirical evidence seems to support the notion that maltreating families exhibit patterns of interaction different from those of nonmaltreating families. This was demonstrated in the high negativity and low positivity of the neglecting parents in the Burgess and Conger (1978) study. In addition, study of the reciprocity of the child-parent relationship revealed differences in child-to-father interactions among neglectful, abusive, and control families.

However, this model, like many others, explains child maltreatment mainly in terms of abuse and not neglect. Neglect is merely included as another type of abuse, with the same etiology as, for example, physical abuse. Mounting evidence has suggested that neglect and abuse are separate entities and should be evaluated as such (Bousha & Twentyman, 1984). The failure to recognize these differences and to develop a rigorous theoretical perspective, despite the appearance of neglectful families in comparisons of interactional patterns among maltreating families, may limit the generalizability of this model.

Three-Factor Model of Child Neglect

Theoretical Foundations. Lesnik-Oberstein, Cohen, and Koers (1982) proposed a three-factor model (see Figure 8.3) to address the etiology and forms of child abuse and neglect. These factors are (1) parental aggressive feelings, (2) parental inhibition of overt aggressive acts, and (3) the focus of parental aggression on the child. The authors utilize Kohlberg's stages of moral reasoning to

Figure 8.3
Schematic Representation of Three-Factor Model

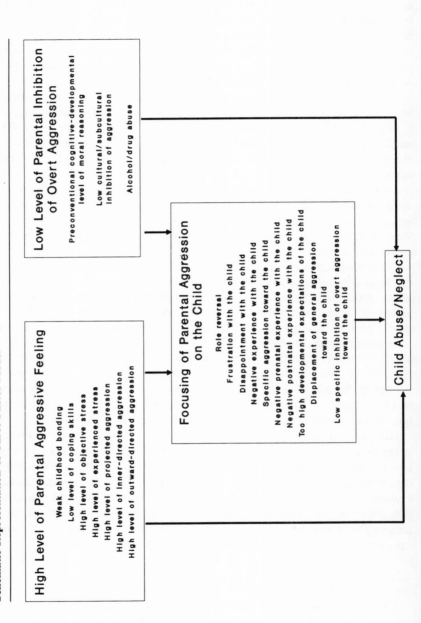

High Level of Parental Aggressive Feeling

Weak childhood bonding
Low level of coping skills
High level of objective stress
High level of experienced stress
High level of projected aggression
High level of inner-directed aggression
High level of outward-directed aggression

Low Level of Parental Inhibition
of Overt Aggression

Preconventional cognitive-developmental
level of moral reasoning

Low cultural/subcultural
inhibition of aggression

Alcohol/drug abuse

Focusing of Parental Aggression
on the Child

Role reversal
Frustration with the child
Disappointment with the child
Negative experience with the child
Specific aggression toward the child
Negative prenatal experience with the child
Negative postnatal experience with the child
Too high developmental expectations of the child
Displacement of general aggression
toward the child
Low specific inhibition of overt aggression
toward the child

Child Abuse/Neglect

help explain various circumstances relating to the roles of parental aggression and inhibition in child abuse and neglect. Basically, child neglect is considered the dysfunctional manifestation of the same qualitative phenomena of the three factors that are more appropriately used for the explanation of child abuse etiology.

Basic Principles. According to this model, the parent experiences a high level of aggressive feeling, coupled with a low level of inhibition of overt aggressive acts. These two factors, combined with their focus upon a child, are suggested as the basic cause of child maltreatment.

Each of these three factors has several subfactors contributing to its manifestation in child abuse and neglect. The first factor, a high level of parental aggressive feeling toward the child, is the result of a combination of the following seven subfactors: (1) low level of coping skills (e.g., low marital adjustment), (2) high level of objective stress (e.g., great socioeconomic change), (3) high level of experienced stress (e.g., social isolation), (4) weak bonding in childhood (e.g., a feeling of being unloved by one or both parents), (5) high level of outward aggression (e.g., greater use of violent tactics to deal with marital conflicts), (6) high level of projected aggression (e.g., paranoid hostility), and (7) high level of inner-directed aggression (e.g., frustration with low self-esteem).

The second factor, low parental inhibition of overt aggressive acts, is the result of the combination of the following three subfactors: (1) preconventional cognitive-developmental level of moral reasoning (taken from Kohlberg [1976], this refers to a developmental stage in which social and moral rules are experienced as "external to the self"); (2) low cultural/subcultural inhibition of overt aggression (e.g., more autocratic child-rearing practices); and (3) substance abuse (e.g., alcohol and psychoactive drug use).

The third factor, the focusing of parental aggression on the child, involves two circumstances: (1) aggression from other sources displaced on the child, and (2) aggression brought on by the child himself when, for example, the parent's expectation of the child is frustrated.

More specifically, the authors propose ten subfactors to account for these two general circumstances: (1) negative prenatal experience with the child (e.g., mother experiences pregnancy as unpleasant); (2) negative postnatal experience with the child (e.g., early removal of the child from the mother); (3) excessively high developmental expectations of the child (e.g., expectations for the child to achieve developmental milestones earlier than normal); (4) role reversal (e.g., parental expectation of the child to take care of the parent); (5) negative experience with the child (e.g., delivery complications); (6) disappointment with the child (e.g., child of undesired sex); (7) frustration with the child (e.g., failure to achieve milestones); (8) specific aggression toward the child (e.g., spanking); (9) displacement of other aggression toward the child (from both present and past sources); and (10) low specific inhibition of aggression toward the child (e.g., low tolerance level).

Lesnik-Oberstein, Cohen, and Koers explain the etiology and forms of child abuse and neglect in terms of the relationship between parental aggressive feeling and inhibition of aggressive acts. A high ratio of aggression to inhibition results in violent maltreatment, such as physical abuse, while a lower ratio results in nonorganic failure to thrive and physical neglect.

Further, this lower ratio can be characterized in terms of relative relationships between two aggression and inhibition situations. The first involves a higher level of parental aggressive feeling coupled with a level of inhibition of aggressive acts that is also high, but not high enough to prevent maltreatment. The second situation involves a lower level of parental aggressive feeling, along with a level of inhibition of aggressive acts that is so low that maltreatment results. In both cases, it is assumed that the net level of aggression is lower than the level present in cases of abuse, but still high enough to result in nonorganic failure to thrive and physical neglect.

Empirical Evidence. As of this writing (in 1990), no empirical evidence has been found in the literature that would support or refute this theory. The authors' original plan was to test the 50 hypotheses derived from this theory through a battery of tests to parents and a single test to children over three years old. No empirical reports have been found to test these hypotheses. The lack of follow-up report on this theory prohibits the presentation of empirical evidence in its favor. (However, personal communication from Lesnik-Oberstein to Tzeng indicates that an empirical study has been completed and the report will soon be available.)

Evaluation. This three-factor model attempts to provide a comprehensive explanation of the etiology and forms of child abuse and neglect. It has the following strengths: (1) It takes into account the presence of a wide variety of factors and subfactors; (2) it provides a schematic model to delineate the causal relationships among these various factors and subfactors; and (3) it presents 50 hypotheses for empirical testing.

However, in its attempt to be comprehensive, the theory is deficient in several important aspects. First, the relationships between the three major factors are not clearly explained. Although the occurrence of abuse and neglect is proposed as a ratio of aggression to inhibition, no specific criteria were given that would compute various values of ratios for the different forms and subcategories of child abuse and neglect. Specifics of the mechanisms of this inhibition are left unexplained. Second, practical applications of the model have been neither proposed nor discussed. Third, several of the subfactors are vague and seemingly redundant (e.g., the separation of disappointment, negative experience, and frustration with the child, when they may be essentially the same phenomenon). Finally, no empirical support of this model has been provided, either at its proposal or since then.

In addition, this model is primarily for abuse, not neglect. The aggression-inhibition ratio is more suited for physical abuse, involving acts of commission, than for neglect, which usually pertains to acts of omission. The suggestion that aggression is responsible for neglect is at odds with the present state of knowledge about neglect. The concept of putting abuse and neglect on the continuum defined by the ratio of aggression over inhibition is also problematic in attempting to account for the multiple causes and correlates of child abuse and neglect.

Part VI

Content and Process Evaluations and Summaries

Chapter Nine

Introduction to the Psychosemantic Process Model of Human Behavior

The purpose of this chapter is to present a brief introduction to a theoretical model that will be used in Chapter 10 for a summary evaluation of the content issues of all theoretical perspectives on child abuse and neglect presented in previous chapters. This model, entitled "The Psychosemantic Process Model of Human Behavior" by Tzeng (cf. Tzeng, Hanner & Fortier, 1988), is a conceptual framework for organizing various issues and variables that are involved in social behaviors. Due to its generality and applicability, it has been used with satisfaction in studying various substantive topics in social and behavioral sciences (e.g., cultural adaptation processes of immigration families, human aggression, and interpersonal love relationships).

For the evaluation of theoretical accounts of child abuse and neglect etiologies, this model will be used as a scientific tool (1) to decompose the concerned content issues of all theoretical perspectives into many operationally defined units (components), (2) to organize the issues, postulations, and empirical evidence of each theoretical perspective in terms of the basic conceptual framework of the model (e.g., subjective and objective cultures at different levels of human ecology), and (3) to summarize the evaluation results of all theoretical perspectives in terms of their structural comprehensiveness and functional sophistication. Therefore, familiarity with this model as introduced in this chapter is important in order for readers to follow the summary evaluation of all theoretical perspectives presented in the next chapter.

The following are brief descriptions of four important aspects of the theoretical framework of this model—two types of culture, five levels of human ecologies, ten model components, and six functional steps of the model.

SUBJECTIVE AND OBJECTIVE CULTURES

The characteristics of individual human beings and their social environments can generally be dichotomized into two types of cultures: objective and subjective. *Objective culture* contains all visible characteristics of people and objects in a given social environment, such as materials, skin color, sex, housing, and cars. *Subjective culture*, on the other hand, contains various mental conditions of individuals or groups that cannot be directly observed, such as thoughts, feelings, beliefs, hopes, and understandings. These two types of cultures are closely interrelated in human behavioral dispositions and life experiences.

PSYCHOSEMANTIC PROCESS AND EVALUATION SYSTEMS

In the process of social learning and interactions with various life environments (people as well as inanimate objects), human beings constantly go through a mental process of *evaluating* other people and/or objects encountered. This evaluation process, identified as the *psychosemantic process* in this book, consists of five sequential stages: (1) perception of an input stimulus (verbal or nonverbal, animate or inanimate object); (2) uncoding (understanding) of the stimulus through analysis of its characteristics on the basis of familiar references (e.g., age and sex in objective culture and likes and attitude in subjective culture); (3) integration of the decoded meaning in reference to preexisting semantic features (criteria) that were previously established about similar stimuli; (4) formulation of behavioral dispositions about the stimulus; and (5) decoding (expression) of dispositions as some overt reaction toward the objects.

Except for the fifth stage, expression, all mental activities in the psychosemantic process—perception, understanding, integration, and formulation of behavioral dispositions—are important mental functions that are governed by two types of meaning systems. First is the *cognitive system*, which represents a person's evaluation of events or situations through some objective criteria (semantic features). Such criteria are usually observable and/or easily measurable with known properties within a given society. For example, a child can be evaluated in terms of body height, food intake, and physical strength. The key function of the cognitive system involves evaluation of content issues, integration of current and past conditions, and formulation of expectations or predictions regarding these issues and concerns.

The *affective system* represents an individual's feelings, attitude, and emotional reactions toward objects or situations. For example, people may use evaluation descriptions to distinguish an event as being fun or dull, an object as being good or bad, and a person as being nice or not nice. In daily life situations, the average individual will always judge new life events in terms of such an affective system developed over a variety of life situations. Therefore, the affective system usually governs subjective emotional status of each individual across different times, situations, and life contexts. Such an affective system significantly influences the generation of individual's behavioral dispositions and overt coping behaviors.

FIVE ECOLOGICAL LEVELS
OF HUMAN LIFE EXPERIENCES

Human life experiences can be characterized in reference to five system levels of human ecology:

Idiosystem of individuals: This system covers the characteristics of the environment that are specific to a given individual. The nature of these characteristics can be either subjective, such as personality traits, attitudes, interests, values, and moral standards, or objective, such as age, sex, race, and physical features. The idiosystem comprises all characteristics that are fundamental to individual identity and its interactions with the outside world.

Microsystem of family: This ecological system represents the characteristics of family structures, functions, and home conditions. The terms *family* and *home* are meant to include all types of living circumstances in the contemporary society—nuclear family, single-parent family, cohabitants, and other arrangements. The characteristics of each family will include not only those that are common to other families, but also those that are specific to each household.

Exosystem of community and occupational environment: This system includes the environments of neighborhood, community, occupations, and various commercial/ industrial facilities. These environments cover both subjective and objective conditions in each community that determine the total living situations of the individual under normal life functions.

Macrosystem of culture: This system represents an overall composition of people within a pluralized, heterogeneous country. The composition may be differentiated in terms of such objective cultural variables as ethnicity, sex roles, life-styles, socioeconomic status, and political persuasion across different geographic regions. Within each macrosystem, the individuals prescribe some definite societal roles, subjective cultural values, attitudes, beliefs, and behavioral patterns that are homogeneous to all members of the same population.

Geopolitical system: This system represents the identities of different countries at the international level. Within this system, each nation will be perceived as a behavioral entity that has a set of common identifiable characteristics (patterns or styles) in both subjective (e.g., values and perceptions) and objective (e.g., national gross product and industries) cultures. Intercommunications among different nations will usually rely on such characteristics.

CULTURE ECOLOGY UNITS

By separating subjective and objective cultures and by dividing human life experiences into five ecological systems, a two-by-five matrix can further be derived to categorize the life conditions of human beings. As shown in Table 9.1, each entry represents a *culture by ecology unit* that can describe specific issues and concerns of human behavior and interactions. For example, in daily family life and social interactions, we can use the *subjective by microsystem unit* to describe the attitudes and beliefs of the people involved about various family

Table 9.1
Examples of Human Life Experiences in Ten Culture-Ecology Units

Ecology/ Culture	Idiosystem of Individuals	Microsystem of Family	Exosystem of Community	Macrosystem of Culture	Geopolitical System
Subjective Culture	Needs Wants Perception of self	Family norms Values Expectations	Neighbor- hood values Career goals	Culture Values Taboos	Stereotypes of national issues
Objective Culture	Life style Leisure activities	Food Clothing Family activities	Crime rate Occupational relations	Trans- portation Taxation	Inter- national trade, Tourism

issues. These family issues could be the perceptions of roles of individual family members and the priority of family values. Other examples for the ten culture-ecology units are given in Table 9.1

PROCESS MODEL AND FUNCTIONAL STEPS

The theoretical concepts presented above can be applied to the evaluation of the nature, conditions, and consequences of human aggressive behaviors, including child maltreatment. Such application results in the development of the psychosemantic process model for human behavior in Figure 9.1. This model organizes various aspects of human behaviors, dispositions, and their backgrounds into ten individual model domains. Before the nature of each domain is discussed, the six functional steps that delineate the entire process of human aggressive behavior are presented.

Antecedent stimulus: This step represents the emergence of an aversive circumstance (i.e., immediate stressor) that causes an imbalance in feeling or thinking. This stressor requires attitudinal and/or behavioral adaptations through some form of aggressive or nonaggressive actions.

Supporting baseline characteristic: Each individual has developed some form of thinking and feeling patterns and behavioral adaptation mechanisms through a long-term social learning process. The results of such development become implicit foundations for social

Figure 9.1
Ten Model Components of the Psychosemantic Process Model

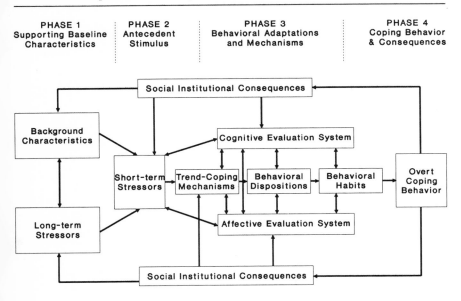

behaviors and interactions. These foundations can be further divided into three categories in terms of their relative significance in daily life situations: (1) *background characteristics:* general conditions of each individual's subjective as well as objective culture in reference to the five ecological levels (from personality to national origin) that usually do not create significant stress in general life situations; (2) *long-term stressors:* certain life events and/or conditions that have a relatively long-term and negative impact on the individual (e.g., long-term illness); and (3) *short-term stressors:* events and/or conditions that have a relatively short but very significant impact on the individual (e.g., family car breakdown or a short-term hospitalization).

Evaluation processes: This functional step refers to the mental process used by each individual to evaluate antecedent stimuli (stressors). This process will rely on the use of supporting baseline characteristics of each individual to perform two types of evaluations: (1) *Cognitive evaluation* will analyze the antecedent stimuli objectively and then integrate all related information and formulate expectations and response strategies, and (2) *affective evaluation* will determine each individual's subjective feeling and attitudes about the antecedent stimuli and related circumstances, which will facilitate the cognitive evaluation system in formulation of coping strategies.

Behavior generation and monitoring process: This step involves three functional mechanisms in response to any short-term stressor: (1) retrieval of previous coping strategies from life history, (2) generation of behavioral response dispositions, and (3) monitoring of a behavioral disposition through habits. This step represents the linkage between each individual's present behavioral response plan and past behavioral tendency (and habit) in facing similar stressful events or situations.

Overt coping behavior: This functional step represents the performance of eventual, overt coping behavior, which may be violent or nonviolent. Again, the behavior is initially stimulated by the antecedent stimulus, linked to the supporting baseline characteristics, evaluated by both affective and cognitive systems, monitored by prior behavioral habits, and finally carried out as an overt stress-coping activity.

Social consequences: Any social behavior is interactional in nature with respect to various ecological circumstances. Therefore, each individual's stress-coping behavior has social consequences in each ecological environment. These consequences will influence the subsequent functional process in generating social behaviors for all individuals involved, either positively or negatively, directly or indirectly.

More detailed discussion of the contents and the dynamics of the above six functional steps will be made after the presentation of individual components that follows.

NATURE AND DYNAMICS OF INDIVIDUAL COMPONENTS

The psychosemantic model in Figure 9.1 is continuous in time and space. By *continuous in time* it means that all components in the model are constantly active and they are functionally linked from the first component of *background characteristics* to the last component of *overt coping behavior*. There are eight components in between that contribute to the eventual manifestation of overt behavior.

By *continuous in space,* it means that all components in this model deal with issues involved in the ten culture-ecology units at the same time in varying degrees. Although the structural characteristics of these components are independent of each other, their functions are not. Therefore, it is important to specify the structural characteristics of individual components and their functional relationships. For this reason, the major contents of each component and their dynamics are illustrated in the following sections.

Background Characteristics

Each individual has various background characteristics that are responsible for aggressive or nonaggressive behaviors. These characteristics can be illustrated in terms of the ten culture-ecology units:

1. *Idiosystem by objective culture* represents various social identifiers of each individual, such as sex, race, physique, behavior patterns, life-styles, and routine activities.

2. *Idiosystem by subjective culture* contains the individual's values, beliefs, needs, expectations, and perception of self and others.

3. *Microsystem by objective culture* represents observable family characteristics, such as housing, family members, activities, and socioeconomic status.

4. *Microsystem by subjective culture* covers family norms, values, identities, roles, and expectations.

5. *Exosystem by objective culture* covers issues on neighborhoods, crime rates, community development, and occupational opportunities.

6. *Exosystem by subjective culture* consists of neighborhood values, norms, perceived peer pressure, career goals, and need for achievement.

7. *Macrosystem by objective culture* covers such social indicators as transportation, taxation, energy, and national wealth and security.

8. *Macrosystem by subjective culture* contains cultural norms, values, taboos, and sex roles.

9. *Geopolitical system by objective culture* reflects various kinds of indexes occurring through international interactions such as trade, conflicts, and travel.

10. *Geopolitical system by subjective culture* represents various international stereotypes, cultural exchanges, and international ethics.

Each individual's background characteristics, as mentioned above, are identifiable through various sources. These characteristics usually determine the individual's competence and performance in interaction with other people. Generally speaking, each individual's behavioral patterns in normal life situations are predictable in terms of his or her background characteristics. Furthermore, members of any social group tend to share similar characteristics on the same issues that enable them to develop common goals, objectives, and activity patterns.

On the other hand, members from two different culture groups (which may be broadly defined in terms of race, age, sex, or other social issues) may have different background characteristics. In intergroup interactive situations, such differences frequently become stressful factors that might bring about strain, conflicts, or prejudices.

Long-term Stressors

Subjective background characteristics of each individual are acquired through a continuous social learning process in all five ecological environments. When some permanent changes occur at an ecological level, the changes may influence the stability of the subjective culture of the individual. For example, the loss of a job may induce changes in a person's value system and confidence in future job performance.

When an individual's objective cultural characteristics change, they may become long-term stressors that require new adaptations. These changes may be due to natural or accidental causes, such as the aging process or an unexpected physical handicap. Like subjective stressors, these objective changes also contribute to the development of aggressive behaviors.

Under usual circumstances, individuals have developed adaptive behaviors and habits as part of background characteristics that will facilitate "normal" interactions with outside ecological environment. They will also facilitate a reasonable control of long-term stressors. This is especially true where the individual's baseline characteristics are compatible with the external circumstances in routine life situations.

Short-term Stressors

Under some circumstances, the individual's life situation may undergo abrupt and possibly severe changes that require urgent behavioral adaptations (e.g., breaking into a new job, short-term illness, or visiting a foreign country). Such changes are usually temporary in time and can occur in any one of the ten culture ecology units. These changes can be referred to as short-term stressors.

There are several measurement instruments that have been developed to evaluate the impact of various short-term stressors on an individual's mental health and coping behaviors. For example, Holmes and Rahe (1967) developed the Social Adjustment Rating Scale in which 43 stressors (life events) are ranked in order of their "life change units" (severity of stress-producing level). The events of death of spouse and divorce are the two highest units on the life change scale, whereas the events of vacation, Christmas, and minor violations of the law are at the bottom of the list.

When short-term stressors (life events) occur, they represent a "deviation" or "interruption" in the individual's routine behavioral patterns. *Deviation* implies an unusual change from prior characteristics of the individual or environment. Deviation changes can take a favorable or unfavorable direction. *Interruption,* on the other hand, implies a change from the current status to some new behavioral pattern. In either case, the individual, and possibly the environment, is required to change in order to overcome (or adjust to) the acute nature of the short-term stressor.

Trend-Coping Mechanisms

Each individual develops a set of behavioral strategies (mechanisms) from repeated coping with long-term and short-term stressors in life history. Theoretically, how well a person's trend-coping mechanisms work can be evaluated in terms of their capability to resolve various "pressures" in daily lives, whether these pressures are new or old, familiar or unfamiliar, and/or similar or dissimilar events. When facing old, familiar, and generally similar situations, these mechanisms will be automatically applied. When facing new, unfamiliar, and dissimilar short-term stressors, the individual usually uses cognitive and affective evaluation systems to determine if trend-coping mechanisms can be applied to each short-term stressor.

Cognitive Evaluation System

Human cognition controls the processes of information identification, appraisal, and integration. According to Tzeng (1977), the process of human judgment involves at least three major elements: (1) the individual making the judgment, (2) the objects (events or stressors) being judged, and (3) the criteria (semantic features) the individual uses in making judgments. For any domain of life situations (e.g., cognitions about kinships), the individual will always formulate *implicit theories* (internal perceptions and feelings) about them. These theories serve as evaluation criteria in judgment of the objects or events involved.

With respect to any new short-term stressor, the individual will first employ relevant implicit theories to assess the nature and conditions of the stressors in order to select relevant coping mechanisms for responses. This cognitive evaluation process involves three major functions: (1) appraisal of the stressors in reference to the existing implicit theories in order to derive some meanings for the stressors; (2) integration of meanings of the *new* stressors with implicit theories of the *old* life experiences; and (3) expectations about the stressors in terms of their strengths, weaknesses, progressions, and consequences.

The cognitive system is developed through long-term interactions with environments and situations. This system is relatively stable in time and space under normal social circumstances. However, as social ecologies change over time, they are also subject to continuous modifications.

Affective Evaluation System

This system represents the emotional aspect of evaluation about stressors and related issues. Like the cognitive system, the affective system is developed from lifelong learning processes through interactions with other individuals and objects (events, situations, and external environments).

The role of the affective evaluation system in human behavior has been investigated in depth by Osgood (Osgood, Miron & May, 1975). In the context of human aggression and violence, three affective components identified by Osgood are directly relevant: (1) Evaluation is the attitude toward objects and events classified as *good* or *bad, desirable* or *undesirable,* and *nice* or *awful;* (2) potency refers to the intensity and strength of things—*potent* or *impotent, strong* or *weak,* and *heavy* or *light;* and (3) activity refers to various events in life experiences being identified as *active* or *passive, fast* or *slow,* and *noisy* or *quiet.* These three affective components play an important role in evaluating baseline characteristics, short-term stressors, and coping mechanisms.

Furthermore, the human affect system generates three behavioral dispositions: (1) *approach,* the tendency to be positive and ready to endorse certain overt behaviors (e.g., a person is "ready" to render assistance to the child who falls); (2) *retreat,* the passive tendency to withdraw involvement from a given situation (e.g., some individual tends to avoid an argument situation); and (3) *attack,* the aggressive tendency to attack the counterparts or situations (e.g., some individual is prone to criticize others). Under normal, familiar life situations, the affective system tends to maintain the *approach* disposition. But under the pressures of severe short-term stressors, the individual might retreat or attack, depending upon what outcome was expected by the individual's cognitive and affective evaluation systems.

Usually the attack disposition is the emotional arousal that generates such feelings as anger, contempt, disdain, and hate. These emotions have been frequently reported as causal factors in human aggression and violence. On the other hand, the retreat disposition is the emotional inhibition that might generate such passive emotions as fear, shame, self-pity, and grief. These emotions have frequently been considered as major symptoms of depression and social withdrawal.

Social aggression and violence have been associated directly with attack; however, suicide and self-targeted destructive behavior can be linked with both attack and retreat. Specifically, suicide has been considered in the literature as an inward-oriented aggressive behavior that might come from global frustration in life. In addition, suicide has also been believed to be the ultimate means of escaping from reality. Such retreating behavior is the direct consequence of inhibition of the approach emotions of desire, affection, curiosity, and pride.

Therefore, to understand the generative process of human behavior, it is important to assess the nature and characteristics of the affective system of each individual or group. In short, the assessments should be done in reference to three affective components (evaluation, potency, and activity) and three behavioral dispositions (approach, retreat, and attack) toward general social environments and specific stressors.

Behavioral Dispositions

In facing an unfamiliar short-term stressor, the individual may have to produce new adaptations quickly. When this happens, the cognitive evaluation system identifies the intellectual and cognizant aspects of the conditions in relation to various baseline characteristics and trend-coping mechanisms. As a result, this cognitive evaluation will generate understanding (implicit theory), strategies, and response procedures that will eventually lead to overt coping behaviors. The intended action from this process is represented by the term *behavioral disposition* in the model.

This behavioral disposition is further facilitated, either positively or negatively, by the affective evaluation system, which will characterize the disposition as being good or bad, strong or weak, and active or passive. As a result, the individual tends to display either approach, attack, or withdrawal behavior.

Behavioral Habits

Behavior is made up of routine responses to familiar stimuli and situations. These responses range from the abstract level of mental activities to the concrete level of physical routines, such as walking styles and physical gestures. Generally speaking, routine responses can be categorized in terms of (1) the individual's familiarity with the stimulus, (2) the occurrence frequency of the stimulus in general life situations, (3) the individual's response patterns under normal circumstances, and (4) the generality of the stimulus to other stimulus conditions. The linkage between stimuli and routine responses will increase when the stimulus is repeated frequently and is much like other familiar stimuli.

Such behavioral linkage is called a *trend habit*. Theoretically, all individuals have developed many action and reaction habits in life situations. These habits will monitor all behavioral dispositions after they are formed in response to various stimuli (or short-term stressors). The monitoring functions of a habit will intensify, neutralize, or block any intended action. Therefore, it is useful to identify the habits that a person responds with under specific situations and stimuli. Furthermore, if habits can be categorized, they can help in the evaluation, interpretation, and prediction of a person's aggressive behaviors.

Overt Coping Behaviors

Behavioral dispositions can be manifested through observable coping behaviors that are either verbal or nonverbal. These overt behaviors can be explained in terms of a five-step hierarchial continuum of human aggression: (1) assertiveness, (2) competition, (3) intrusion, (4) domination, and (5) violence.

How these coping behaviors are labeled depends upon the norm values of the community at the ecological level. For example, each family has its own values and expectations of behavior; each community has its own rules of thumb for relationships between people and groups, and each culture group has its own verbal and nonverbal standards for behavior. Furthermore, due to subjective and/or objective cultural differences, different individuals or groups may consider the same behavioral act to be at different levels of the aggression hierarchy (e.g., an employee asking about rights or benefits is considered assertive in Western culture, but may be considered intrusive of the employer's power in Eastern culture).

The individual adapts to the environment when his or her attitudes and behaviors are consistent with norm values of higher ecological levels. Conflicts between individual values and community values may mean that the individual needs to adjust within the environment. Of course, both individual behaviors and social norms may change continuously over time. Therefore, the definitions and the scope of various aggressive behaviors in society may change as well. Because an individual's overt behavior is usually stable over time, it is possible to characterize the individual's adaptation mechanisms across different ecological levels.

Social Institutional Consequences

The behavioral norms, values, and expectations of a given society can be identified. This is true even for various subcultural groups of individuals that may vary in terms of economic status and political orientation. The identified norms, values, and expectations become the groups' standards for adopting specific behaviors. These standards can be formal (such as laws, regulations, and rules) or informal (such as customs and traditions passed through generations).

Each social institution at the individual, family, community, and cultural levels has certain behavior standards that its members must comply with or follow. Each standard can further be characterized in terms of its historical development. That is, from the *developmental perspective,* a higher-level social institution is established by the composition of many low-level institutions (e.g., a community is established by many families, and each family consists of many individuals). Similarly, subjective cultural characteristics of high-level social institutions are developed from the composition and integration of those of lower-level institutions. Therefore, the formation and change of social values, customs, and laws reflect the evolutional process of human subjective culture initiated at the lower ecological level.

Conversely, from the *perspective of societal functions,* once the subjective cultural characteristics of higher ecological levels are established from lower-level institutions, they become the norms (standards) of all member institutions and have "governing" power to monitor the behaviors of lower-level institutions.

It should be noted that standards of different ecological levels are not necessarily always congruent, because they continue to evolve with changes in time and situations. Because of this variance, an individual's behavior is always compared with and/or adjusted against the standards of family traditions and community. Child-rearing practices and expectations, as social behaviors, are thus subject to the same processes of development and comparisons with the standards of higher-level social institutions (family, residing community, and/or society).

In the process of monitoring and comparing standards, each individual's behavior will always have social consequences that can be grouped into three general categories: (1) *"acceptable" approach behaviors* that are within the normal range of standards of the social institution at higher ecological levels, (2) *"offensive" attack behaviors* that, in varying degrees of aggression and violence, are direct violations of social norms and values, and (3) *"insufficient" retreat behaviors,* such as withdrawal, passivity, and inhibition, that fall below the normal expectations of culturally endorsed behaviors.

These three consequences of social behaviors are usually labeled by various qualifiers in communications. For example, *good, pleasant,* and *smart* describe acceptable behaviors; *agitating, frustrating,* and *rude* describe offensive behaviors; and *naive, timid,* and *insane* are used to describe insufficient behaviors. While the individual's acceptable (approach) behaviors are positively reinforced by social institutions at the higher ecological levels, the offensive attack behaviors are negatively evaluated.

Given positive, neutral, or negative feedback on the overt behavior, an individual may modify (increase or decrease) the intensity of future behavior and, simultaneously, may change the evaluation process that controls the original behavioral dispositions. Therefore, feedback from all ecological levels, either positive or negative, can determine the direction and force of social movement in general. It could especially affect the maintenance patterns of social norms, values, and expectations about interaction patterns between people.

RELATIONSHIPS AMONG COMPONENTS

Each of the ten components in Figure 9.1 is independent regarding its structure, role, and content. On the other hand, all the components work together to determine an individual's eventual overt behavior. By working together, they emphasize (1) continuity in the structural contents of different components, (2) sequence of behavioral processes over time, (3) equal importance of all components, and (4) integration of functional relationships across all components.

These ten components are categorized into four *operational phases* that correspond with how people handle daily life experiences:

1. *supporting baseline characteristics,* which include background characteristics and long-term stressors;

2. *antecedent stimuli,* such as short-term stressors;

3. *behavioral adaptations and mechanisms,* which include the cognitive evaluation system, the affective evaluation system, trend-coping mechanisms, behavioral dispositions, and behavioral habits; and

4. *coping behavior and consequences,* which include overt coping behavior and social institutional consequences.

This model is comprehensive, dynamic, and process oriented, and it can be applied to general social behaviors. It can explain normal circumstances, as well as deviant functions, in different social institutions. Because this model proposes to handle issues at different ecological levels at the same time, it can be used to study not only *individual* dispositions but also the "behaviors" of *social institutions.* This includes handling issues at the microsystem, exosystem, and macrosystem levels. Its application to the summary and integration of various theoretical perspectives of child abuse and neglect is described in the next chapter.

Chapter Ten

Summary and Evaluation of Theories via the Psychosemantic Process Model

This chapter presents an overall summary and evaluation of the 46 individual theories, models, and perspectives in reference to the psychosemantic process model. These theories represent the major viewpoints concerning the etiology of child abuse and neglect in the literature.

These theories and their paradigms originated from different academic disciplines, such as medicine, social work, sociology, anthropology, biology, psychology, education, and nursing. In the preceding chapters, each theory was assessed in terms of four content issues: (1) theoretical foundations, (2) basic principles and models, (3) empirical findings, and (4) evaluation of strengths and weaknesses.

In order to identify the general trends of theoretical accounts of child abuse and neglect etiology, it seems necessary to summarize the results from evaluating all individual theories across the nine paradigms in terms of the theoretical framework of the psychosemantic process model (i.e., ten culture-ecology units and the ten model components). Therefore, the content issues of all 46 theories are evaluated and summarized using the following steps: (1) evaluation of topical issues (key words) addressed in each theory and paradigm, (2) sorting of these topical issues first into the ten different culture-ecology units and then into the ten model components of the psychosemantic process model, and (3) organization of all topical issues within each sorting category (i.e., the culture-ecology unit and the model component) into distinctive themes for presentations.

Characteristics of the topical issues of each theory are also evaluated in this chapter to depict the predominant contribution of certain culture-ecology units to the etiology of each type of child maltreatment. Finally, the topical issues from all theories are organized in reference to the theoretical framework of the psychosemantic process model. The utility of the resulting organization is discussed in terms of future development of an integrated theory for each type of child maltreatment.

EVALUATION OF MAJOR TOPICAL ISSUES IN TERMS OF THE TEN CULTURE-ECOLOGY UNITS

Summary of Topical Issues

Table 10.1 organizes major topical issues of the nine paradigms and their member theories in reference to the ten culture-ecology units of the psychosemantic process model.

The results presented in this table indicate that different ecological characteristics of maltreatment have been addressed by different theories in the following hierarchical order:

1. Objective idiosystem—36 (78%) of the 46 theories were involved and 182 topical issues addressed.

2. Subjective idiosystem—35 (76%) of the theories were involved and 223 topical issues addressed.

3. Objective microsystem—33 (72%) of the theories were involved and 147 topical issues addressed.

4. Subjective microsystem—21 (46%) of the theories were involved and 56 topical issues addressed.

5. Objective macrosystem—18 (39%) of the theories were involved and 55 topical issues addressed.

6. Subjective macrosystem—15 (33%) of the theories were involved and 31 topical issues addressed.

7. Objective exosystem—14 (30%) of the theories were involved and 33 topical issues addressed.

8. Subjective exosystem—11 (23%) of the theories were involved and 13 topical issues addressed.

Subjective and objective geopolitical systems have not been the focus of any theory and thus have zero frequencies in the table.

Overall, objective factors are more salient than subjective ones. Objective culture involves about 55 percent of the theories, whereas subjective culture has an average of only 45 percent of the theories. Of the total 740 topical issues compiled in Table 10.1, 44 percent deal with the subjective culture, and 56 percent deal with the objective culture. This indicates a preference to address factors such as life-styles, activities, crime rates, and social structures rather than needs, wants, perceptions, values, norms, and goals. A possible exception to this general trend is found at the idiosystem (individual ecological) level where subjective factors superseded objective ones by a margin of 223 to 182 in the number of total topical issues.

When the ecological levels are broken down without regard to the subjective/objective culture factor, the characteristics of individuals and families are considered of primary theoretical concern, being addressed by 43 (93%) and 36

(78%) of the theories, respectively. Factors at the macrosystem-cultural level were emphasized by 23 (50%) of the theories, but only 17 (37%) attended to the exosystem-community level.

In terms of the theoretical status of child abuse and neglect literature, the major weaknesses in dealing with the culture-ecological system seem to lie in the lack of addressing (1) subjective and objective geopolitical factors, (2) subjective and objective exosystem factors, and (3) subjective and objective macrosystem factors.

Looking at the number of culture-ecological units involved in each theory, only 14 (30%) of the reviewed theories consider 5 or more of the total possible 10 units of issues to be of significant importance (cf. Table 10.1). This clearly indicates the noncomprehensive nature of the theories in dealing with the complex problem of child abuse and neglect. In addition, it should be noted that while some of the theories consider both subjective and objective factors in their analysis, few draw this important distinction formally in their theoretical postulations.

Nature of Topical Issues in Each Culture-Ecology Unit

The 740 topical issues are further analyzed in terms of their similarities and differences within each culture-ecology unit. This analysis assesses the impact of each ecological level, both subjective and objective, on the causality and prevalence of child abuse and neglect. This analysis is also meant to identify the nature and dynamics of individual theories such that future intervention efforts of the abuse/ neglect problems can be systematically applied. Furthermore, the analysis can aid in depicting areas in need of identifying, and also maintaining, healthy conditions for human beings of all ages.

Overall, the topic issues should represent some unique characteristics of abuse/neglect patterns within each culture-ecology unit:

Subjective idiosystem: The subjective culture at the individual level consists of 223 abuse/neglect-related topics, which can readily be differentiated in terms of 9 psychosocial themes: (1) *needs, drives, and motivations* (e.g., primary sexual orientation, needs for power and/or control, fear of mature sexuality, functional values of abuse, need to maintain social image, attention/affection starvation, and developmental characteristics of victim); (2) *frustration and aggression* (low levels of impulse control and frustration tolerance, motivation to abuse, and abnormal coping); (3) *inhibition and depression* (internal and external inhibitors); (4) *psychiatric problems* (psychopathic deviance, schizophrenia, and affective disturbances); (5) *unique personality characteristics* (low self-esteem, egocentrism, chronic insecurity, and manipulation); (6) *social skills* (irresponsible or incompetent parenting); (7) *cognitive evaluation* (distorted perceptions of childhood, limited mental abilities, perception of stress, rationalizations, stages of parental thinking, perceptions and expectancies of others and self, and perception of power and control); (8) *childhood experiences* (relations with parents and history of abuse and neglect); and (9) *affective evaluation* (feelings of isolation, emotional congruence with abusive act, and intimate childhood associations).

Table 10.1

Summary of Topic Issues in Ten Culture-Ecology Units

	Idiosystem		Microsystem		Exosystem		Macrosystem		GP. system		Total	
	Sub.	Obj.	Sub.	Obj.	Sub.	Obj.	Sub.	Obj.	Sub.	Obj.	Issues	Units
(A) Physical Abuse Theories												
(1) Psychiatric	24	4	-	1	-	1	-	-	-	-	30	4
(2) Intrapsychic	9	7	-	-	-	-	-	-	-	-	16	2
(3) Social Systems	1	5	-	-	-	-	2	9	-	-	17	4
(4) Resource	1	4	-	2	-	-	-	-	-	-	7	3
(5) 3-Component	2	10	-	-	-	-	-	-	-	-	12	2
(6) Social Psychological	-	12	-	15	2	-	-	-	-	-	29	3
(7) Symbiosis	1	3	-	6	-	-	1	-	-	-	11	4
(8) Social Interaction	-	3	-	11	-	-	-	-	-	-	14	2
(9) 3-Factor	-	23	6	-	1	1	-	1	-	-	32	5
(10) Exchange/Control	4	2	-	-	-	-	2	4	-	-	12	4
(11) General Stress	5	4	2	1	-	-	1	-	-	-	13	5
(12) Offender Typologies	8	1	1	-	-	3	-	1	-	-	14	3
(13) Systems	17	4	10	17	1	2	5	6	-	-	62	8
(14) Attachment	4	2	-	5	1	1	-	4	-	-	17	6
(15) Parental Accept.-Rej.	3	-	5	5	-	-	-	-	-	-	13	3

(18) Cognitive Behavioral	-	15	2	1	-	1	-	19	4
(19) Discrimitative Parent.	-	2	2	4	-	1	-	8	3
(20) Social Learning	12	15	1	1	1	1	-	33	8
(21) Situational Analysis	3	-	-	-	1	-	-	3	1
(22) Coercion	4	1	5	-	-	-	-	10	3
(23) Ecological	7	4	-	6	6	2	4	30	7
(24) Choice	3	4	-	4	3	2	2	19	7
(25) Multilevel	-	4	-	3	2	3	1	15	5

(B) Incest Taboo Theories

(1) Biological	-	1	-	-	-	-	1	2	2
(2) Normative	-	-	-	1	2	-	7	10	3
(3) Biosocial	3	5	-	-	-	-	-	8	2

(C) Incestuous Abuse Theories

(1) Humanistic	4	2	1	2	-	-	1	10	5
(2) Patriarchial	-	-	-	7	-	1	5	13	3
(3) Biosocial/Attach.	8	1	1	2	-	-	-	12	4
(4) Family Survival	9	-	3	8	-	-	-	20	3
(5) Endogamous	8	5	3	9	-	-	-	25	4
(6) Grounded Theoretical	3	1	3	2	1	1	3	15	8

(continued)

221

Table 10.1 (continued)

(D) Sexual Abuse Theories

									Total	No.
(7) Psychoanalytic	11	-	-	-	-	-	-	-	11	1
(8) Psychiatric	10	-	-	-	-	-	-	-	10	1
(9) Socialization	-	-	-	3	-	-	-	-	10	3
(10) Four Preconditions	8	7	3	1	-	6	1	-	20	5
(11) Offender Types	10	-	2	-	-	1	-	-	12	2
(12) Female Abusers	18	5	1	2	-	-	-	-	26	4

(E) Psychological Maltreatment Theories

									Total	No.
(1) Ecological Context	1	4	2	4	-	2	-	-	13	5
(2) Family Breakup	1	-	-	4	-	-	-	-	5	2
(3) Ecological/Def. Needs	6	2	-	6	-	6	-	-	20	4

(F) Neglect Theories

									Total	No.
(1) Personalistic	4	1	-	1	-	-	-	-	9	4
(2) Social Interaction	3	3	1	4	1	-	1	3	13	6
(3) Three-Factor	6	3	1	4	1	2	-	-	17	6

									Total	
Total topical issues	223	182	56	147	13	33	31	55	740	
Total no. theories	35	36	21	33	11	14	15	18		
% theories involved	76%	78%	46%	72%	23%	30%	33%	39%		

Objective idiosystem: Falling within the objective idiosystem unit are 182 topics, which may be placed under 2 general themes: (1) *predisposing factors* (genetic and physical characteristics of child and abuser) and (2) *current precipitators* (objective stress, lack of sexual gratification, and alcohol/drug abuse).

Subjective microsystem: At the subjective microsystem level, 56 topical issues emerged under 3 themes: (1) *parent-child interactions* (parent-child bond, parent-child-sibling interactions, discipline measures, focusing aggression on child, and socialization factors); (2) *parental relations* (sexual, emotional, and marital discord); (3) *whole family interactions* (general family dynamics and structure, confusion of family roles, and blurring of generational boundaries); and (4) *goals of the family* (expectancies and fear of breakdown by all members).

Objective microsystem: Within this unit, 147 topical issues were identified and placed under 4 themes: (1) *family structure* (patriarchal, chaotic or endogenous family type, and reconstituted family); (2) *genetic relationship* between abuser and victim (natural parents and stepparents); (3) *family functional issues* (failed abuse inhibition, abuse being functional for the family, and all members playing a role in the abuse); (4) *family stressors* (social isolation, family size, socioeconomic status, lack of social supports, inadequate health care, unhealthy interactions between members, and alienating neighborhoods).

Subjective exosystem: The subjective culture-by-community ecological level contains 3 themes: (1) *the child's interactions with peers,* (2) *the child's subjective experiences* in the family, school, day care, and so on, and (3) *class and community norms* (community tolerance of abuse, subculture of violence).

Objective exosystem: This unit of analysis contains 33 topic issues under 3 themes: (1) *formal community organizations* (local supports for families, individuals, and school environment), (2) *informal community social supports* (friends and neighbors), and (3) *susceptibility to exposure* (public attention of the abuse, social distance between abuser and control agencies, and nearness of relatives and friends).

Subjective macrosystem: At this junction, 10 topic issues are placed into 2 themes: (1) *condonation* (cultural values, attitudes, or world views that excuse child abuse/neglect, social tolerance of sexual interest in children, and social tolerance of deviance while intoxicated) and (2) *promotion or blocking of solutions* (repressive sexual norms, generational inequality, violence norms, taboos, and conflict resolution norms).

Objective macrosystem: This entry includes (1) *social structures* that promote or maintain inequalities and (2) *weak criminal sanctions* for child abuse/neglect offenders.

Of the theories reviewed and their applications in empirical research, no studies have been found that address the interactive relationships of the child abuse and neglect issues at the geopolitical level.

However, some empirical studies do address intercultural differences, as well as similarities, in various aspects of child abuse and neglect problems (e.g., Rohner, 1980; Kitahara, 1987; Korbin, 1977; Loening, 1981).

EVALUATION OF TOPICAL ISSUES IN TERMS OF TEN PSYCHOSEMANTIC MODEL COMPONENTS

Summary of Topical Issues

The principal topical issues of the 46 theories are further organized into the 10 model components of the psychosemantic process model. The results, presented in Table 10.2, display the following general trends: (1) The domain of *background characteristics* is the component most emphasized by the theories; (2) other components have differential patterns of importance for different theories; (3) no single theory addresses all ten components simultaneously; and (4) individual theories stress an average of five components. Specifically, cognitive evaluation is considered important by nearly half (43%) of the theories, and affective evaluation is considered by only 30 percent of the theories. Stressors, both long-term (63%) and short-term (52%), are taken into account by most of the theories. Trend-coping mechanisms are addressed by nearly half (43%) of the theories, but the social institutional consequences of child maltreatment are addressed by only 24 percent of the 46 theories reviewed.

Background characteristics: There are 3 major themes encompassing 295 topic issues: (1) individual characteristics (psychiatric problems, genetic factors, personality traits, parenting skills, and experiences in childhood); (2) interpersonal relations (poor parental relations, family structure and function, and parent-child interactions); and (3) cultural, community, and family norms.

Long-term stressors: Three primary themes comprising 153 topical issues are identified: (1) interpersonal relations (marital problems, vocational conflicts, incompatible expectations, social isolation, and overcrowded living conditions); (2) socioeconomic stress (loss of income, increases in expenditures, and relative poverty); and (3) health stressors (chronic, physical, or mental illness of the child or other family member and substance abuse).

Short-term stressors: Five major patterns of short-term stressors are emphasized: (1) temporary illness, (2) infidelity (committed by either party), (3) temporary loss of income (being laid off work for a short period), (4) legal stress (small claims court and traffic violations), and (5) other immediate precipitators (e.g., frustrations and interruptions).

Trend-coping mechanisms: Three major topical issues are addressed under this category: (1) child maltreatment functioning as a stress-coping mechanism (father obtaining emotional support by sexually abusing his daughter when he is rejected by his wife), (2) offender's primary sexual orientation (the sex to which the individual is attracted), and (3) father unwilling to go outside the family for sex.

Behavioral dispositions: Three major theoretical positions are employed: (1) the focusing of aggression onto the child (i.e., displacement of frustrations), (2) genetic relationship that predisposes the offender to certain behavioral responses, and (3) the role of parent-child attachment in the development of responses to stress.

Behavior habits: Two major issues are classified as pertaining to this component: (1) early parent-child bonding being strongly influential in the development of dispositions and habits (positive attachment for a sense of trust and security in the child) and (2) high level of general parental aggression leading to child abuse.

Cognitive evaluation: Fifty-eight major issues fall under three themes: (1) perceptions (distorted perceptions of childhood, perceiving that the reward of abuse outweighs the costs, perceived stress, perceived loss of power, and perception of self and others); (2) stages of parental thinking and moral cognitive development; and (3) overcoming external inhibition forces.

Affective evaluation: Thirty-three major topical issues are identified in terms of four themes: (1) needs (displacement of affect, child maltreatment for fulfilling an emotional need, the need for maintaining a positive social image, affect linked to intimate childhood associations, and abnormal need to feel powerful and in control); (2) fears (fear of mature sexuality and fear of family breakdown shared by all family members); (3) congruency between abusive acts and emotional states and having a guilt-free conscience; and (4) emotional characteristics and prebirth conditions of mothers.

Overt coping behavior: Each form of child maltreatment may be considered an overt coping behavior when it is the result of one of the short-term stressors noted above (e.g., abuse as a response to immediate frustration).

Social institutional consequences: Child abuse and neglect acts have been associated with the consequences of five societal conditions: (1) low cultural inhibition of aggression (many aggressive acts are not socially inhibited); (2) cultural, class, and community norms and values toward violence and human sexuality (media portrays physical force as the normal, right, and successful way to solve problems, and males are socialized to sexualize power, intimacy, and affection); (3) social distance between aggressor and power sources in human ecological contexts (individuals in control of power and resources are socially permitted to be aggressive); (4) societal reinforcement of abusive behavior (abusive/neglectful behaviors generate personal satisfaction for some abusers, and child abuse reduces unwanted behavior); and (5) negative social consequences of abuse and neglect (perpetrators are jailed or shunned by or ejected from community).

Conclusions

Overall, in terms of the ten model components of the psychosemantic process model, three areas are especially lacking in the current child abuse and neglect literature: (1) behavioral habits (considered important only by 11% of the theories), (2) affective evaluation (considered important by 30% of the theories), and (3) social institutional consequences (considered important by only 24% of the theories).

PHYSICAL ABUSE

Analysis of the physical abuse theories in terms of the 10 culture-ecology units reveals the following patterns in Table 10.1 for each theory under individual theoretical paradigms:

Individual determinants paradigm: The psychiatric theory covers 30 topical issues under 4 culture-ecology units, with a concentration on subjective idiosystem variables.

Table 10.2
Summary of Topic Issues in Ten Model Components

	Background Characteristics	Long-term Stressors	Short-term Stressors	Trend-Coping Mechanisms	Behavioral Dispositions	Behavioral Habits	Cognitive Evaluation	Affective Evaluation	Overt Coping Behavior[a]	Social Instit. Consequences	Total Issues	Components
(A) Physical Abuse Theories												
(1) Psychiatric	13	17	-	-	-	-	-	-	-	-	30	2
(2) Intrapsychic	5	3	-	-	1	-	2	3	-	2	16	6
(3) Social Systems	14	3	-	-	-	-	-	-	-	-	17	2
(4) Resource	1	6	-	-	-	-	-	-	-	-	7	2
(5) Three-Component	6	1	3	-	-	-	2	-	-	-	12	4
(6) Social Psychological	10	17	2	-	-	-	-	-	-	-	29	3
(7) Symbiosis	6	4	-	1	-	-	-	-	-	-	11	3
(8) Social Interaction	3	8	3	-	-	-	-	-	-	-	14	3
(9) Three-Factor	5	-	8	8	8	1	2	-	-	1	33	7
(10) Exchange/Control	6	-	2	-	-	-	1	2	-	1	12	5
(11) General Stress	-	5	2	5	-	-	-	-	-	1	13	4
(12) Offender Typologies	5	1	3	2	2	-	1	-	-	-	14	6
(13) Systems Theory	39	8	3	1	4	-	1	1	-	5	62	8
(14) Attachment	12	-	-	-	2	-	-	-	-	3	17	3
(15) Parental Accept.-Reject.	2	-	-	-	8	-	1	-	-	2	13	4
(16) Transactional	3	7	1	1	-	-	-	2	-	-	14	5
(17) Encounter	6	-	1	-	2	-	-	-	-	-	9	3
(18) Cognitive Behavioral	1	2	2	-	8	-	6	-	-	-	19	5
(19) Discriminative Parenting	5	3	-	-	-	-	-	-	-	-	8	2
(20) Social Learning	6	-	3	-	-	-	16	-	-	4	29	4
(21) Situational Analysis	-	-	2	-	-	-	-	-	-	1	3	2
(22) Coercion	-	5	3	1	1	-	-	-	-	-	10	4
(23) Ecological	15	6	2	-	1	-	5	1	-	-	30	6
(24) Choice	13	4	1	1	1	-	2	1	-	-	23	7
(25) Multilevel	12	1	-	1	1	-	-	-	-	-	15	4
(B) Incest Taboo Theories												
(1) Biological	1	-	-	-	-	-	-	-	-	1	2	2
(2) Normative	6	-	-	-	-	-	-	-	-	4	10	2
(3) Biosocial	2	-	-	-	3	3	-	-	-	-	8	3

226

Theory	1	2	3	4	5	6	7	8	9
(1) Humanistic	3	2	-	-	2	-	1	10	5
(2) Patriarchial	13	-	-	-	-	-	-	13	1
(3) Biosocial/Attach.	7	-	-	4	-	-	-	12	3
(4) Family Survival	8	3	3	1	1	-	-	20	6
(5) Endogamous	7	4	-	5	1	4	-	25	6
(6) Grounded Theoretical	8	-	-	1	-	2	3	15	5
(D) Sexual Abuse Theories									
(1) Psychoanalytic	4	-	-	3	1	-	-	11	4
(2) Psychiatric	4	-	-	1	3	-	2	10	4
(3) Socialization	6	3	1	1	-	-	-	10	3
(4) Four Preconditions	8	1	4	4	4	3	-	20	5
(5) Offender Types	4	-	1	2	-	-	5	12	4
(6) Female Sexual Offenders	7	7	1	1	4	2	4	26	7
(E) Psychological Maltreatment Theories									
(1) Ecological Context	2	8	1	1	-	1	-	13	5
(2) Family Breakup	-	5	-	-	-	-	-	5	1
(3) Ecological/Deficiency Needs	4	13	-	-	1	2	-	20	4
(F) Neglect Theories									
(1) Personalistic	4	2	1	2	2	-	-	9	4
(2) Social Interaction	4	4	4	-	-	-	-	12	3
(3) Three-Factor	5	-	8	8	8	1	-	33	7
Total topical issues	295	153	64	49	72	58	33	25	756
Total no. theories	42	29	24	20	23	20	14	11	
% theories involved	91%	63%	52%	43%	50%	43%	30%	24%	

[a] Overt Coping Behavior refers to the actual act of child abuse or neglect.

The intrapsychic theory covers 16 topical issues under 2 units, with a concentration on subjective and objective idiosystem variables.

Sociocultural determinants paradigm: The social systems theory covers 17 topical issues under 4 units, with a concentration on objective macrosystem variables.

Individual-environment interaction paradigm: Resource theory covers 7 topical issues under 3 units, with a concentration on objective idiosystem variables. The three-component theory covers 12 topical issues under 2 units, with a concentration on objective idiosystem variables. The social psychological theory covers 29 topical issues under 3 units, with a concentration on objective idiosystem and objective microsystem variables. The symbiosis theory covers 11 topical issues under 4 units, with a concentration on objective microsystem variables. The social interaction theory covers 14 topical issues under 2 units, with a concentration on objective microsystem variables. The three-factor theory covers 32 topical issues under 5 units, with a concentration on objective idiosystem variables. Exchange/control theory covers 12 topical issues under 4 units, with a concentration on subjective idiosystem and objective macrosystem variables. The general stress theory covers 13 topical issues under 5 units, with a concentration on subjective and objective idiosystem variables.

Offender typologies paradigm: The offender typologies theory covers 14 topical issues under 3 units, with a concentration on subjective idiosystem variables.

Family systems paradigm; The systems theory covers 62 topical issues under 8 units, with a concentration on subjective idiosystem and subjective and objective microsystem variables.

Parent-child interaction paradigm: Attachment theory covers 17 topical issues under 6 units, with a concentration on subjective idiosystem, objective microsystem, and objective macrosystem variables. The parental acceptance-rejection theory covers 13 topical issues under 3 units, with a concentration on subjective and objective microsystem variables. Transactional theory covers 14 topical issues under 3 units, with a concentration on objective idiosystem variables. Encounter theory covers 9 topical issues under 4 units, with a concentration on objective idiosystem variables. The cognitive/behavioral/ developmental theory covers 19 topical issues under 4 units, with a concentration on objective idiosystem variables.

Sociobiological paradigm: The discriminative parenting theory covers 8 topical issues under 3 units, with a concentration on objective microsystem variables.

Learning/situational paradigm: The social learning theory covers 33 topical issues under 8 units, with a concentration on subjective and objective idiosystem variables. The situational theory covers 3 topical issues under 1 unit, concentrating on subjective idiosystem variables.

Ecological determinants paradigm: The ecological theory covers 30 topical issues under 7 units, with a concentration on subjective idiosystem, objective microsystem, and objective exosystem variables. Multilevel theory covers 15 topical issues under 5 units, with a concentration on objective idiosystem, objective microsystem, and subjective macrosystem variables.

Overall, the theories of physical abuse concentrate mostly on the subjective and objective characteristics of individual perpetrators. This includes such objective variables as having an exceptionally disturbing childhood experience (e.g., being abused) or various psychiatric problems (e.g., poor impulse control, substance abuse, or poor self-esteem). Subjective factors at this level include distorted thinking processes of the child offender (e.g., rationalizations, justifications, and inaccurate beliefs) and/or the personal resources of the offender (e.g., parenting skills and stress-coping mechanisms).

Objective characteristics of the family (microsystem) are also stressed to a comparatively large degree. Marital conflict, divorce and separation rates, family isolation, disorganized family structure, socioeconomic status of families, family composition (e.g., number and age of parents, size, age of children), and punishment methods prevail in the theoretical literature. The few subjective aspects of family (microsystem) conditions under scrutiny include attitudes toward child disciplinary tactics and familial beliefs about the appropriateness of aggression as a means to resolve family conflicts.

Objective community (exosystem) variables are not stressed often. When they are, it is usually in reference to factors such as subcultural acceptance of violence, child-rearing practices, community isolation, and institutional cases of abuse (e.g., abuse in schools or day-care centers). Subjective community variables are not a concentration of any of the physical abuse theories.

Used to some, but a relatively limited, extent are objective cultural (macrosystem) variables, such as poverty, unemployment, social isolation, and other indexes of social and economic stress, and subjective cultural variables, such as cultural attitudes toward violence, discipline, and conflict resolution norms.

INCEST TABOO

Analysis of the incest taboo theories in terms of the ten culture-ecology units reveals the following patterns for each theory:

Individual determinants paradigm: The biological theory covers two topical issues under two units, with a concentration on objective idiosystem and objective macrosystem variables.

Sociocultural determinants paradigm: Normative theory covers ten topical issues under three units, with a concentration on objective macrosystem variables.

Individual-environment paradigm: Biosocial theory covers eight topical issues under two units, with a concentration on subjective and objective idiosystem variables.

Overall, theories of the incest taboo concentrate their efforts on three culture-ecology units: the subjective idiosystem of individuals, the objective idiosystem of individuals, and the objective macrosystem of societal variability.

Theories that stress objective culture at the individual level note the negative physical effects of incest on offspring, such as deformities, sickliness, infertility, poor intelligence, and death. Regarding the subjective culture of individuals, two main themes have been most prevalent: (1) emphasis on certain values and attitudes, including the impact of the taboo on the development of appropriate individualization, and (2) the theory that incest by stepfathers is more prevalent than incest by natural fathers because nonblood relatives are subject to weaker normative taboos against incest.

Beyond the individual level, objective cultural traits associated with the incest taboo include exogamy, the taboo of marriage to certain kinfolk, and the shift of dependency from the family to the community. Therefore, the major function of the incest taboo is to encourage intergroup interactions and cooperations that are necessary for economic survival and for the further development of society.

INCESTUOUS ABUSE

Analysis of the incestuous abuse theories in terms of the ten culture-ecology units reveals the following patterns for each theory in Table 10.1:

Individual determinants paradigm: The humanistic theory covers 10 topical issues under 5 units, with a concentration on subjective idiosystem variables.

Sociocultural determinants paradigm: The patriarchal theory covers 13 topical issues under 3 units, with a concentration on objective microsystem and macrosystem variables.

Individual-environment interaction paradigm: The biosocial theory covers 12 topical issues under 4 units, with a concentration on subjective idiosystem variables.

Family systems paradigm: Family survival theory covers 20 topical issues under 3 units, with a concentration on subjective idiosystem and objective microsystem variables. Endogamous theory covers 25 topical issues under 4 units, with a concentration on subjective idiosystem and objective microsystem variables.

Overall, the theories of incestuous abuse concentrate most strongly on subjective idiosystem and objective microsystem variables, and to a lesser degree on objective macrosystem factors.

Under the culture-ecology unit of subjective idiosystem, the perpetrator (i.e., the father in the family) has been characterized as having high rates of desertion anxiety, a regressed ego state, an unwillingness to act sexually outside the family, and as being confused about his masculine identity. The nonparticipating mother has been said to have great needs of dependency and to be unconsciously sanctioning the incest. The victimized daughter has been labeled as pseudomature, lacking impulse control, and as having poor ego functioning.

In terms of objective family characteristics, it has been theorized that the incestuous family experiences mother-daughter role reversal, isolation, extreme patriarchy, and often includes other deviant backgrounds (e.g., parental conflict and physical abuse). Macrological factors that have been theoretically linked to incestuous behaviors include the prevalence of sexual and generational inequality in society as a whole.

SEXUAL ABUSE

Analysis of the incest taboo theories in terms of the 10 culture-ecology units reveals the following patterns for each theory:

Individual determinants paradigm: Psychoanalytic theory covers 11 topical issues under 1 unit, concentrating on subjective idiosystem variables. The psychiatric theory covers 10 topical issues under 1 unit, concentrating also on subjective idiosystem variables.

Sociocultural determinants paradigm: Socialization theory covers 10 topical issues under 3 units, with a concentration on subjective macrosystem variables.

Individual-environment interaction paradigm: The four preconditions theory covers 20 topical issues under 5 units, with a concentration on subjective and objective idiosystem variables.

Offender typologies paradigm: Offender typology theory covers 12 topical issues under 2 units, with a concentration on subjective idiosystem variables. Female abusers theory covers 26 topical issues under 4 units, with a concentration on subjective idiosystem variables.

Overall, under the category of sexual abuse, theories are most likely to stress subjective idiosystem factors. Objective idiosystem and subjective macrosystem variables are emphasized also, but to a lesser degree.

The most common subjective idiosystem factors considered important to the understanding of sexual abuse etiology include (1) having psychological problems (e.g., excessive impulses, high anxiety, substance abuse, and/or psychosexual disorder), (2) lacking personal resources (e.g., self-esteem, impulse control, and social skills), (3) perception of stressors, (4) affective processes (e.g., a fear of mature sexuality, regressed ego state, and emotional transference), (5) motivation to abuse, and (6) the overcoming of internal and external inhibitors.

Objective idiosystem factors include having severe early childhood disturbances (e.g., being victimized or having a psychologically disturbed parent). Subjective macrosystem factors include socialization norms that promote the transference of male sexuality into sexual abuse. For example, it has been suggested that men are socialized to consider sex only as a means of self-gratification (rather than gratifying one's partner), to view sexual partners as objects, to seek partners inferior in size and age, and to be dominant in sexual relations.

PSYCHOLOGICAL MALTREATMENT

Analysis of the psychological maltreatment theories in terms of the 10 culture-ecology units reveals the following patterns for each theory in Table 10.1:

Ecological determinants paradigm: Ecological context theory covers 13 topical issues under 5 units, with a concentration on objective idiosystem and objective microsystem variables. Family breakup theory covers 5 topical issues under 2 units, with a concentration on objective microsystem variables. Ecologi-

cal/deficiency needs theory covers 20 topical issues under 4 units, with a concentration on subjective idiosystem, objective microsystem, and objective exosystem variables.

Overall, psychological maltreatment theories focus on objective microsystem
variables at a substantially greater rate than other culture-ecology units. However, subjective and objective idiosystem factors and objective exosystem factors
are also areas of concentration.

At the subjective idiosystem level, theories of psychological maltreatment
tend to focus on the perpetrators' negative perceptions of themselves, their families, and their surroundings. For example, one theory places the perception of
children on a bipolar continuum. On one end of the continuum children are
considered utterly perfect, needing no help whatsoever, and on the other end,
they are considered a constant source of frustration and trouble, totally dependent, bad, demanding, and problematic.

At the objective idiosystem level, the risk of maltreatment has been said to
increase when the child is excessively active or naturally shy or suffers from
some sort of handicap. These characteristics may be an extra source of stress for
the parent. It has also been suggested that the risk of psychological maltreatment
is associated with either the child or the parent having developmental problems,
being under stress, or suffering from a psychological disorder.

Objective microsystem factors are central to the theories of psychological
abuse, because they tend to consider family interactions and the composition of
the family. Risks of maltreatment are heightened when interactions between
family members are conflictual or when the family is under unusual strain due to
socioeconomic disadvantages, large number of children, or inexperience or single status of the parents.

The most common objective exosystem factor regards community support
systems. The risk of psychological maltreatment is said to have an inverse
relationship with community support systems. In other words, risk will be higher
when the availability of community support is low. Community support may be
either formal (i.e., public organizations, such as family stress centers) or informal (e.g., friends, and neighbors).

NEGLECT

Analysis of neglect theories in terms of the 10 culture-ecology units reveals the
following patterns for each theory:

Individual determinants paradigm: The personalistic theory covers 9 topical issues
under 4 units, with a concentration on subjective idiosystem and objective macrosystem
variables.

Individual-environment interaction paradigm: The social interaction theory covers 13
topical issues under 6 units, with a concentration on subjective and objective idiosystem
and objective microsystem variables. The three-factor theory covers 17 topical issues

under 6 units, with a concentration on subjective idiosystem and objective microsystem variables.

Overall, the theories of neglect focus mainly on subjective and objective idiosystem variables and on objective microsystem and macrosystem variables.

The theories of neglect most often concentrate on variables at the culture-ecology unit of the subjective idiosystem, such as character disorders or personality deficits. The three most commonly identified are the apathy-futility syndrome, the impulse-ridden character, and infantile emotional functioning. Specific characteristics of neglectful individuals include feelings of worthlessness, inhibited emotional responses, superficial relationships, intense loneliness, and passive-aggressive expressions of anger.

At the culture-ecology unit of the objective idiosystem, it has been theorized that neglectful offenders are often verbally inaccessible to others, resulting in their reduced capacity to solve social conflicts. Other objective characteristics of the neglectful person include psychophysiological problems, low intelligence, low education, and a history of lack of employment.

Objective microsystem variables such as large family size, poverty, single-parent household, and isolation from support networks are also said to play an important role in facilitating the development of child neglect.

At the objective macrosystem level, poverty is most frequently considered as the major causal factor for neglect. It represents the absence of material goods, which often intensifies the feelings of powerlessness and self-devaluation among the lower classes. Isolation among this group can further intensify the inaccessibility of material goods and also problems with mental health. Therefore, these macrological factors are said to function as moderating variables to increase the negative impact of the parent's personality deficits.

FUNCTIONAL QUALITIES OF THE PSYCHOSEMANTIC PROCESS MODEL

Organization of the topical issues in terms of theoretical framework of the psychosemantic process model is intended to provide an objective measure to evaluate the comprehensiveness and organizational structures of contents for each theory. This organization can have multiple functions. For example:

1. It can serve as the operational structure for each theory that can be used to develop empirical research programs in the future, including design of control and experimental variables and subject populations.
2. It can establish postulates to link causal relationships between various variables.
3. It can help form hypotheses for empirical testing through various quantitative methodologies.

Information derived from such research efforts can be used to integrate the current knowledge within each theory and also across different theories, and further to improve the sophistication and predicting power of scientific knowledge about child abuse and neglect etiologies.

The psychosemantic process model has successfully organized all topical issues addressed by all 46 theories, although some topical issues raised by various theories have been quite vague and many of them may be categorized in different ways. It is the intention of the psychosemantic process model to integrate currently available knowledge in the literature into a scientific system about human cognitive and behavioral processes that are related to child maltreatment.

More specifically, the system of knowledge integrated in the model can serve two functions. First, it can improve the area of evaluating existing theories and of developing new ones. Unless certain model components are unnecessary or invalid, each child maltreatment theory should contain topical issues for each model component. The theory should also account for the linkage across all model components. In the present state of theorization of child abuse and neglect, the majority of theories have not addressed all model components, much less their linkages and integrations. Therefore, the compilation of topical issues of all existing theories through the model components of the psychosemantic process model can serve as the resource base for improving existing theories and also for developing new theories.

Second, the psychosemantic process model, with the compilation of topical issues for each of the ten components, can serve as an empirical guide for continuing collection of child victimization profiles in various clinical settings. It can also serve as an operational framework for designing rigorous research programs to test theoretical postulates and hypotheses that can be generated from various theories.

In short, the summary compilation of the contemporary theoretical accounts of child victimization from the literature clearly indicates the following: First, all theories have attempted to address some aspects of child abuse and neglect etiological issues, but none have successfully accounted for all important components as advocated by the psychosemantic process model. Second, the profiles of topical issues, compiled from all theories into the ten culture-ecology units and also into the ten psychosemantic process model components, are rich resources that represent systematic organizations of current knowledge about child abuse and neglect etiologies. They can be used for further evaluation and improvement of individual theories and, perhaps more important, for developing new, more comprehensive and integrated theories in the future.

Chapter Eleven

Perspectives from the Psychosemantic Process Model

This chapter presents two aspects of integrations of all topical issues and their implications that were discussed in Chapters 9 and 10. Over the past few decades, child maltreatment has been a major study topic for many disciplines. As a result, different theorizations and much clinical and empirical evidence have been reported in the literature. Many, and frequently conflicting, recommendations have further been derived for clinical use in dealing with child abuse and neglect problems.

The difficulty with using these theorizations and their accompanied recommendations can be explained in part by the complex and diverse nature of the content issues integrated in Chapter 10. Therefore, in order for professionals to utilize the integrated information across the 46 theories for clinical or academic purposes, it seems necessary to delineate the *definition issues* of child abuse and neglect from a larger and higher ecological perspective in human society.

Under this premise, this chapter is devoted, first, to the introduction of a *general topical structure* of child abuse and neglect content issues that are frequently raised by professionals in all disciplines and also by the general public, and, second, to the development of a *conceptual network* of all services that are needed for societal efforts on the problem of child abuse and neglect.

While the first part represents a formal organization of child abuse and neglect content issues, the second part represents a system of networking all service needs within each community.

The content structure and the service network suggested in this chapter will further be used in Chapter 14 to illustrate the conflicting roles of different theorizations in legal processes and in Chapter 15 to summarize diverse strategies for implementing various social service programs as they were advocated under the guidance of the nine theoretical paradigms.

GENERAL TOPICAL STRUCTURE OF CONTENT ISSUES

From a social behavioral science point of view, child abuse and neglect are socially undesirable behaviors that involve issues pertaining to a simple question of *who did what to whom*. The term *who* represents the individuals and/or institutions that act out undesirable behaviors against children, the term *what* represents the undesirable behaviors manifested by the offenders against the children, and the term *whom* represents the children who are victimized by the offenders. Each of these three terms—*who, what,* and *whom*—represents a significant domain of issues involved in the child abuse and neglect literature. They can be further delineated as follows:

Who: Offenders

As shown in Figure 11.1, there are three general types of *offenders* who might be responsible for child abuse and neglect:

System Offenders. Within each social ecology where children reside, there are numerous institutional systems that assist, govern, or monitor social behaviors and interactions (e.g., systems of education, welfare, transportation, health, marriage, religion, law enforcement, and economic structures). Each system has a significant impact on the individual members within the system, as well as on other systems. Therefore, each system can positively serve the individuals and families and also possibly generate negative impacts on some families and/or individuals that might lead to the direct or indirect consequences of child abuse or neglect.

Figure 11.1
Conceptual Inquiries about Child Abuse and Neglect

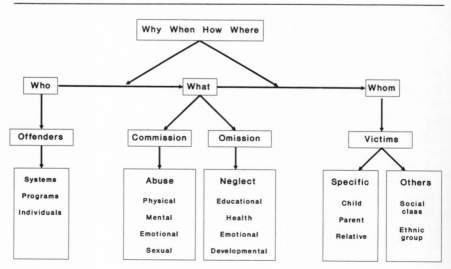

Program Offenders. Within each public and/or private social institution or system, there are always some ongoing programs (projects) that will generate impacts on individuals and other institutions. For example, within a child abuse and neglect crisis center, programs may include volunteer participation, Parents Anonymous activities, parenting assistance, or respite care for children. Of course, the intent of the general assistance program is always positive, but the consequence of the program implementation may not always be beneficial to all families and individuals involved. Due to various reasons, the objectives of programs may miss the anticipated remediation or alleviation of social problems related to children. Under such circumstances, improper or misguided program implementation may result in institutional offenses against children. For example, an overdominant and punishing approach to treatment of children's alcohol and drug problems may generate irreversible damage to children's ego development.

Individual Offenders. The incident of child victimization is always associated with identifiable individuals who are directly responsible for the abusive or neglectful acts. These individuals may be family members, relatives, or workers in child service and education institutions. Other individuals who have no family or child-care relationships may also be responsible for abusive acts against children (e.g., sexual abuse or physical and/or verbal attacks from strangers). In addition, child protection laws in most states provide that people who witness a child abuse incident are subject to punishment if they do not report the incident to proper authorities. Therefore, if these individuals do not report the incident, they are, according to law, responsible for continued child victimization even though they do not contribute to the direct abusive act.

What: Types of Offenses

While child *abuse* is the result of *commission* (action) of undesirable/ unacceptable behaviors against children, *neglect* is the result of *omission* (inaction) of necessary behaviors for the benefit of children. It is clear that between active commission and passive omission, there is a continuum of behaviors that involve the interactions between children and adults (or child-care and education institutions). On this continuum, excessive behaviors are not permissible (e.g., overpunishment of children for running outside during cold weather), and excessive inaction is equally harmful to children (e.g., letting children be exposed to cold for long periods of time without proper intervention).

Between abuse and neglect, there is a range of desirable and permissible behaviors that are needed for the benefit of children. The difficult issue is to determine the critical point that will differentiate between acceptable and unacceptable behaviors on the part of adults and institutions. In most state laws, there are general criteria regarding the unacceptable abusive or neglectful behaviors against children (for information on national trends of state laws for protecting child victimization, readers are referred to Tzeng and Hanner, 1988). Violation of these criteria may result in criminal prosecution of offenders, and at the same time the child may be declared to have the legal status of "child in need of services" (CHINS). As a result, mandatory intervention and protection of the child must be made by various public protection agencies.

Adults in families and education and care institutions have a definite responsibility to perform permissible actions for the well-being of children. These individuals should know their responsibilities as well as their limits of behaviors regarding children (e.g., good touch vs. bad touch in caring for a young child).

Therefore, due to the multifaceted nature of child development and statutory requirements for protecting children, abuse and neglect (on the issue of *what*) can be broadly categorized according to five areas: *physical/health, emotional, educational, sexual,* and *social.* In most cases, different "types" of child maltreatment are interrelated. Identification and intervention programs for different typologies should thus address all areas of etiological issues simultaneously.

Whom: Victimizations

Generally speaking, child abuse and neglect involves two types of target persons: self and others. While *self-victimization* may be due to environmental stress from physical, mental, or emotional difficulties, *victimization of others* is often the result of inappropriate background characteristics and environmental influences. As discussed earlier, short-term stressors of the individual, due to either real or imaginary circumstantial conditions, may trigger abusive or neglectful reactions that might be further intensified by improper coping behaviors and habits.

On the issue of child abuse and neglect, a child's self-victimization (e.g., head banging among emotionally disturbed children) is rarely reported. In fact, in most states it is not considered a legal problem.

On the other hand, *victimization of others* can be divided into two subcategories: (1) specific individuals as target victims (e.g., children, spouse, aged parents, siblings, and specific individuals in an institution) and (2) social classes or groups in a certain ecological system (e.g., victimization against a certain ethnic, low socioeconomic, or age group). Child abuse and neglect falls mostly under the subcategory of victimization against specific individual children. But it may also fall under the subcategory of institutional maltreatment against all children (e.g., all children of a certain day-care facility might suffer abuse and/or neglect under the maltreatment of the system, the program, and/or the individual caretaker).

From a strictly behavioral point of view, the purpose of intervention is simply to sever the linkage of *who did what to whom:* elimination of abuse and neglect (*what*) between the two counterparts *who* and *whom.*

Unfortunately, statistics have repeatedly suggested that the reoccurrence of child abuse and neglect had its recursive origin in the adult's own victimization at an early age. It may also implant the child's own abusive dispositions against the next generation. Therefore, it is clear that intervention in child abuse and neglect circumstances requires a comprehensive investigation of other important issues as proposed in the psychosemantic model. That is, other issues surrounding the *who did what to whom* linkage should be addressed simultaneously. The issues include (1) *why* the offender acts or doesn't act in certain ways, (2) *how* the incidents of child abuse and neglect occur, and (3) *where* and *when* the maltreatments happen. In short, we should address all of the issues that would answer the questions pertaining to *who, what, whom, why, when, how,* and *where* in child abuse and neglect incidents. For this purpose, the summary organization of content issues of different theoretical paradigms clearly requires the impartial knowledge resources in the literature that can be used to address these seven *W*s.

PSYCHOSEMANTIC APPROACH TO SERVICE NETWORK

Incidents of child abuse and neglect are well recognized as being pervasive to varying degrees across all types of families regardless of age, sex, race, economic status, education, and marital condition of the adults. It is clear that most etiological theorizations evaluated in this book are not sufficient to address issues on the seven *W*s because each theory alone cannot account for all aspects of the child victimization process.

Furthermore, within each community, it is theoretically possible, and also practically desirable, to identify common profiles for families and individuals that have similar characteristics related to the seven *W*s. Therefore, it is necessary to develop an integrated theory that will not only consider the strengths of individual theories, but also their constraints and weaknesses for practical application in each community. Under this objective, the following five *fundamental principles* are identified for future social services in combating child abuse and neglect problems within each community:

1. *comprehensiveness* in service programs to cover needs in all seven service domains, which are described later as identification, intervention, treatment, prevention, evaluation, follow-up, and dissemination,

2. *coordination* among service-providing agencies across all domains,

3. *community-based* development of systems, programs, and activities under the consideration of profile characteristics of each community at all ecological levels,

4. *a child- and family-centered* approach in implementation of services with an emphasis on continual long-term improvement and growth processes, and

5. *a multidisciplinary* approach to the development of an integrated theory across different theorizations that can be used by various disciplinary professionals for planning practical strategies in dealing with child abuse and neglect problems.

The topical issues and concerns of different theorizations that have been organized in Chapter 10 (under five ecological levels and two aspects of culture) can theoretically be synthesized into a system of service network that will clearly delineate the seven Ws for each type of maltreatment. For future endeavors toward the development of some system of service network, two components of the psychosemantic process model—behavioral dispositions and affective evaluation—are especially important, because they address the structural and dynamical characteristics of human intrinsic motivations and behavioral dispositions. Therefore, delineation of child victimization processes in terms of the effective evaluation system and behavioral dispositions of the individuals involved (parents, victims, and significant others) will greatly facilitate the systemization of all etiological accounts proposed by different theories. For this reason, three human behavioral dispositions and three basic emotions are briefly introduced as follows:

Three Basic Behavioral Dispositions. As explained in Chapter 9, human behaviors are manifestations of three directional dispositions: (1) *approach*—the readiness for spontaneous and outward actions that can be characterized as being friendly, helpful, happy, and willing; (2) *attack*—the readiness for aggressive or defensive actions that can be characterized as being unfriendly, hostile, critical, and damaging; and (3) *withdrawal*—the readiness for retreat or inhibited actions that can be categorized as depressed, indifferent, ignoring, and unhelpful.

When these dispositions are manifested in overt behaviors by parents in dealing with children, *approach disposition* is likely to result in normal, open-minded, and caring activities; *attack disposition* may result in punitive, closed-minded, and hostile behaviors; and *retreat dispositions* may result in indifferent, absent-minded, and insensitive behavioral patterns.

Three Basic Human Emotions. Manifestation of each behavioral disposition—either "approach" with a socially desirable action, "attack" with abusive behavior, or "retreat" with indifferent attitude—is facilitated by three basic emotions. They are

1. *desire,* the positive attitudes toward self, others, and environment that will facilitate the individual's spontaneous and approaching behaviors in "acting," "reacting," "searching," "helping," and "enjoying";

2. *anger,* the emotional status that derives from frustration or rejection of expressed or implicit desires. This emotion can be characterized in terms of such manners as "hostile," "explosive," "hot-tempered," "domineering," and "single-minded"; and

3. *fear,* a status of depression, anxiety, and uncertainty that will appear in such behavioral patterns as "inaction," "wandering," "avoidance," "ignorance," and "indifference".

These three emotions are directly related to the three behavior dispositions in child-rearing and disciplinary activities. As shown in Table 11.1, *desire* usually elicits active and appropriate parenting practices, such as loving, caring, and guiding; *anger,* due to whatever internal and/or external reasons, might elicit critical, hostile, disciplinary actions that are abusive in nature; and *fear* might elicit passive and withdrawal patterns in parenting that can be characterized by indifference, ignorance, and negligence behaviors.

Table 11.1
Relations between Behavioral Dispositions and Emotions

Behavioral Disposition	Basic Emotions	Behavioral Manifestations
Approach	Desire	Appropriate parenting practices (loving, caring, providing)
Attack	Anger	Abusive and punitive behaviors (verbal attack and physical violence)
Retreat	Fear	Inhibition of desirable behaviors (indifference, ignorance, negligence)

Under normal circumstances, each individual (child as well as adult) has these three emotions exhibited in daily life. However, significant individual differences exist in (1) the tolerance level in accepting real (or imaginary) rejection from others, (2) the persistence level in pursuing desires, and (3) the level of recovering from inhibition and frustration.

Because of such differences, each individual develops distinct coping strategies and habits in handling life situations. In some individuals, unfulfilled desires and needs might lead to severe frustrations and/or inhibitions that can generate abusive attack or neglectful withdrawal in child-rearing practice.

Intervention, prevention, and treatment of child abuse and neglect will require in-depth analyses of the underlying dynamics of each offender in terms of these emotions, dispositions, and general coping behaviors and habits. Analyses of this nature will provide fundamental information as to the real causes of child abuse and neglect and of associated circumstances that contribute to the manifestations and severity of child abuse and neglect.

It should be noted that these three emotions represent the motivational status of child abuse and neglect offenders who may have diverse patterns of associations with target individuals (children and other significant individuals, such as the offender's parents or spouse) and circumstances in different ecological levels (families, workplace, and community). Interactions and/or displacements of these emotions across different target individuals and circumstances frequently result in multiple causalities of child victimization. Many theoretical paradigms successfully demonstrate the complex nature of such interactions.

Therefore, it is important to conduct comprehensive analysis of all topical issues of abuse and neglect in terms of some overall theoretical framework such as the psychosemantic process model. Such analysis should be done not only for different homogeneous subgroups of perpetrators, victims, and abusive and neglectful behaviors, but also for specific characteristics and dynamics of each subgroup. Integration of analytic results should yield valuable profiles that will shed light on the *why, when, where,* and *how* issues for each case of child victimization in any situation.

Seven Comprehensive Service Domains

With such information, a community-based and child/family-centered planning of programs becomes possible. In this respect, Tzeng, Hanner, & Fortier (1988) advocated that a comprehensive community network of services should consist of *seven service domains,* as in Figure 11.2.

1. Identification. The identification domain focuses on the analysis of profile characteristics of victimized children, offenders, and their interactions with respect to three model components of the psychosemantic model: *background characteristics* (e.g., health and intellectual development of the child), *long-term stressors* (health problems, emotional difficulties, etc.), and *short-term stressors* (family crisis related to abuse and neglect). In order to have a full understanding of all the issues involved, the analysis should involve the subjective and objective aspects of cultures of victimized children, offenders, families, and the community. Such information is a prerequisite to the identification of the etiology of child abuse and neglect and also to the development of effective service delivery programs and strategies.

2. Intervention. This domain emphasizes the missions of immediate rescue of victimized children and of the deterrence of abusive or neglecting circumstances. Many programs have been established for these purposes, including crisis centers for child care, crisis counseling, volunteer assistance, parent aides, Parents Anonymous, and telephone hotlines. However, an effective intervention effort must rely on the integration of all community resources across all service and support systems.

Because of the fact that different professionals have different missions in dealing with child abuse and neglect incidents, there exist many intervention models in current use. For example, the medical model emphasizes the assessment and treatment of physical wounds, the psychiatric model emphasizes the treatment of personality disorder of the offenders, the social model emphasizes the improvement and resolution of societal disparities (e.g., unemployment and housing and educational segregations), the *legal model* emphasizes parental rights in continuing custody of child victims, and the criminal model emphasizes the punishment of the offenders.

However, each model alone cannot contribute to all aspects of intervention needs. For example, the psychiatric model accounts for less than 15 percent of the incidents, the social model cannot fully resolve the child abuse and neglect

Figure 11.2
Seven Service Domains of Child Maltreatment

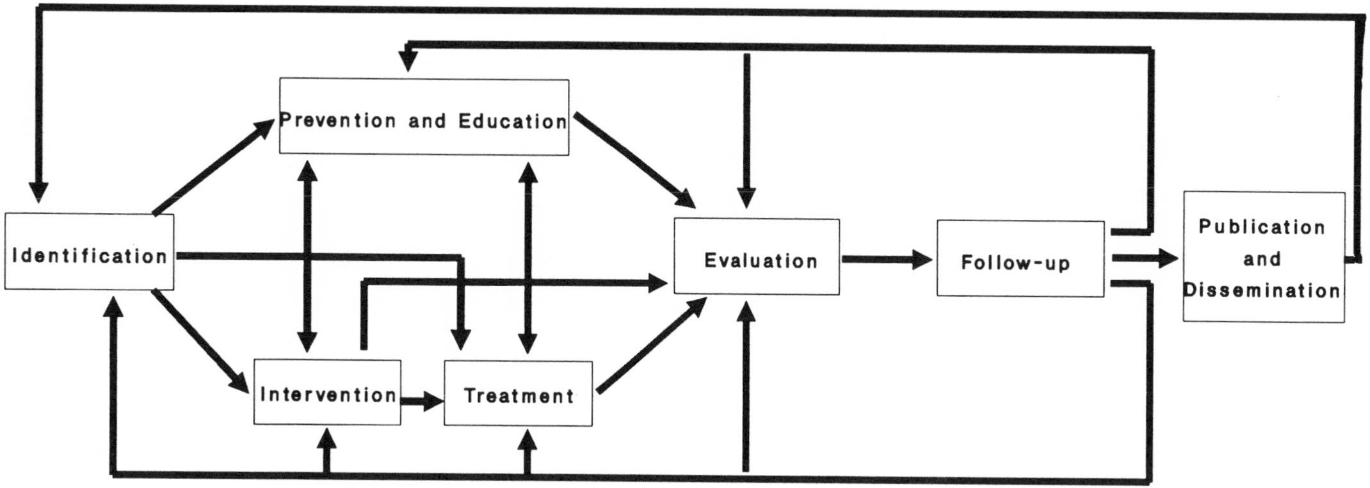

problems by merely working on social disparity issues, the situational model cannot predict many clear behavioral consistencies across various situations, the *legal model* usually fails to uphold family continuity and simultaneously fails to eliminate abusive cycles, and the criminal model fails to deter the occurrence of over 1.7 million cases per year. The sheer emphasis on the criminal model would drain a tremendous amount of human and economic resources without proven evidence of cost-efficient consequences.

3. Treatment. This domain calls for the development and implementation of a comprehensive case treatment and management program that will utilize resources from both the public and private sectors (e.g., hospital, mental health centers, schools, juvenile court, child protection services, and private therapists). For this purpose, it is ideal to develop a multidisciplinary community-based treatment network that will coordinate the service functions of all individual providers. Separate efforts can then be united to work for each type of family.

4. Prevention and Education. Because of individual and family differences in various child abuse and neglect issues, it is necessary to develop a comprehensive prevention and education network within each community. Within this network, many preventative services should be provided such that different subtypes of victimizations or vulnerabilities can be dealt with simultaneously. In addition, this domain emphasizes the implementation of various instructional programs for training professionals, paraprofessionals, volunteers, and the community at large regarding the issue of prevention, identification, and intervention of child abuse and neglect. For such purposes, the community-based information—profile characteristics of victims, perpetrators, at-risk families, and community responses—should be used to maximize the impact of prevention and education efforts.

5. Evaluation. This domain includes two types of evaluation: (1) *process evaluation* of all implementation procedures and strategies across all service domains and (2) *outcome evaluation* of the impact of various programs on changes in individuals, families, and the community. For both evaluations, specific criteria should be established such that the degree of success of individual programs can be objectively assessed.

In addition, evaluation results from separate programs should be aggregated and analyzed from a broad community system-operation perspective. Under this premise, evaluation should focus on overall community resource utilization, program availability and efficiency, and impact and accountability for future program improvement.

6. Follow-up. Ideally, implementation of intervention, treatment, and prevention programs on child abuse and neglect should always result in positive changes at various ecological levels. For example, for vulnerable abusive adults, the services should help them to develop socially acceptable and effective coping mechanisms in dealing with stressful circumstances.

When specific programs for individuals are carried out with suitability and efficiency, intervention in child abuse and neglect usually yields at least a temporary modification of problematic circumstances. However, in some instances, the individual's habits may not be easily and completely replaced with desirable ones. In either case, the effort of outcome evaluation is not sufficient to detect recidivism or qualitative improvement of adverse circumstances. Thus it is necessary to follow the course of changes and related consequences on a long-term basis such that the process and outcome evaluations can continue to ensure the permanent improvement of the situation.

Similarly, follow-up efforts should be carried out at the family and community levels. Since child abuse and neglect is not just the problem of individuals involved, but also an indication of institutionalized dysfunctions in the family and/or community, follow-up efforts should therefore focus not only on comprehensive analysis of all issues and related ecologies involved, but also on longitudinal analysis of progress patterns on a continuing basis.

7. Publication and Dissemination. This domain emphasizes the communication of the information from the above-mentioned six domains of services to professionals and the public. The literature has been criticized for its lack of comprehensive integration and presentation of information from different professionals across different time frames. As a result, professionals in various service facilities frequently operate under the constraints of partial knowledge, biased interest, and/or narrowly focused strategies. To reverse such deficiencies, it is necessary to integrate knowledge from multidisciplinary perspectives and to disseminate such knowledge to all practitioners in different service functions.

Under this premise, the following implementation strategies become important: development of regional resource centers, development of computerized data retrieval systems, organization of a community-based prevention and education network, development of constant in-service training/workshop programs, and publication of documentations in professional journals as well as in the public media.

In an ideal community-based service network, the above seven service domains should be independent of each other in their missions, but interdependent in their purposes and functions. The sum combination of their missions and functions possesses all the necessary properties advocated in the psychosemantic process model: multidisciplinary orientation, comprehensive programs, coordination network, community-based planning, and family-centered approach.

Chapter Twelve

The Nature of Scientific Knowledge and Theories

Tzeng and Jackson (1991) have presented a common methodological framework for the construction and evaluation of scientific theories. This chapter reviews the basic issues on the philosophy, development, and evaluation of contemporary social scientific theories and utilizes the Tzeng and Jackson framework as the model and criteria to evaluate the contemporary child abuse and neglect theorizations presented in the previous chapters.

KNOWLEDGE ACQUISITION AND THE SCIENTIFIC METHOD

Four methods of knowledge acquisition—tenacity, authority, introspection, and science—have prevailed over the course of history. Science is the method by which the most valid and reliable answers to questions regarding human ecological phenomena can be derived.

The scientific method is a rigorous analysis of ecological, animate, as well as inanimate, phenomena and their relationships. This method has three important characteristics: (1) *objectivity* in knowledge-acquiring methods and procedures, (2) *validity* of acquired knowledge with verification and reproduction properties, and (3) *functional generality* of acquired knowledge in usage within each class of ecological phenomena. With these properties, the scientific method is preferred over other methods of knowledge acquisition.

THE PHILOSOPHY OF SCIENCE

Two general philosophical approaches to science have been prevalent in pursuing knowledge acquisition and synthesis: The empirical approach stresses the atheoretical gathering and sorting of facts for which science is considered a *goal*. The theoretical approach considers science as a *method* and stresses knowledge acquisition through empirical theory testing. Theories provide (1) a framework in which to work, (2) economy and efficiency, (3) a clarification of relationships, and (4) the potentiality for predicting and controlling events.

FORMAL THEORIZATION IN THE SOCIAL SCIENCES

There is great diversity among thinkers concerning the variations, developments, modifications, and terminology of the logical structure and empirical foundations of theories. A primary concern of theorization in the social sciences involves the relationship between facts and theories. Facts and theories are viewed as reciprocally complementary in the process of discovery. Both are vital for progression in the social sciences. The four major historical influences on contemporary social theory development are clinical observation, Gestalt psychology, experimentalism, and quantitative methodology.

FORMS OF THEORIES

The meaning of the term *theory* has been approached from many angles. Table 13.1 (Section I) defines the six major conceptualizations of what social scientists mean when they use the term. The two most prevalent forms of social theories are the *summative-induction* and the *functional-deduction* form.

Summative-inductive theories use only those statements (laws) that have been subjected to and overwhelmingly supported by rigorous empirical testing and cumulative evidence. Functional-deductive theories provide a formalized set of logically intertwined definitions, statements, and propositions, which are deliberately subjected to theoretical analyses. Other theoretical modes include the axiomatic form, the model, and the functional theory. Each type of theory has its positive and negative attributes. Overall, the preferred form is the functional-deduction form, because it (1) allows for greater flexibility, (2) permits the use of hypothetical constructs, (3) is generally more efficient and economical, (4) is more applicable to practical problems, and, perhaps most important, (5) is better able to provide an understanding of causality (Tzeng & Jackson, 1990).

THE COMPONENTS OF A THEORY

Although theories may differ in the degree of their scopes and functions, all theories share some basic characteristics in studying a certain domain of ecological phenomena. The core components of a theory generally include (1) operational definitions, (2) postulates, (3) basic principles, (4) hypothetical constructs, (5) independent, dependent, and intervening variables, (6) the hypothesis, and (7) empirical laws. The relationships among these seven components are shown in Figure 12.1.

Each of these basic components is defined in Chapter 13 in Table 13.1 (Section

Figure 12.1
Components of a Scientific Theory

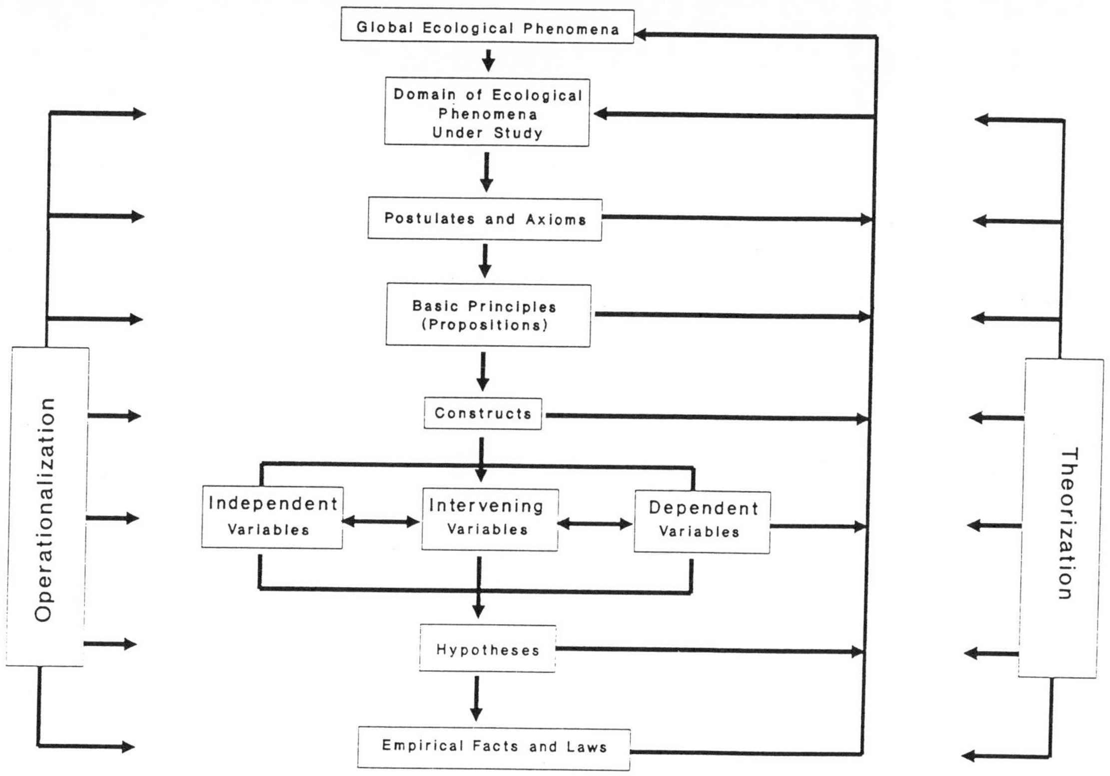

II). These components are interrelated in logical, hierarchial order such that "old" existing theories can be evaluated and "new" theories can be developed.

Dynamics of seven components: The organization of the common components of scientific theories, depicted in Figure 12.1, represents mostly a *deductive* approach to theoretical development and utilization. However, this organization can also be used to characterize the *inductive* form of theoretical generalizations. Empirically, in a scientific study of theoretical constructs and their relationships, two approaches have been most prevalent: conformatory analysis and exploratory investigation.

Conformatory analysis is usually used to validate theoretical constructs and their relationships that are embedded in an existing theory. On the other hand, the exploratory analysis of empirical data can be used to generate new constructs with initially loose conceptions of postulates and principles. Through empirical validations and/or new identifications, resultant facts and laws are used to develop a formal network of theoretical postulates, propositions, and constructs for subsequent inferences to other similar content issues under the same ecological domain.

THE FUNCTIONS OF A THEORY

Social scientists generally agree that a good theory should fulfill six basic functions: (1) decomposition of content issues (operationalization, definitions, and categorization), (2) nomologicalization (systemization of various content issues), (3) establishment of causal relationships, (4) explanation and "postdiction," (5) prediction, and (6) fruitfulness in generation of further research and theorization (Tzeng & Jackson, 1990). In addition, the potential for controlling events is also a desirable seventh, although not always possible, function of a theory. These seven functions are depicted in Figure 12.2.

In evaluating the extent to which the theories of child abuse and neglect fulfill these seven functions, the definitions provided in Table 13.1 (Section III) will be used.

SCIENTIFIC SELF-REGULATION MECHANISMS

The scientific method, through the process of knowledge acquisition, requires that theories build in objective self-regulating mechanisms. These mechanisms usually include (1) the use of experimental and control groups with which research is conducted and results are analytically compared to insure differentiation between them; (2) the use of verification or replication methods to determine the extent to which experimental results are valid and reliable; (3) the utilization of hypothesis testing, by which theoretical postulates and predictions of relationships are empirically evaluated and may be proven incorrect; (4) the documentation of theory, data, methodological procedures, and empirical results such that all aspects of the scientific investigation may be critically examined or

Figure 12.2
Functions of a Scientific Theory

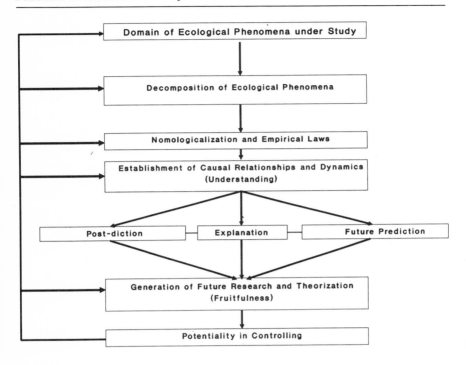

replicated by others. These self-regulatory mechanisms are defined in Table 13.1 (Section IV).

THEORY CONSTRUCTION

There is no single set of proper procedures for developing a good theory. In the literature, there is not even a consensus on what constitutes a theory. Some generally acceptable guidelines may, however, be drawn from the literature. Theorization is not an easy task. It takes many hard hours of concentrated study, examination, and reexamination. It is the antithesis of sloppy thinking, lazy reading, and unconstrained philosophizing. Nine basic steps are recommended by Tzeng and Jackson (1991): (1) specification of the field of study, (2) comprehensive review of the existing literature, (3) development of postulates as theoretical foundations, (4) formulation of a system of organization, (5) development of the theory's basic principles (or propositions), (6) generation of hypotheses from the basic principles, (7) empirical testing of the hypotheses, (8) evaluation and reformulation of propositions, and (9) construction of valid and reliable predictive statements (laws).

THEORY EVALUATION

The major criteria by which any theory may be evaluated are defined in Table 13.1 (Section V). These criteria include (1) comprehensiveness and integration, (2) parsimony, (3) falsifiability and testability, (4) applicability to empirical data (accuracy), (5) fruitfulness, (6) clarity, and (7) operationalization.

All good theories have the utmost objective of being scientific. Therefore, they should strive to achieve the general goals of science: to organize, predict, explain, and provide understanding. Perhaps most important is the theory's capability of generating predictions about when, where, and/or how the event is to transpire. The more successfully a theory is able to predict ecological phenomena, the more successfully the theory may be evaluated (Neel, 1969; Lana, 1976). Post facto accounts are merely descriptive and thus are not sufficient as criteria for a good theory (Neel, 1969).

A good theory should also fulfill all of the theoretical functions outside the general goals of science: They should decompose information, map out systematic relationships, fill in gaps between facts, specify assumed relationships, make accurate predictions, spark empirical research, and ideally provide the potential to control events.

THE FALLACIES AND PITFALLS OF THEORIES

Theories are extremely helpful, indeed essential, in the progression in scientific studies of ecological phenomena. However, as with any good thing, there are some potential drawbacks and inaccuracies associated with theoretical undertakings.

For reasons involving economy and clarity, scientific discoveries are often presented in an idealized simple format. As a result, theories and scientific breakthroughs may appear to have been developed from a common logic applied to all empirical investigations. Such beliefs and other misrepresentations are regarded as common fallacies concerning the nature of theories and their constructions (cf. Marx, 1970). Five common fallacies of scientific theory are the inaccurate beliefs that scientific progress is (1) straightforward, (2) strictly logical in nature, (3) emphasizing only very accurate theories, (4) relying only on grand theories that explain "everything," and (5) always based on experiments designed such that a theory is given full support and/or rejected.

Most theories, especially those describing human subjective cultures, have some potentially adverse conditions (pitfalls) associated with theory formulation. Two common pitfalls of theorizing include (1) becoming emotionally attached to a theory to the point that it is regarded as an "absolute truth" and is adhered to at all costs and (2) the "bandwagon" effect, which refers to the problem of individuals being drawn to a theory because of its popularity, rather than its scientific validity.

ISSUES AND LIMITATIONS IN THEORETICAL ANALYSES

The human ecological environments where social scientific theories are developed and applied can be characterized in terms of various ontological issues that are frequently used in the philosophy of science. Similarly, the theories developed for explaining the ecological environments have to deal with the same and other basic issues. In evaluation of child abuse and neglect theories and models, there are ten common issues that any one behavioral theory should address at some point. These issues are (1) mind versus body, (2) subjectivism versus objectivism, (3) quantification versus qualification, (4) reductionism versus nonreductionism, (5) molar versus molecular, (6) determinism versus teleology, (7) utility versus purity, (8) nature versus nurture, (9) reward versus nonreward, and (10) theoretical singularity versus pluralism. These issues have to be dealt with in varying degrees by every theory on child abuse and neglect etiologies.

The limitations of contemporary social research discussed by Tzeng and Jackson (1991) include the overabundance of indication and the lack of concern with empirical proof, theoretical intricate complexity, prediction utility, and cooperative interaction among different disciplines. There is a further need for coherent linkage between theory, measurement, and statistics. Also, the issue of value neutrality is an important aspect of any research program.

CONCLUSIONS

The delineation of the above issues serves two major purposes. The first is to provide a general view of the position regarding the development and evaluation of a scientific theory in the social and behavioral sciences. The second purpose is to use the information presented in this chapter as the model and criteria for evaluation of all theories on child abuse and neglect presented in this book. Of course, this integration of the nature of scientific knowledge about different theories can be used by other researchers to facilitate their evaluation of existing theories, and also for the development of new theories in the social and behavioral sciences.

For such purposes, the theories and paradigms of child abuse and neglect described in preceding chapters will be evaluated in terms of individual criteria under five general areas: (1) theoretical form (summative inductive, functional deductive, axiomatic, model, and functional), (2) decomposition of theoretical components (hypotheses, operational definitions, hypothetical constructs, independent/dependent variables, and postulates), (3) functions of scientific theories (decomposition, explanation, understanding, prediction, fruitfulness, control, and laws), (4) scientific self-regulation mechanisms (control groups, verification, hypothesis testing, and objectivity/replicability), and (5) theory evaluative criteria (falsifiability, fruitfulness, clarity, operationalization, integration/comprehensiveness, parsimony, and accuracy). The results of this evaluation are the topic of Chapter 13.

Chapter Thirteen

Evaluation of Theoretical Paradigms from Science

This chapter presents a "process" evaluation of the child abuse and neglect theories, models, and paradigms presented in chapters one through nine, in terms of theory constructions in social and behavioral sciences. For this purpose, each theory is evaluated in terms of five major domains of theory construction: (1) form of theory development, (2) decomposition of theoretical components, (3) functions of scientific theories, (4) scientific theory self-regulation mechanisms, and (5) theory evaluative criteria (cf. Tzeng & Jackson, 1991). Within each domain, separate content criteria are developed and used to characterize each theory in terms of three levels of sufficiency in theory construction. Statistical results initially obtained from analyzing individual theories are further used to derive summary statistics for each paradigm across its member theories for each type of maltreatment. In this chapter, a detailed evaluation method is presented first and is followed by summary of the evaluation results on appropriate paradigms for each of the six maltreatment types.

METHOD AND PROCEDURE

The five process evaluation domains for construction of a scientific theory will be used for the evaluation of individual theories and paradigms. The major content criteria for these evaluation domains are described in Table 13.1.

For the domain of theory development forms, each theory is categorized by one of the six theoretical forms. For evaluating individual theories against four other content domains—decomposition of theoretical components, functions of scientific theories, scientific theory self-regulation mechanisms, and theory evaluation criteria—each criterion is considered as a continuum that represents the relative level of satisfaction (from 0% to 100%). Therefore, each theory is judged individually against all 23 content criteria of the four process evaluation domains in Table 13.1. The result on each criterion is further coded in one of three ranks:

Table 13.1
Process Evaluation Domains and Content Criteria for Scientific Theory Construction

----

I. Forms of Theory Development

1. Summative inductive form: Many pieces of empirical data are reduced to a set of generalized statements that have overwhelming empirical support. This form goes from specific to general statements.

2. Functional deductive form: A formalized set of logically intertwined definitions, causal statements, and propositions that are deliberately subjected to empirical testing. This form goes from general to specific statements.

3. Axiomatic form: This form, derived from mathematics, is nearly identical to the functional deductive form, except that the propositions are strictly arranged in a hierarchical order.

4. Model: The theory uses some structures, often borrowed from another discipline, as a means of studying the field in question.

5. Functional theory: The theory is similar to the functional deductive form, except that it is very specific to an empirical study.

6. Perspective: A conceptualization of a topic that lacks scientific formalization in terms of relational statements, objectivity, systemization, and empirical testing.

II. Decomposition of Theoretical Components[a]

1. Postulates: Basic assumptions about the theories that are given and accepted without testing.

2. Operational definitions: Theoretical constructs defined in terms of objective measures that can be empirically demonstrated and tested.

3. Basic principles (propositions): Heuristic relational statements about the ecological characteristics under inquiry.

4. Hypothetical constructs: Statements of relationship involving intangible processes (e.g., fear, hunger, and cognitive map) and usually referred to as "psychological realities" that cannot be directly observed, but merely inferred.

5. Independent, dependent, and intervening variables: The independent variable is an experimental condition manipulated by the researcher for assessment of its impact on other measures known as dependent variables.

Table 13.1 (continued)

6. <u>Hypothesis</u>: A formal empirical statement that predicts a relationship among two or more variables.

7. <u>Empirical facts and laws</u>: A group of empirically derived reliable and valid details tied together by generalized statements describing regularities among observable phenomena.

III. <u>Functions of Scientific Theories</u>

1. <u>Decomposition</u>: The extent to which a theory provides a way of decomposing the global content issues in the field of study into many organizational elements for assessment.

2. <u>Nomologicalization and Law</u>: The extent to which a theory has linked the components and concepts generated through the decompositon process and has generated empirical laws.

3. <u>Understanding</u>: The extent to which a theory is able to identify the causal processes among variables.

4. <u>Explanation</u>: The extent to which a theory explains past events.

5. <u>Prediction</u>: The extent to which a theory attempts to make specific future predictions in the field of study.

6. <u>Fruitfulness</u>: The extent to which the theory stimulates further research and theorization.

7. <u>Control</u>: The potential a theory has to control future events.

IV. <u>Scientific Self-Regulation Mechanisms</u>

1. <u>Control groups</u>: The extent to which empirical studies, designed to support the theory, involve data comparisons with control groups.

2. <u>Verification</u>: Any attempt to provide empirical evidence for the theory.

3. <u>Hypothesis testing</u>: The extent to which the theory tests specific relationships among variables.

4. <u>Objectivity and replicability</u>: The extent to which the constructs of the theory are measured using standard procedures that are amenable to criticism and replication.

(continued)

Table 13.1 (continued)

V.   Theory Evaluative Criteria

1. <u>Integration/comprehensiveness</u>: The degree of grandness or specificity of the theory and the level of culture-ecology units addressed.

2. <u>Parsimony</u>: The extent to which a theory attempts to account for complex ecological phenomena in terms of parsimonious constructs.

3. <u>Falsifiability</u>: The extent to which a theory can be objectively tested or may be proven wrong.

4. <u>Accuracy</u>: The extent to which a theory's predictions are successful, valid, and reliable.

5. <u>Fruitfulness</u>: The extent to which a theory stimulates further research and theorization.

6. <u>Clarity</u>: The extent to which a theory is clear and its statements and variables explicitly defined and consistently used.

7. <u>Operationalization</u>: Defining of variables in terms of objective measures.

----

aFor subsequent evaluation of child abuse and neglect theories, only five of seven theoretical components were used because the basic principles (propositions) criterion appears under the postulates component, and the empirical facts/laws criterion is combined with the "laws component" under the function of the scientific theories category.

with a $+$, 0, or $-$ sign. A $+$ indicates that the theory met the criterion to a very satisfactory degree (75% or higher on the evaluation continuum), a 0 indicates that the theory met the criterion to an average level of satisfaction (between 25% and 75% on the evaluation continuum), and a $-$ indicates that the theory did not meet the minimum level of satisfaction (less than 25% on the continuum).

The present coding system is qualitative in nature. It is used to probe the general level of "achievement" by individual theories against the "process requirements" for constituting scientific theories in social and behavioral sciences. Therefore, it does not represent the substance level of validity of individual theories.

It should be noted that assignment of codings for individual theories under various content evaluation criteria is an extremely difficult task for the following reasons:

1. The theories, models, or perspectives reviewed in this book were developed without a priori common references as identified in scientific theory construction process,

2. different theories have attempted to address different aspects of theoretical and empirical issues in varying degrees of rigor and depth, and

3. global assessment of individual theories will have to involve comparisons of content similarities and differences across different theories. Because of the lack of common references, the derivation of an overall coding for each theory is quite subjective, and thus it may also be subjected to scientific evaluation by itself.

In addition, many theories were developed from completely different theoretical perspectives that make certain evaluative criteria inappropriate (e.g., hypothesis testing of psychiatric postulations and development of empirical laws for biological theories of the incest taboo). Therefore, it seems impossible and also unrealistic to put all individual theories into the same rating schemes for comparisons.

However, the utmost goal of this research effort is to develop child abuse and neglect studies as an integrated discipline by itself in the future. Under this premise, it is not only helpful, but also necessary, to identify the state of affairs of child abuse and neglect etiologies in terms of the process characteristics in developing a scientific theory.

With this mission in mind and despite the constraints involved, individual theories and their paradigms are assessed against the 23 content criteria of the four process evaluation domains (sections II through V in Table 13.1).

The entire evaluation procedure is set for deriving first the codings of individual theories on all evaluative criteria and then summary statistics of each theory across all criteria within each domain for subsequent cross-theory and cross-paradigm comparisons. Empirically, this procedure includes the following six operational steps:

1. Individual theories are analyzed against each content criterion using the previously described three-rank rating scale (+, 0, and −).

2. For each theory, the codings of + and 0 on individual content criteria are transformed to numerical rank scores of 2 and 1, respectively. Summation of such rank scores across the content criterion for each evaluation domain generates the raw rank score for each theory.

3. The raw rank score of each theory is then converted to the proportion with respect to the total possible rank score. This proportion represents the overall achievement score of each theory in a specific domain of theory construction processes.

4. In order to identify the general trend of individual theories across the four evaluation domains (excluding the domain of theoretical form), a total rank score is obtained for each theory across all four domains. In reference to the total possible rank scores, an overall proportion of each theory is finally obtained as a satisfactory index in scientific theory construction process.

5. The above four steps are completed for each theory within each maltreatment type. Based on the results of individual theories, statistics are also compiled for each

Table 13.2
Evaluation of Paradigms in Terms of Theoretical Form

Paradigm	Form of Theory Development					
	Deduction	Induction	Axiomatic	Model	Functional	Perspect
(A) Physical Abuse						
(1) Individual determinants				X		
(2) Sociocultural						X
(3) Individual-environment				X		X
(4) Offender typologies				X		
(5) Family systems						X
(6) Parent-child interactions	X			X		X
(7) Sociobiological				X		
(8) Learning/situational	X					X
(9) Ecological						X
Subtotal	2 (15%)	0 (0%)	0 (0%)	5 (38%)	0 (0%)	6 (
(B) Incest Taboo						
(1) Individual determinants		X				
(2) Sociocultural		X				
(3) Individual-environment	X					
Subtotal	1 (33%)	2 (67%)	0 (0%)	0 (0%)	0 (0%)	0 (
(C) Incestuous Abuse						
(1) Individual determinants						X
(2) Sociocultural						X
(3) Individual-environment	X					
(4) Family systems						X
(5) Ecological		X				
Subtotal	1 (20%)	1 (20%)	0 (0%)	0 (0%)	0 (0%)	3
(D) Sexual Abuse						
(1) Individual determinants				X		X
(2) Sociocultural						X
(3) Individual-environment						X
(4) Offender typologies		X				X
Subtotal	0 (0%)	1 (17%)	0 (0%)	1 (17%)	0 (0%)	4
(E) Psychological Maltreatment						
(1) Ecological						X
Subtotal	0 (0%)	0 (0%)	0 (0%)	0 (0%)	0 (0%)	1
(F) Neglect						
(1) Individual determinants						X
(2) Individual-environment				X		X
Subtotal	0 (0%)	0 (0%)	0 (0%)	1 (33%)	0 (0%)	2 (
Total	4 (13%)	4 (13%)	0 (0%)	7 (23%)	0 (0%)	16 (

paradigm by summary of information across its member theories. These results are presented in Tables 13.2 to 13.7.

6. Finally, information for each paradigm is compiled across all maltreatment types.

Discussion of the results presented in this chapter focus first on paradigm information for individual maltreatment types. Overall summary and discussion about the status of child abuse and neglect theories are presented at the end of this chapter.

Table 13.3
Evaluation of Paradigms in Terms of Theoretical Components

Paradigm	Decomposition of Theoretical Components					Total +/0/-	Rank Score	Achi. (%)
	Hypotheses	Operational Definitions	Hypothetical Constructs	In/Dependent Variables	Postulates			
) Physical Abuse								
1) Individual determinants	-	-	+	+	+	3/0/2	6 (60%)	
2) Sociological	-	0	-	+	+	2/1/2	5 (50%)	
3) Individual-environment	0	-	+	+	+	3/1/1	7 (70%)	
4) Offender typologies	-	-	+	+	+	3/0/2	6 (60%)	
5) Family systems	-	-	-	-	-	0/0/5	0 (0%)	
6) Parent-child interaction	0	0	+	+	0	2/3/0	7 (70%)	
7) Sociobiological	0	0	0	0	+	1/4/0	6 (60%)	
8) Learning/situational	+	0	+	+	+	4/1/0	9 (90%)	
9) Ecological	-	-	0	+	+	2/1/2	5 (50%)	
Subtotal +	1 (11%)	0 (0%)	5 (55%)	7 (78%)	7 (78%)	20 (44%)	51 (57%)	
0	3 (33%)	4 (44%)	2 (22%)	1 (11%)	1 (11%)	11 (24%)		
-	5 (55%)	5 (55%)	2 (22%)	1 (11%)	1 (11%)	14 (31%)		
Incest Taboo								
) Individual determinants	0	0	0	0	0	0/5/0	5 (50%)	
) Sociocultural	+	-	-	+	0	2/1/2	5 (50%)	
) Individual environment	0	0	0	0	0	0/5/0	5 (50%)	
Subtotal +	1 (33%)	0 (0%)	0 (0%)	1 (33%)	0 (0%)	2 (13%)	15 (50%)	
0	2 (67%)	2 (67%)	2 (67%)	2 (67%)	3 (100%)	11 (73%)		
-	0 (0%)	1 (33%)	1 (33%)	0 (0%)	0 (0%)	2 (13%)		
Incestuous Abuse								
) Individual determinants	0	-	0	0	0	0/4/1	4 (40%)	
) Sociocultural	-	-	-	+	0	1/1/3	3 (30%)	
) Individual-environment	0	0	0	+	+	2/3/0	7 (70%)	
) Family systems	-	-	0	+	+	2/1/2	5 (50%)	
) Ecological	-	-	0	+	+	2/1/2	5 (50%)	
Subtotal +	0 (0%)	0 (0%)	0 (0%)	4 (80%)	3 (60%)	7 (28%)	24 (48%)	
0	2 (40%)	1 (20%)	4 (80%)	1 (20%)	2 (40%)	10 (40%)		
-	3 (60%)	4 (80%)	1 (20%)	0 (0%)	0 (0%)	8 (32%)		
Sexual Abuse								
) Individual determinants	0	-	+	+	+	3/1/1	7 (70%)	
) Sociocultural	0	-	-	+	+	2/1/2	5 (50%)	
) Individual-environment	+	-	+	+	+	4/0/1	8 (80%)	
) Offender typologies	0	-	+	0	0	1/3/1	5 (50%)	
Subtotal +	1 (25%)	0 (0%)	3 (75%)	3 (75%)	3 (75%)	10 (50%)	25 (62%)	
0	3 (75%)	0 (0%)	0 (0%)	1 (25%)	1 (25%)	5 (25%)		
-	0 (0%)	4 (100%)	1 (25%)	0 (0%)	0 (0%)	5 (25%)		
Psychological Maltreatment								
Ecological	0	-	0	+	+	2/2/1	6 (60%)	
Subtotal +	0 (0%)	0 (0%)	0 (0%)	1 (100%)	1 (100%)	2 (40%)	6 (60%)	
0	1 (100%)	0 (0%)	1 (100%)	0 (0%)	0 (0%)	2 (40%)		
-	0 (0%)	1 (100%)	0 (0%)	0 (0%)	0 (0%)	1 (20%)		
Neglect								
Individual determinants	+	0	0	+	+	3/2/0	8 (80%)	
Individual-environment	+	+	+	+	+	5/0/0	10 (100%)	
Subtotal +	2 (100%)	1 (50%)	1 (50%)	2 (100%)	2 (100%)	8 (80%)	18 (90%)	
0	0 (0%)	1 (50%)	1 (50%)	0 (0%)	0 (0%)	2 (20%)		
-	0 (0%)	0 (0%)	0 (0%)	0 (0%)	0 (0%)	0 (0%)		
Total 2 +	5 (21%)	1 (4%)	9 (37%)	18 (75%)	16 (67%)	49 (41%)	133 (59%)	
1 0	11 (46%)	8 (33%)	10 (42%)	5 (21%)	7 (29%)	41 (34%)		
-	8 (33%)	15 (62%)	5 (21%)	1 (4%)	1 (4%)	30 (25%)		
all Achievement Score	21 (44%)	10 (21%)	28 (58%)	41 (85%)	39 (81%)	133 (59%)		

Table 13.4
Evaluation of Paradigms in Terms of Scientific Theory Functions

Paradigm		Decomposition	Prediction	Explanation	Understanding	Fruitfulness	Control	Laws	Total +/0/-	Rank Ach Score (%)
(A) Physical Abuse										
(1) Individual determinants		0	0	0	-	0	-	-	0/4/1	4 (28%
(2) Sociocultural		0	0	+	0	+	0	-	2/4/1	8 (57%
(3) Individual-environment		+	0	+	0	0	-	-	2/3/2	7 (50%
(4) Offender typologies		+	-	0	0	-	-	-	1/2/4	4 (28%
(5) Family systems		+	-	+	-	-	-	-	2/0/5	4 (28%
(6) Parent-child interact.		0	0	0	0	0	-	-	0/5/2	5 (36%
(7) Sociobiological		-	0	0	0	0	-	-	0/4/3	4 (28%
(8) Learning/situational		+	+	+	+	0	+	-	5/1/1	11 (79%
(9) Ecological		+	-	0	0	0	-	-	1/3/3	5 (36%
Subtotal	+	5 (55%)	1 (11%)	4 (44%)	1 (11%)	1 (11%)	1 (11%)	0 (0%)	13 (21%)	52 (41%
	0	3 (33%)	5 (55%)	5 (55%)	6 (67%)	6 (67%)	1 (11%)	0 (0%)	26 (43%)	
	-	1 (11%)	3 (33%)	0 (0%)	2 (22%)	2 (22%)	7 (78%)	9 (100%)	24 (34%)	
(B) Incest Taboo										
(1) Individual determinants		-	-	0	0	0	-	-	0/3/4	3 (21%
(2) Sociocultural		0	0	0	0	+	-	-	1/4/2	6 (43%
(3) Individual-environment		0	0	0	0	+	0	-	1/5/1	7 (50%
Subtotal	+	0 (0%)	0 (0%)	0 (0%)	0 (0%)	2 (67%)	0 (0%)	0 (0%)	2 (9%)	16 (38%
	0	2 (67%)	2 (67%)	3 (100%)	3 (100%)	1 (33%)	1 (33%)	0 (0%)	12 (57%)	
	-	1 (33%)	1 (33%)	0 (0%)	0 (0%)	0 (0%)	2 (67%)	3 (100%)	7 (33%)	
(C) Incestuous Abuse										
(1) Individual determinants		0	0	0	0	+	0	-	1/5/1	7 (50%
(2) Sociocultural		-	-	0	0	+	0	-	1/3/3	5 (36%
(3) Individual-environment		0	0	0	0	+	0	-	1/5/1	7 (50%
(4) Family systems		0	-	0	0	0	-	-	0/4/3	4 (28%
(5) Ecological		+	0	0	0	-	0	-	1/4/2	6 (43%
Subtotal	+	1 (20%)	0 (0%)	0 (0%)	0 (0%)	3 (60%)	0 (0%)	0 (0%)	4 (11%)	29 (41%
	0	3 (60%)	3 (60%)	5 (100%)	5 (100%)	1 (20%)	4 (80%)	0 (0%)	21 (60%)	
	-	1 (20%)	2 (40%)	0 (0%)	0 (0%)	1 (20%)	1 (20%)	5 (100%)	10 (29%)	
(D) Sexual Abuse										
(1) Individual determinants		0	0	0	0	+	0	-	1/4/2	6 (43%
(2) Sociocultural		0	-	0	0	+	0	-	1/4/2	6 (43%
(3) Individual-environment		+	+	+	+	+	+	-	6/0/1	12 (86%
(4) Offender typologies		0	0	0	0	0	-	-	0/5/2	5 (36%
Subtotal	+	1 (25%)	1 (25%)	1 (25%)	1 (25%)	3 (75%)	1 (25%)	0 (0%)	8 (29%)	29 (52%
	0	3 (75%)	2 (50%)	3 (75%)	3 (75%)	1 (25%)	1 (25%)	0 (0%)	13 (46%)	
	-	0 (0%)	1 (25%)	0 (0%)	0 (0%)	0 (0%)	2 (50%)	4 (100%)	7 (25%)	
(E) Psychological Maltreatment										
(1) Ecological		+	0	0	0	0	-	-	1/4/2	6 (43%
Subtotal	+	1 (100%)	0 (0%)	0 (0%)	0 (0%)	0 (0%)	0 (0%)	0 (0%)	1 (14%)	6 (43%
	0	0 (0%)	1 (100%)	1 (100%)	1 (100%)	1 (100%)	0 (0%)	0 (0%)	4 (57%)	
	-	0 (0%)	0 (0%)	0 (0%)	0 (0%)	0 (0%)	1 (100%)	1 (100%)	1 (29%)	
(F) Neglect										
(1) Individual determinants		0	0	0	0	+	0	-	1/5/1	7 (50%
(2) Individual-environment		+	+	+	0	+	0	-	4/2/1	10 (71%
Subtotal	+	1 (50%)	1 (50%)	1 (50%)	0 (0%)	2 (100%)	0 (0%)	0 (0%)	5 (36%)	17 (61%
	0	1 (50%)	1 (50%)	1 (50%)	2 (100%)	0 (0%)	2 (100%)	0 (0%)	7 (50%)	
	-	0 (0%)	0 (0%)	0 (0%)	0 (0%)	0 (0%)	0 (0%)	2 (100%)	2 (14%)	
Total	+	9 (37%)	3 (12%)	6 (25%)	2 (8%)	11 (46%)	2 (8%)	0 (0%)	33 (15%)	149 (46%
	0	12 (50%)	14 (58%)	18 (75%)	20 (83%)	10 (42%)	9 (37%)	0 (0%)	83 (38%)	
	-	3 (12%)	7 (29%)	0 (0%)	2 (8%)	3 (12%)	13 (54%)	24 (100%)	52 (24%)	
Total Rank Score (Ach. Score)		30 (63%)	20 (42%)	30 (63%)	24 (50%)	32 (67%)	13 (17%)	0 (0%)	149 (46%)	

Table 13.5
Evaluation of Paradigms in Terms of Scientific Self-Regulation Factors

Paradigm	Self-Regulation Mechanisms						
	Control Groups	Verification	Hypothesis Testing	Objectivity/ Replicability	Total +/0/-	Rank Score	Ach. (%)
A) Physical Abuse							
(1) Individual determinants	-	-	-	-	0/0/4		0 (0%)
(2) Sociocultural	0	+	0	0	1/3/0		5 (62%)
(3) Individual-environment	-	-	-	-	0/0/4		0 (0%)
(4) Offender typologies	-	-	-	-	0/0/4		0 (0%)
(5) Family systems	-	-	-	-	0/0/4		0 (0%)
(6) Parent-child interaction	0	0	0	0	0/4/0		4 (50%)
(7) Sociobiological	0	0	0	0	0/4/0		4 (50%)
(8) Learning/situational	0	0	0	0	0/4/0		4 (50%)
(9) Ecological	0	0	-	-	0/2/2		2 (25%)
Subtotal +	0 (0%)	1 (11%)	0 (0%)	0 (0%)	1 (3%)		19 (26%)
0	5 (55%)	4 (44%)	4 (44%)	4 (44%)	17 (47%)		
-	4 (44%)	4 (44%)	4 (44%)	5 (55%)	18 (50%)		
B) Incest Taboo							
(1) Individual determinants	-	0	-	-	0/1/3		1 (12%)
(2) Sociocultural	0	0	-	-	0/2/2		2 (25%)
(3) Individual-environment	0	0	+	0	1/3/0		5 (62%)
Subtotal +	0 (0%)	0 (0%)	1 (33%)	0 (0%)	1 (8%)		8 (33%)
0	2 (67%)	3 (100%)	0 (0%)	1 (33%)	6 (50%)		
-	1 (33%)	0 (0%)	2 (67%)	2 (67%)	5 (42%)		
C) Incestuous Abuse							
(1) Individual determinants	-	-	-	-	0/0/4		0 (0%)
(2) Sociocultural	-	0	-	0	0/2/2		2 (25%)
(3) Individual-environment	+	+	+	0	3/1/0		7 (87%)
(4) Family systems	-	0	-	-	0/1/3		1 (12%)
(5) Ecological	-	0	-	-	0/1/3		1 (12%)
Subtotal +	1 (20%)	1 (20%)	1 (20%)	0 (0%)	3 (15%)		11 (27%)
0	0 (0%)	3 (60%)	0 (0%)	2 (40%)	5 (25%)		
-	4 (80%)	1 (20%)	4 (80%)	3 (60%)	12 (60%)		
D) Sexual Abuse							
(1) Individual determinants	-	-	-	-	0/0/4		0 (0%)
(2) Sociocultural	-	0	-	-	0/1/3		1 (12%)
(3) Individual-environment	-	+	-	-	1/0/3		2 (25%)
(4) Offender typologies	-	0	-	0	0/2/2		2 (25%)
Subtotal +	0 (0%)	1 (25%)	0 (0%)	0 (0%)	1 (6%)		5 (16%)
0	0 (0%)	2 (50%)	0 (0%)	1 (25%)	3 (19%)		
-	4 (100%)	1 (25%)	4 (100%)	3 (75%)	12 (75%)		
E) Psychological Maltreatment							
(1) Ecological	-	0	-	-	0/1/3		1 (12%)
Subtotal +	0 (0%)	0 (0%)	0 (0%)	0 (0%)	0 (0%)		1 (12%)
0	0 (0%)	1 (100%)	0 (0%)	0 (0%)	1 (25%)		
-	1 (100%)	0 (0%)	1 (100%)	1 (100%)	3 (75%)		
F) Neglect							
(1) Individual determinants	-	0	-	-	0/1/3		1 (12%)
(2) Individual-environment	0	0	-	0	0/3/1		3 (37%)
Subtotal +	0 (0%)	0 (0%)	0 (0%)	0 (0%)	0 (0%)		4 (25%)
0	1 (50%)	2 (100%)	0 (0%)	1 (50%)	4 (50%)		
-	1 (50%)	0 (0%)	2 (100%)	1 (50%)	4 (50%)		
Total +	1 (4%)	3 (12%)	2 (8%)	0 (0%)	6 (6%)		48 (23%)
0	8 (33%)	15 (62%)	4 (17%)	9 (37%)	36 (37%)		
-	15 (63%)	6 (25%)	18 (75%)	15 (62%)	54 (56%)		
Total Rank Score (Ach. Score)	10 (21%)	21 (44%)	8 (17%)	9 (19%)	48 (23%)		

Note: Throughout this chapter, the same coding strategies are applied in assessment of paradigms and individual theories. A "+" means that the paradigm utilized the criteria (e.g., control groups) more than 75 percent of the time, a "0" means that the paradigm utilized the criteria (e.g., control groups) between 25 and 75 percent of the time, a "−" means that the paradigm utilized the criteria (e.g., control groups) less than 25 percent of the time.

263

Table 13.6
Evaluation of Paradigms in Terms of Evaluative Criteria

Paradigms	Falsifiability	Fruitfulness	Clarity	Operational	Integration/ Comprehensive	Parsimony	Accuracy	Total +/0/-/?	Total Ach. Rank (%)
(A) Physical Abuse									
(1) Individual determinants	0	0	+	-	0	0	-	1/4/2/0	6 (43%)
(2) Sociocultural	+	+	+	0	-	0	0	3/3/1/0	9 (64%)
(3) Individual-environment	0	0	+	-	+	+	0	3/3/1/0	9 (64%)
(4) Offender typologies	-	-	+	-	+	0	?	2/1/3/1	5 (36%)
(5) Family systems	+	+	+	-	+	0	?	4/1/1/1	9 (64%)
(6) Parent-child interactions	0	0	+	0	0	0	0	1/6/0/0	8 (57%)
(7) Sociobiological	0	0	+	0	-	0	0	1/5/1/0	7 (50%)
(8) Learning/situational	0	0	+	0	0	0	0	1/6/0/0	8 (57%)
(9) Ecological	-	0	0	-	+	0	?	1/3/2/1	5 (36%)
Subtotal +	2 (22%)	2 (22%)	8 (89%)	0 (0%)	4 (44%)	1 (11%)	0 (0%)	17 (27%)	66 (52%)
0	5 (55%)	6 (67%)	1 (11%)	4 (44%)	3 (33%)	8 (89%)	5 (55%)	32 (51%)	
-	2 (22%)	1 (11%)	0 (0%)	5 (55%)	2 (22%)	0 (0%)	1 (11%)	11 (17%)	
(B) Incest Taboo									
(1) Individual determinants	-	0	+	0	-	-	0	1/3/3/0	5 (36%)
(2) Sociocultural	-	+	0	-	0	0	-	1/3/3/0	5 (36%)
(3) Individual-environment	0	+	+	-	+	0	0	3/4/0/0	10 (71%)
Subtotal +	0 (0%)	2 (67%)	2 (67%)	0 (0%)	1 (33%)	0 (0%)	0 (0%)	5 (24%)	20 (48%)
0	1 (33%)	1 (33%)	1 (33%)	2 (67%)	1 (33%)	2 (67%)	2 (67%)	10 (48%)	
-	2 (67%)	0 (0%)	0 (0%)	1 (33%)	1 (33%)	1 (33%)	1 (33%)	6 (29%)	
(C) Incestuous Abuse									
(1) Individual determinants	0	+	0	-	-	0	?	1/3/2/1	5 (36%)
(2) Sociocultural	0	+	+	-	-	0	0	2/3/2/0	7 (50%)
(3) Individual-environment	0	+	+	0	0	0	0	2/5/0/0	9 (64%)
(4) Family systems	0	0	0	-	0	0	0	0/6/1/0	6 (43%)
(5) Ecological	0	-	0	-	+	0	?	1/3/2/1	5 (36%)
Subtotal +	0 (0%)	3 (60%)	2 (40%)	0 (0%)	1 (20%)	0 (0%)	0 (0%)	6 (18%)	32 (46%)
0	5 (100%)	1 (20%)	3 (60%)	1 (20%)	2 (40%)	5 (100%)	3 (60%)	20 (61%)	
-	0 (%)	1 (20%)	0 (0%)	4 (80%)	2 (40%)	0 (0%)	0 (0%)	7 (21%)	
(D) Sexual Abuse									
(1) Individual determinants	0	+	+	-	0	0	0	2/4/1/0	8 (57%)
(2) Sociocultural	0	+	+	-	0	0	0	2/4/1/0	8 (57%)
(3) Individual-environment	0	+	+	-	+	0	0	3/3/1/0	9 (64%)
(4) Offender Typologies	0	0	0	-	0	0	0	0/6/1/0	6 (43%)
Subtotal +	0 (0%)	3 (75%)	3 (75%)	0 (0%)	1 (25%)	0 (0%)	0 (0%)	7 (25%)	31 (55%)
0	4 (100%)	1 (25%)	1 (50%)	0 (0%)	3 (75%)	4 (100%)	4 (100%)	17 (61%)	
-	0 (0%)	0 (0%)	0 (0%)	4 (100%)	0 (0%)	0 (0%)	0 (0%)	4 (14%)	
(E) Psychological Maltreatment									
(1) Ecological	0	0	+	-	+	0	0	2/4/1/0	8 (57%)
Subtotal +	0 (0%)	1 (100%)	0 (0%)	0 (0%)	1 (100%)	0 (0%)	0 (0%)	2 (28%)	8 (57%)
0	1 (100%)	0 (0%)	1 (100%)	0 (0%)	0 (0%)	1 (100%)	1 (100%)	4 (57%)	
-	0 (0%)	0 (0%)	0 (0%)	1 (100%)	0 (0%)	0 (0%)	0 (0%)	1 (14%)	
(F) Neglect									
(1) Individual determinants	0	+	0	0	+	0	0	2/5/0/0	9 (64%)
(2) Individual-environment	0	+	0	0	0	0	0	1/6/0/0	8 (57%)
Subtotal +	0 (0%)	2 (100%)	0 (0%)	0 (0%)	1 (50%)	0 (0%)	0 (0%)	3 (21%)	16 (60%)
0	2 (100%)	0 (0%)	2 (100%)	2 (100%)	1 (50%)	2 (100%)	2 (100%)	10 (78%)	
-	0 (0%)	0 (0%)	0 (0%)	0 (0%)	0 (0%)	0 (0%)	0 (0%)	0 (0%)	
Total +	2 (8%)	12 (50%)	16 (67%)	0 (0%)	9 (37%)	1 (4%)	0 (0%)	40 (24%)	176 (52%)
0	18 (75%)	10 (42%)	8 (33%)	9 (37%)	10 (42%)	22 (92%)	17 (71%)	94 (56%)	
-	4 (17%)	2 (8%)	0 (0%)	15 (62%)	5 (21%)	1 (4%)	2 (8%)	29 (17%)	
Total Rank Score (Ach. Score)	22 (46%)	34 (71%)	40 (83%)	9 (19%)	28 (58%)	24 (50%)	17 (35%)	176 (52%)	

Table 13.7
Total Rank Scoring of Paradigms in Each Maltreatment Type for Each Evaluative Domain

Theory	Self-Regulation	Functions of Science/Theory	Theoretical Components	Evaluative Criteria	Total Rank	Total Ach.(%)
		Evaluative Domain				
Maximum Score Possible	8 (100%)	14 (100%)	10 (100%)	14 (100%)	46	(100%)
(A) Physical Abuse						
(1) Individual determinants	0 (0%)	4 (28%)	6 (60%)	6 (43%)	16	(35%)
(2) Sociocultural	5 (62%)	8 (57%)	5 (50%)	9 (64%)	27	(59%)
(3) Individual-environment	0 (0%)	7 (50%)	7 (70%)	9 (64%)	23	(50%)
(4) Offender typologies	0 (0%)	4 (28%)	0 (0%)	5 (36%)	9	(19%)
(5) Family systems	0 (0%)	4 (28%)	6 (60%)	9 (64%)	19	(41%)
(6) Parent-child interaction	4 (50%)	5 (36%)	7 (70%)	8 (57%)	24	(52%)
(7) Sociobiological	4 (50%)	4 (28%)	6 (60%)	7 (50%)	21	(46%)
(8) Learning/situational	4 (50%)	11 (79%)	9 (90%)	8 (57%)	32	(69%)
(9) Ecological	2 (25%)	5 (36%)	5 (50%)	5 (36%)	17	(37%)
(subtotal)	19 (26%)	52 (41%)	51 (57%)	66 (52%)		
(B) Incest Taboo						
(1) Individual determinants	1 (12%)	3 (21%)	5 (50%)	5 (36%)	14	(30%)
(2) Sociocultural	2 (25%)	6 (43%)	5 (50%)	5 (36%)	18	(39%)
(3) Individual-environment	5 (62%)	7 (50%)	5 (50%)	10 (71%)	27	(59%)
(subtotal)	8 (33%)	10 (38%)	15 (50%)	20 (48%)		
(C) Incestuous Abuse						
(1) Individual determinants	0 (0%)	7 (50%)	4 (40%)	5 (36%)	16	(35%)
(2) Sociocultural	2 (25%)	5 (36%)	3 (30%)	7 (50%)	17	(37%)
(3) Individual-environment	7 (87%)	7 (50%)	7 (70%)	9 (64%)	30	(65%)
(4) Family systems	1 (12%)	4 (28%)	5 (50%)	6 (43%)	16	(35%)
(5) Ecological	1 (12%)	6 (43%)	5 (50%)	5 (36%)	17	(37%)
(subtotal)	11 (27%)	29 (41%)	24 (48%)	32 (46%)		
(D) Sexual Abuse						
(1) Individual determinants	0 (0%)	6 (43%)	7 (70%)	8 (57%)	21	(46%)
(2) Sociocultural	1 (12%)	6 (43%)	5 (50%)	8 (57%)	19	(41%)
(3) Individual-environment	2 (25%)	12 (86%)	8 (80%)	9 (64%)	31	(67%)
(4) Offender typologies	2 (25%)	5 (36%)	5 (50%)	6 (43%)	18	(39%)
(subtotal)	5 (16%)	29 (52%)	25 (62%)	31 (55%)		
(E) Psychological Maltreatment						
(1) Ecological	1 (12%)	6 (43%)	6 (60%)	8 (57%)	21	(46%)
(F) Neglect						
(1) Individual determinants	1 (12%)	7 (50%)	8 (80%)	9 (64%)	25	(54%)
(2) Individual-environment	3 (37%)	10 (71%)	10 (100%)	8 (57%)	31	(67%)
(subtotal)	4 (25%)	17 (61%)	18 (90%)	16 (60%)		59%
(Overall)	(23%)	(46%)	(59%)	(53%)		(46%)

PHYSICAL ABUSE

The physical abuse maltreatment category includes nine paradigms of theorization: (1) individual determinants, (2) sociocultural determinants, (3) individual-environment interaction, (4) offender typologies, (5) family systems, (6) parent-child interaction, (7) sociobiological determinants, (8) learning/ situational model, and (9) ecological perspectives. Together, these nine paradigms represent 24 individual theories.

Form of Theoretical Development

In reference to the six basic forms of theory construction—summative inductive, functional deductive, axiomatic, model, functional, and perspective—some paradigms include theories with different theoretical forms. Therefore, the orientation forms in Table 13.2 (A) do not add up to nine. Two (15%) physical abuse paradigms are *functional* deductive, five (38%) are primarily models, and six (46%) are classified as perspectives. No theories utilize the inductive, axiomatic, or functional modes of theorization.

The functional deductive theoretical form, evaluated most positively in the previous chapter, is utilized by only two paradigms (i.e., the parent-child interaction and the learning/situation paradigms).

In terms of the member theories of the paradigms, three physical abuse theories utilize deductive theorization: (1) transactional, (2) social learning, and (3) coercion. Each of these theories are also ranked in the top ten of physical abuse theories in terms of an overall satisfaction index across the four evaluative domains.

Decomposition of Theoretical Components

As shown in Table 13.3 (A), five theoretical components are used for evaluation of the decomposition process in theory construction. They are (1) hypotheses, (2) operational definitions, (3) hypothetical constructs, (4) independent/dependent variables, and (5) postulations.

The majority of the theoretical paradigms do utilize the components of independent/dependent variables (loosely, not empirically, defined) and postulates (also loosely defined) to an adequate degree. That is, 78 percent of the paradigms are given positive evaluations, and 11 percent neutral evaluations, in terms of using independent/dependent variables. On the postulates component, 78 percent of the theories are ranked highly (+), 11 percent moderately (0), and 11 percent minimally (−).

Hypothetical constructs are utilized significantly (+) by 55 percent of the paradigms, moderately (0) by 22 percent, and minimally or not at all (−) by 22 percent.

On the negative side, two very important components, hypotheses and operational definitions, are not utilized by a majority of the paradigms, with 0 percent for the positive (+) rankings, 55 percent for the negative (−) rankings, and 33 percent for the neutral (0) ranks on the hypothetical construct, and 44 percent on the operational definitions.

Total rank scores for the nine individual paradigms range from 0 (0%) to 9 (90%). The overall achievement score across all nine paradigms is 57 percent.

The individual determinants paradigm has a total achievement score of 6 (or 60% in achievement score), with positive ratings on the theoretical components of hypothetical constructs, independent/dependent variables, and postulates, and negative ratings on the components of hypotheses and operational definitions.

The sociocultural paradigm has an overall achievement score of 50 percent, with positive evaluations on the components of independent/dependent variables and postulates, a neutral evaluation on the operational definitions component, and negative evaluations on the hypothetical constructs and hypotheses components.

The individual-environment interaction paradigm has a total achievement score of 7 (70%), with positive ratings on the components of independent/dependent variables, postulates, and hypothetical constructs, a neutral rating on the hypotheses component, and a negative rating on the operational definitions component.

The offender typologies paradigm, failing to address any of the theoretical components at a significant level, has all negative evaluations, for a total achievement score of 0 percent.

The family systems paradigm has a total achievement score of 60 percent. It does well in the areas of hypothetical constructs, independent/dependent variables, and postulates, but falls short in the hypotheses and operational definitions components.

The parent-child interaction paradigm, with an overall achievement score of 70 percent, receives the second highest ranking in this theory decomposition domain along with the individual-environment interaction paradigm. It receives positive ratings on the components of hypothetical constructs and independent/dependent variables, and neutral ratings on the components of hypotheses, operational definitions, and postulates. The sociobiological paradigm has a total achievement score of 60 percent. It receives neutral scores in all areas except for the postulations component, which is given a positive evaluation.

The sociobiological, parent-child interaction, and learning/situational paradigms have neutral to positive ratings on all five components. That is, the learning/situational paradigm receives a nearly perfect overall achievement score of 90 percent for the domain of theoretical components. It ranks positively in all areas except for the operational definitions component, which receives a neutral mark.

Finally, the ecological paradigm scores relatively low, with a total achievement rank score of 50 percent. It receives two positive ratings on the components of independent/dependent variables and postulates, one neutral rating on the hypothetical constructs component, and two negative ratings on the operational definitions and hypotheses components.

In summary, across the nine physical abuse paradigms, an overall achievement score of 57 percent suggests poor to moderate fulfillment of the requirement of theoretical decomposition. However, some paradigms are apparently superior to others. For example, while the learning/situational paradigm has an achievement score of 90 percent, the offender typologies paradigm has a 0 percent score value.

Overall, there is a clear need for all theories to devote more concentration on the empirical aspects of theoretical components, especially in hypotheses and operational definitions, and perhaps also in specifying the exact role of hypothetical constructs in their empirical orientations. The independent/dependent variables and postulates components, on the other hand, have been sufficiently delineated, but could be better grounded in an empirical milieu whereby specifications of various operational conditions could be thoroughly established.

Functions of Scientific Theories

A good theory should fulfill seven basic scientific theoretical functions. It should (1) decompose the data on a given subject, (2) explain past events, (3) provide a means of understanding current events, (4) make predictions concerning future events, (5) stimulate further research and theorization, (6) provide the potential for controlling events, and (7) establish empirical laws concerning events.

The mean average of achievement scores across the nine physical abuse paradigms is 5.78 (41%) out of a possible maximum score of 14 (or 100% achievement score, cf. Table 13.4 [A]). This suggests that the nine paradigms of physical abuse as a whole do not adequately meet the requirements dictated by the functions of scientific theories. However, some paradigms have established decent foundations, with over 50 percent in achievement scores.

Three paradigms that are "best" at fulfilling the function requirements of scientific theories are the learning/situational (total achievement score of 79%), sociocultural (57% achievement score), and individual-environment (50% in achievement score). The least favorable paradigms are the individual determinants, offender typologies, family systems, and sociobiological, each with an achievement score of only 28 percent (see Table 13.4 [A]).

Of the seven functions, decomposition of content issues is the most successful component, accomplished by five of the nine paradigms. Most of the paradigms do a good job (about 50% of achievement score) at four other components— explaining the past, understanding the present, predicting the future, and stimulating further research.

On the other hand, all paradigms of child physical abuse are exceedingly lacking in the functions of controlling the event (with 78% negative ratings) and establishing empirical laws (with 100% negative ratings).

These results clearly suggest that current theoretical perspectives need a comprehensive analysis of issues in order to establish empirical laws about child physical abuse phenomena such that the control of continuing abuse may become possible.

Scientific Self-Regulation Mechanisms

In reference to the four scientific self-regulation mechanisms—control groups, verification, hypothesis testing, and objectivity/replicability, all nine physical abuse paradigms rate very poorly.

Out of the 36 codings from the combinations of nine (paradigms) by four (mechanisms) in Table 13.5 (A), only one entry (3%) is rated positively (+), about half of the entries (47%) are rated as neutral (0), and half (50%) are rated negatively (−). The average rank score is 2.11 and the average achievement score is 26 percent from a possible maximum rank score of 8, or 100 percent in achievement.

Between-paradigm comparisons indicate that the sociocultural paradigm is the best in terms of all four self-regulation mechanisms, especially in its attempt at verification through empirical analyses. The parent-child interaction, sociobiological, and learning/situational paradigms all do relatively well (each has neutral codings across all four criteria). However, four clinically based paradigms—the individual determinants, individual-environment interactions, offender typologies, and family systems—rate very poorly, with 0 scores in overall achievement.

Specifically, hypothesis testing has been the minimal concern for most theoretical paradigms of child physical abuse. It is used rarely (−) by 55 percent of the paradigms and only occasionally (0) by 44 percent of the paradigms. None of the paradigms have positive codings on the hypothesis testing component.

This result is consistent with the fact that the components of stipulating objective, replicable methods and of using control groups receive minimal rank codings from most paradigms. That is, no paradigm is rated positively (+) on these criteria; 55 percent of the paradigms receive neutral ratings on the control groups component, and 44 percent receive neutral ratings on the objectivity and replicability component. Forty-four percent of the paradigms are rated negatively on the control groups component, and 55 percent are rated negatively on the objectivity/replicability component.

The verification component (assessing theoretical propositions by objective methods) also receives little attention. Only the sociocultural paradigm is rated positively. Of the remaining eight paradigms, half are considered neutral in adopting various verification procedures and the other half are considered significantly deficient in this vital area.

Theory Evaluative Criteria

Seven evaluative criteria mentioned in Table 13.1 are used to identify the strengths and deficiencies of the nine physical abuse paradigms. The seven criteria are (1) falsifiability (can the theory be objectively tested and possibly proven wrong?), (2) fruitfulness (has the theory stimulated the field and generated further research and theorization?), (3) clarity (is the theory clearly and logically presented?), (4) operationalization (does the theory operationalize its concepts and variables?), (5) integration/comprehensiveness (does the theory manage to include and integrate all of the important findings within its scope?), (6) parsimony (is the theory kept as simple as possible or does it contain any parsimony components?), and (7) accuracy (is the theory correct or accurate in its predictions?).

The nine physical abuse paradigms accumulate a grand total of a 52 percent achievement score, indicating a rather dismal overall situation in the domain of evaluative criteria (see Table 13.6 [A]).

Among the seven criteria, *clarity* is most satisfactory, because 89 percent of the paradigms are positively evaluated (the only exception is that the ecological paradigm is given a neutral evaluation). None of the remaining criteria receive over 50 percent of the paradigms with positive (+) ratings. In fact, the next best criterion is integration/comprehensiveness, but it has only 44 percent of the paradigms being evaluated positively.

The operationalization criterion receives the least amount of positive or neutral ranks. Therefore, it has the highest negative (−) rating from 55 percent of the paradigms. This seems to reflect the lack of rigorous empirical research in the field of child physical abuse. Generally speaking, operationalization is associated primarily with experimental or other types of empirical studies.

The extent of the accuracy criterion is difficult to access because of the great lack of empirical testing of theories. Therefore, three paradigms (including 12 member theories) are given questionable (?) codings to reflect such deficiency. None of the paradigms are given a positive mark for accuracy. One is given a negative mark (the individual determinants paradigm) and five other paradigms are given neutral marks (sociocultural, individual-environment, parent-child interaction, sociobiological, and learning/situational).

Comparisons across all seven evaluation criteria indicate that none of the nine paradigms are outstanding or even approach 75 percent of the overall achievement scores. The three leading paradigms, which have the highest achievement score of 64 percent, are the sociocultural, individual-environment, and family systems paradigms.

In addition, three other paradigms have achievement scores of 50 percent or more: parent-child interaction (57%), learning/situational (57%), and sociobiological (50%).

The remaining paradigms score less than 50 percent. The individual determinants paradigm receives 43 percent, the offender typologies paradigm receives 36 percent, and the ecological paradigm also receives 36 percent.

In summary, all nine paradigms of child physical abuse are deficient in the areas of operationalism, accuracy, fruitfulness, integration/comprehensiveness, and falsifiability. This is definitely related to the general lack of empiricism in the field. However, this result may also indicate a transitional stage in child abuse and neglect theorization. For future development of a comprehensive theory, the current state of knowledge (especially in clarity and parsimony criteria) indicates that base data have been accumulated and basic organizational schemes have been worked out. Therefore, the realm of theory building seems to be proceeding in the direction of better and more stringent qualifications.

INCEST TABOO

The incest taboo category consists of three paradigms—individual determinants, sociocultural, and individual-environment interaction—representing the biological, normative, and biosocial theories.

Theoretical Form

The three paradigms of incest taboo cover two basic types of theoretical forms. The theories under the individual determinants and sociocultural paradigms are of the inductive type, whereas the theory under the individual-environment paradigm is classified as a deductive type (see Table 13.2 [B]).

Essentially this result means that two (67%) of the three theories designed to explain the etiology and maintenance of incest taboo phenomena are formed by analyzing empirical social phenomena and then reducing the information to abstract statements.

Decomposition of Theoretical Components

In terms of the five theoretical components, each of the incest taboo paradigms has a total achievement score of 50 percent in Table 13.3 (B). Between the individual determinants and individual-environment paradigms, no variability exists because both were given neutral scores across all five components.

The sociocultural paradigm is evaluated positively in terms of hypotheses and independent/dependent variables, negatively in terms of operational definitions and hypothetical constructs, and neutrally in terms of operational definitions.

Functions of Scientific Theory

The average achievement score for the three paradigms is 38 percent (see Table 13.4 [B]). This low score is indicative of the nature of the query under investigation. It is difficult to conceive of an incest taboo as a dependent variable that may be, for example, predicted to occur under certain circumstances.

Among the three components, the individual-environment interaction paradigm has better functions (50%) than the sociocultural paradigm (43%), which is superior to the individual determinants paradigm (21%).

The function of being *fruitful* is the only area that receives any positive ratings. Both the sociocultural and individual-environment paradigms are rated positively in this respect. Overall, positive evaluations account for only 9 percent of the total 21 evaluation entries. The majority of the evaluations under this domain for the incest taboo category are of a neutral nature (57%). Seven (or 33%) of the 21 entries are given negative evaluations. Specifically, the functions of *controlling future events* and *generating empirical laws* receive most negative ratings.

These three paradigms also do not do well under the functions of *decomposition* and *prediction*. For these two functions, two of the paradigms are rated neutral and one negative. It should be noted that successful "prediction" reflects some successful empirical studies investigating aspects of incest taboos. It does not mean that the paradigms are engaged in predicting an incest taboo per se.

Self-Regulation Mechanisms

The three paradigms of the incest taboo are also rated poorly on four *self-regulation* criteria, with a mean average achievement score of 33 percent. Of the 12 evaluation entries in Table 13.5 (B), only one (8%) manages a positive scoring: The individual-environment paradigm engages in *hypothesis testing*. This is due primarily to the fact that a number of anthropological studies have conducted empirical studies of the biosocial theory in natural settings (for example, Fox, 1967; Westermarck, 1921; Wolf, 1970). On the contrary, the other two paradigms (individual determinants and sociocultural) receive negative ratings on the hypothesis testing criterion.

The *utilization of control groups* (two neutral evaluations and one negative evaluation) and *verification procedures* (three neutral evaluations) receives the most, albeit still not compelling, support from these paradigms. This reflects the efforts of the biological theory to comparatively test the physical effects of incest using nonincestuous comparative control groups (e.g., Shull & Neel, 1965; Adams & Neel, 1967). It also reflects the research effort of the biosocial theory under the individual-environment paradigm (for example, by Parker & Parker, 1986).

Evaluative Criteria

Under the domain of evaluative criteria, the three incest taboo paradigms again do rather poorly, obtaining an achievement score of 48 percent (see Table 13.6 [B]). Of the total seven by three (21 entries) matrix structure, 5 (24%) entries are rated positive, 10 (48%) neutral, and 6 (29%) negative. This indicates that the overall evaluation of incest taboo theories is quite inadequate. As far as individual evaluation criteria are concerned, *fruitfulness, clarity,* and *integration* receive positive ratings, whereas the *falsifiability* criterion receives the most negative rating. The above results clearly suggest an emphasis on subjective introspection about incest taboo by biological and normative theorists.

INCESTUOUS ABUSE

There are six theories of incestuous abuse organized under five paradigms. The individual determinants paradigm includes the humanistic theory; the sociocultural paradigm includes the patriarchal theory; the individual-environment paradigm includes the biosocial/attachment theory; the family systems paradigm includes the family survival and endogamous theories; and the ecological paradigm includes the grounded theoretical model.

Theoretical Form

Of the five incestuous abuse paradigms, three (60%—individual determinants, sociocultural, and family systems) are labeled as perspectives, one (20%—individual-environment interaction) as a deductive form, and one (20%—the ecological paradigm) as an inductive form of theory (see Table 13.2 [C]).

This indicates a significant lack of formal theorization in the field of child incestuous abuse. The exceptions, represented by the *deductive* biosocial/attachment theory of Parker and Parker (1986) and the *inductive* grounded theoretical model of Vander Mey and Neff (1986), represent some of the best efforts in the field. While the biosocial/attachment theory tends to be more empirical in nature, it lacks somewhat in comprehensiveness. Conversely, while the grounded theoretical model tends to be comprehensive, it tends to lack empirical rigor. Some type of synthesis of these two approaches may be attainable in the near future. Overall, however, the deductive, empirical approach provides the greatest potential for generating accurate progression in the field.

Decomposition of Theoretical Components

The five paradigms of incestuous abuse do not fare well in terms of the decomposition of theoretical components. The overall average achievement score is 48 percent across all five domain factors (see Table 13.3 [C]). Of a total of 25 evaluation units for five theoretical paradigms on five components, only 7 (28%) are positive evaluations, 10 (40%) are neutral evaluations, and 8 (32%) are negative evaluations.

Two theoretical components used by most of the incest paradigms are independent/dependent variables and postulates, with the former being used profusely by 80 percent of the paradigms (i.e., the sociocultural, individual-environment interaction, family systems, and ecological paradigms) and scarcely by one (20%) of the paradigms (i.e., the individual determinants). On the other hand, the postulation component is utilized amply by three (60%) of the paradigms (individual-environment interaction, family systems, and ecological) and to a smaller extent by two (40%) of the paradigms (individual determinants and sociocultural).

Hypothetical constructs are used moderately by four (80%) of the paradigms (individual determinants, individual-environment interaction, family systems, and ecological) and are excluded by one (20%) of the paradigms (the sociocultural). As stated previously, hypothetical constructs are not necessarily considered an indispensable attribute by all scientists, and therefore evaluation in terms of such a mechanism should be done with caution.

Two theoretical components least used by any of the paradigms are hypothesis and operational definitions. Testing hypotheses are disregarded at least 75 percent of the time by the sociocultural, family systems, and ecological paradigms (60% of the paradigms) and moderately by the individual determinants and individual-environment paradigms.

Operational definitions are disregarded by four (80%) paradigms (individual determinants, sociocultural, family systems, and ecological), and somewhat by one (20%) of them (the individual-environment paradigm).

Functions of Scientific Theory

The five incestuous abuse paradigms are given an overall achievement score of 41 percent (see Table 13.4 [C]). Only 4 (11%) of all 35 possible ratings are given a positive rating, 21 (60%) are rated neutral, and 10 (29%) are rated negatively.

Overall, only the fruitfulness function is given a reasonably acceptable rating of 60 percent, with three of the paradigms scoring pluses, one a zero, and one a minus. This indicates that these paradigms have generally been successful in terms of generating research and further theorization. However, their research efforts have apparently not been of significant value or rigor as indicated by the uniform negative evaluations (100%) on the development of empirical "laws" across all five paradigms and also by 40 percent negative and 60 percent neutral evaluations on the "prediction" function.

On the decomposition function, only the ecological paradigm fulfills it in a positive way, three (60%) of the paradigms (individual determinants, individual-environment interaction, and family systems) are partially committed (neutral), and the sociocultural paradigm is quite neglectful (negative) in terms of decomposition.

The function of providing the potential to control events (e.g., incestuous abuse) is not a positive attribute of any of the paradigms, with four (80%) paradigms being neutral in this respect and one paradigm being negatively evaluated.

Finally, the five paradigms (100%) uniformly lack *explanatory power* and also fail to perform the understanding function. Individually, the individual-environment interaction and the individual determinants paradigms rank the highest, even though each obtains only a total achievement score of 50 percent. The ecological paradigm ranks second, with an achievement score of 43 percent, and the sociocultural and family systems paradigms rank last, with achievement scores of 36 percent and 28 percent, respectively.

Self-Regulation Mechanisms

Overall, the average achievement score for the five paradigms is only 27 percent, indicating a general lack of concern about self-regulation issues in theory development for incestuous abuse (see Table 13.5 [C]). Individually, the individual-environmental perspective is the only paradigm that has a decent achievement score (87%). The remaining four paradigms obtain extremely poor scores (all less than 26%). Therefore, it is clear that the individual determinants, family systems, and ecological paradigms are inadequate across all four self-regulation mechanisms. This reflects the clinical, as well as exploratory, nature of these paradigms and their failure to incorporate rigorous scientific methodology into theoretical postulations. In short, these paradigms usually excel in organizing, classifying, and conceptualizing complex phenomena, such as incest, but lack the means of specifying and testing exact relationships among their respective theoretical constructs or components. Therefore, these paradigms usually fail to produce empirical evidence to substantiate their theoretical assertions.

Evaluative Criteria

An overall achievement score of 46 percent is obtained for the five theoretical paradigms across the seven evaluative criteria. Of the 35 possible evaluative entries generated in Section C of Table 13.6, 6 (18%) are positive, 20 (61%) are neutral, and 7 (21%) are negative evaluations.

Most of the paradigms (60%) are considered fruitful in providing good stimulation to the field. For example, the sociocultural paradigm, although it has not been comprehensive or operational most of the time, has generated much research and healthy debate.

None of the other criteria are considered to be successfully fulfilled by any of the paradigms. Falsifiability and parsimony are both rated as neutral across all five paradigms.

In terms of clarity, two paradigms (sociocultural and individual-environment interaction) are rated positively and the others are rated as neutral.

The sociocultural, individual-environment interaction, and family systems paradigms are considered somewhat accurate, but not to an adequate degree. The individual determinants and ecological paradigms could not be evaluated in this realm because of their lack of empirical research.

In terms of operationalization of variables, four (80%) of the paradigms fail extensively. Only one paradigm—the individual-environment interaction—manages to obtain a neutral score in this category.

Finally, the ecological paradigm scores the only positive mark under the criterion of integration/comprehensiveness. The individual-environment interaction and family systems paradigms both obtain neutral scores, and the individual determinants and sociocultural paradigms are rated with negative marks for this area.

Overall, the five theoretical paradigms are about at the same level of inadequacy across the seven criteria for constructing any theory as a rigorous science.

SEXUAL ABUSE

There are four paradigms of sexual abuse involving six theories: (1) individual determinants (psychoanalytic and psychiatric theories), (2) sociocultural (socialization theory), (3) individual-environment interaction (four preconditions model), and (4) offender typologies (theories of sexual offender types and female abusers). The following evaluation focuses on these four paradigms.

Theoretical Form

Three forms of theorization are utilized by four paradigms of child sexual abuse (Table 13.2 [D]): The individual determinants paradigm utilizes both forms of model and perspective; the sociocultural and individual-environment paradigms utilize only the perspective form; while the offender typology paradigm utilizes the inductive and perspective forms.

Overall, the perspective form is used by all paradigms, and the model form is utilized by only one paradigm. This suggests that, as is the case for other child abuse and neglect types, formal theorization is still a significantly deficient area.

Decomposition of Theoretical Components

A grand achievement score of 62 percent is obtained with half of 25 evaluation entries marked positive, 25 percent marked neutral, and 25 percent marked negative (see Table 13.3 [D]).

Three components used most often by the four paradigms are: (1) independent/dependent variables, (2) postulates, and (3) hypothetical constructs. Each of these components is utilized by 75 percent of the paradigms under consideration.

The hypotheses component is used to a significant extent by only one paradigm (the individual-environment interaction) and to a mediocre extent by the other paradigms. None of the paradigms, however, approach the utilization of operational definitions with any serious effort. Therefore, except for the operational definitions component, four other components are emphasized by all sexual abuse paradigms.

Functions of Scientific Theory

The overall total achievement score is 52 percent across all paradigms of sexual abuse under the domain of scientific theorization functions (see Table 13.4 [D]). Of the 28 possible evaluative entries, 8 (29%) are positive, 13 (46%) are neutral, and 7 (25%) are negative. This clearly indicates a lack of general functional utility in the field.

It appears that the most successfully established criterion is the fruitfulness function, with a majority (75%) of the paradigms (individual determinants, sociocultural, and individual-environment interaction) being positively evaluated and none of the paradigms being negatively evaluated in this respect.

Three criteria that are least successfully fulfilled are the establishment of laws, the potential to control, and the ability to predict events. None of the paradigms has generated any empirical laws; only one paradigm (individual-environment interaction) is successful in predictions and in establishing a potential for controlling events. The individual-environment paradigm also successfully attains the functions of decomposition, explanation, and understanding. Therefore, a cross-paradigm comparison clearly indicates that the individual-environment interaction perspective, which is represented here by Finkelhor's (1986) four-preconditions theory of child sexual abuse, has been most successful in terms of fulfilling the functional criteria of a scientific theory. Its total achievement score of 86 percent is twice as high as that of the next highest (sociocultural) paradigm.

Self-Regulation Mechanisms

Overall, the four paradigms of sexual abuse evaluated very poorly in reference to the four self-regulation criteria. The average total achievement score is only 16 percent. There are only one positive (6%) and three neutral (19%) ratings out of all 16 possible evaluative entries in Table 13.5 (D). The remaining 12 entries (75%) are given negative ratings.

A cross-paradigm comparison indicates that the individual determinants paradigm is most inadequate on all four evaluation criteria: the use of control groups, verification, hypothesis testing, and objectivity/replicability.

The sociocultural paradigm does not fare much better, ranking negatively in all but the verification category. A neutral ranking in verification reflects this paradigm's empirical analysis of sociocultural phenomena (e.g., macrological statistics from governmental sources or telephone surveys). These types of analysis are informative, but generally are not conducted in a clearly defined theoretical framework that specifies predictive causal relationships.

The individual-environment paradigm is also rated negatively for every mechanism except that of verification, which receives a positive rating. This seems to be due to the fact that the four preconditions model (Finkelhor, 1986) is able to successfully verify propositions through integration of previous research, but fails to provide direct empirical testing of predictive hypotheses.

The offender typologies paradigm is given negative ratings in the areas of control groups and hypothesis testing. Neutral ratings are received under the areas of verification and objectivity/replicability. Groth (1982) has provided a little objective evidence for his typology of sexual offenders (fixated versus regressed), but the research efforts have lacked formal hypotheses and good control groups with which the experimental subjects could be compared.

Overall, the three most deficient areas are the use of control groups (100% negative), hypothesis testing (100% negative), and the use of objective and replicable methodology (75% negative and 25% neutral). Verification of propositions (with 25% positive, 50% neutral, and 25% negative ratings) remains an area of concern.

Evaluative Criteria

An overall achievement score across all four paradigms of sexual abuse has an average of 55 percent, with a range of 43 percent to 64 percent (see Table 13.6 [D]). Two criteria are most successfully attained, with 75 percent of the paradigms having established fruitfulness to an acceptable level and being sufficiently clear in their theoretical presentation.

The most severely lacking evaluation criterion is operationalization. It has negative ratings for all four paradigms. The criteria of falsifiability, parsimony, and accuracy are also not well considered by the paradigms. They all received neutral evaluations from the four paradigms.

PSYCHOLOGICAL MALTREATMENT

The three psychological maltreatment theories—ecological context, family breakup, and ecological/deficiency needs—are all placed under the ecological determinants paradigm.

Theoretical Form

The ecological paradigm is foremost a perspective on child maltreatment, rather than a formal theory that works toward predictive statements of testing explicit hypotheses (as in the deductive form) or the establishment of abstract statements from cumulative knowledge (as in the inductive formulation of theory). This is reflected in the acceptance of various theoretical types and introspective statements about verbal and or/nonverbal maltreatment of children.

Decomposition of Theoretical Components

The total achievement score of the ecological paradigm is 60 percent in Table 13.3 (E). It is derived from positive evaluations on two theoretical components (independent/dependent variables and postulates), neutral evaluations on the components of hypotheses and hypothetical constructs, and a negative evaluation on the operational definitions component.

The ecological paradigm specifies various independent and dependent variables (but generally not in a formal empirical way) and also suggests postulations that may involve multiple levels of ecology and cultures in order to account for the etiology of psychological maltreatment. Unfortunately, more empirically directed components are disregarded or infrequently utilized by this paradigm.

Functions of Scientific Theory

The total achievement score for the ecological paradigm is 43 percent (see Table 13.4 [E]), which represents a rather poor rating of its functional characteristics.

The ecological paradigm does well in decomposing all relevant theoretical, as well as empirical, issues, and therefore, receives a positive evaluation (100%) on the decomposition function. Unfortunately, this is its only positive evaluation on the seven functional components.

Four neutral scores are obtained on the functions of prediction, explanation, understanding, and fruitfulness, and two negative scores are obtained on the controls and laws functions. Therefore, the current psychological maltreatment theorization does not offer lawful relationships among various etiological issues and their control strategies for practical purposes.

Self-Regulation Mechanisms

Psychological maltreatment has recently received attention from the ecological paradigm. In terms of self-regulation criteria in the process of scientific theory construction, this paradigm rates very poorly. In fact, the total achievement score for this paradigm is only 12 percent (see Table 13.5 [E]). This is due to the fact that it does not receive any positive evaluation on any of the four self-regulatory mechanisms. Instead, it receives one neutral rating for theoretical verification procedure and negative ratings on the remaining criteria—use of control groups, hypothesis testing, and objectivity/replicability.

The uniformly inferior ratings of this paradigm in the self-regulation phase of theoretical construction points to an important problem with this type of approach. The ecological theorists generally try to be comprehensive and sensitive in all aspects of theoretical and contextual issues, but in doing so, they frequently become fragmental and disorganized. Therefore, they fail in the important task of integrating knowledge and evidence in a concrete way at the empirical level. In effect, what often happens is that most ecological theorists end up with a long list of topics or concerns linked to all forms of child maltreatment, including those at the individual (perpetrator and victim), family (nuclear, extended, and contemporary single-parent households), community (subculture and workplace), and societal (governmental and informal) levels. At the current level of theory development, they conclude that "everything" causes or influences child maltreatment.

Evaluative Criteria

On the seven evaluative criteria as a whole, the ecological paradigm receives a total achievement score of 57 percent (see Table 13.6 [E]). On individual criteria, this paradigm receives two positive marks, four neutral marks, and one negative evaluation. The one negative evaluation on the operationalization criterion indicates that the independent/dependent viables stressed by the ecological theorists are expressed as abstractions, rather than as concrete measures with empirical ramifications. Overall, much improvement is needed if the ecological approach is to progress as a variable theoretical paradigm for dealing with child psychological maltreatment problems in the future.

NEGLECT

There are two paradigms of neglect involving three theories. The individual determinants paradigm represents the personalistic theory, and the individual-environment paradigm includes the social interaction and three-factor theories of child neglect.

Theoretical Form

Two forms of theoretical development are used by the two paradigms of neglect: The individual determinants paradigm utilizes the perspective form and the individual-environment paradigm uses both forms of model and perspective for conceptualizing child neglect issues in Table 13.2 (F).

Decomposition of Theoretical Components

The two neglect paradigms are evaluated as being relatively favorable in terms of decomposition of theoretical components in Table 13.3 (F). They receive a total achievement score of 90 percent, representing the highest rating among the six maltreatment categories. It has 80 percent positive and 20 percent neutral evaluations in ten possible ratings. In fact, the components of hypotheses, independent/dependent variables, and postulates are given positive evaluations across both paradigms. The use of hypothetical constructs is evaluated as neutral for the individual-environment paradigms. The operational definitions component is evaluated positively for the individual-environment interaction paradigm and neutrally for the individual determinants paradigm.

Functions of Scientific Theory

Overall, the two paradigms of neglect compile a total achievement score of 61 percent in Table 13.4 (F). Out of all 14 possible evaluation entries, 36 percent receive positive evaluations, 50 percent neutral evaluations, and 14 percent negative evaluations.

The fruitfulness characteristic is the most positive attribute in terms of the functions of scientific theory for the two paradigms of neglect. Both the individual determinants and individual-environment paradigm are evaluated positively in this respect. The most negative attribute is the function of generating empirical laws. Neither paradigm has succeeded in this respect. The functions of decomposition, prediction, and explanation are rated positively for the individual-environment paradigm and neutrally for the individual determinants paradigm. The understanding and control functions are evaluated neutrally for both paradigms.

Self-Regulation Mechanisms

The two paradigms represent different theoretical orientations regarding the etiology and dynamics of child neglect. Their combined achievement score is only 25 percent (see Table 13.5 [F]). No positive evaluations are given to either of the paradigms for any of the four self-regulatory factors. Four neutral and four negative evaluations are given over the 8 possible evaluative entries. The best evaluation was obtained in the area of verification, in which both paradigms are given neutral ratings.

The worst evaluation is in hypothesis testing, for which both paradigms are given negative scores. The other two areas—control groups and objectivity/replicability—are neutrally evaluated for the individual-environment paradigm and negatively evaluated for the individual determinants paradigm.

Evaluative Criteria

An overall achievement score of 60 percent is obtained for the two paradigms of neglect in Table 13.6 (F). Of the total 14 possible evaluation entries, 21 percent are positive, 78 percent are neutral, and none have negative evaluations.

On individual evaluation criteria, both paradigms are considered very fruitful in that they provide good stimulation to the field. For example, although both member theories of the individual determinants paradigm have not been comprehensive or operational most of the time, they have generated much research and healthy debate.

The individual determinants paradigm is also rated favorably in the integration/comprehension criterion, whereas the individual-environment paradigm is given a neutral rating for this area. As for the rest of the evaluative criteria, both paradigms are given neutral marks.

SUMMARY AND DISCUSSION

In order to identify general trends of child abuse and neglect theorizations in the contemporary literature, three overall evaluations are the focus of this section: (1) overall achievement of all child abuse and neglect theoretical paradigms on the 23 evaluation criteria, (2) overall achievement of the nine theoretical paradigms on the four evaluative domains, and (3) overall achievement of the six maltreatment types on the four evaluative domains for theory development. After these three topics are discussed, a summarative evaluation of all theories and paradigms will be made at the end of this chapter.

Overall Achievement on 23 Evaluative Criteria
in Theory Construction

In order to evaluate all theories and paradigms of child abuse and neglect as a whole, their achievement scores on each of the 23 evaluative criteria are summarized to derive an overall score of all theories on each criteria. Briefly, the achievement score on each evaluative criterion is obtained by (1) calculating the total number of plus and minus rank codings of all paradigms on each criterion in Tables 13.3 to 13.7 across all nine paradigms and also across all six maltreatment types, (2) converting the individual plus and zero codings to rank scores of 2 and 1, respectively (the minus codings are not involved in calculation), (3) deriving each evaluation criterion's total rank score by summing over its rank scores of 2 and 1 for plus and zero codings, and (4) dividing the total rank score of each evaluation criterion by its maximally possible rank score (assuming all codings are pluses) and yielding a proportion as the achievement score of all paradigms on a given evaluation criterion.

For example, for the hypothesis criterion in Table 13.3, its total rank codings across all nine paradigms and six maltreatment types are 5 pluses, 11 zeroes, and 8 minuses. Its total rank score is 21 ($5 \times 2 + 11 \times 1$), and its overall achievement score is 44 ($21/\{2 \times [5 + 11 + 8]\}$). As a result, a total of 23 achievement scores are obtained for all theories and paradigms evaluated in this book on the 23 evaluation criteria (cf. the bottom of Tables 13.3 to 13.7).

In order to further depict general successful levels of all child abuse and neglect theorizations reviewed in this book as a whole, the range of achievement scores (1 to 100) is partitioned into three hierarchical (equal intervals) levels, with the first level, 67 to 100, representing excellent achievement; the second level, 34 to 66, representing moderate achievement; and the third level, 0 to 33, representing poor achievement. The 23 evaluation criteria are then assigned individually into these three hierarchical groups in accordance with their overall achievement scores. The resultant assignments, as presented in Table 13.8, can be discussed as follows:

Of the 23 evaluation criteria, 4 (17.39%) fall in the *excellent* category. These criteria include (1) the identification of *independent* and *dependent variables* and (2) the statement of theoretical *postulations* from the first theory construction domain (decomposition of theoretical components). The excellence criteria also include *clarity* and *fruitfulness* from the evaluation domain (the criterion of fruitfulness also appears in the function domain). These four criteria as a whole are related to the specification of content issues (variables) and postulations of their relationships in the theoretical account of child abuse and neglect etiologies. Results from such efforts are generally fruitful in generating further theorizations, discussions, and even debate.

On the other hand, 7 (30.44%) of the 23 evaluation criteria fall in the *poor* category. These criteria are closely related to the procedures and goals that are necessary to carry out the empirical evaluation of a scientific theory. That is, the current status of child abuse and neglect theorizations is rather weak in (1) theoretical constructs, which are not operationally defined to the extent that can be empirically demonstrated and tested; (2) the self-regulation mechanisms that have not been used, such as objective procedures for replication, control group comparisons for cross-validation, and hypothesis testing for rigorous assessment

Table 13.8

Achievement Levels of Child Abuse and Neglect Theoretical Paradigms on 23 Evaluative Criteria

Evaluation Domain of Theory Construction	Excellent (67%-100%)	Level of Achievement — Moderate (34%-66%)	Poor (0%-33%)
Decomposition of theoretical component (Average = 59%)	Independent/dependent variables (85%), Postulates (81%)	Hypothetical constructs (58%), Hypotheses (44%)	Operational definitions (21%)
Function of scientific theories (Average = 46%)	Fruitfulness (67%)	Decomposition (63%), Explanation (63%), Understanding (50%), Prediction (42%)	Control (17%), Law (0%)
Self-regulation mechanisms (Average = 23%)		Verification (44%)	Control group (21%), Objectivity/replicability (19%), Hypothesis testing (17%)
Evaluation criteria (Average = 53%)	Clarity (83%), Fruitfulness (71%)	Integration/comprehensive (58%), Parsimony (50%), Falsifiability (40%), Accuracy (35%)	Operationalization (19%)
Overall Ratio	17.39%	52.17%	30.44%

of specific relationships among variables; and, consequently, (3) generation of empirical laws that could be used to control further epidemics of child abuse and neglect.

Despite the above-mentioned weaknesses, the contemporary child abuse and neglect theorizations have shown moderate achievements (between 34% and 66%) in that (1) many theorists have proposed some theoretical constructs and their relationships that are presumably embedded in child abuse and neglect phenomena; (2) many proposed theorizations can serve the function of a "close look" at various aspects of child abuse and neglect issues in order to provide global explanations of past events, understanding of current phenomena, and prediction of some future trends; (3) many of such functions are parsimonious, comprehensive, and, to some extent, accurate in reflecting realities; and, consequently, (4) the current theorizations have successfully provided some clinical accounts of child abuse and neglect etiologies (e.g., associations between victimization history, current personality characteristics, and future abusive cycles).

Overall, child abuse and neglect theorizations, up to the 1980s, appear to have reached the level of gradual conceptualization and identification of certain important variables. Many theories and hypotheses have been generated and used in clinical settings and also in social service planning. In short, these efforts have achieved what can be called "conceptualization" and "subjective advocation" stages in theory construction.

° What is lacking is to treat the contents of all theorizations as subject matters in science that will be submitted to rigorous and empirical assessment through further decomposition of contents, networking of various constructs, and establishment of objective operational procedures. In other words, the study of child abuse and neglect theorizations should become a scientific discipline by and in itself, although this discipline will necessarily involve theoretical and empirical issues of many other disciplines. To achieve this goal, the question arises as to where the study of child abuse and neglect stands in terms of the completeness and efficiency of different theorizations. The following evaluation summarizes the overall achievement level of the nine theorization paradigms in reference to the four scientific evaluation domains.

Overall Evaluation of Nine Theoretical Paradigms

Table 13.9 presents an overall assessment of the nine theoretical paradigms against each of the four evaluative domains. For this evaluation, achievement scores of individual paradigms on each evaluative domain are summarized across appropriate types of maltreatment from Table 13.7. To facilitate interpretations, a total achievement score is further obtained for each paradigm by averaging its achievement scores on the four evaluation domains. Such total achievement scores of the nine paradigms are finally categorized into three levels of theory construction quality in science. That is, the range of overall achievement scores (1 to 100%) is divided into three equal intervals, and each represents a unique level of quality in theory construction (i.e., *poor* quality for scores between 0% and 33%, *moderate* quality for scores between 34% and 66%, and *excellent quality* for scores above 67%). These three levels are coded by a minus sign, a zero, and a plus sign, respectively, under the *Quality Level* heading in Table 13.9.

Of the nine paradigms, the learning/situational theorization is the only one that obtained an excellent rating (67%). The remaining eight paradigms reached a moderate level of overall achievement (between 34% and 66%).

The ecological paradigm is least effective in scientific theory construction mainly for the following reasons: The low score in the domain of self-regulation (only 16%) refers to methods and procedures usually used in the social sciences (e.g., control groups, establishment of objective research procedures, analysis of empirical data through hypothesis testing, and verification of research outcomes through cross-validation). In fact, there are very few empirical studies that were specifically designed under the theoretical guidelines of the ecological paradigm. In its present state of development, this paradigm emphasizes the complex correlates of the child abuse and neglect problem, often devising long lists of contributing factors at different levels of analysis (e.g., intraindividual, family dynamics, subcultural violence, and sociopolitical structures). In effect, this paradigm suggests that nearly everything causes child abuse (especially psychological maltreatment). As a result, the content issues of this paradigm become almost impossible to test empirically in any research program.

Table 13.9

Overall Achievement of Nine Theoretical Paradigms on Four Evaluative Domains

Paradigm	Evaluative Domain					
	Self-Regulation	Functions of Science/Theory	Theoretical Components	Evaluative Criteria	Total Ach. Score Ave.	Quality Level
(1) Individual determinants	12% -	50% 0	70% +	64% 0	49%	0
(2) Sociocultural	37% 0	43% 0	50% 0	57% 0	47%	0
(3) Individual-environment	40% 0	64% 0	80% +	64% 0	62%	0
(4) Offender typologies	25% -	43% 0	40% 0	50% 0	40%	0
(5) Family systems	12% -	43% 0	80% +	71% +	52%	0
(6) Parent-child interaction	50% 0	36% 0	70% +	57% 0	53%	0
(7) Sociobiological	50% 0	28% -	60% 0	50% 0	47%	0
(8) Learning/situational	50% 0	71% +	90% +	57% 0	67%	+
(9) Ecological	16% -	41% 0	53% 0	42% 0	38%	0
Average	23%	46%	59%	53%	46%	

Note: the codings $-$, 0, $+$ represent three hierarchical levels of quality in scientific theory construction that have achievement score ranges of 0% to 33%, 34% to 66%, and 67% to 100% respectively.

The learning/situational paradigm received the best total achievement score mainly for the following three reasons: (1) This paradigm emphasizes interactions within and between the individual and the environment; (2) the acquisition of etiological dispositions are due to environmental influences, and therefore the emphasis on learned and innate interactions increases the observation variables in field/empirical research; and (3) this paradigm is closer to the rigorous empirical research in contemporary social and behavioral sciences.

Comparisons between the overall achievement scores of the four evaluation domains (each was derived by averaging the scores of the nine paradigms) indicates that the decomposition of the theoretical components domain ranks the highest in efficiency, followed by the domains of evaluative criteria and functions of scientific theory. The self-regulation domain was by far the poorest across all nine paradigms (with four "poor" and five "moderate" quality ratings). This is mostly due to the fact that very little empirical research has been conducted in the field for specific theories. Most of the empirical studies that are supposedly testing a specific theory are not scientific. They usually fail to utilize control groups, do not test prespecified hypotheses, and generally lack the use of the objective operational definitions.

The functions of scientific theories domain ranked third in efficiency (with one "excellent," one "poor," and seven "moderate" quality ratings). This is because some functions are adequately fulfilled by the paradigms as a whole (e.g., decomposition and fruitfulness), while others are not sufficiently fulfilled (e.g., laws, control, and prediction), and still others are, more or less, evenly fulfilled (e.g., understanding and explanation). A similar pattern is evident for the domain of evaluative criteria, in which most of the variables are evenly fulfilled (i.e., the variables of falsifiability, parsimony, and accuracy; all were rated as mostly neutral), others lean toward the positive end (i.e., fruitfulness, clarity, and integration/comprehensiveness), while others are more negative (i.e., operationalization).

The high ranking for the decomposition of theoretical components domain (with five "excellent" and four "moderate" quality ratings) suggests that the nine paradigms do generally attempt to decompose their theories, perspectives, or models into different components, such as postulates, hypothetical constructs, independent and dependent variables, and hypotheses. However, in many cases these components were loosely defined in order to accommodate borderline theoretical considerations.

Overall Evaluation of Six Maltreatment Typologies

The evaluation of the six maltreatment categories in terms of their overall achievement scores and quality ratings is presented in Table 13.10. As can be seen, all six categories reached about the same moderate level of achievement (between 41% and 59%).

This moderate level of achievement across all six victimization types is mainly due to two major reasons: (1) Except for the self-regulation domain, which has "poor" quality ratings for all six types, relatively uniform achievement ratings were found for all six maltreatment categories across three other evaluative domains, and (2) relatively concurrent emphases on different maltreatment types were made in the contemporary field of child abuse and neglect.

First, the six maltreatment categories have more or less comparable scores (equal ratings of "moderate" quality) on three evaluative domains: The decomposition of theoretical components domain has an overall mean achievement score of 59 percent, in the range between 48 percent and 90 percent. The neglect category has an extra high (90%) achievement score. The domain with the next largest score range between different maltreatment types is the functions of scientific theory (23%), in which the category of incest taboo received the lowest (38%) achievement score and the victimization category of neglect received the highest (61%) achievement score. Overall, all six types have moderate quality ratings.

The other two evaluation domains (self-regulatory mechanisms and evaluative

Table 13.10
Achievement Levels of Six Maltreatment Types on Four Evaluative Domains for Theory Development

Maltreatment Type	Evaluative Domains				Overall Ach. Quality %
	Self-Regulation	Functions of Science/Theory	Theoretical Components	Evaluative Criteria	
Physical Abuse	26% (-)	41% (0)	59% (0)	52% (0)	44% (0)
Incest Taboo	33% (-)	38% (0)	50% (0)	48% (0)	43% (0)
Incestuous Abuse	27% (-)	41% (0)	48% (0)	46% (0)	41% (0)
Sexual Abuse	16% (-)	52% (0)	62% (0)	55% (0)	47% (0)
Psychological Maltreatment	12% (-)	43% (0)	60% (0)	57% (0)	43% (0)
Neglect	25% (-)	61% (0)	90% (+)	60% (0)	59% (0)
Overall	23%	46%	59%	53%	46%

Note: Codings in parentheses represent trichotomous quality levels with the " + " for the achievement score greater than 67%, "0" for achievement scores between 34% and 66% and "−" for achievement scores between 0% and 33%.

criteria) had very little variations in their achievement rankings across the six maltreatment types. Under the self-regulatory mechanisms, the category of psychological maltreatment received the lowest (12%) achievement score, and the domain of incest taboo received the highest (33%) achievement score. All those achievement scores reflect "poor" quality in the self-regulation aspect of theory construction. The domain of evaluative criteria has an average of 53 percent achievement score, with the lowest score of 46 percent from the incestuous abuse category and the highest score of 60 percent from the neglect category.

Secondly, the five general subfields of child abuse and neglect (i.e., sexual abuse, physical abuse, neglect, incestuous abuse, psychological maltreatment) have generally developed concurrently and have been closely related in terms of methodology and academic discipline interest. As a result, their rate of progression has been more or less equal as reflected in their similar average achievement scores.

However, it should be noted that the neglect category appears to be somewhat superior to the others. This is due to its superiority in three domains (decomposition of theoretical components, functions of scientific theory, and evaluative criteria). In fact, it had the highest achievement scores in three of the four domains (except the self-regulation domain, where it had about a median achievement rating, 25%).

It should also be noted that this higher achievement of the neglect maltreatment type may be skewed by the fact that it consists of only three theories under two paradigms, the individual determinants and individual-environment interaction paradigms. The individual-environment interaction paradigm is relatively robust, and the neglect category has two of its theories within it.

CONCLUSION

The above evaluation of all contemporary child abuse and neglect theorizations suggests the following general patterns:

Theory formation. In terms of the forms of theory development, there exists a clear deficiency in formal theorization. Over half (52%) of the proposed "theories" in the field are not scientific theories at all, but rather are mere perspectives. Perspectives are usually not scientific and do not offer precise definitions and systematic integrations of causal relationships. Furthermore, they lack objectivity, systemization, and empirical testing.

About one-fourth (23%) of the reviewed "theories" are classified as models. These models have often used some framework for studying certain issues of child maltreatment, but have failed to make formalized assertions or to test propositions.

Only about one-fourth (26%) of the 46 "theories" can be classified as actual theories that make systematic statements of causality and utilize a degree of empiricism. Half of these are of the summative inductive form and half are of the functional deductive form.

Levels of Achievement Quality

As indicated in Table 13.8, the four evaluation domains are dispersed among the three levels of achievement quality. The highest level is decomposition of theoretical components (average = 59%), followed by evaluation criteria (average = 53%), functions of scientific theories (average = 46%), and finally self-regulation mechanisms (average = 23%).

Five of the 23 criteria are ranked under the category of excellent achievement. They are independent/dependent variables (85%), postulates (81%), clarity (83%), and fruitfulness as a theoretical function (71%) and as an evaluative criterion (67%). This indicates that the field of child abuse and neglect has progressed to the point of specifying various factors that seem to be involved in the etiology of child maltreatment and has delineated some broad theoretical assumptions concerning the nature of the problem. Furthermore, the theoretical perspectives have been clearly presented and also have stimulated the field in terms of healthy debate, empirical research, and further theorization.

A moderate level of achievement is established for the following 11 criteria: (1) hypothetical constructs (58%), (2) hypotheses (44%), (3) decomposition (63%), (4) explanation (63%), (5) understanding (50%), (6) prediction (42%), (7) verification (44%), (8) integration/comprehensiveness (58%), (9) parsimony (50%), (10) falsifiability (40%), and (11) accuracy (35%). As this clearly demonstrates, the field comprises mostly moderate attempts in theorizing and also in somewhat less sophisticated empirical hypothesis testing.

A poor level of achievement is recorded for the following criteria: (1) operational definitions (21%), (2) control of future events (17%), (3) establishment of empirical laws (0%), (4) use of control groups (21%), (5) objectivity/ replicability (19%), (6) hypothesis testing (17%), and operationalization (19%). As this list indicates, the major shortcoming of child abuse and neglect theorizations is that they are not well established in the sense of social scientific theory, philosophy, or methodology.

The two best paradigms are the learning/situational and individual-environment interaction paradigms (cf. Table 13.9). Both are more closely oriented toward academic empiricism and formalization than those theories developed out of more clinically orientated introspections. This strongly indicates a need for better integration of clinical fields and basic research disciplines.

Finally, as pointed out in Table 13.10, the need for better theorization is constant across all six maltreatment categories: physical abuse, incest taboo, incestuous abuse, sexual abuse, psychological maltreatment, and neglect. These categories have essentially minimal achievement in each of the four evaluative domains. This deficiency undoubtedly reflects the fact that most theories have been developed for specific purposes of individual disciplines from working experiences in some narrowly defined focuses. In other words, the processes of theoretical development are mostly dependent upon subjective introspections of limited experiences in various working environments. Consequently, theoretical perspectives may produce workable postulates and assertions for individual disciplines, but they are frequently fragmented and conflicting when compared with those from other disciplines.

Ideally, a comprehensive scientific theory should be developed that would consist of the strengths of all existing theories and would improve on their weaknesses, such that the theory could help explain the gaps and produce workable hypotheses that lead to more knowledge about the problems in and across all disciplines. With more knowledge and more empirical laws, efforts to reduce the prevalence of child maltreatment can be more successful. It is therefore apparent that good theorization is an essential component in the fight against child abuse and neglect.

Part VII

Cameo Application and Conclusions

Chapter Fourteen

Impact of Differential Theories on the Legal Profession: A Cameo Evaluation of Expert Witnesses

Various theories, models, and perspectives have significant differences in their etiological accounts and empirical strategies for addressing substantive issues on child abuse and neglect. As an illustration of the impacts of different theoretical perspectives for practical use, this chapter presents a summary of Tzeng's (1989) evaluation of the roles of different theories in legal processes that involve expert witnesses. For this reason, the issues of expert witnesses related to child abuse and neglect are discussed in reference to two topics: (1) definitions and characteristics of expert witnesses and (2) knowledge and responsibilities of all individuals using expert witnesses in legal proceedings.

DEFINITIONS AND CHARACTERISTICS OF EXPERT WITNESSES

The knowledge provided by the expert witness is intended to increase understanding of the evidence presented in court so that the judicial decision is accurate and fair. It may also permit a court to reach a determination that could not be made without the expert's opinion (e.g., causation of child maltreatment and standard of care for children). In terms of qualifications, any individual who possesses special knowledge, skills, and/or experience can be called upon as an expert witness to render opinions on certain aspects of issues in child victimization processes. Therefore, professionals in many disciplines are theoretically qualified as expert witnesses. Professionals in various disciplines are uniquely qualified in their own areas of expertise related to specific, pertinent areas of child victimization. However, they are not qualified in the areas that are beyond their disciplinary orientations. Under this premise, professionals oriented with different theoretical foundations are all qualified in their special areas of competency.

There is a need for the expert witness to help establish the four basic requirements of legal evidence—identification of duties of individuals/institutions, verification of breach of duty, establishment of causalities, and evidence of harm. Therefore, the primary purposes of expert witnesses are (1) to establish causality, (2) to establish standards, and (3) to postulate incident occurrences and related processes. In addition, the expert witness may function to (1) verify or nullify the claims of other witnesses, (2) confirm or contradict interpretations of factual data, (3) evoke sympathy or condemnation from the jury, (4) divide or consolidate the relevant evidence, and (5) advocate or impartially educate in court proceedings.

Different theoretical orientations can create different bases for experts in searching special knowledge for their testimony. Therefore, professionals in different theoretical disciplines can perform legitimate, illegitimate, or both functions to supply "expert knowledge" for use in the decision process of the court.

Although no uniform theory is available to provide consistent answers to disputed issues between conflicting parties, there should be a common goal for all professionals acting as expert witnesses. That is, *all theories and expert witnesses should work toward the best interest of the child.* However, different professionals may disagree as to what is in a child's best interest. Under this premise, legal professionals need to know the fundamental similarities and differences of all theories and models of child abuse and neglect such that expert witnesses can be called upon who will select the most accurate and impartial view of the child's best interest. In short, the knowledge provided by the expert witness should serve the functions of *verification, confirmation, conversion, and education* in order to increase maximal judicial validity of evidence presented in court.

RESPONSIBILITIES OF LEGAL PROFESSIONALS IN USING EXPERT WITNESSES

In legal proceedings dealing with victimization, the court may require concrete and comprehensive information from experts in order to establish the evidence of responsibility, causality, liability, and damages. Therefore, the legal and other professionals involved will need to have accurate knowledge of the (1) perpetrator (e.g., intention), (2) victim (e.g. impact), (3) victimization processes (e.g., form of maltreatment), and (4) social and legal dispositions (e.g., removal of the victimized child from the abusive environment).

Resolution for these issues relies heavily on subjective explanations and interpretations of circumstantial evidence and facts. Because of the subjective nature in explanations or inferences, the experts used by the legal profession will thus generate possibly controversial and incompatible opinions about various objective phenomena of child abuse and neglect.

Therefore, in dealing with the diverse theoretical backgrounds of the experts,

Table 14.

Criteria for Evaluating Background Orientations of Expert Witnesses

Theoretical orientation	Basic focus	Causalities	Whom to blame
1. Individual determinants	Perpetrator's characteristics Reinforcement of maltreating behavior Intergenerational cycle	Dysfunctional/deviant individuals Continuation of maltreatment cycle	Perpetrator Family of perpetrator's childhood
2. Sociocultural	Five basic human needs Seven primary social systems Group inequalities	Dysfunctional/deviant society	Dysfunctional social systems that promote inequalities and block basic human needs
3. Individual-environment	Social, personal & economic resources Perpetrator's characteristics Stressors Social and community values/norms Family interactions Consequences of maltreatment	Dysfunctional/deviant individuals	Perpetrator Social, community, & family norms, values, & interactions Long- & short-term stress Characteristics of the child
4. Offender typologies	Intergenerational cycle Personal resources Stress	Dysfunctional individuals	Perpetrator Situations Social forces
5. Family systems	Family variables Characteristics of family members Stress Social factors Consequences of maltreatment	Dysfunctional family systems Dysfunctional individuals Dysfunctional society	Family characteristics Characteristics of family members Stress Social forces
6. Parent-child interactions	Parent-child interactions/relationship Child's perception of parent	Dysfunctional family relations	Characteristics of the parent Characteristics of the child Parent-child relationship Community systems Situational stress
7. Sociobiological	Genetic relationship of individuals Resources	Dysfunctional individuals	Perpetrator-victim genetic relationship Adversive external factors
8. Learning/situational	Social learning Situational factors Resources Abusive potential	Dysfunctional individuals, families, communities & society	Socialization experiences Perpetrator, consequences Aggressive cues Family, school, mass media Situations, frustration Specific elicitors Coercive cycle
9. Ecological	Individual factors Family factors Community factors Sociocultural factors Societal factors	Dysfunctional individuals, families, communities & society	Perpetrator/child characteristics Family Community

lawyers need to have a clear understanding of evaluation criteria for assessment of expert testimony. That is, each expert should and can be characterized in terms of his/her "theorization of child abuse and neglect," which is usually derived from adoption of one or more of the specific theoretical paradigms presented in previous chapters.

In consideration of the different theoretical perspectives on causalities and liabilities, Table 14.1 presents a summary of the positions taken by the nine theoretical paradigms on the following three evaluation criteria: (1) the basic focus of individual theoretical paradigms, (2) the assumed contributing circumstances (causality) of maltreatment, and (3) the individuals or institutions that are liable for child maltreatment consequences.

These positions clearly indicate that different theoretical perspectives, in addition to their common characteristics, have unique focuses and strategies in dealing with child victimization processes and related issues. Apparently there is some degree of knowledge of paradoxical difficulties (Tzeng, 1989) under which the legal and judicial judgment in civil and criminal proceedings will focus on responsible individuals and/or institutions. In this process, the purposes and functions of expert testimony will not necessarily generate uniform conclusions from the same phenomenon. Therefore, application of the nine theoretical paradigms (across many conflicting theories, models, and perspectives) is a necessary, albeit difficult, task.

With the knowledge of the above differential perspectives in using expert witnesses, all legal professionals are strongly encouraged to expand their professional orientations from unidisciplinary to multidisciplinary perspectives. Since clinical and psychological testimonies are frequently based on some theories that may have no empirically verified foundations, legal professionals in future handling of child abuse and neglect cases, with or without the assistance of other professions, should always evaluate the admissibility of expert testimony in reference to multidisciplinary theories and knowledge. Therefore, the judicial validity of future expert testimony will rely heavily on the competency and willingness of lawyers in testing its admissibility in the areas of *necessity, reliability, validity, understandability,* and *importance.*

Above all, it relies on the ability of lawyers to identify different origins of various theoretical foundations used and to differentiate their feasibilities for application to the legal issues involved.

Chapter Fifteen

Summary and Conclusions

In the preceding chapters, 46 theories, models, and perspectives compiled from the literature of child abuse and neglect were organized under five major types of child victimization—physical abuse (25 theories), incestuous abuse (6 theories), sexual abuse (6 theories), neglect (3 theories), and psychological maltreatment (3 theories). Three additional theories for explaining the origin of incest taboo were also included as a separate type of theorization. These 46 individual theories were further organized into nine theoretical paradigms, each representing a major theoretical approach to the explanation of child abuse and neglect etiologies.

For description of all theories and paradigms, a common evaluation format was used that includes four general topics: *theoretical foundations* about human nature and its development processes, *basic principles* of each theoretical account about the etiology of child maltreatment and its correlates, *empirical evidence* available in the literature to support, or dispute, each theoretical account, and *general evaluation* of the theoretical foundations, basic principles, and empirical evidence of each theory and paradigm. The evaluation judgments were made by the authors of this book and/or summarized from the literature.

Under this organizational structure, Chapter 1 presented basic concepts and the prevalence of child abuse and neglect from the social and historical perspectives; Chapter 2 presented summary descriptions of the nine individual paradigms in their accounts of the six maltreatment typologies; Chapter 3 presented the descriptions of 25 individual physical abuse theories; Chapter 4 presented the descriptions of 3 incest taboo theories; Chapter 5 presented the 6 incestuous abuse theories; Chapter 6 described the 6 sexual abuse theories; Chapter 7 discussed 3 psychological maltreatment theories; and Chapter 8 described 3 neglect theories.

In order to present an overview of all theories and paradigms, two additional analyses were performed: (1) *substantive evaluation* of the content issues of all individual theories and paradigms and (2) *process evaluation* of the properties of all theories in reference to the requirements for constructing a rigorous scientific theory. For the first purpose, a psychosemantic process model of human behavior was introduced in Chapter 9, and the analysis of all 46 theories, in terms of the ten model components, was presented in Chapter 10. For the second purpose, Chapter 11 introduced basic requirements for constructing scientific theories in social and behavioral science, and Chapter 12 reported the results from the evaluation of the nine theoretical paradigms in science. Finally, to illustrate the utility and impact of different theories and paradigms, Chapter 14 briefly discussed some major issues in using different theories for expert testimony in legal proceedings about child abuse and neglect.

As a summary of evaluations presented in the preceding chapters regarding the status of existing theories, their strengths and weaknesses, major similarities and conflicts, and quality and efficiency under the scrutiny of a rigorous scientific theory construction, the following six topics will be presented in this concluding chapter: (1) issues on definitions and typologies of child abuse and neglect, (2) empirical research limitations, (3) specific research deficiencies, (4) specific focuses for communitywide services, (5) status of contemporary theorizations, and (6) prospects for developing integrated theories.

DEFINITION AND TYPOLOGY ISSUES

Because of the wide variety of views of child abuse and neglect, there exists considerable debate as to the nature of the problem, its causes, management, and definitions. The central question is why different professionals hold such widely different and often conflicting views on the problem.

A major confusion results from the various definitions of child maltreatment that may focus on actual behaviors, intentions, cultural norms, or outcomes (Keller & Erne, 1983). Using different definitions and typologies will eventually lead to different and frequently conflicting theoretical perspectives and will inevitably lead to different (conflicting) empirical strategies for identification and intervention of the problem.

Even though all forms of child maltreatment are generally handled by the same service systems, contemporary research tends to focus on a specific type of maltreatment (physical, sexual, emotional, or neglect). As a result, specific dynamics are reported as involving different types of maltreatment. For example, Martin and Walters (1982) found that (1) *abandonment* was most reliably associated with promiscuity and/or alcoholism of the mother; (2) *physical abuse* was mostly associated with parent-child conflict and a nonbiological relationship between the perpetrator and the child; (3) *emotional maltreatment* was associated with emotional/psychological problems of the child and intellectual inadequacies of the child; (4) *neglect* was most closely associated with intellectual status of the parents; and (5) *sexual abuse* was associated with a promiscuous/alcoholic father. Such distinctive associations between maltreatment typologies and specific dispositions or behavior have been criticized as being too narrow-minded in search of the etiologies of child maltreatment phenomena.

Various federal and state government agencies categorize maltreatment in terms of acts of commission (abuse) and omission (neglect). These agencies generally provide working guidelines for public and private clinics and research professionals. Many researchers have also utilized the abuse-neglect dichotomy (Halperin, 1979; Watkins & Bradbard, 1982). However, the acceptance of this distinction is not universal among academic and service professionals. Currently, there is considerable dispute among experts in the field as to whether abuse and neglect constitute entirely different (qualitative) phenomena (the dichotomous argument), or simply manifest different (quantitative) degrees of the same phenomena (the continuum argument).

There is evidence to support both the dichotomous and continuum arguments, but no consensus has been reached. This is an important area of concern because each argument leads to different analysis and treatment of the issues. For example, if abuse and neglect are dichotomous phenomena with clearly different etiologies, then different analysis of related issues would be desirable. However, if they are simply variable manifestations of the same underlying characteristics of human ecologies, then researchers must concentrate their efforts on analysis and treatment of the common etiological factors, with no separate concentration on unique characteristics.

Between the dichotomous and continuous arguments, the psychosemantic process model presented in Chapter 9 compiles pertinent issues from the literature that represent (1) the major content issues addressed by all theoretical perspectives, (2) the organization of all content issues in terms of the ten model components (from background characteristics, long-term stressors, short-term stressors, trend-coping mechanisms, affective and cognitive evaluation systems, behavioral disposition, habits, overt behaviors of abuse and/or neglect, to social consequences), and (3) the delineation of these issues in terms of subjective and objective cultures at the five ecological levels.

Therefore, similarities and differences between different theoretical paradigms can be specified from comparisons of their models, principles, and strategies regarding the etiologies of child abuse and neglect in reference to the ten psychosemantic model components and the ten cultural-by-ecological units. With comprehensive information from such analyses, the dichotomous versus continuous argument about the definitions of child abuse and neglect becomes a complex matter. That is, the dichotomous position is feasible in describing certain phenomena for some model components (especially regarding the dichotomy of commission as abuse and omission as neglect for the "overt behavior" component), whereas the continuous position is not only desirable but also necessary in addressing the underlying characteristics of mental processes involved in the child abuse and neglect behaviors (especially on the attack-approach-inhibition continuum for the component of affective evaluation of circumstances and also for the component of generating behavior dispositions).

Therefore, from the psychosemantic process model point of view, the debate on the definition issues between dichotomy and continuity does not deserve further attention in research community of child abuse and neglect. What is needed now and in the future is the systemization of knowledge available in the literature through the use of scientific methods and strategies presented in Chapter 12.

EMPIRICAL RESEARCH LIMITATIONS

In order to develop accurate, reliable, and valid strategies in the prediction, prevention, intervention, and treatment of child abuse and neglect, there is a need to place greater emphasis on utilization of scientific empirical research methods and strategies, as opposed to relying on other types of information, such as subjective speculation, religious dogma, authoritarian decree, or clinical assumptions. Therefore, it seems helpful to summarize the current status of basic research in the field of child abuse and neglect.

Gelles (1982) has pointed out six major limitations to research and theory in the field of family violence including child abuse and neglect:

Sampling errors of caught cases: According to Gelles (1982), approximately 90 percent of all child maltreatment studies are based on small, nonrepresentative samples of people who have been labeled as victims or perpetrators of abuse or who sought public assistance through the filing of child abuse reports. These types of studies hopelessly confound causalities with those variables that have been publicly identified or labeled as deviant (Gelles, 1973; Spinetta & Rigler, 1972).

Lack of control/comparison groups in evaluation of empirical data: In addition to sampling errors, studies in the field of child abuse and neglect often fail to compare study samples with control groups (e.g., a nonabusing group). As evaluated in Chapter 13, empirical verification through cross-group comparisons is a basic consideration in any scientific endeavor. These studies are thus unable to establish causal associations or show that differences exist among abusing and nonabusing populations.

Lack of generalizability to other populations: Because of the sampling problems inherent in most studies of child maltreatment, the empirical findings and subsequent conclusions reached by investigators are often not generalizable to a larger, general population.

The application of simplistic, unicausal theoretical models to explanations of complex problems: The etiology of child abuse and neglect has traditionally been, and often still is, explained in terms of a single factor such as mental illness, being abused as a child, substance abuse, stress, low income, or patriarchy. While nearly each one of these factors is certainly related to child abuse, it is extremely doubtful that any one alone can fully account for child abuse and neglect etiologies as a whole.

Research validity suffering from the "Woozle Effect:" The woozle effect refers to the phenomenon that occurs when a simple empirical result or statement is repeated by many authors until it gains the status of a "law," without rigorous assessment of its internal (construct) properties or its external (concurrent) validity. The woozle effect has been quite common among researchers and clinicians as they attempt to find ideas and data to fill important theoretical and practical gaps in their work (Gelles, 1980, 1982).

The perpetuation of myths: According to Gelles (1982), the various limitations of family violence research (including child abuse and neglect) have culminated in a number of myths and fallacies concerning the extent, patterns, and causes of family violence in clinical communities (e.g., general immaterial evidence of causalities and treatment impacts). As a result, the transformation of empirically based findings for clinically focused utilities usually fails, despite the fact that both researchers and clinicians share a common subject matter and desire to help families. Therefore, a goal for future efforts in the field may be to enhance joint interaction and cooperation among researchers and clinicians in order to reduce incompatibilities between the two professions.

SPECIFIC RESEARCH DEFICIENCIES

Gelles's (1982) analysis of empirical research limitations in studying different aspects of child abuse and neglect is supported by other professionals. The following six aspects of specific deficiencies and needs have been identified for future research endeavors:

Stepfamilies: Giles-Sims and Finkelhor (1984) have advocated the following research priorities in the study of child abuse in stepfamilies: (1) The absolute (actual amounts) and relative (amounts compared with other families) level of economic resources available to the family, (2) the nature of norms for the stepparent's disciplinary role and the strength of sanctions associated with the norms, (3) the differential use of resources to benefit natural children over stepchildren, particularly when overall resources are scarce, and (4) the link between the extent of and acceptance of the stepparent's authority and child abuse. These issues have not been well addressed in the literature.

Pathological population: Much of the child sexual abuse research has been carried out on patients undergoing psychotherapy. The results of such studies tend to be skewed because they do not necessarily represent either the abused target population or the nonabused population. For example, in the case of incest, victims seeking psychotherapeutic assistance may be the ones who have been most traumatized by the incest or who have made the most healthy adjustments because of their very involvement in therapy (de Young, 1982).

Criminal system population: A number of studies used incarcerated perpetrators or court cases as target populations. Since it is believed that most cases of child abuse go unreported, subjects sampled from the criminal justice system cannot be considered as representative of "typical" child abuse and neglect cases (de Young, 1982).

Because of these sampling problems, despite the existence of extensive research reports cited in the empirical evidence sections of different theoretical models, the causes of child abuse and neglect are not well understood (French, 1984). Therefore, it can be concluded that the etiology of child maltreatment is a complex problem that involves multiple causal and associating factors. Future empirical research efforts should consider the importance of interactions among different theoretical and practical perspectives, including psychological, medical, social, and environmental.

Dissemination discrepancies: Two common ways have been used to disseminate research knowledge for clinical practice: publication of research results in clinical journals and/or books and clinical workshops or conferences conducted by researchers. These two types of transferring scientific research knowledge and skills have frequently failed the intended purposes. Gelles (1982) contends that researchers and clinicians usually share little else beyond a subject matter and concerned issues. They use different terms and concepts, are generally interested in different issues, and tend to disagree on what the most important questions are.

Disciplinary dependency: Child abuse and neglect has not developed as a discipline by itself. It relies heavily on the adaptation of other research topics or theories in social and behavioral sciences. For example, in the field of physical abuse, some researchers (e.g., Feshbach, 1980) have advocated the use of general principles of aggression, because it has been extensively studied in social psychology. However, others (e.g., Gelles & Straus, 1979; Burgess, 1979) have argued that since interactions among family members are so different from those among nonfamily members (upon which the aggression data is generally based), a separate analysis of family violence is necessary.

These major differences can be attributed to the following unique characteristics of the family: (1) family members look to one another for protection, support, and love; (2) the family is a geographically independent unit; (3) family members spend a greater amount of time together; (4) the family membership is nonvoluntary; (5) there exist greater age and gender discrepancies within the family; (6) personal space is more likely to be invaded in the family; and (7) inequality is ascribed in family roles. Because of these unique characteristics, the principles and dynamics of aggression between nonfamily members cannot be reasonably transferred to family violence and thus cannot be automatically used for studying child abuse and neglect problems.

The role of stress: Much of what social researchers presently know about the relationship between stress and family violence is at the level of theoretical speculation, rather than sociological or psychological law (Farrington, 1986). Numerous studies have indicated that stressors, such as heavy child-care responsibilities and economic problems, are a factor in child physical abuse and neglect. Stress and frustration have also been associated with spouse abuse (Straus, 1980a, 1980b). However, Straus and others (1980) found no relationship between stress and sibling abuse. In addition, the results from the analysis of various sexual abuse theories indicate that stress is not viewed as a significant factor in the etiology of child sexual abuse by the majority of the theories. Therefore, stress seems to be strongly related to physical abuse and neglect, but not to sexual abuse (Farrington, 1986).

There is also an important distinction to be drawn between the amount of stress and the type of stress (a quantitative vs. qualitative issue). Holmes and Rahe (1967), in their situational "life events" approach, contend that stressors are all basically the same in terms of their overall impact, whereas others have suggested that the impact of stressors will vary with the type of stressors involved.

According to Farrington (1986), major factors that influence how an individual or family will react to stress include (1) gender, (2) socioeconomic status, and (3) the extent to which violence is considered a legitimate response to stress, both at the subcultural and the family levels. Therefore, it appears that the impact of stress on child abuse and neglect is mediated by many kinds of subjective and objective variables, such as sex of the perpetrator and victim, economic and social conditions, and family and cultural norms. Although various forms of stress have been associated with child abuse and neglect, the exact nature of the relationships among these variables has not been explicitly delineated. Therefore, the role of stress remains an important issue to study in the field of child maltreatment.

In summary, due to the complexity of the problem and the simultaneous urgency of the empirical investigation, theoretical postulation, and clinical application, research efforts have frequently been hampered by (1) partial focus on specific issues or ecological systems; (2) different orientations toward incompatible disciplines; (3) reliance on biased theoretical foundations and/or conflicting postulates; (4) separate or disjointed efforts among professionals in service, education, and research; (5) implementation of research programs through the use of unscientific methods and strategies; and (6) overcommitment to partial and/or incomplete empirical results. These limitations have severely undercut progress in developing a comprehensive theory that would encompass the strengths of individual theorizations and simultaneously overcome their weaknesses.

SPECIFIC FOCUSES FOR COMMUNITYWIDE SERVICES

Tzeng, Hanner, & Fortier (1988) stressed that an ideal social service system for combating child abuse and neglect problems in the future should be based on a comprehensive communitywide service model that should consider seven service domains simultaneously (cf. Figure 11.2). These service domains include the following:

1. Identification—analysis of various characteristics of victimized children, offenders, and their relationships across all family, social, and cultural environments.
2. Intervention—immediate rescue of victimized children and the deterrence of abusive or neglectful circumstances.
3. Treatment—clinical treatment and social environmental management of individuals and families involved through public and private resources.
4. Prevention/education—implementation of various preventive services and instructions to reduce the vulnerability of child victims and also to educate professionals, paraprofessionals, volunteers, and the community at large regarding service issues on child abuse and neglect.
5. Evaluation—both process evaluation of all implementation procedures and strategies, and outcome evaluation of the impact of various programs on changes in individuals, families, and community;

6. Follow-up—continuous assessment of changes and related impacts by communitywide services in order to insure permanent prevention of child abuse and neglect situations.

7. Publication/dissemination—dissemination of information on the theories, contents, methods, strategies, and outcomes of the above six service domains to appropriate agencies and the public at large.

For each of these seven service domains, there exist many theorizations that have specific focuses and strategies in dealing with underlying child maltreatment etiologies (cf. Table 15.1). For example, the individual determinants paradigm focuses on the offender as the target of analysis, whereas the sociocultural determinants paradigm emphasizes the analysis of social phenomena. The family systems paradigm, on the other hand, emphasizes all family variables and members, including the victimized child. Such discrepancies in identification of child abuse and neglect have resulted in significant differences in advocating various methods, procedures, and strategies for other service domains such as intervention, treatment, and prevention. Table 15.1 presents a summary of various strategies proposed (or indirectly suggested) by the nine theoretical paradigms for each of the seven service domains.

Identification

In the task of identification, the individual determinants paradigm focuses on the individual offender, whereas the sociocultural paradigm analyzes specific social factors. Taking somewhat of a mediating stance between the individual and social extremes, the individual-environment paradigm considers the offender, the victim, and trigger situations.

Like other clinical views, the offender typologies paradigm generally looks at the individual perpetrator in identification of child maltreatment. The family systems paradigm, on the other hand, takes into account the family as a whole, as well as each of its individual members. The parent-child interaction paradigm is also interested in familial relationships, but concentrates primarily on the consequences of bonding processes between the mother and child.

The sociobiological paradigm may look at many identifying variables, but specializes in analysis of the parent-child relationship from a phylogenetic point of view. The learning/situational paradigm identifies child maltreatment by studying the perpetrator's past learning experiences (direct and observational), and also focuses on cognitive processes. Finally, the ecological paradigm checks out multiple forces, including those at the individual, family, community, and societal levels.

Overall, the nine paradigms require the identification of various characteristics by analyses of the offender (advocated by five paradigms), social phenomena (two paradigms), family variables (two paradigms), the parent-child relationship (two paradigms), community situations (one paradigm), victims (one paradigm), and maltreatment situations (one paradigm).

Intervention

The nine theoretical paradigms differ significantly in their approaches to the intervention of child maltreatment. For example, it is conceivable that nearly all of the nine paradigms would utilize some type of crisis counseling. The one exception is that the sociocultural paradigm would probably advocate meeting the needs of the individuals via the alteration of various sociocultural norms and institutions.

In addition to crisis counseling, the individual determinants paradigm would likely suggest separating the perpetrator and the family. On the other hand, the family systems paradigm would lean toward some sort of family crisis intervention strategy, and both the offender typologies and individual-environment paradigms may stress the need for community crisis centers to intervene in family dysfunction. Other popular intervention strategies include parenting aides, as frequently advocated by the parent-child interaction paradigm and the learning/situational paradigm, and resource assistance, as suggested by the sociobiological paradigm. The ecological paradigm would likely recommend such intervention strategies as child-care centers, volunteer assistance, and parent aides.

Overall, the nine paradigms address ten major aspects of interventions: crisis counseling (by seven paradigms), parent aides (three paradigms), community crisis centers (two paradigms), meeting the needs of the individual (one paradigm), alteration of social institutions (one paradigm), family crisis intervention (one paradigm), separation of perpetrator and the family (one paradigm), resource assistance (one paradigm), child-care centers (one paradigm), and volunteer assistance (one paradigm).

Treatment

Based on different theorizations of child abuse and neglect etiologies, the nine theoretical paradigms stress different treatment strategies. For example, the individual determinants paradigm would most often advocate some psychiatric and/or psychological treatment for the perpetrator, whereas the sociocultural paradigm would focus on "treating" society; the individual-environment paradigm, as well as the offender typologies paradigm, would focus on both socially and individually based treatments. The family systems paradigm would be inclined to treat the whole family as a unit and to advocate treatment of society.

The parent-child interaction paradigm and the sociobiological paradigm would be disposed to treatment strategies involving improvement of the parent-child relationship through enhancing parenting skills and other personal and environmental changes. The learning/situational paradigm might accentuate learning skills, resources, the child's behavior, and societal forces at work. Lastly, the ecological paradigm advocates the treatment of the individual, the family, the community, and society as a whole.

Table 15.1
Approaches of Theoretical Paradigms to Seven Service Domains in Child Abuse and Neglect

Paradigm	Identification	Intervention	Treatment	Prevention
1. Individual determinants	Analysis of offender	Separate perpetrator & family; Crisis counseling	Perpetrator's pathology	Focus on treatment; Break intergeneration cycle
2. Sociocultural	Analysis of social phenomena	Meet the needs of individuals; Alter social institutions	Sociocultural systems	Change social systems
3. Individual-environment	Analysis of offender, victim & situation	Crisis counseling; Community crisis centers	Perpetrator's pathology, skills & resources; Sociocultural variables; Child's characteristics; Family interactions	Enhance personal resources; Education; Change social values/norms; Reduce stress; Alter expected consequences
4. Offender typologies	Analysis of offender	Crisis counseling; Community crisis centers	Perpetrator's personality & behavior; Sociocultural forces	Enhance personal resources; Reduce stress; Change social values/norms
5. Family systems	Analysis of family variables	Family crisis intervention	Family; Individual family members; Sociocultural forces	Enhance family resources; Enhance personal resources; Reduce stress
6. Parent-child interaction	Analysis of parent-child relationship	Crisis counseling; Parent aides	Parent-child interactions; Sociocultural forces; Parental skills, resources; Child's characteristics; Perpetrator's pathology	Enhance parent-child relations; Reduce stressors; Enhance resources
7. Sociobiological	Analysis of parent-child relationship	Crisis counseling; Resource assistance	Parent-child relationship; Parental resources	Ensure close genetic relations; Reduce stress; Enhance resources
8. Learning/situational	Analysis of offender's past learning experiences	Crisis counseling; Parent aides	Perpetrator's behavior, learning, skills, resources; Social/situational forces; Child's behavior	Reduce exposure to aggressive models; Teach options to aggression
9. Ecological	Analysis of offender, family, community & social forces	Crisis counseling; Child care centers; Volunteer assistance	Perpetrator's pathology, skills, resources; Family interactions/norms	Alter adversive characteristics of perpetrator, child, family, community & society

Paradigm	Evaluation	Continuation & Follow-up	Dissemination
1. Individual determinants	Therapeutic strategies and impact	Clinical evaluations of groups and individuals	Clinical reports & presentations
2. Sociocultural	Social change strategies and impact	Effectiveness of social programs	Reporting/presenting sociocultural data
3. Individual-environment	Educational procedures and impact	Effectiveness and importance of education, clinical & community programs	Reporting/presenting various theoretical & empirical data
4. Offender typologies	Offender counseling techniques/progress	Monitoring of clinical programs	Clinical reports and presentations
5. Family systems	Family intervention procedures and their success	Assessment and monitoring of family dynamics	Clinical/theoretical reports
6. Parent-child interaction	Counseling & parental assistance programs and their impact	Patterns and dynamics of parent-child relationship	Clinical, empirical & theoretical
7. Sociobiological	Programs designed to improve personal resources & behavior	Patterns and dynamics of offender-victim relationship	Empirical/theoretical reports
8. Learning/situational	Social learning techniques designed to reduce dysfunctional & improve positive interaction	Patterns and dynamics of individual, family, community & social efforts	Empirical/theoretical reports
9. Ecological	Various individual, family, community & social programs, techniques & outcomes	Long-term evaluations of individual, family, community & social programs	Summary, integration of empirical and theoretical data

Overall, the nine paradigms address five major aspects of treatment: the perpetrator's psychopathology and/or behavior (six paradigms), sociocultural systems (seven paradigms), the perpetrator's resources (five paradigms), intrafamily interactions (five paradigms), and the child's characteristics (four paradigms).

Prevention

The individual determinants paradigm, focusing on treatment as a preventive measure, would be most concerned with tertiary level techniques, such as breaking the intergenerational cycle of abuse. The prevention of future child maltreatment might also involve the alteration of sociocultural values, norms, and/or systems, as advocated most strongly by the sociocultural paradigm and to a lesser degree by the the individual-environment and offender typologies paradigms. This could include enhancement of personal resources, public education, reducing stress, and influencing the expected consequences of abuse.

In fact, the reduction of stress and enhancement of resources as prevention measures have been strongly recommended by the family systems paradigm (with a special emphasis on family resources), the parent-child interaction paradigm (on general parent-child relations), and the sociobiological paradigm (with the possible monitoring of genetic relations).

The learning/situational paradigm promotes reducing the availability of aggressive behavioral models and violent modes of conflict resolution. It also promotes the teaching of nonviolent options to dealing with conflicts and frustrations. Finally, for prevention purposes, the ecological paradigm endorses the alteration of adverse characteristics of the perpetrator, the child, the family, the community, and society.

Overall, the nine paradigms address 11 major aspects of prevention that include focus on treatment of the perpetrator (one paradigm), breaking the intergenerational cycle (one paradigm), changing social systems (four paradigms), enhancing personal resources (five paradigms), increasing education (one paradigm), reducing stress (six paradigms), altering expected consequences (one paradigm), enhancing parent-child relations (one paradigm), ensuring close genetic relations (one paradigm), reducing exposure to aggressive models (one paradigm), and teaching alternatives to aggression models (one paradigm).

Evaluation

As suggested in Table 15.1, evaluation activities for the nine paradigms would involve different objectives based on their treatment and prevention strategies. For the individual determinants paradigm, evaluation would definitely involve therapeutic strategies and their impact.

The sociocultural paradigm would evaluate the needs and the impact of social changes; the individual-environment paradigm would evaluate educational programs on coping with various situations; the offender typologies paradigm would evaluate counseling strategies and progress for offenders; the family systems paradigm would emphasize the evaluation of the family's new orientation and dynamics; the parent-child interaction paradigm would look toward improvement of communication and parental assistance programs; the sociobiological paradigm would evaluate programs designed to improve personal resources and behavior; the learning/situational paradigm would likely evaluate the effects of various social learning techniques on the reduction of dysfunctional behavior and attitudes; and the ecological paradigm would evaluate various programs and techniques designed to have a positive impact on the individual, the family, the community, and society at large.

Overall, the nine paradigms concentrate on six evaluation topics: therapeutical strategies for offenders (by three paradigms), educational programs and impact (two paradigms), resource improvement (two paradigms), techniques for improving interpersonal relations (two paradigms), social change strategies and impact (one paradigm), and family intervention procedures and their success (one paradigm).

Continuation and Follow-up

Under this domain, the individual determinants paradigm and the offender typologies paradigm would continue a long-term clinical evaluation of groups and individuals. The sociocultural paradigm, however, would be more apt to continuously advocate the importance of effective social programs. Proponents of the individual-environment paradigm may continue to concentrate on the implementation of various educational, clinical, and community service programs, whereas the family systems paradigm would focus on the monitoring of family dynamics.

Both the parent-child interaction paradigm and the the sociobiological paradigm would continue to assess the patterns and dynamics of the victim-perpetrator relationship. Finally, the learning/situational paradigm and the ecological paradigm would provide long-term evaluations of the processes and impact of various programs for individuals, families, communities, and society.

Overall, three major topics have been suggested in the follow-up of child abuse and neglect efforts: assessment and monitoring of family dynamics, including the parent-child relationship (by five paradigms), clinical evaluations of groups and individuals (four paradigms), and effectiveness of social, educational, and community programs (four paradigms).

Dissemination

Generally speaking, the methods of knowledge distribution are pretty much the same across disciplines with different theoretical orientations. Major dissemination methods include publications, reports, presentations, and group discussions. However, the contents and the target audience of these reports vary, depending upon the disciplinary orientations of the professionals involved. For example, the paradigms of individual determinants, offender typologies, and family systems tend to focus on a clinical audience with introspective knowledge from clinical case analyses, whereas the sociocultural paradigm tends to focus on political policy and a social service-oriented audience with aggregated statistics compiled from the general population.

Overall, the nine paradigms delineate the following dissemination efforts: clinical reports and presentations (four paradigms), various theoretical and empirical data (four paradigms), reporting and presenting sociocultural data (two paradigms), and summary and integration of empirical and theoretical data (one paradigm).

It is clear that different theoretical backgrounds across different professions, or even within the same profession, might generate diverse, and possibly conflicting, strategies for implementing various programs for each of the seven service domains. Therefore, working with child abuse and neglect cases, a professional in any capacity—either for clinical practice or academic research—will have to face issues pertaining to the following five questions: (1) What domain of services will be needed? (2) What theoretical perspective(s) will have the most accurate and useful knowledge? (3) Which professionals will have most experience and skills in applying different theories to clinical situations? (4) How will other service domains be coordinated to provide an effective communitywide service system? (5) How can different, and possibly conflicting, theories be used, either separately or jointly, to maximize the efforts of various professions?

Answers to these questions require a complete understanding of empirical, as well as theoretical, issues that face all professionals in handling child abuse and neglect cases on a daily basis.

STATUS OF CONTEMPORARY THEORIZATIONS

As a study topic in health and behavioral sciences, child abuse and neglect has a relatively short history in both theoretical development and empirical research. However, diverse theories and abundant empirical findings, as reviewed in this book, indicate that the state of affairs in theory formulation and field research has made rather impressive progress in recent years.

Unfortunately, this progressive movement is far from complete. As is evident from the process evaluation of the theories, models, and perspectives in Chapter 13, there are a number of clear structural barriers in the way these theoretical perspectives have been constructed that have hampered sound progression in theoretical development.

Many of the problems associated with poor theoretical construction reflect a lack of formalization to the extent that propositions have not been empirically tested, replicated, or revised in a systematic manner. Very few of the "theories" could even be called theories in the formal sense. Most could be classified as perspectives, and many are models designed for conceptualization but not prediction, explanation, or understanding.

There is also a problem in not formally decomposing, to an adequate degree, various phenomenal characteristics of child abuse and neglect in terms of important theoretical components (i.e., hypothetical constructs, operational definitions, independent/dependent variables, postulates, and hypotheses). Usually, these components have not been defined or formally specified, and thus they are not objectively assessed as a true science. As a result, the ability to make accurate generalizations and inferences from existing knowledge is significantly negated.

If most of the "theories" in a field are indeed not actual theories and lack the proper theoretical components, it is no surprise to learn that the existing theorizations as a whole generally fail in performing simultaneously all seven basic functions of a scientific theory (i.e., decomposition of knowledge, explanation of past phenomenon, understanding of current relationships, prediction of future events, fruitfulness in generating new research and theorization, establishment of valid and reliable laws, and control over future maltreatment dispositions and behaviors).

Despite such overall deficiencies, some significant progress at the individual function level has been made in the literature. For example, the function of decomposing the data base of knowledge has been accomplished very well by many theories (e.g., social learning for physical abuse and grounded theory for incestuous abuse). It reveals that knowledge has been accumulated and organized from an established data base. This is an important first step for the future development of a comprehensive scientific theory. In addition, the different perspectives on child maltreatment have also been fruitful in sparking debate and in inspiring new empirical research and theoretical conceptualizations.

Therefore, it seems fair to conclude that although various organizational schemes of theoretical knowledge and empirical evidence are not universally accepted, child abuse and neglect as a scientific field of study has established a good repertoire of content issues and has organized empirical data in a relatively consistent manner. Having progressed this far, the field is currently beginning to produce some good theories that offer both explanations of past events and predictions of future directions. Perhaps most important, it offers understanding of the complexity of causal relationships among different variables. In short, as far as the development of a comprehensive scientific theory is concerned, the field has passed beyond its infancy stage of explorations in diverse disciplinary orientations. What is needed in the future is the rigorous integration and development of scientific theories that will perform all important functions of a mature science simultaneously.

In order to reach maturity, future theoretical development needs to embark on a more rigorous path that will fully utilize scientific methods such as control groups, verification procedures, hypothesis testing, and objectivity and replicability of procedures. It is only through the use of such methods that theories can be objectively tested and established with maximal functional efficiency.

In this process of development, the field needs to emphasize the integration of all existing theories and empirical evidence as reviewed in this book and also needs to adopt an approach that will use both summarative inductive and functional deductive forms of theory construction.

PROSPECTS FOR DEVELOPING INTEGRATED THEORIES

The present evaluation of theoretical issues and their empirical evidence reveals that most efforts in the area of child abuse and neglect tend to focus on treatment and intervention issues. These efforts usually employ a small number of clinical subjects and rarely address the complex nature of all aspects of theoretical issues (Parker & Parker, 1986; Finkelhor, 1984). However, in recent years, there are a growing number of notable exceptions that simultaneously consider quality theoretical issues, solid empirical research, and overall integration (e.g., Finkelhor, 1984; Russell, 1986; Hart, Brassard & Germain, 1987; Garbarino, Guttmann & Seeley, 1986; Gelles, 1983; Gil, 1987; Vietze et al. 1982). Nevertheless, there still exist significant gaps between anecdotal description of clinical cases and scientific inference from empirical findings in a broader context universe. Also there appear to be significant discrepancies between knowledge and performance in societal efforts for intervention, prevention, and treatment of child abuse and neglect problems.

The foundations and principles of the individual theories, models, and perspectives reviewed in this study are by themselves unable to provide a comprehensive, satisfactory conceptualization that will address all important facets of issues simultaneously. This is clearly due to the fact that child abuse and neglect is a very complex problem—it is not just a problem for victimized children or perpetrators, but rather, is a problem of the whole family, the community, and the larger ecocultural environment (Tzeng, Hanner, & Fortier, 1988). The majority of theoretical accounts have been designed to explain one particular type of maltreatment and/or particular etiological issues about a specific type of maltreatment.

All of the above controversial and inconclusive theoretical issues of the contemporary literature reflect a desperate need to develop a comprehensive integrated theory that will address the etiology and dynamics of maltreatment and will also address different societal service functions simultaneously.

To overcome these difficulties and deficiencies, a comprehensive, integrated theory is required for serving four important functions in combating child abuse and neglect: (1) linkage of seemingly diverse and conflicting disciplines; (2) organization and evaluation of empirical data, both existing and incoming; (3) development and implementation of intervention, treatment, and prevention strategies; and (4) foundations for continuing scientific research and follow-up evaluation.

This ideal theory should also emphasize the importance of multiple factors and their interactions in both subjective and objective cultures at all ecological levels. As such, this theory should be well suited for planning various educational, clinical, community, and social programs that will effectively combat the problem of child abuse and neglect at any geographic region. It is anticipated that through both process and product evaluations, etiological factors that cause child maltreatment may be halted and eliminated, while factors that oppose child maltreatment may be promoted and maintained.

In short, an ideal theory should be developed for each type of maltreatment, and different theories for various maltreatment typologies should have their commonalities and specificities that will provide accurate information and necessary foundations for the redesigning and implementation of effective programs in all seven service domains of the child abuse and neglect issues (identification, intervention, treatment, prevention, evaluation, follow-up, and dissemination).

As is becoming clear, child abuse and neglect is a problem that requires simultaneous consideration of all individuals and societal institutions (families, communities, and societies). A level of international relations may also be shown to be of significant importance as interactions increase on a worldwide basis and basic human rights become increasingly stressed internationally.

The psychosemantic process model and related conceptualizations presented in Chapters 9, 10, and 11 appear to be important to the above-mentioned pursuit of developing a comprehensive integrated theory for each type of child maltreatment. The structures of two cultures over five ecological units across ten model components have successfully organized the existing theoretical concepts and empirical evidence in a logical way. We believe that such organization reflects significant progress in the field and thus enhances the understanding of child maltreatment as a complex multilevel problem that requires complex multilevel solutions. Using such scientific knowledge and empirical evidence as foundations, it is possible to develop at least five integrated theories, one each for physical abuse, sexual abuse, incestuous abuse, neglect, and psychological maltreatment. Toward this goal, the psychosemantic process model may be used as the major scientific organizational tool to systemize the pertinent topical issues and concerns of all existing theories and empirical data.

References

Aber, J. L., & Allen, J. P. (1987). Effects of maltreatment on young children's socioemotional development: An attachment theory perspective. *Developmental Psychology, 23,* 3, 406–414.

Adams, M. S., & Neel, J. V. (1967). Children of incest. *Pediatrics, 40,* 55–67.

Ainsworth, M. D. (1967). *Infancy in Uganda: Infant care and the growth of love.* Baltimore: Johns Hopkins University Press.

Ainsworth, M. D. S. (1979). Infant-mother attachment. *American Psychologist, 34,* 932–937.

Ainsworth, M. D. S., Blehar, M., Walters, E., & Wall, S. (1978). *Patterns of attachment.* Hillsdale, NJ: Erlbaum.

Alexander, P. (1985). A systems theory conceptualization of incest. *Family process, 24,* 39–47.

Alfaro, J. D. (1981). Report on the relationship between child abuse and neglect and later socially deviant behavior. In R. J. Hunner & Y. E. Walker (Eds.), *Exploring the relationship between child abuse and delinquency,* 175–219. Monteclair, NJ: Allanheld Osmun.

Alland, A. (1972). *The human imperative.* New York: Columbia University Press.

Altemeier, W. A., Vietze, P. M., Sherrod, K. B., Sandler, H. M., Falsey, S., & O'Connor, S. (1979). Prediction of maltreatment during pregnancy. *Journal of the American Academy of Child Psychiatry, 18,* 205–218.

Alter-Reid, K., Gibbs, M. S., Lachenmeyer, J. R., Sigal, J., & Massoth, N. A. (1986). Sexual abuse of children: A review of the empirical findings. *Clinical Psychology Review, 6,* 249–266.

American Humane Association. (1980). *National analysis of official child neglect and abuse reporting.* Department of Health and Human Services. Washington, DC: Government Printing Office. (Pub. No. OHD 80-30271)

American Humane Association. (1986). *Highlights of official child neglect and abuse reporting, 1984.* Denver: American Humane Association.

Anderson, C., & Mayes, P. (1982). Treating family sexual abuse: The humanistic approach. *Journal of Child Care, 1,* 2, 31–46.

316   References

Araji, S., & Finkelhor, D. (1985). Explanations of pedophilia: Review of empirical research. *Bulletin of the American Academy of Psychiatry and Law, 3*, 1, 17–37.
Ardrey, R. (1966). *The territorial imperative.* New York: Columbia University Press.
Aries, P. (1962). *Centuries of childhood: A social history of family life.* New York: Knopf.
Atwood, R., & Howell, R. (1971). Pupillometric and personality test scores of female aggressing pedophiliacs and normals. *Psychonomic Science, 22*, 115–116.
Ayoub, C., & Jacewitz, M. M. (1982). Families at risk of poor parenting: A descriptive study of sixty at risk families in a model prevention program. *Child Abuse and Neglect, 6*, 413–422.
Ayoub, C. C. & Milner, J. S. (1985). Failure to thrive: Parental indicators, types and outcomes. *Child Abuse and Neglect, 9*, 491–499.
Azar, S. T. (1986). A framework for understanding child maltreatment: An integration of cognitive, behavioural and developmental perspectives. *Canadian Journal of Behavioral Science, 18*, 4, 340–355.
Azar, S. T., Fantuzzo, J., & Twentyman, C. T. (1984). An applied behavioural approach to child maltreatment: Back to basics. *Advances in Behaviour Research and Therapy, 6*, 3–11.
Azar, S. T., Robinson, D. R., Hekimian, E., & Twentyman, C. T. (1984). Unrealistic expectations and problem solving ability in maltreating and comparative mothers. *Journal of Consulting and Clinical Psychology, 52*, 687–691.
Bakan, D. (1971). *Slaughter of the innocents.* San Francisco: Jossey-Bass.
Bandura, A. (1961). Transmission of aggression through imitation of aggressive models. *Journal of Abnormal and Social Psychology, 63*, 3, 935–941.
Bandura, A. (1973). *Aggression: A social learning analysis.* Englewood Cliffs, NJ: Prentice-Hall.
Bandura, A. (1983). Psychological mechanisms of aggression. In R. G. Geen & E. I. Donnerstein (Eds.), *Aggression: Theoretical and empirical reviews* (Vol. 1). New York: Academic Press.
Barash, D. (1979). *The whispering within.* New York: Harper & Row.
Barnett, E. R., Pittman, C. B., Ragan, C. K., & Salus, M. K. (1980). *Family violence: Intervention strategies.* Department of Health and Human Services. Washington, DC: Government Printing Office. (Pub. No. OHDS 80-30258)
Basini, J., & Kentsmith, D. (1980). Psychotherapy with wives of sexual deviants. *American Journal of Psychotherapy, 24*, 1, 20–25.
Bateson, P. (1983). Optimal outbreeding. In P. Bateson (Ed.), *Mate choice.* Cambridge: Cambridge University Press.
Bauer, W. D., & Twentyman, C. T. (1985). Abusing, neglectful, and comparison mothers' responses to child-related and non-child-related stressors. *Journal of Consulting and Clinical Psychology, 53*, 3, 335–343.
Behling, D. W. (1979). Alcohol abuse as encountered in 51 instances of reported child abuse. *Clinical Pediatrics, 18*, 87.
Bell, A. D., & Hall, C. S. (1976). The personality of a child molester. In M. S. Weinberg (Ed.), *Sex research: Studies from the Kinsey Institute.* Oxford, England: Oxford University Press.
Bell, G. (1973). Parents who abuse their children. *Canadian Psychiatric Association Journal, 18*, 223–228.

Belsky, J. (1978). Three theoretical models of child abuse: A critical review. *Child Abuse and Neglect, 2,* 37–49.

Belsky, J. (1980). Child maltreatment: An ecological integration. *American Psychologist, 35,* 320–335.

Belsky, J. (1984). The determinants of parenting: A process model. *Child Development, 55,* 83–96.

Belsky, J., Rovine, M., & Taylor, D. (1984). The Pennsylvania infant and family development project, III: The origins of individual differences in infant-mother attachment. *Child Development, 55,* 718–728.

Bennie, E. H., & Sclare, A. B. (1969). The battered child syndrome. *American Journal of Psychiatry, 125,* 7, 975–979.

Berkowitz, L. (1981). How guns control us. *Psychology Today,* June, 11–12.

Berlin, F. S. (1982). Sex offenders: A biomedical perspective. In J. Greer & I. Stuart (Eds.), *Sexual aggression: Current perspectives on treatment* (Vol. 1), *Victim treatment* (Vol. 2). New York: Van Nostrand Reinhold.

Berman, P. W. (1980). Sex differences in responses to the young. *Psychological Bulletin, 88,* 668–698.

Berry, G. W. (1975). Incest: Some clinical variations on a classical theme. *Journal of the American Academy of Psychoanalysis, 3,* 2, 151–161.

Berry, J. W. (1979). Research in multicultural societies: Implications of cross-cultural methods. *Journal of Cross-Cultural Psychology, 10,* 4, 415–434.

Biaggio, A. M. B. (1983). Brazil: Competing theories of aggression and initial research findings. In A. P. Goldstein & M. H. Segall (Eds.), *Aggression in global perspective.* New York: Pergamon Press.

Birrell, R. G., & Birrell, J. H. W. (1968). The maltreatment of children: A hospital survey. *Medical Journal of Australia, 2,* 1023–1029.

Blau, P. M. (1964). *Exchange and power in social life.* New York: Wiley.

Blumberg, M. L. (1974). Psychopathology of the abusing parent. *American Journal of Psychotherapy, 28,* 21–29.

Boehm, B. (1964). The community and the social agency define neglect. *Child Welfare,* November.

Bousha, D. M., & Twentyman, C. T. (1984). Mother-child interactional style in abuse, neglect, and control groups: Naturalistic observations in the home. *Journal of Abnormal Psychology, 93,* 1, 106–114.

Bowen, N. H. (1987). Pornography: Research review and implications for counseling. *Journal of Counseling and Development, 65,* 345–350.

Bowlby, J. (1951). Maternal care and mental health. *Bulletin of the World Health Organization, 3,* 355–533.

Bowlby, J. (1953). *Child care and the growth of love.* London: Penguin.

Bowlby, J. (1969). *Attachment and loss,* Vol. 1: *Attachment.* New York: Basic Books.

Bowlby, J. (1970). Disruption of affectional bonds and its effects on behavior. *Journal of Contemporary Psychotherapy, 2,* 2, 75–86.

Bowlby, J. (1973). *Attachment and loss,* Vol. 2: *Separation.* New York: Basic Books.

Bowlby, J. (1980). *Attachment and loss,* Vol. 3: *Loss, sadness and depression.* New York: Basic Books.

Brant, R., & Tiza, V. (1977). The sexually misused child. *American Journal of Orthopsychiatry, 47,* 1, 80–90.

318   References

Brassard, M. R., & Gelardo, M. S. (1987). Psychological maltreatment: The underlying construct in child abuse and neglect. *School Psychology Review, 16*, 2, 127–136.

Brassard, M. R., Tyler, A., & Kehle, T. J. (1983). School programs to prevent intra-familial child sexual abuse. *Child Abuse and Neglect, 7*, 241–245.

Breese, P., Stearns, G. B., Bess, B. H., & Packer, L. S. (1986). Allegations of child sexual abuse in child custody disputes: A therapeutic assessment model. *American Journal of Orthopsychiatry, 56*, 4.

Broadhurst, D. D. (1975). Project protection in Maryland: A school program to combat child abuse. *The Education Digest, 61*, 2, 20–23.

Bronfenbrenner, U. (1977). Toward an experimental ecology of human development. *American Psychologist, 32*, 7, 513–532.

Bronfenbrenner, U. (1979). *The ecology of human development: Experiments by nature and design*. Cambridge: Harvard University Press.

Brown, A., & Finkelhor, D. (1986). Impact of child sexual abuse: A review of the research. *Psychological Bulletin, 99*, 1, 66–77.

Browning, D., & Boatman, B. (1977). Incest: Children at risk. *American Journal of Psychiatry, 134*, 1, 69–72.

Brownmiller, S. (1975). *Against our will*. New York: Simon & Schuster.

Buckley, W. (1967). *Sociology and modern systems theory*. Englewood Cliffs, NJ: Prentice-Hall.

Burgess, R. (1978). Project interact: A study of patterns of interaction in abusive, neglectful and central families. Final report to the National Center of Child Abuse and Neglect, U.S. Department of Health, Education and Welfare.

Burgess, R. L. (1979). Project interact: A study of patterns of interaction in abusive, neglectful and control families. *Child Abuse and Neglect, 3*, 781–791.

Burgess, R. L., & Conger, R. D. (1978). Family interaction in abusive, neglectful and normal families. *Child Development, 49*, 1163–1173.

Burgess, R. L., & Garbarino, J. (1983). Doing what comes naturally? An evolutionary perspective on child abuse. In Finkelhor, D., Gelles, R. J., Hotaling, G. T., & Straus, M. A. (Eds.), *The dark side of families: Current family violence research*. Beverly Hills, CA: Sage.

Burgess, A. W., Groth, N. A., Holmstrom, L. L., & Sgroi, S. M. (1978). *Sexual assault of children and adolescents*. Lexington, MA: Lexington Books.

Buric, O., & Zecevic, A. (1967). Family authority, marital satisfaction, and social network in Yugoslavia. *Journal of Marriage and the Family, 29*, 2, 325–336.

Burland, J. A., Andrews, R. G., & Headsten, S. J. (1973). Child abuse: One tree in the forest. *Child Welfare, 52*, 585–592.

Burr, W. R., Ahern, L., & Knowles, E. M. (1977). An empirical test of Rodman's theory of resources in cultural context. *Journal of Marriage and the Family, 29*, 2, 325–336.

Cavallin, H. (1966). Incestuous fathers: A clinical report. *American Journal of Psychiatry, 122*, 10, 1132–1138.

Chagnon, N. (1977). *Yanomano: The fierce people*. New York: Dell.

Chandler, L. A. (1981). The source of stress inventory. *Psychology in the Schools, 18*, 2, 164–168.

Chapman, J. (1979). Ill-treatment of children: The social and legal context in England and Wales. *Child Abuse and Neglect, 3*, 51–60.

Cicchetti, D. (1987). Developmental psychopathology in infancy: Illustration from the study of maltreated youngsters. *Journal of Consulting and Clinical Psychology,* *55,* 6, 837–845.

Cicchetti, D., & Carlson, V. (1989). *Child maltreatment: Theory and research on the causes and consequences of child abuse and neglect.* New York: Cambridge University Press.

Cohen, T. (1983). The incestuous family revisited. *Social Casework: The Journal of Contemporary Social Work,* March.

Cohler, J. (1987). Sex, love and incest. *Contemporary Psychoanalysis, 24,* 4, 604–621.

Conger, J. C., & Keanon, S. P. (1981). Social skills intervention in treatment of isolated or withdrawn children. *Psychological Bulletin, 90,* 3, 478–495.

Conger, J. J. (1981). Freedom and commitment: Families, youth and social change. *American Psychologist, 36,* 1475–1484.

Conger, R. D., Burgess, R. L., & Barrett, C. (1979). Child abuse related to life change and perceptions of illness: Some preliminary findings. *Family coordinator, 28,* 1, 73–78.

Conger, R. D., Lahey, B. B., & Smith, S. S. (1981). An intervention program for child abuse: Modifying maternal depression and behavior. Paper presented at the National Conference for Family Violence Researchers, Durham, NH.

Conte, J. R. (1985). The effects of sexual abuse on children: Preliminary findings. Unpublished paper, available from the author at School of Service Administration, 969 E. 60th St., Chicago, IL, 60637.

Conte, J. R. (1986). Sexual abuse and the family: A critical analysis. *Journal of Psychotherapy and the Family, 2,* 2, 113–126.

Conte, J. R., & Schuerman, J. R. (1987). Factors associated with an increased impact of child sexual abuse. *Child Abuse and Neglect, 11,* 201–211.

Coon, P. M. (1985). Children of parents with multiple personality disorder. In R. P. Kluft (Ed.), *Childhood antecedents of multiple personality.* Washington, DC: American Psychiatric Association.

Crittenden, P. M. (1984). Sibling interaction: Evidence of a generational effect in maltreating infants. *Child Abuse and Neglect, 8,* 433–438.

Cromwell, R. E., & Olson, D. H. (1975). *Power in families.* Beverly Hills, CA: Sage.

Daly, M., & Wilson, M. (1980). Discriminative parental solicitude: A biological perspective. *Journal of Marriage and the Family, 42,* 277–280.

Daly, M., & Wilson, M. (1981). Child maltreatment from a sociobiological perspective. *New Directions in Child Development, 11,* 93–112.

Davitz, J. R. (1952). The effects of previous training on postfrustration behavior. *Journal of Abnormal and Social Psychology, 47,* 309–315.

DeChesnay, M. (1985). Father-daughter incest: An overview. *Behavioral Sciences and the Law, 3,* 391–402.

Delsardo, J. D. (1974). Protective casework for abused children. In J. E. Leavitt (Ed.), *The battered child.* New York: General Learning.

DeMause, L. (1974). *The history of childhood.* New York: Harper & Row.

Denelsky, G., & Denenberg, V. (1967). Infantile stimulation and adult exploratory behavior: Effects of handling upon tactual variation seeking. *Journal of Comparative Physiological Psychology, 63,* 309–312.

Denson-Gerber, J., & Hutchinson, S. (1979). Sexual and commercial exploitation of children: Legislative responses and treatment challenges. *Child Abuse and Neglect, 3,* 61–66.

Dentan, R. K. (1979). *The Semai: A nonviolent people of Malaya.* New York: Holt, Rinehart & Winston.

de Young, M. (1982). *The sexual victimization of children.* Jefferson, NC: McFarland.

Dietrich, K. N., Starr, R. H., Jr., & Kaplan, M. G. (1980). Maternal stimulation and care of abused infants. In T. Field (Ed.), *High risk infants and children: Adult and peer interactions.* New York: Academic Press.

Dion, K. K. (1974). Children's physical attractiveness and sex as determinants of adult punitiveness. *Developmental Psychology, 10,* 772–778.

Disbrow, M. A., Doerr, H., & Caulfield, M. (1977). Measuring the components of parent's potential for child abuse and neglect. *Child Abuse and Neglect, 1,* 279–296.

Ditson, J., & Shay, S. (1984). Use of a home-based computer to analyze community data from reported cases of child abuse and neglect. *Child Abuse and Neglect, 8,* 503–509.

Dobash, R. E., & Dobash, R. P. (1979). *Violence against wives: A case against the patriarchy.* New York: Free Press.

Dollard, J., Doob, L., Moller, N., Mowrer, O. H., & Sears, R. R. (1939). *Frustration and aggression.* New Haven, CT: Yale University Press.

Dougherty, N. (1983). The holding environment: Breaking the abusive cycle of abuse. *Social Casework: The Journal of Contemporary Social Work,* May, 283–290.

Dubanoski, R. A. (1982). Child maltreatment in European- and Hawaiian- Americans. *Child Abuse and Neglect, 5,* 457–465.

Duberman, R. E. (1975). *The reconstituted family: A study of remarried couples and their children.* Chicago: Nelson-Hall.

Durkheim, E. (1963). *Incest: The nature and origin of the taboo.* New York: L. Stuart.

Egeland, B., & Erickson, M. F. (1987). Psychologically unavailable caregiving. In M. R. Brassard, R. Germain, & S. N. Hart (Eds.), *Psychological maltreatment of children and youth.* New York: Pergamon Press.

Egeland, B., Sroufe, L. A., & Erickson, M. (1983). The developmental consequence of different patterns of maltreatment. *Child Abuse and Neglect, 1,* 459–469.

Eisnitz, A. J. (1984). Father-daughter incest. *International Journal of Psychoanalysis and Psychotherapy, 10,* 495–503.

Ellis, H. (1942). *Studies in the psychology of sex* (2 vols.). New York: Random House.

Elmer, E. (1966). Hazards in determining child abuse. *Child Welfare,* January, 29–34.

Elmer, E. (1967). *Children in jeopardy: A study of abused minors and their families.* Pittsburgh: University of Pittsburgh Press.

Elmer, E. (1977). *Fragile families, troubled children: The aftermath of infant trauma.* Pittsburgh: University of Pittsburgh Press.

Engfer, A., & Schneewind, K. (1982). Causes and consequences of harsh parental punishment: An empirical investigation in a representative sample of 570 German families. *Child Abuse and Neglect, 6,* 2, 129–139.

Erikson, E. (1963). *Childhood and society.* New York: Norton.

Erikson, E. (1968). *Identity: Youth and crisis.* New York: Norton.

Eron, L. (1987). Television as a source of maltreatment of children. *School Psychology Review, 16,* 195–202.

Evans, S. L., Reinhart, J. B., & Succop, R. A. (1972). Failure to thrive: A study of 45 children and their families. *Journal of the American Academy of Child Psychiatry, 11,* 440–457.

Fagan, J. A., Stewart, D. K., & Hansen, K. V. (1983). Violent men or violent husbands? In D. Finkelhor, R. J. Gelles, G. T. Hotaling, & M. A. Straus (Eds.), *The dark side of families: Current family violence research*. Beverly Hills, CA: Sage.

Fanaroff, A., Kennel, J., & Klaus, M. (1972). Follow-up of low birth weight infants: The predictive value of maternal visiting patterns. *Pediatrics, 49*, 287–290.

Farrington, K. (1980). Stress and family violence. In M. Strauss & G. Hotaling, *Social causes of husband-wife violence*. Minneapolis: University of Minnesota Press.

Farrington, K. (1986). The application of stress theory to the study of family violence: Principles, problems and prospects. *Journal of Family Violence, 1*, 2, 131–147.

Fenichel, D. (1945). *The psychoanalytic theory of neurosis*. New York: Norton.

Ferrier, P. E., Schaller, M., & Girardet, I. (1985). Abused children admitted to a pediatric inpatient service in Switzerland: A ten-year experience and follow-up evaluation. *Child Abuse and Neglect, 9*, 373–381.

Feshbach, S. (1980). Must the child be the victim of political violence? An issue in adult moral consciousness. *Journal of Clinical Child Psychology, 9*, 125–127.

Field, T. (1980). *High risk infants and children: Adult and peer interactions*. New York: Academic Press.

Finkelhor, D. (1978). Psychological, cultural and family factors in incest and family sexual abuse. *Journal of Marriage and Family Counseling*, Oct., 41–49.

Finkelhor, D. (1979). *Sexually victimized children*. New York: Free Press.

Finkelhor, D. (1980). Risk factors in the sexual victimization of children. *Child Abuse and Neglect, 4*, 265–273.

Finkelhor, D. (1982). Sexual abuse: A sociological perspective. *Child Abuse and Neglect, 6*, 95–102.

Finkelhor, D. (1983). Common features of family abuse. In D. Finkelhor, R. J. Gelles, G. T. Hotaling, & M. A. Straus (Eds.), *The dark side of families: Current family violence research*. Beverly Hills, CA: Sage.

Finkelhor, D. (1984). *Child sexual abuse: New theory and research*. New York: Free Press.

Finkelhor, D. (1986). Sexual abuse: Beyond the family systems approach. In T. S. Trepper & M. J. Barrett (Ed.) *Treating incest: A multimodal systems perspective*. New York: Haworth.

Finkelhor, D., & Araji, S. (1986). Explanations of pedophilia: A four factor model. *The Journal of Sex Research, 22*, 2, 145–161.

Finkelhor, D., Gelles, R. J., Hotaling, G. T., & Straus, M. A., eds. (1983). *The dark side of families: Current family violence research*. Beverly Hills, CA: Sage.

Finkelhor, D., & Redfield, D. (1984). How the public defines sexual abuse. In D. Finkelhor (Ed.), *Child sexual abuse: New theory and research*. New York: Free Press.

Finkelhor, D., & Russell, D. (1984). Women as perpetrators. In D. Finkelhor, *Child sexual abuse: New theory and research*, 171–187. New York: Free Press.

Fisher, G. (1969). Psychological needs of heterosexual pedophiliacs. *Digest of the Nervous System, 3*, 419–421.

Fisher, G., & Howell, L. (1970). Psychological needs of homosexual pedophiliacs. *Digest of the Nervous System, 3*, 623–625.

Fontana, V. J. (1971). *The maltreated child* (2nd ed.). Springfield, IL: Thomas.

Fontana, V. J., & Bersharav, D. J. (1979). *The maltreated child*. Springfield, IL: Thomas.

Fowler, C., Burns, S., & Roehi, J. (1983). The role of group theory in incest counseling. *International Journal of Family Therapy, 5*, 2, 127–135.

Fox, G. L. (1973). Another look at the comparative resource model: Assessing the balance of power in Turkish families. *Journal of Marriage and the Family, 35,* 718–730.

Fox, J. (1962). Sibling incest. *British Journal of Sociobiology, 13*, 128–150.

Fox, R. (1967). *Kinship and marriage.* London: Pelican.

Fox, R. (1980). *The red lamp of incest.* New York: Dutto.

Fraczek, A. (1985). Moral approval of aggressive acts: A Polish-Finnish comparative study. *Journal of Cross-Cultural Psychology, 16*, 1, 41–54.

Freedman, D. A., & Freedman, N. (1969). Behavioral differences between Chinese-American and European-American newborns. *Nature, 224*, 1227.

French, C. (1984). Child abuse: The development of competing paradigms. *International Social Work, 27*, 2, 1–8.

Freud, S. (1893). Studies in hysteria. In *Standard edition,* Vol. 3, 45–68. London: Hogarth Press.

Freud, S. (1894). The neuropsychoses of defense. In *Standard edition,* Vol. 2, 131–135. London: Hogarth Press.

Freud, S. (1896). Heredity and the aetiology of the neurosis. In *Standard edition,* Vol. 3, 142–156. London: Hogarth Press.

Freud, S. (1938). *Totem and taboo.* In *The basic writing of Sigmund Freud* (Trans. A. A. Brill). New York: Random House.

Freud, S. (1939). *An outline of psychoanalysis.* New York: Norton.

Freud, S. (1953). Three essays on the theory of sexuality. In *Standard edition,* Vol. 7. London: Hogarth Press.

Freund, K. (1967). Erotic preference in pedophilia. *Behavior Research Theory, 5*, 339–348.

Freund, K., & Langevin, R. (1976). Bisexuality in homosexual pedophilia. *Archives of Sexual Behavior, 5*, 415–423.

Freund, K., Langevin, R., & Cibiri, S. (1967). Heterosexual aversion in homosexual males. *British Journal of Psychiatry, 122*, 163–169.

Friedman, P. (1959). Sexual deviations. In S. Arieti (Ed.), *American handbook of psychiatry,* Vol. 1. New York: Basic Books.

Friedrich, W. N., & Boriskin, J. A. (1976). The role of the children in abuse: A review of the literature. *American Journal of Orthopsychiatry, 46*, 580–590.

Frisbie, L. V., Vanasek, F. J., & Dingman, H. F. (1967). The self and the ideal self: Methodological study of pedophiles. *Psychological Reports, 20*, 3, 699–706.

Frude, N. (1982). The sexual nature of sexual abuse. *Child Abuse and Neglect, 6*, 211–223.

Gaddini, R. (1983). Incest as a developmental failure. *Child Abuse and Neglect, 7*, 357–358.

Galdston, R. (1965). Observations on children who have been physically abused and their parents. *American Journal of Psychiatry, 122*, 440–443.

Garbarino, J. (1976). Some ecological correlates of child abuse: The impact of economic stress on mothers. *Child Development, 47*, 178–185.

Garbarino, J. (1977). The human ecology of child maltreatment. *Journal of Marriage and the Family, 39*, 721–736.

Garbarino, J. (1982). *Children and families in the social environment.* New York: Aldine.

Garbarino, J. (1984). Adolescent abuse: Troubled youth, troubled families. Paper presented at the 92nd annual convention of the American Psychological Association, Toronto, Canada.

Garbarino, J., Guttman, E., Seeley, J. W. (1986). *The psychologically battered child: Strategies for identification, assessment, and intervention.* San Francisco: Jossey-Bass.

Garbarino, J., & Sherman, D. (1980). High-risk neighborhoods and high-risk families: The human ecology of child maltreatment. *Child Development, 51,* 188–198.

Garbarino, J., & Vondra, J. (1983). Psychological maltreatment of children and youth. Paper presented at the International Conference on Psychological Abuse of Children and Youth, Indiana University, Indianapolis, IN.

Gebhard, P., Gagnon, J., Pomeroy, W., & Christenson, C. (1965). *Sex offenders: An analysis of types.* New York: Harper & Row.

Geis, G., & Monahan, J. (1976). The social ecology of violence. In T. Lickona (Ed.), *Man and Morality.* New York: Holt, Rinehart & Winston.

Geiser, R. I. (1979). *Hidden victims: The sexual abuse of children.* Boston: Beacon Press.

Gelardo, M. S., & Sanford, E. E. (1987). Child abuse and neglect: A review of the literature. *School Psychology Review, 16,* 2, 137–155.

Gelles, R. J. (1973). Child abuse as psychopathology: A sociological critique and reformulation. *American Journal of Orthopsychiatry, 43,* 4, 611–621.

Gelles, R. J. (1975). Violence and pregnancy: A note on the extent of the problem and needed services. *Family Coordination, 24,* 1, 81–86.

Gelles, R. J. (1978). Violence toward children in the United States. *American Journal of Orthopsychiatry, 48,* 4, 580–592.

Gelles, R. J. (1980). Violence in the family: A review of research in the 70s. *Journal of Marriage and the Family, 41,* 75–88.

Gelles, R. J. (1982). Toward better research on child abuse and neglect: A response to Besharov. *Child Abuse and Neglect, 6,* 4, 495–496.

Gelles, R. J. (1983a). An exchange/social control theory. In D. Finkelhor, R. J. Gelles, G. T. Hotaling, & M. A. Straus (Eds.), *The dark side of families: Current family violence research.* Beverly Hills, CA: Sage.

Gelles, R. J. (1983b). Applying research on family violence to clinical practice. *Journal of Marriage and the Family, 44,* 9–20.

Gelles, R. J. (1985). *Intimate violence in families.* Beverly Hills, CA: Sage.

Gelles, R. J. (1987). The family and its role in the abuse of children. *Psychiatric Annals, 17,* 4, 229–232.

Gelles, R. J., & Cornell, C. P. (1985). International perspectives on child abuse. *Child Abuse and Neglect, 7,* 4, 375–386.

Gelles, R. J., & Hargreaves, W. A. (1981). Maternal employment and violence towards children. *Journal of Family Issues, 2,* 4, 509–530.

Gelles, R. J., & Maynard, P. E. (1987). A structural family systems approach to intervention in cases of family violence. *Family Relations, 36,* 270–275.

Gelles, R. J., & Straus, M. A. (1979). Determinants of violence in the family: Toward a theoretical integration. In W. R. Burr et al. (Eds.), *Contemporary theories about the family.* New York: Free Press.

Germain, R., Brassard, M., & Hart, S. (1985). Crisis intervention for maltreated children. *School Psychology Review, 14,* 3, 291–299.

Gil, D. G. (1970). *Violence against children: Physical child abuse in the United States*. Cambridge: Harvard University Press.

Gil, D. G. (1971). Violence against children. *Journal of Marriage and the Family, 33*, 637–657.

Gil, D. G. (1975). Unraveling child abuse. *American Journal of Orthopsychiatry, 45*, 346–356.

Gil, D. G. (1987). Maltreatment as a function of the structure of social systems. In M. R. Brassard, R. Germain, & S. N. Hart (Eds.), *Psychological maltreatment of children and youth*. New York: Pergamon Press.

Giles-Simes, J., & Finkelhor, D. (1984). Child abuse in stepfamilies. *Family Relations, 33*, 407–413.

Gillespie, W. H. (1964). The psycho-analytic theory of sexual deviation with special reference to fetishism. In I. Rosen (Ed.), *The psychology and treatment of sexual deviation*. New York: Oxford University Press.

Giovannoni, J. M. (1971). Parental mistreatment: Perpetrators and victims. *Journal of Marriage and the Family, 33*, 649–657.

Giovannoni, J. M., & Billingsley, A. (1970). Child neglect among the poor: A study of parental adequacy in families of three ethnic groups. *Child Welfare, 49*, 196–204.

Giovannoni, J. R., Billingsley, A., & Purvine, M. (1969). *Child protective services*. Unpublished manuscript, School of Social Welfare, University of California, Los Angeles.

Glick, I. D., & Kessler, D. R. (1974). *Marital and family therapy*. New York: Grune & Stratton.

Glueck, B. C. (1954). Psychodynamic patterns in sex offenders. *Psychiatric Quarterly, 28*, 1–21.

Glueck, B. C. (1965). Pedophilia. In R. Slovenko (Ed.), *Sexual behavior and the law*. New York: Harper & Row.

Goldstein, A. P., & Segall, M. H., eds. (1983). *Aggression in global perspective*. New York: Pergamon Press.

Goldstein, H. S. (1983). Father's absence and cognitive development of children over a 3- to 5-year period. *Psychological Reports, 52*, 3, 971–976.

Goldstein, M. J., Kant, H. S., & Hartman, J. J. (1973). *Pornography and sexual deviance*. Los Angeles: University of California Press.

Goode, W. J. (1971). Force and violence in the family. *Journal of Marriage and the Family, 33*, 624–636.

Goodman, G. S., & Rosenberg, M. S. (1987). The child witness to family violence. In D. J. Sonkin (Ed.), *Domestic violence on trial: Psychological and legal dimensions of family violence*. New York: Springer.

Goodwin, J., & DiVasto, P. (1979). Mother-daughter incest. *Child Abuse and Neglect, 3*, 953–957.

Gordon, M., & Creighton, S. J. (1988). Natal and non-natal fathers as sexual abusers in the United Kingdom: A comparative analysis. *Journal of Marriage and the Family, 50*, 99–105.

Goshen-Gottstein, E. R. (1980). Treatment of young children among western Jewish mothers in Israel: Sociocultural variables. *American Journal of Orthopsychiatry, 50*, 2, 323–340.

Goy, R., & McEwen, B. S. (1977). *Sexual differentiation of the brain*. Cambridge, MA: MIT Press.

Gray, J. P. (1981). Male security and art style in traditional societies. *Journal of Social Psychology, 114,* 1, 35–42.

Green, A. H. (1980). *Child maltreatment: A handbook for mental health and child care professionals.* New York: Aronson.

Green, A. H. (1984). Child abuse by siblings. *Child Abuse and Neglect, 8,* 311–317.

Green, A. H., Gaines, R. W., & Sandgrund, A. (1974). Child abuse: Pathological syndrome of family interaction. *American Journal of Psychiatry, 131,* 882–886.

Griswold, B., & Billingsley, A. (1967). Psychological functioning of parents who mistreat their children and those who do not. Unpublished manuscript, Berkeley, CA.

Groth, N. A. (1978). Patterns of sexual assault against children and adolescents. In A. W. Burgess, N. A. Groth, L. L. Holmstrom, & S. M. Sgroi, *Sexual assault of children and adolescents.* Lexington, MA: Lexington Books.

Groth, N. A. (1982). The incest offender. In S. M. Sgroi (Ed.), *Handbook of clinical intervention in child sexual abuse.* Lexington, MA: Lexington Books.

Groth, N. A., & Birnbaum, H. J. (1979). *Men who rape: the psychology of the offender.* New York: Plenum Press.

Groth, N. A., & Burgess, A. W. (1977). Motivational intent in the sexual assault of children. *Criminal Justice and Behavior, 4,* 3, 253–264.

Groth, N. A., Hobson, W., & Gary, T. (1982). The child molester: Clinical observations. In J. Conte & D. Shore (Eds.), *Social work and child sexual abuse.* New York: Haworth.

Gruber, A. R. (1981). Sexual victimization of youth. *Child Abuse and Neglect, 3,* 65–73.

Gruber, K., & Jones, R. J. (1983). Identifying determinants of risk of sexual victimization of youth: A multivariate approach. *Child Abuse and Neglect, 7,* 1, 17–24.

Guttman, H. A. (1986). Epistemology, systems theories and the theory of family theory. *American Journal of Family Therapy, 14,* 1, 13–22.

Haley, J. (1967). Toward a theory of pathological systems. In G. Zuk & I. Boszormenyinagy (Eds.), *Family therapy and disturbed families.* Palo Alto, CA: Science & Behavior Books.

Hall, C. S., & Lindzey, G. (1985). *Introduction to theories of personality.* New York: Wiley.

Hally, C., Polansky, N. F., & Polansky, N. A. (1980). *Child neglect: Mobilizing services,* Washington, DC: Government Printing Office. (DHHS Publication No. OHDS 80-30257)

Halperin, M. (1979). *Helping maltreated children: School and community involvement.* St. Louis: Mosby.

Hammer, R. F., & Glueck, B. C., Jr. (1957). Psychodynamic patterns in sex offenders: A four-factor theory. *Psychiatric Quarterly, 31,* 325–345.

Harcourt, M. (1986). Child sexual abuse. In J. J. Jacobson (Ed.), *Psychiatric sequelae of child abuse.* Springfield, IL: Thomas.

Hardin, G. (1977). *The limits of altruism: An ecologist's view of survival.* Bloomington: Indiana University Press.

Harlow, H. F. (1969). Age-mate or peer affectional system. In D. S. Lehrman, R. A. Hinde, and E. Shaw (Eds.), *Advances in the study of behavior,* Vol. 2, 333–383. New York: Academic Press.

Harlow, H. F. (1974). Induction and alleviation of depressive states in monkeys. In N. F. White (Ed.), *Ethology and psychiatry,* 197–208. Toronto: University of Toronto.

326   References

Harlow, H., & Harlow, M. K. (1970). Developmental aspects of emotional behavior. In P. Black (Ed.), *Physiological correlates of emotion*. New York: Academic Press.

Harlow, H. F., Harlow, M. K., Dodsworth, R. O., & Arling, G. L. (1966). Maternal behavior of rhesus monkeys deprived of mothering and peer associations in infancy. In C. M. Harlow (Ed.), *From learning to love*. New York: Praeger.

Harris, M. (1974). *Cows, pigs, wars, and witches: The riddles of culture*. New York: Random House.

Hart, S. N., Brassard, M. R., & Germain, R. (1987). Psychological maltreatment in education and schooling. In M. R. Brassard, R. Germain, & S. N. Hart (Eds.), *Psychological maltreatment of children and youth*. New York: Pergamon Press.

Hart, S. N., Germain, R. B., & Brassard, M. R. (1987). The challenge: To better understand and combat psychological maltreatment of children and youth. In M. R. Brassard, R. Germain, & S. N. Hart, (Eds.), *Psychological maltreatment of children and youth*. New York: Pergamon Press.

Haukes, G. R., & Taylor, M. (1975). Power structure in Mexican and Mexican American farm labor families. *Journal of Marriage and the Family, 37*, 807–811.

Havighurst, R. (1972). *Developmental tasks and education*. New York: David McKay.

Heinicke, C. M. (1984). The role of pre-birth parent characteristics in early family development. *Child Abuse and Neglect, 8*, 169–181.

Henderson, J. (1975). Community transference: Toward a psychiatry of the community. *International Journal of Social Psychiatry, 21*, 1, 14–20.

Henry, J. (1940). Some cultural determinants of hostility in Pilaga Indian children. In R. Hunt (Ed.), *Personalities and cultures: Readings in psychological anthropology*, 166–181. Garden City, NY: Natural History Press.

Hepworth, J., Ryder, R. G., & Dreyer, A. S. (1984). The effects of parental loss on the formation of intimate relationships. *Journal of Marital and Family Therapy, 10*, 1, 73–82.

Herman, J. L. (1981). *Father-daughter incest*. Cambridge: Harvard University Press.

Herman, J., & Hirschman, L. (1977). Father-daughter incest. *Signs, 2*, 1–22.

Herman, J., & Hirschman, L. (1981). Families at risk for father-daughter incest. *American Journal of Psychiatry, 138*, 967–970.

Herrenkohl, R. C., Herrenkohl, E. C., & Egolf, B. P. (1983). Circumstances surrounding the occurrence of child maltreatment. *Journal of Consulting and Clinical Psychology, 51*, 424–431.

Holland, R. E. (1988). Children in peril: Historical background. In O. C. S. Tzeng & J. J. Jacobsen (Eds.), *Sourcebook for child abuse and neglect*. Springfield, IL: Thomas.

Holmes, T. H., & Rahe, R. H. (1967). The social readjustment rating scale. *Journal of Psychosomatic Research, 11*, 213–218.

Homans, G. C. (1958). Social behavior as exchange. *American Journal of Sociology, 62*, 597–606.

Hopkins, T. K. (1964). *The exercise of influence in small groups*. Totowa, NJ: Bedminster.

Horney, K. (1937). *The neurotic personality of our time*. New York: Norton.

Horowitz, J. E. (1985). Sexual abuse of children: A review of symptomatology, offender behavior patterns, and treatment methods. *American Mental Health Counselors Association Journal, 7*, 4, 172–179.

Howells, J. G. (1974). Child-parent separation as a therapeutic procedure. *Child Psychiatry Quarterly, 7,* 4, 7–12.

Howells, J. G. (1978). Developments in family psychiatry in the United Kingdom. *Journal of Marital and Family Therapy, 4,* 1, 133–141.

Howells, K. (1981). Adult sexual interest in children: Considerations relevant to theories of aetiology. In M. Cook & K. Howells (Eds.), *Adult sexual interest in children.* New York: Academic Press.

Hrdy, S. B. (1974). Male-male competition and infanticide among the Langurs of Abu Rajasthan. *Rolia Primatologica, 22,* 19–58.

Hunka, C. D., O'Toole, A. W., & O'Toole, R. (1985). Self help therapy in Parents Anonymous. *Journal of Psychosocial Nursing and Mental Health, 23,* 7, 24–32.

Isaacs, C. (1981). A brief review of the characteristics of abuse-prone parents. *Behavior Therapist, 4,* 5, 5–8.

Jacobsen, J. J. (1986). *Psychiatric sequelae of child abuse.* Springfield, IL: Thomas.

Jung, C. G. (1921). *Psychological types.* New York: Harcourt, Brace & World.

Justice, B., & Justice R. (1976). *The abusing family.* New York: Human Sciences Press.

Justice, B., & Justice, R. (1979). *The broken taboo.* New York: Human Sciences Press.

Kadushin, A., & Martin, J. (1981). *Child abuse: An international event.* New York: Columbia University Press.

Kandel, D., & Lesser, G. (1972). Marital decision-making in American and Danish urban families: A research note. *Journal of Marriage and the Family, 34,* 134–138.

Katan, A. (1973). Children who were raped. *Psychoanalytic Study of the Child, 28,* 208–211.

Katz, R., & Peres, Y. (1985). Is resource theory equally applicable to wives and husbands? *Journal of Comparative Families Studies, 16,* 1, 1–10.

Kaufman, I., Peck, A., & Tagiuri, C. (1954). The family constellation and overt incestuous relations between father and daughter. *American Journal of Orthopsychiatry, 24,* 2, 266–279.

Kazdin, A. E., Moser, J., Colbus, D., & Bell, R. (1985). Depressive symptoms among physically abused and psychiatrically disturbed children. *Journal of Abnormal Psychology, 94,* 3, 289–307.

Keller, H. R., & Erne, D. (1983). Child abuse: Toward a comprehensive model. In Center for Research on Aggression, A. P. Goldstein (Director), *Prevention and control of aggression.* New York: Pergamon Press.

Kempe, C. H., & Helfer, R. E. (1972). *Helping the battered child and his family.* Philadelphia: Lippincott.

Kempe, C. H., Silverman, F. N., Steele, B. F., Droegemueller, W., & Silver, H. K. (1962). The battered child syndrome. *Journal of Marriage and the Family, 18,* 17–24.

Kempe, R., & Kempe, C. H. (1976). Assessing family pathology. In R. E. Helfer & C. H. Kempe (Eds.), *Child abuse and neglect: The family and the community.* Cambridge, MA: Ballinger.

Keshet, J. K. (1980). From separation to stepfamily. *Journal of Family Issues, 1,* 4, 517–532.

Kinard, E. M. (1982). Child abuse and depression: Cause or consequence. *Child Welfare, 61,* 7, 403–413.

Kitahara, M. (1987). Perception of parental acceptance and rejection among Swedish university students. *Child Abuse and Neglect, 11,* 223–227.

Klein, M., & Stern, L. (1971). Low birth weight and the battered child syndrome. *American Journal of Diseases of Childhood, 122,* 15–18.

Kluft, R. P. (1987). The parental fitness of mothers with multiple personality disorder: A preliminary study. *Child Abuse and Neglect, 11,* 273–280.

Kohlberg, L. (1976). Moral stages and moralization. In T. Lichona (Ed.), *Moral development and behavior: Theory, research, and social issues.* New York: Holt, Rinehart, & Winston.

Kokkevi, A., & Agathonos, H. (1987). Intelligence and personality profile of battering parents in Greece: A comparative study. *Child Abuse and Neglect, 11,* 93–99.

Korbin, J. (1977). Anthropological contributions to the study of child abuse. *Child Abuse and Neglect, 1,* 7–24.

Krafft-Ebing, R. (1941). *Psychopathia sexualis: A medico-forensic study.* New York: Pioneer.

Kratcoski, P. C. (1982). Child abuse and violence against the family. *Child Welfare, 61,* 7, 435–444.

Kuffman, M., Peck, L., & Tagiuri, G. E. (1954). The family constellation and overt incest relations between fathers and daughters. *American Journal of Orthopsychiatry, 24,* 266–277.

Kurdek, L. A., Blisk, D., & Siesky, A. E. (1981). Correlates of children's long-term adjustment to their parents' divorce. *Developmental Psychology, 17,* 5, 565–579.

Kurtz, K. H. (1965). *Foundations of psychological research: Statistics, methodology and measurement.* Boston: Allyn & Bacon.

Kuttner, R. E. (1983). Is child abuse a human instinct? *International Journal of Social Psychiatry, 29,* 3, 231–233.

Lana, R. E. (1976). *The foundations of psychological theory.* Hillsdale, NJ: Erlbaum Associates.

Landau, H. R., Salus, M. K., Stiffarm, T., & Kalb, N. L. (1980). *Child protection: The role of the courts.* Washington, DC: Government Printing Office.

Langevin, R. (1983). *Sexual strands: Understanding and treating sexual anomalies in men.* Hillsdale, NJ: Erlbaum.

Langevin, R., Day, D., Handy, L., & Russon, A. E. (1985). Are incestuous fathers pedophilic, aggressive and alcoholic?. In R. Langevin (Ed.), *Erotic preference, gender identity and aggression in men.* Hillsdale, NJ: Erlbaum.

Larrance, D. T., & Twentyman, C. T. (1983). Maternal attributions and child abuse. *Journal of Abnormal Psychology, 92,* 4, 449–457.

Lanyon, R. I. (1986). Theory and treatment in child molestation. *Journal of Consulting and Clinical Psychology, 54,* 2, 176–182.

Lenoski, E. F. (1974). Translating injury data into preventive and health services: Physical child abuse. Unpublished manuscript, University of Southern California School of Medicine, Los Angeles.

Lesnik-Oberstein, M., Cohen, L., & Koers, A. J. (1982). Research in the Netherlands on a theory of child abuse: A preliminary report. *Child Abuse and Neglect, 6,* 199–206.

Lester, D. (1972). Incest. *The Journal of Sex Research, 8,* 4, 268–285.

Levenson, E. A. (1981). Facts or fantasies: On the nature of psychoanalytic data. *Contemporary Psychoanalysis, 17,* 4, 486–500.

Levesley, S. (1984). *Haven in a heartless world: The family besieged.* New York: Basic Books.

Lévi-Strauss, C. (1956). The family. In H. L. Shapiro (Ed.), *Man, culture, and society.* New York: Oxford University Press.

Libet, J. M., & Lewinsohn, P. M. (1973). Concept of social skill with special reference to the behavior of depressed persons. *Journal of Consulting and Clinical Psychology, 40,* 304–312.

Liebert, R. M., Neale, J. M., & Davidson, E. S. (1973). *The early window: Effects of television on children and youth.* New York: Pergamon Press.

Lindzey, G. (1967). Some remarks concerning incest, the incest taboo, and psychoanalytic theory. *American Psychologist, 22,* 1051–1059.

Lobb, M. L., & Strain (1984). Temporal patterns of child abuse and neglect reporting: Implications for personnel scheduling. *Child Welfare, 63,* 453–464.

Loening, W. E. K. (1981). Child abuse among the Zulus: A people in cultural transition. *Child Abuse and Neglect, 5,* 3–7.

Loevinger, J. (1976). *Ego development.* San Francisco: Jossey-Bass.

Loss, P., & Glancy, E. (1982). Men who sexually abuse their children. *Medical Aspects of Human Sexuality, 17,* 323–329.

Lourie, M. D., & Stefano, L. (1978). On defining emotional abuse. Child abuse and neglect: Issues in innovation and implementation. *Proceedings of the Second Annual National Conference on Child Abuse and Neglect.* Washington, DC: Government Printing Office.

Lukianowicz, N. (1972). Paternal incest. *British Journal of Psychiatry, 120,* 301–313.

Lustig, N., Dresser, J., Spellman, S., & Murray, T. (1966). Incest: A family group survival pattern. *Archives of general psychiatry, 14,* 31–40.

Lutier, J. (1961). Function of cultural and psychosocial elements in crimes of incest in a rural environment. *Annual Medical Log, 41,* 80–83.

Lynch, M. A. (1985). Child abuse before Kempe: An historical literature review. *Child Abuse and Neglect, 9,* 1, 7–15.

Lynch, M. A., Lindsay, J. & Ounsted, C. (1975). Tranquilizers causing aggression. *British Medical Journal, 1,* 266.

Lystad, M. H. (1975). Violence at Home: A review of the literature. *American Journal of Orthopsychiatry, 45,* 3, 328–345.

Machotka, P. (1986). Incest as a family affair. *Family Process, 65,* 98–116.

MacMurray, V. D. (1979). The effect and nature of alcohol abuse in cases of child neglect. *Victimology, 4,* 1, 29–45.

Maden, M. F., & Wrench, D. W. (1977). Significant findings on child abuse research. *Victimology, 2,* 196–224.

Maisch, H. (1972). *Incest.* New York: Stein & Day.

Malinowski, B. (1927). *Sex and repression in savage society.* New York: Norton.

Maroulis, H. (1979). Child abuse: The Greek scene. *Child Abuse and Neglect, 3,* 185–190.

Martin, D. (1982). Introduction. In Ginny NiCarthy, *Getting free: A handbook for women in abusive relationships,* xvii–xix. Seattle: Seal Press.

Martin, H. P., Beezley, P., Conway, E. F., & Kempe, C. H. (1975). The development of the abused child. *Advances in Pediatrics, 21,* 25–73.

Martin, J. (1981). Maternal and paternal abuse of children: Theoretical and research perspectives. Paper presented at the National Conference for Family Violence Researchers, Durham, NH.

Martin, M. J., & Walters, J. (1982). Familial correlates of selected types of abuse. *Journal of Marriage and the Family, 44,* 267–276.

Marvasti, J. (1986). Incestuous mothers. Paper presented at the Fourth Annual Symposium in Forensic Psychiatry of the American College of Forensic Psychiatry, April, Sanibel Island, FL.

Mash, E. J., Johnston, C., & Kovitz, K. (1983). A comparison of the mother-child interactions of physically abused and non-abused children during play and task situations. *Journal of Clinical Child Psychology, 12,* 3, 337–346.

Maslow, A. (1954). *Motivation and personality.* New York: Harper & Row.

Maslow, A. (1968). *Toward a psychology of being.* New York: Van Nostrand Reinhold.

Maslow, A. (1970). *A theory of human motivation.* New York: Harper & Row.

Mathews, R. (1987). Female sexual offenders. Paper presented at the Third National Adolescent Perpetrator Network Meeting, Keystone, CO, May 23.

Mathias, B. (1986). Lifting the shade of family violence. *Networker,* May-June.

McCarty, D. (1981). *Women who rape.* Unpublished manuscript.

McCord, J. (1983). A forty year perspective on effects of child abuse and neglect. *Child Abuse and Neglect, 7,* 265–270.

McCreary, C. P. (1975). Personality differences among child molesters. *Journal of Personality Assessment, 39,* 6, 591–593.

Mehta, M. N., Lokeshwar, M. R., Bhatt, S. S., Athavale, V. B., & Kulkarni, B. S. (1979). 'Rape' in children. *Child Abuse and Neglect, 3,* 671–677.

Meiselman, K. C. (1978). *Incest.* San Francisco: Jossey-Bass.

Melton, G. B., & Davidson, H. A. (1987). Child protection and society: When should the state intervene? *American Psychologist,* February, 172–173.

Merril, E. J. (1962). *Protecting the battered child.* Denver: Children's Division, American Humane Association.

Middleton, R. (1962). Brother-sister and father-daughter marriage in Ancient Egypt. *American Sociological Review, 27,* 603–611.

Milner, J. S. (1980). *The child abuse potential inventory.* Webster, NC: Psytec.

Milner, J. S., & Ayoub, C. (1980). Evaluation of "at risk" parents using the Child Abuse Potential Inventory. *Journal of Clinical Psychology, 36,* 4, 945–948.

Milner, J. S., & Wimberley, R. C. (1980). Prediction and explanation of child abuse. *Journal of Clinical Psychology, 36,* 4, 875–884.

Minuchin, S. (1984). *Family kaleidoscope.* Cambridge: Harvard University Press.

Mohr, I. W., Turner, R. E., & Jerry, M. B. (1964). *Pedophilia and exhibitionism.* Toronto: University of Toronto Press.

Montageau, A. (1976). *The nature of human aggression.* New York: Oxford University Press.

Morrison, D. E., & Henkel, R. E. (1969). Significance tests reconsidered. *The American Sociologist, 4,* 131–140.

Morse, C., Sahler, O., & Friedman, S. (1970). A three year follow-up of abused and neglected children. *American Journal of Deceases of Children, 120,* 439–446.

Mrazek, P. J. (1983). Long-term follow-up of an adolescent perpetrator of sexual abuse. *Child Abuse and Neglect, 7,* 2, 239–240.

Muldoon, L., ed. (1979). *Incest: Confronting the silent crime.* Saint Paul: Minnesota Program for Victims of Sexual Assault.

Munroe, R. L., & Munroe, R. H. (1975). *Cross-cultural human development.* Monterey, CA: Brooks/Cole.

Murdoch, G. (1949). *Social structure.* NY: Macmillan.

Myers, D. G. (1983). *Social psychology.* New York: McGraw-Hill.

Navarre, E. L. (1987). Psychological maltreatment: The core component of child abuse. In M. R. Brassard, R. Germain, & S. N. Hart, *Psychological maltreatment of children and youth.* New York: Pergamon Press.

Neel, A. (1969). *Theories of psychology: A handbook.* Cambridge, MA: Schenkman.

Newberger, E. H. (1971). The myth of the battered child syndrome. Paper presented at the 95th Anniversary Symposium, American Humane Association, Columbia, South Carolina.

Newberger, E. H., & Bourne, R. (1978). The medicalization and legalization of child abuse. *American Journal of Orthopsychiatry, 48,* 4, 593–607.

Newberger, E. H., Hampton, R. L., Mary, T. J., & White, K. M. (1986). Child abuse and pediatric social illness: An epidemiological analysis and ecological reformulation. *American Journal of Orthopsychiatry, 56,* 4, 589–601.

Newberger, C. M., & Newberger, E. H. (1981). The etiology of child abuse. In N. S. Ellerstein (Ed.), *Child abuse and neglect: A medical reference.* New York: Wiley.

Niem, T. C., & Collard, R. (1971). Parental discipline of aggressive behaviors in four year old Chinese and American children. Paper presented at the annual meeting of the American Psychological Association, Washington, DC.

Nurse, S. M. (1964). Familial patterns of parents who abuse their children. *Smith College Studies in Social Work, 35,* 11–25.

Nye, F. I. (1978). Is choice and exchange theory the key? *Journal of Marriage and the Family, 8,* 219–233.

Nye, F. I. (1979a). Choice, exchange, and the family. In W. R. Burr, et al. (Eds.), *Contemporary theories about the family* (Vol. 2). New York: Free Press.

Nye, F. I. (1979b). Family policy research: Emergent models and some theoretical issues. *Journal of Marriage and the Family, 37,* 473–485.

Nye, F. I. (1980). Family mini theories as special instances of choices and exchange theory. *Journal of Marriage and the Family, 42,* 479–489.

Nye, F. I., & McDonald, G. W. (1979). Family policy research: Emergent models and some theoretical issues. *Journal of Marriage and the Family, 41,* 473–485.

Ochiltree, G., & Amato, P. (1985). The child's eye view of family life. *Institute of Family Studies, 36,* 18–29, Melbourne.

Oliver, A. (1982). The sex offender. *International Journal of Law and Psychiatry, 5,* 403–411.

Oppong, C. (1970). Conjugal power and resources: An urban African example. *Journal of Marriage and the Family, 32,* 676–680.

Osgood, C. E., May, W. H., & Miron, M. S. (1975). *Cross-cultural universals of affective meaning.* Urbana: University of Illinois Press.

Ovaschel, H. (1983). Maternal depression and child dysfunction: Children at risk, In B. B. Lahey & A. E. Kazdin (Eds.), *Advances in Clinical Child Psychology* (Vol. 6). New York: Plenum.

Pagelow, M. D. (1984). *Family violence.* New York: Praeger.

Painter, S. L. (1986). Research on the prevalence of child sexual abuse: New directions. *Canadian Journal of Behavioral Science, 18,* 4, 323–339.

Panton, J. H. (1979). MMPI profile of configurations associated with incestuous and nonincestuous child molesting. *Psychological Reports, 45,* 335–338.

Parke, R. (1974). Rules, roles and resistance to deviation in children: Explorations in punishment, discipline and self-control. In A. Pick (Ed.), *Minnesota Symposium on Child Psychology* (Vol. 8). Minneapolis: University of Minnesota Press.

Parke, R. D. (1978). Child abuse: An overview of alternative theoretical models. *Journal of Pediatric Psychology, 3*, 9–13.

Parke, R. D. (1982). Theoretical models of child abuse: Their implications for prediction, prevention, and modification. In R. H. Starr (Ed.), *Child abuse prediction: Policy implications.* Cambridge, MA: Ballinger.

Parke, R. D., & Collmer, C. W. (1975). Child abuse: An interdisciplinary analysis. In E. M. Hetherington (Ed.), *Review of child development research* (Vol. 5). Chicago: University of Chicago Press.

Parker, H., & Parker, S. (1986). Father-daughter sexual abuse: An emerging perspective. *American Journal of Orthopsychiatry, 56*, 4, 531–549.

Parsons, T. (1954). The incest taboo in relation to social structure and the socialization of the child. *British Journal of Sociology, 5*, 101–117.

Passman, R. H., & Mulhern, R. K. (1977). Maternal punitiveness as affected by situational stress: An experimental analogue of child abuse. *Journal of Child Abuse, 86*, 5, 565–569.

Patterson, G. R. (1974). A basis for identifying stimuli which control behaviors in natural settings. *Child Development, 45*, 900–911.

Patterson, G. R. (1977). The aggressive child: Victim and architect of a coercive system. In E. Mash, L. Hamerlynch, & L. Hangry (Eds.), *Behavior modification and families: Theory and research*, 97–115. New York: Brunner/Mazel.

Pattersen, G. R. (1982). *Coercive family process: A social learning approach* (Vol. 3). Eugene, OR: Castalia.

Patterson, G. R. (1986). Performance models for antisocial boys. *American Psychologist, 41*, 4, 432–444.

Patterson, G. R., & Dawes, R. M. (1975). A Guttman scale of children's coercive behaviors. *Journal of Consulting and Clinical Psychology, 43*, 4, 594.

Pedersen, F. A., Anderson, B. J., & Cain, R. L. (1977). An approach to understanding linkages between the parent-infant and spouse relationships. Paper presented at the Society for Research in Child Development, New Orleans, March.

Pelton, L. H. (1978). Child abuse and neglect: The myth of classlessness. *American Journal of Orthopsychiatry, 48*, 608–617.

Penrod, S. (1986). *Social psychology.* Englewood Cliffs, NJ: Prentice Hall.

Pettigrew, J. (1986). Child neglect in rural Punjabi families. *Journal of Comparative Family Studies, 17*, 1, 63–85.

Piaget, J. (1932). *The moral judgment of children.* London: Paul, Trench, Trubner.

Pierce, R. L. (1984). Child pornography: A hidden dimension of child abuse. *Child Abuse and Neglect, 8*, 483–492.

Plotkin, R., & Twentyman, C. T. (1983). Cognitive mediation of discipline in mothers who maltreat their children. Unpublished manuscript. University of Rochester.

Polansky, N. A. (1985). Loneliness and isolation in child neglect. *Social Casework, 66*, 1, 38–47.

Polansky, N. A., Borgman, R. D., De Saix, C., & Sharlin, S. (1971). Verbal accessibility in the treatment of child neglect. *Child Welfare, 50*, 6, 349–356.

Polansky, N. A., Chalmers, M. A., Williams, D. P., and Buttenweiser, E. W. (1981). *Damaged parents: An anatomy of child neglect.* Chicago: University of Chicago Press.

Polansky, N. A., Gaudin, J. M., Jr., Ammons, P. W., & Davis, K. B. (1985). The psychological ecology of the neglectful mother. *Child Abuse and Neglect, 9,* 265–275.

Post, S. (1982). Adolescent parricide in abusive families. *Child Welfare, 61,* 7, 445–455.

Preston, G. (1986). The post-separation family and the emotional abuse of children: An ecological approach. *Australian Journal of Sex, Marriage, and the Family, 7,* 1, 40–49.

Quay, H. C. (1983). A dimensional approach to behavioral disorder: The Revised Behavior Problem Checklist. *School Psychology Review, 12,* 3, 244–249.

Quinsey, V. L. (1977). The assessment and treatment of child molesters: A review. *Canadian Psychological Review, 18,* 204–220.

Quinsey, V. L., Steinman, C. M., & Bergensen, S. G. (1975). Penile circumference, skin conduction, and ranking responses of child molesters and "normals" to sexual and nonsexual visual stimuli. *Behavior Therapy, 6,* 213–219.

Radbill, A. (1974). History of child abuse and infanticide. In C. H. Kempe & R. Helfer (Eds.), *The battered child.* Chicago: University of Chicago Press.

Reid, J. B., Patterson, G. R., & Loeber, R. (1981). The abused child: Victim, instigator, or innocent bystander? *Nebraska Symposium on Motivation, 29,* 47–68.

Reid, J. B., Taplin, P. S., & Loeber, R. (1981). A social interactional approach to the treatment of abusive families. In R. B. Stuart (Ed.), *Violent behavior: Social learning approaches to prediction, management, and treatment.* New York: Brunner/Mazel.

Reidy, T. J. (1977). The aggressive characteristics of abused and neglected children. *Journal of Clinical Psychology, 33,* 4, 1140–1145.

Resnick, E. H., & Sclare, A. B. (1969). Child murder by parents: A psychiatric review of filicide. *American Journal of Psychiatry, 126,* 3, 325–334.

Riemer, S. (1940). A research note on incest. *Comprehensive Psychiatry, 2,* 338–349.

Rist, K. (1979). Incest: Theoretical and clinical views. *American Journal of Orthopsychiatry, 49,* 4, 680–691.

Rohner, R. P. (1980). Worldwide tests of parental acceptance-rejection theory: An overview. *Behavior Science Research, 14,* 1–21.

Rohner, R. P. (1986). *The warmth dimension: Foundations of parental acceptance-rejection theory.* Beverly Hills, CA: Sage.

Rohrbeck, C. A., & Twentyman, C. T. (1986). Multimodal assessment of impulsiveness in abusing, neglecting, and nonmaltreating mothers and their preschool children. *Journal of Consulting and Clinical Psychology, 54,* 2, 231–236.

Rosenberg, M. S. (1987). New directions for research on the psychological maltreatment of children. *American Psychologist, 42,* 2, 166–171.

Rosenberg, M. S., & Germain, R. (1987). Psychological maltreatment: Theory, research and ethical issues in psychology. In M. R. Brassard, R. Germain, & S. N. Hart (Eds.), *Psychological maltreatment of children and youth.* New York: Pergamon Press.

Rosenberg, M. S., & Reppucci, N. D. (1983). Child abuse: A review with special focus on an ecological approach in rural communities. In A. W. Childs & G. B. Melton (Eds.), *Rural Psychology,* 305–336. New York: Plenum.

Rubinstein, B. B. (1975). On the clinical psychoanalytic theory and its role in the inference and confirmation of particular clinical hypotheses. *Psychoanalysis and Contemporary Science, 4,* 3–57.

Rush, F. (1980). *The best kept secret: Sexual abuse of children.* New York: McGraw-Hill.

Russell, B. (1945). *A history of Western philosophy.* New York: Simon & Schuster.

Russell, D. (1975). *The politics of rape.* New York: Stein & Day.

Russell, D. E. H. (1984). The prevalence and seriousness of incestuous abuse: Stepfathers vs. biological fathers. *Child Abuse and Neglect, 8,* 1, 15–22.

Russell, D. E. H. (1986). *The secret trauma: Incest in the lives of girls and women.* New York: Basic Books.

Rutter, N. (1972). *The qualities of mothering.* New York: Aronson.

Salter, A. C., Richardson, C. M., & Martin, P. A. (1985). Treating abusive parents. *Child Welfare, 64,* 4, 327–341.

Sameroff, A. J., & Chandler, M. J. (1975). Reproductive risk and the continuum of caretaking casualty. In F. D. Horowitz, E. M. Hetherington, S. Scarr-Salapatek, & G. Siegel (Eds.), *Review of child development research* (Vol. 4). Chicago: University of Chicago Press.

Sandler, J., Van Dercar, C., & Milhoan, M. (1978). Training child abusers in the use of positive reinforcement practices. *Behavior Research and Therapy, 16,* 169–175.

Sardoff, R. L. (1985). Divorce and the emotionally abused child. In A. Carmi & H. Zimrin (Eds.), *Child and contemporary problems, 39,* 3, 39–77.

Scanzoni, J. (1979). Sex-role influences on married women's status attainment. *Journal of Marriage and the Family, 41,* 4, 793–800.

Schachter, M. (1960). Medical, psychological and social study of incest as seen in the perspective of child psychiatry. *Acta Paedopsychiat, 27,* 146.

Schaller, G. B. (1972). *The Segengeti lion: A study of predatory-prey relations.* Chicago: University of Chicago Press.

Scher, M., & Stevens, M. (1987). Men and violence. *Journal of Counseling and Development, 65,* 351–355.

Schetky, D. H., & Green, A. H. (1988). *Child sexual abuse: A handbook for health care and legal professionals.* New York: Brunner/Mazel.

Schiff, A. W., & Schiff, J. L. (1971). Passivity. *Transactional Analysis Journal, 1,* 71–78.

Schilling, R. G., Schinke, S. P., Blythe, B. J., & Barth, R. P. (1982). Child maltreatment and mentally retarded parents: Is there a relationship? *Mental Retardation, 20,* 201–209.

Schneider, G., Pollock, C., & Helfer, R. E. (1972). The predictive questionnaire: A preliminary report. In R. E. Helfer & H. C. Kempe (Eds.), *Helping the Battered Child and his Family.* Philadelphia: Lippincott.

Schull, W. J., & Neel, J. V. (1965). *The effects of inbreeding on Japanese children.* New York: Harper & Row.

Schultz, N. W. (1980). A cognitive-developmental study of the grandchild-grandparent bond. *Child Study Journal, 10,* 1, 7–26.

Seagull, E. A. (1987). Social support and child maltreatment: A review of the evidence. *Child Abuse and Neglect, 11,* 1, 41–52.

Segall, M. H. (1983). Aggression in global perspective: A research strategy. In A. P. Goldstein & M. H. Segall (Eds.), *Aggression in global perspective.* New York: Pergamon Press.

Segner, L. L. (1968). Two studies of the incest taboo. *Dissertation Abstracts, 29b,* 796.

Sgroi, S. M. (1982a). Family treatment of child sexual abuse. *Journal of Social Work and Human Sexuality, 1,* 109–128.

Sgroi, S. M. (1982b). *Handbook of clinical intervention in child sexual abuse.* Lexington, MA: Lexington Books.

Shengold, L. (1980). Some reflections on a case of mother/adolescent son incest. *International Journal of Psychoanalysis, 61,* 461–76.

Shepher, J. (1971). Mate selection among second generation kibbutz adolescents and adults: Incest avoidance and negative imprinting. *Archives of Sexual Behavior, 1,* 293–307.

Shepher, J. (1983). *Incest: A biosocial view.* New York: Academic Press.

Sherrod, D. (1982). *Social psychology.* New York: Random House.

Sidel, R. (1972). *Women and child care in China.* New York: Hill & Wang.

Skinner, B. F. (1938). *The behavior of organisms: An experimental analysis.* New York: Appleton-Century-Crofts.

Skinner, B. F. (1957). *Verbal behavior.* New York: Appleton-Century-Crofts.

Smith, S. L. (1984). Significant research findings in the etiology of child abuse. *Social Caseworker: The Journal of Contemporary Social Work, 18,* 337–346.

Specktor, P. (1979). *Incest: Confronting the silent crime.* Minneapolis: Minnesota Program for Victims of Sexual Abuse.

Spinetta, J. J., & Rigler, D. (1972). The child abusing parent: A psychological review. *Psychological Bulletin, 77,* 296–304.

Sroufe, L. A. (1979). Emotional development. In J. Osofsky (Ed.), *Handbook of infant development.* New York: Wiley.

Starr, R. H., Jr. (1982). *Child abuse prediction: Policy implications.* Cambridge, MA: Ballinger.

Steele, B. F. (1976). *Working with abusive parents from a psychiatric point of view.* Washington, DC: U.S. Dept. of Health, Education, and Welfare, Children's Bureau.

Steele, B. F. (1978). The child abuser. In I. Kutash & L. B. Schlesinger (Eds.), *Violence: Perspectives on murder and aggression,* 285–300. San Francisco: Jossey-Bass.

Steinmetz, S. K. (1974). Intra-familial patterns of conflict resolution: United States and Canadian comparisons. Paper presented at the Annual Meeting of the Society for the Study of Social Problems, Montreal.

Steinmetz, S. K. (1977). *The cycle of violence: Assertive, aggressive, and abusive family interaction.* New York: Praeger.

Steinmetz, S. K., & Straus, M. A. (1973). *Violence in the family.* New York: Harper & Row.

Stenens-Long, J. (1973). The effect of behavioral context on some aspects of adult's disciplinary practice and affect. *Child Development, 44,* 476–484.

Stevens, M., & Gebhart, R. (1985). *Rape education for men: Curriculum guide.* Columbus: Ohio State University Rape Education Prevention Project.

Storr, A. (1965). *Sexual deviation.* London: Heineman.

Strasburg, P. A. (1978). *Violent Delinquents.* New York: Monarch Books.

Straus, M. A. (1973). A general systems theory approach to a theory of violence between family members. *Social Science Information, 12,* 6, 105–125.

Straus, M. A. (1979). Measuring intrafamily conflict and violence: The conflict tactics (CT) scales. *Journal of Marriage and the Family, 42,* 873–885.

Straus, M. A., Gelles, R. J., & Steinmetz, S. K. (1980). *Behind closed doors: Violence in American families.* Garden City, NY: Doubleday.

Stringer, S. A., & La Greca, A. M. (1985). Correlates of child abuse potential. *Journal of Abnormal Child Psychology, 13*, 2, 217–226.

Summit, R., & Kryso, J. (1978). Sexual abuse of children: A clinical spectrum. *American Journal of Orthopsychiatry, 48*, 2, 237–51.

Swan, R. W. (1985). The child as active participant in sexual abuse. *Clinical Social Work Journal, 13*, 62–77.

Szasz, T. (1961). *The myth of mental illness: Foundations of a theory of personal conduct.* New York: Delta.

Thomas, C. (1972). Child abuse and neglect, part 1: Historical overview, legal matters, and social perspectives. *North Carolina Law Review, 50*, 293.

Thorndike, E. L. (1949). The law of effect. In *Selected writings from a connectionist's psychology.* New York: Appleton-Century-Crofts.

Tierner, K. J., & Crowin, D. L. (1983). Exploring intra-familial child sexual abuse: A systems approach. In D. Finkelhor, R. J. Gelles, G. T. Hotaling, & M. A. Straus (Eds.), *The dark side of families: Current family violence research*, 102–116. Beverly Hills, CA: Sage.

Toby, J. (1966). Violence and the masculine ideal: Some qualitative data. In M. Wolfgang (Ed.), *Patterns of Violence: The annals of the American Academy of Political and Social Science* (Vol. 364). Philadelphia: American Academy of Political and Social Science.

Toobert, S., Bartelme, K. F., & Jones, E. S. (1959). Some factors related to pedophilia. *International Journal of Psychiatry, 4*, 272–279.

Trivers, R. L. (1971). Parental investment and sexual selection. In B. Campbell (Ed.), *Sexual selection and the descent of man: 1871–1971*, 136–179. Chicago: Aldine.

Tzeng, O. S. C. (1977). A quantitative method for separation of semantic subspaces. *Applied Psychological Measurement, 1*, 171–184.

Tzeng, O. S. C., & Hanner, L. J. (1988). National trends of state laws for protecting child victimization. In O. S. C. Tzeng & J. J. Jacobsen, *Sourcebook for child abuse and neglect: Intervention, treatment, and prevention through crisis programs.* Springfield, IL: Thomas.

Tzeng, O. S. C., Hanner, L. J., & Fortier, R. H. (1988). Nature and etiology of human aggression and violence: A comprehensive model for studying child abuse and neglect problems. In O. S. C. Tzeng & J. J. Jacobsen, *Sourcebook for child abuse and neglect: Intervention, treatment, and prevention through crisis programs.* Springfield, IL: Thomas.

Tzeng, O. C. S. (1989). Conflicting theories of child abuse and neglect and the expert witness. In Indiana Continuing Legal Education Forum (Ed.), *Child abuse and neglect.* Indianapolis: Indiana Continuing Legal Education Forum.

Tzeng, O. C. S., & Jackson, J. W. (in press). Common methodological framework for theory construction and evaluation in the social and behavioral sciences. *Genetic, Social, and General Psychology Monographs.*

Tzeng, O. S. C., & Jacobsen, J. J. (1988). *Sourcebook for child abuse and neglect: Intervention, treatment, and prevention through crisis programs.* Springfield, IL: Thomas.

Tzeng, O. S. C., Jacobsen, J. J., & Ware, R. (1988). Summary and prospects. In O. S. C. Tzeng & J. J. Jacobsen, *Sourcebook for child abuse and neglect: Intervention, treatment, and prevention through crisis programs.* Springfield, IL: Thomas.

U.S. Department of Health and Human Services. (1988). *Study findings: Study of the national incidence and prevalence of child abuse and neglect: 1988.* Office of Human Development Services, Administration for Children, Youth and Families, Children's Bureau. Washington, DC: National Center on Child Abuse and Neglect, U.S. Department of Health and Human Services.

Vallois, H. V. (1961). The social life of early man: The evidence of skeletons. In S. L. Washburn (Ed.), *Social life of early man.* Chicago: University of Chicago Press.

Van den Berghe, P. L. (1983). Human inbreeding avoidance: Culture in nature. *Behavioral and Brain Sciences, 6,* 1, 91–123.

Vander Mey, B. J., & Neff, R. L. (1982). Adult-child incest: A review of the research and treatment. *Adolescence, 17,* 717–735.

Vander Mey, B. J., & Neff, R. L. (1986). *Incest as child abuse.* New York: Praeger.

Van Stolk, M. (1972). *The battered child in Canada.* Toronto: Canadian Publishers.

Vietze, P., Falsey, S., Sandler, H., O'Connor, S., & Altemeier, W. (1980). Transactional approach to the prediction of child maltreatment. *Infant Mental Health Journal, 1,* 248–261.

Vietze, P. M., O'Conner, S., Hopkins, J. B., Sandler, H. M., & Altemeir, W. A. (1982). Prospective study of child maltreatment from a transactional perspective. In R. H. Starr (Ed.), *Child abuse prediction: Policy implications.* Cambridge, MA: Ballinger.

Virkkunen, M. (1974). Incest offenses and alcoholism. *Medicine, Science and Law, 14,* 124–128.

Wallerstein, J. S., & Kelly, J. B. (1980). Effects of divorce on the visiting father-child relationship. *American Journal of Psychiatry, 137,* 12, 1534–1539.

Walters, D. R. (1975). *Physical and sexual abuse of children: Causes and treatment.* Bloomington: Indiana University Press.

Watkins, H. D., & Bradbard, M. R. (1982). Child maltreatment: An overview with suggestions for intervention and research. *Family Relations, 31,* 323–333.

Watts, D. L., & Courtois, C. A. (1981). Trends in the treatment of men who commit violence against women. *Personnel and Guidance Journal, 60,* 245–249.

Weiner, I. (1962). Father-daughter incest: A clinical report. *Psychiatric Quarterly, 36,* 607–632.

Weis, K., & Borges, S. S. (1973). Victimology and rape: The case of the legitimate victim. *Issues in Criminology, 8,* 2, 71–115.

Welch, G. J. (1985). Contingency contracting with a delinquent and his family. *Journal of Behavior Therapy and Experimental Psychiatry, 16,* 3, 253–259.

Westermarck, E. (1921). *The history of human marriage.* London: Macmillan.

White, E. A. (1948). The definition and prohibition of incest. *American Anthropologist, 50,* 416–435.

White, R. B., & Cornely, D. A. (1981). Navajo child abuse and neglect study: A comparison group examination of abuse and neglect of Navajo children. *Child Abuse and Neglect, 5,* 9–17.

Wiggins, J. A. (1983). Family violence as a case of interpersonal aggression: A situational analysis. *Social Forces, 62,* 1, 102–123.

Will, D. (1983). Approaching the incestuous and sexually abusive family. *Journal of Adolescence, 6,* 229–246.

Wilson, E. O. (1975). *On human nature.* Cambridge: Harvard University Press.

Wilson, M., Daly, M., & Weghorst, S. J. (1980). Household composition and the risk of child abuse and neglect. *Journal of Biosocial Science, 4,* 23–33.

Wolf, A. P. (1966). Childhood association, sexual attraction and the incest taboo: A Chinese case. *American Anthropologist, 50,* 383–398.

Wolf, A. P. (1970). Childhood association and sexual attraction: A further test of the Westermarck hypothesis. *American Anthropologist, 72,* 3, 371–385.

Wolfe, D. A. (1981). Child abuse. In E. Mash & G. Terdal (Eds.), *Behavioral assessment of childhood disorders.* New York: Guilford Press.

Wolfe, D. A. (1985). Child-abusive parents: An empirical review and analysis. *Psychological Bulletin, 97,* 3, 462–482.

Wolfe, F. (1985). *Twelve female sexual offenders.* Presented at Next Steps in Research on the Assessment and Treatment of Sexually Aggressive Persons, March 3–5, St. Louis, MO.

Wooley, P. V., & Evans, W. A. (1955). Significance of skeletal lesions in infants resembling those of traumatic origin. *Journal of American Medical Association, 158,* 539–543.

Wright, L. (1976). The "sick but slick" syndrome as a personality component of parents of battered children. *Journal of Clinical Psychology, 32,* 41–45.

Wulkan, D., & Bulkey, J. (1981). Analysis of incest statutes. In J. Bulkey (Ed.), *Child sexual abuse and the law,* 52–80. Washington: American Bar Association.

Yorukoglu, A., & Kemph, J. P. (1966). Children not severely damaged. *Journal of the American Academy of Child Psychiatry, 5,* 111–124.

Young, L. (1964). *Wednesday's children: A study of child neglect and abuse.* New York: McGraw-Hill.

Zalba, S. (1971). Battered children. *Transaction, 8,* 68–71.

Zillmann, D., & Bryant, J. (1984). Effects of massive exposure to pornography. In N. M. Malamuth & E. Donnerstein (Eds.), *Pornography and sexual aggression.* Orlando, FL: Academic.

Zimrin, H. (1984). Child abuse: A dynamic process of encounter between needs and personality traits within the family. *The American Journal of Family Therapy, 12,* 1, 37–47.

Index

abandonment, 86, 298
Aber, J. L., 76, 78, 79
abuse: compared with neglect, 44, 57, 237, 299; fallacies/myths, 45, 301; hotlines, 148; potential, 49, 50, 102
accidental abusers, 70
Adams, M. S., 116, 272
adolescent female offenders, 167, 169
adultery, 123
affective evaluation, 15, 38, 127, 131, 204, 208, 211–13, 219, 224, 225, 240, 299
Agathonos, H., 35
age: of children/victims, 52, 63, 86, 97, 166, 229; inequality, 43, 44; of parents, 51, 82, 195, 229
aggression: by child, 78, 85, 111, 179; cues, 27, 98, 99, 100; cultural norms, 63, 177, 225; displacement of, 21, 48, 199; general principles applied to family violence, 302; impulses, 15, 34, 40, 92–93, 96, 156; learning of, 27, 94–97, 99, 223–24, 237, 308; passive, 81, 169, 190; reinforced, 27, 89, 98; response to frustration, 42, 95, 98–99; sexual, 145, 148, 159; sociobiology of, 25–26, 90; three factors of, 59–60
Ainsworth, M. D., 55, 76
alcohol abuse, in child maltreatment, 20, 34, 48, 146, 154, 155, 163, 192, 199

Alexander, P., 140
Alfaro, J. D., 6
Alland, A., 26, 93
Allen, J. P., 76, 78
Alorese culture, 122
Altemeier, W. A., 83
altruism, 25, 90, 97, 144
Amato, P., 179
American culture, 4, 43, 46–47, 52, 64–66, 68, 130, 148
American Humane Society, 5
Anderson, C., 15, 111, 125, 126, 127
anger, 38, 55, 63, 240
anthropological perspective, 8, 90, 97, 133, 217
anxiety, 24, 102
apathy-futility syndrome, 190, 192, 193
Apgar scores, 82
Araji, S., 129, 130, 153, 156, 158, 163
Ardrey, R., 25
Aries, P., 3
Aristotle, 3
assessment, 9, 71, 167
at-risk populations, 5, 17, 35, 82, 83, 91, 97, 100, 191. *See also* risk factors
attachment, 23, 26, 55, 76, 78–79, 81, 92. *See also* bonding
attachment theory, 76–79, 121, 131, 133, 228
attitudinal theory of sexual abuse, 127, 130

attribution error of sexual abusers, 90
Atwood, R., 155
authoritarianism, 19, 46, 58, 101, 129,
    155, 300
Ayoub, C., 92
Azar, S. T., 23, 87, 88, 89

baby sitting, 168
background characteristics, 208, 209,
    210, 215, 224, 242, 299
bad homes vs. good institutions, 79
Bakan, D., 111
Bandura, A., 26, 94, 95
Bantu culture (of East Africa), 115
Barsh, D., 25, 90
Bartelme, K. F., 155
"Battered Child Syndrome, The," 4, 33
Bauer, W. D., 197
behavioral: characteristics of children, 85,
    105; intentions of sexual abusers, 161
Bell, A. D., 88, 152
Bell, G., 36
Belsky, J., 28, 76, 85, 104, 105
Bennie, E. H., 52
Berkowitz, L., 26
Berlin, F. S., 161
Berman, P. W., 92
Berry, G. W., 142, 159
Biaggio, A. M. B., 96
Bible, 3, 4, 38
Billingsley, A., 44, 192
biological perspective, 26, 42, 55, 95,
    97, 115–18, 122, 161, 217, 229, 272
biosocial/attachment theory, 19, 115,
    118, 120–24, 131–33, 229, 230, 272,
    273
bipolar continua, 13
bipolar continuum, of parental percep-
    tions of children, 29
Birnbaum, H. J., 152
Birrell, R. G., 112
Birrell, J. H. W., 112
birth: control education, 53; defects, con-
    genital, 117; illegitimate, 61; rate, 30;
    trauma, 82, 117; weight, 19, 20, 82,
    99, 100, 112
bisexuality of sexual offenders, 166

Blau, P. M., 62
Blumberg, M. L., 155
Boatman, B., 36
Boehm, B., 192
bonding, 25, 55, 76, 91, 99, 131–32,
    199. See also attachment
borderline personality, 39
Borges, S. S., 159
Borgman, R. D., 191
Boriskin, J. A., 64
Bousha, D. M., 89, 197
Bowen, N. H., 159
Bowlby, J., 23, 24, 55, 76, 79, 131
boyfriends as sexual abusers, 156
Bradbard, M. R., 7, 299
Brant, R., 136, 142
Brassard, M. R., 6, 100, 176, 180, 181,
    183, 312
Breese, P., 165
Bronfenbrenner, U., 28, 103, 177
brother-sister: incest, 159; marriages, 118
Browning, D., 36
Brownmiller, D., 159, 160
Bryant, J., 159
Buckley, W., 72, 120
Burgess, R. L., 8, 14, 25, 33, 36, 37,
    57, 58, 89, 90, 91, 92, 101
Burgess, A. W., 158, 195, 196, 197, 302
Buric, O., 47
Burland, J. A., 36
Burr, W. R., 47

Cain, R. L., 111
Canada, 111
castration anxiety, 151
catharsis, 38, 94
Catholics, 129
Caulfield, M. A., 111
Cavallin, H., 136, 153
Chagnon, N., 96
Chandler, L. A., 23, 179
character disorder, 34, 85, 138, 155, 190
child: care, 21, 28, 70, 78, 79, 107, 174,
    176, 184; characteristics, 19–21, 24,
    25, 27, 29, 50, 51, 53, 55, 57, 59,
    64, 80, 85, 91, 97, 99, 101, 105, 161,
    163, 177, 194, 223; development, 55,

103, 131, 133; handicapped, 26, 29, 49, 64, 91, 99, 100; in need of services (CHINS), 238; labor, 43
Child Abuse Potential Inventory, 101–3
childhood, 21, 22, 24, 33, 49, 59, 61, 74, 76, 77, 82, 95, 138, 152, 153, 219
child maltreatment types, 7, 10
child management, 50, 55, 100
child protection, 237, 238, 244
child-rearing practices, 3, 19, 28, 34, 42, 44, 53, 61, 70, 105, 109, 129, 193, 194, 199, 215, 241
children: of incestuous couples, 116, 118; as property, 29, 128, 129; rejected, 80; rights of, 8; 3-month- to 3-year-old, 52
child welfare, 4, 18, 28, 44, 65, 78, 148
China, 65, 111
choice theory, 106–8
Christianity, 4
church involvement, 176, 183
Cicchetti, D., 36
circular vs. linear view of abuse, 103
civil rights, 43
class values and norms, 52, 195
classical conditioning, 26, 94
classroom activities, 77. See also school; education factors
clinical analysis, 21, 33, 36, 37, 39, 70, 74, 300
coercion theory, 27, 100–103
cognitive/behavioral/developmental theory, 76, 87–90, 228
cognitive factors, 15, 16, 19, 21, 22, 24, 26, 28, 76, 78, 88, 89, 97, 127, 132, 133, 181, 204, 208, 215, 219, 225
Cohen, T., 22, 58, 60, 75, 135, 136, 137, 142, 143, 197
Cohler, J., 152, 153
Collard, R., 65, 111
Collmer, C. W., 8, 50, 112, 155
collusive mother, 129
commission-omission distinction, 7, 181, 200, 237
common methodological framework, 247
communication skills, 100
community: attitudes/values/norms, 8, 19, 27, 44, 51, 52, 74, 99, 176, 214,

223; factors, 10, 14, 16, 23, 28, 29, 37, 40, 53, 67, 84, 103, 108, 110, 120, 127, 174, 176, 177, 179, 184, 194, 195, 242; isolation, 19, 112; programs, 22, 107, 110, 127, 148, 223, 239, 298, 303, 304, 309
competition, 18, 42, 43
conduct disorder, 53, 102
conflict, 23, 63, 74, 90; resolution, 74, 177, 229
congenital birth defects, 117
Conger, R. D., 89, 101, 195, 196, 197
Congress (U.S.), 43
conjugal power relations, 47, 48
Consortium for Child Abuse and Neglect Resources, 10
Conte, J. R., 23, 58, 75, 137, 138, 139, 140
cooperation, 43, 45, 97
coping skills, 39, 57, 59, 69, 105, 126, 136, 142, 176, 195, 199, 208, 212, 216
Cornell, C. D., 35
Cornely, D. A., 58
Courtois, C. A., 159
counseling, 72, 127, 305. See also treatment
Creighton, S. J., 121, 123, 130, 159
criminality and crime, 34, 42, 65, 93, 130, 145, 176, 183, 191, 238, 242, 244, 301
crisis centers, 49, 50, 237, 305
Cromwell, R. E., 47
cross-cultural perspective, 26, 35, 65, 81, 92, 96, 111, 115, 118, 120, 121, 122, 130, 149, 150, 214
cross-generational coalitions, 29, 178
cross-paradigm comparisons, 259
crowded living, 20, 26, 92
cultural: influences, 5, 17, 21, 24, 29, 40, 42, 43, 45, 48, 61, 70, 84, 86, 97, 105, 108, 110, 118, 120, 128, 131, 158–60, 183, 192, 194, 210; inhibition of overt aggression, 59, 199; institutions, 22, 24, 45, 127, 183; norms, 4, 8, 18, 24, 42, 64, 65, 107, 118, 130, 131, 135, 137, 147, 156,

cultural: norms (*continued*)
    159, 160, 177, 183, 209, 298, 303;
    scriptings, 19, 54, 55, 56; violence,
    29, 44, 110, 111, 176, 184
culturalogical theory, 119
culture-ecology units, 205–7, 209, 210,
    217–19, 225, 229, 230, 231, 233,
    234, 299, 313
cycle of maltreatment, 27, 34, 55, 70,
    96, 138, 142, 153, 191, 193, 244

Daly, M., 25, 90, 91, 92
Davidson, E. S., 64, 111
Davitz, J. R., 111
day-care centers, 21, 70, 174, 184
death in early infancy, 117, 118
DeChesnay, M., 35
deficiency needs theory, 180–85
defining: child abuse and neglect, 7–8,
    30, 176, 200, 235, 298–300; domi-
    nance-subjugation, 146; incest, 129,
    146; physical abuse, 7, 8, 21; psycho-
    logical maltreatment, 6, 8, 29, 173,
    177, 181
delivery complications, 61, 199
Delsardo, J. D., 85
DeMause, L., 3, 129
democracy, 43, 45, 64
Denelsky, G., 132
Denenberg, V., 132
Denson-Gerber, J., 159
Dentan, R. K., 96
Department of Health and Human Ser-
    vices, 5
dependency needs, 19, 35, 50, 81
depression, 16, 36, 38, 42, 66, 179
DeSaix, C., 191
desertion anxiety, 23, 74
detectives, 127
detention home, 70
developmental factors, 8, 24, 28, 29, 34,
    38, 77, 82, 95, 97, 103, 107, 152,
    164, 173, 176, 185, 214
developmental-organizational theory, 76
deviance, 6, 23, 85, 154
de Young, M., 134, 135, 136, 137, 138, 301
diet, 20, 30, 112

Dietrich, K. N., 89
Dingman, H. F., 155
Dion, K. K., 112
Disbrow, M. A., 111
discipline, child, 3, 4, 16, 27, 29, 65,
    70, 96, 107, 110, 111, 137, 184, 194,
    195, 196, 223, 229, 240, 301, 302,
    310
disciplines, academic, 9. *See also* multi-
    disciplinary approaches
discriminative parenting theory, 25, 90,
    91, 228
distorted beliefs, 48, 105, 146
distribution of goods, services, and
    rights, 43
distributive justice, 62
Ditson, J., 149
DiVasto, P., 122
division of labor, 120
divorce, 18, 44, 58, 74, 93, 100, 102,
    156, 210
Doerr, H., 111
Dollard, J., 26, 48
domestic violence, 42, 45, 104
dominance, 26, 50, 146
Dougherty, N., 79
drive theories, 42, 94
drug abuse, 30, 112, 144, 199. *See also*
    alcohol abuse; substance abuse
DSM III, 35
Dubanoski, R. A., 34, 38, 155
Duberman, R. E., 92

Eastern culture, 150, 214
ecocultural systems, 54
ecological: deficiency needs theory, 181,
    183, 232; determinants paradigm, 13,
    28–30, 103, 143, 173, 228, 231, 267,
    270, 273–75, 278, 279, 284, 304,
    305, 308, 309; levels, 71, 205, 299,
    314; perspectives, 21, 28, 103–5,
    173–77, 218, 228, 231, 265
economic factors, 5, 17, 29, 43, 44, 45,
    47, 52, 65, 108, 120, 123, 128, 130,
    135, 153, 174, 214
education factors, 8, 9, 18, 42–44, 47,
    48, 52, 53, 82, 93, 95, 100, 147, 158,

163, 176, 184, 191, 217, 244, 245, 294

Edwards Personal Preference Schedule, 155

effects of maltreatment, 3, 78, 116, 137, 229, 272. *See also* impact

egalitarian values, 43, 45, 129, 147, 129

Egeland, B., 76, 77, 78

ego development, 21, 23, 37–39, 191

Egolf, B. P., 88

Egypt, 115, 120

Eisnitz, A. J., 152

Ellis, H., 155

Elmer, E., 35, 45, 50, 99, 112

emotional: abuse, 173, 183, 298 (*see also* psychological maltreatment); factors, 24, 33, 35, 55, 70, 77, 81, 86, 90, 131, 161, 176, 177, 179, 191

empathy, 34, 155

empirical approach, 247, 283, 298, 300–303

employment, 29, 52, 68, 191, 195. *See also* unemployment; work

encounter theory, 76, 84–87, 228

endogamous family theory, 22, 133, 140–43, 230

Engfer, A., 52

environmental factors, 24, 27, 44, 46, 54, 156, 301

Erickson, E., 76, 77, 181

Erne, D., 7, 9, 17, 36, 298

Eron, L., 97

esteem needs, 125, 180

ethnicity, 43, 82, 184

ethnocentric biases, 115

ethnographic studies, 96

ethological studies, 90, 91, 123

etiological issues, 8, 9, 13, 16

Europe, 3, 47

evaluation, 9, 208, 224, 239, 244, 255, 259, 297, 300, 303, 308, 309

Evans, S. L., 34, 36

evolutionary perspective, 26, 47, 90, 92, 116, 120

exchange-control theory, 19, 45, 62–66, 108, 119, 228

existential perspectives, 15

exogamy, 119

exosystem, 181, 183, 205, 209, 216

experimentalism, 248

expert witnesses, 293–96

"explaining by naming" trap, 36, 71

exploitation, 43, 146, 167, 182

extended families/relations, 28, 30, 67, 75, 110, 148, 178

extramarital affairs, by incest fathers, 138

Fagan, J. A., 184

familial issues, 14, 24, 27, 40, 43, 46, 47, 52, 94, 144, 150, 183

family: characteristics, 23, 30, 43, 163, 168, 176; conflict, 28, 53, 55, 69, 141, 229; factors, 16, 19, 22–24, 36–37, 54, 69, 84, 105, 108, 142–45, 160, 167, 183, 223, 303; interactions, 28, 29, 41, 53, 57, 58, 62, 63, 75, 110, 153, 194, 196, 223; members, 28, 44, 84, 110; privacy, 45, 63, 64, 65, 86, 145, 148; problems, 51, 75, 90, 95, 130, 134–37; roles, 147, 194; separation, 44, 58, 177, 179; single-parent, 25, 57–58, 91, 102, 107, 193; size, 18, 22, 25, 28, 29, 55, 57, 68, 69, 91, 137, 176; structure, 4, 22, 29, 63, 67, 128, 134, 223; as unique institution, 27, 302; unit, 22, 23, 72, 135; values, 22, 28; violence, 27, 37, 45, 65, 98, 100, 127

family breakup theory, 177–80, 231

family survival theory, 133, 134–40, 230

family systems, 13, 22, 23, 28, 54, 72, 74–76, 126–27, 133, 155, 163, 177, 228, 230, 265, 267, 270, 272, 274, 275, 304, 305, 308, 309

Fanaroff, A., 112

fantasies, 15, 34

Fantuzzo, J., 87

Farrington, K., 66, 68, 69, 302

father-daughter: dyad, 145, 146, 150; incest, 22, 120, 134

Federal Child Abuse Prevention and Treatment Act, 7

Federal Children's Bureau, 4

feelings, 29, 36, 39, 55, 82, 178, 191

female offenders, 154, 164, 167–70, 231
feminist perspective, 8, 45, 140
Fenichel, D., 151
Feshbach, S., 302
Field, T., 88
financial problems, 42, 48, 100
Finkelhor, D., 14, 19, 20, 26, 36, 37, 47, 48, 58, 68, 69, 92, 93, 94, 120, 123, 129, 130, 131, 138, 149, 152, 153, 155, 156, 158, 159, 160, 161, 163, 164, 167, 169, 170, 277, 301, 312
Finnish study on aggression, 97
Fisher, G., 155
fixated child offenders, 21, 164–66
follow-up service domain, 239, 244, 304, 309
Fontana, V. J., 111
Fortier, R., 10, 203
foster care, 79
fourfold typology of family dissolution, 179
four preconditions theory, 19, 133, 160–64, 231, 277
Fox, G. L., 47, 121, 272
Fraczek, A., 97
France, 122
Freedman, D. A., 65, 111
French, C., 4, 9, 33, 79, 301
Freud, S., 152, 155, 181
Freund, K., 163
Friedman, P., 158
Friedrich, W. N., 64
Frisbie, L. V., 155
frustration, 17, 21, 22, 27, 34, 38, 42, 53, 68, 70, 95, 96, 98, 99, 104, 108, 174, 199, 200
frustration-aggression theory, 26, 48, 69, 71, 219

Gaines, R. W., 111
Galdston, R., 52
Garbarino, J., 6, 8, 25, 28, 29, 37, 90, 91, 92, 99, 103, 112, 149, 174, 176, 177, 184, 312
Gary, T., 152
Gebhard, P., 138

Gebhart, R., 159
Geis, G., 111
Geiser, R. I., 165
Gelardo, M. S., 42, 45, 95, 100
Gelles, R. J., 8, 22, 27, 35, 37, 42, 45, 47, 50, 51, 52, 53, 62, 63, 64, 75, 130, 194, 195, 196, 300, 301, 302, 312
general stress theory, 19, 66–69, 228
generational boundaries, in incest families, 138
genetic factors, 25, 90, 91, 97, 116, 118, 122, 223
Germain, R., 6, 176, 180, 181, 183, 312
Gestalt psychology, 248
Gil, D. G., 17, 41, 43, 44, 45, 52, 312
Giles-Sims, J., 26, 47, 48, 68, 69, 92–94, 120, 123, 301
Gillespie, W. H., 151
Giovannoni, J. R., 17, 41, 43, 44, 192
Glancy, E., 152
Glick, I. D., 72
Glueck, B. C., 151, 152, 163
Goldstein, M. J., 65, 163
Goode, W. J., 46, 47, 65, 111
Goodman, G. S., 95
Goodwin, J., 122
Gordon, M., 121, 123, 130
Gray, J. P., 99
Greece, 3, 26, 35; ancient, 118
Green, A. H., 20, 111
Griswold, B., 44
Groth, N. A., 20, 21, 152, 158, 164–67, 277
grounded theory, 143–50, 311
Gruber, A. R., 136
guilt feelings, 24, 27, 66, 86, 126, 137
Guttmann, H. A., 6, 8, 28, 29, 99, 153, 174, 176, 177, 184, 312

Hall, C. S., 95, 97, 152
Halperin, M., 7, 299
Hammer, R. F., 152
Hanner, L., 10, 203, 237
Hansen, K. V., 184
Harcourt, M., 3
Hargreaves, W. A., 63

Harlow, H., 23, 24, 55, 132
Harlow, M. K., 55, 132
Harris, M., 96
Hart, S., 6, 176, 180, 181, 183, 312
Hartman, J. J., 163
Haukes, G. R., 47
Havighurst, R., 181
Hawaii, 120
Headsten, S. V., 36
health care, 28, 44, 184
Heinicke, C. M., 77, 78, 92
Helfer, R. E., 4, 5, 49, 50
Henderson, J., 130
Henry, J., 97
Hepworth, J., 179
Herman, J., 58, 128, 129, 130, 139, 164
Herrenkohl, E. C., 88
Herrenkohl, R. C., 88
Hirschman, L., 58, 128
historical perspective, 3, 4, 14, 26, 29, 43, 45, 46, 110, 120, 128, 248, 297, 310
Hobson, T., 152
holding environment program, 79
holistic perspectives, 180
Holland, R. E., 3, 4
Holmes, T. H., 210, 302
Homans, G. C., 62
home environment, 192
homeostasis, 23, 75, 140
Hopi culture, 122
Horowitz, J. E., 97, 136, 142
hostility, 80, 81, 136, 153, 199
housing, 146, 176
Howells, J. G., 79, 90, 152, 155
Hrdy, S. B., 92
humanistic theory, 15, 17, 79, 125–27, 160, 230, 272
human nature, 25, 42, 94, 106, 119
human needs, basic, 17, 41, 42, 43, 125
Hunka, C. D., 49, 50
husband-wife relationship, 47, 78, 99, 111
Hutchinson, S., 159
hyperactivity, 19, 24, 30, 34, 38, 85, 111
hypothesis testing, 20, 250, 266, 282

identification of abuse, 238, 239, 242, 298, 303, 304
identification with aggressor, 137, 152, 168
idiosystem, 205, 209, 219, 223
illness, 42, 44, 61
immaturity, 34
immigration families, 203
impact, 4, 6–7, 9, 16, 66, 78, 79, 84, 85, 88, 89, 108, 109, 116, 127, 132, 138, 145, 147, 177, 179, 181, 230, 236, 293, 298
imprinting, 121
impulse control, 18, 23, 24, 36, 38, 51, 88, 155, 190, 191
impulsive, 19, 34, 38, 49, 50, 58, 176, 192, 193
incest, 22, 183, 301, 311; as aggression, 145; anxiety, 151; avoidance, 121, 132; barriers, 144; compared to extrafamilal sexual abuse, 166; envy, 142; family, 23, 137, 140, 230; as means of reducing tension, 141; myths, 116; offenders/perpetrators, 137, 159; responsibility for, 147; role of child, 139; taboo, 10, 115, 229, 231, 259, 271, 286, 288, 297; trauma, 158, 159; victims, 136, 137, 139, 146, 153
incestuous: brothers and uncles, 167; family structures, 140, 142; fathers, 23, 135, 138; stepfathers, 138
incident reports, 189. See also prevalence
inclusive fitness, 25, 90, 91
income, 17, 29, 42, 44, 46–48, 100, 105, 107, 149, 158, 163
individual determinants paradigm, 13–19, 33, 115, 125, 151, 189, 225, 229–32, 265, 266, 268, 270, 271–77, 280–81, 304–5
individual-environment interaction paradigm, 13, 19–20, 46, 115, 121, 131, 160, 193, 228–32, 265, 267, 271–72, 274, 276–77
individual factors, 14, 19, 20, 21–22, 28, 46, 70, 75, 160, 176, 273
inductive vs. deductive reasoning, 144, 250

inequality, 17, 18, 41, 43, 45, 46, 63–
  65, 97, 145–48, 158, 303
infanticide, 26, 118
infantilism, 190, 191, 192, 193
instinct theories, 15, 76, 91, 93, 94
institutional abuse, 21, 43, 70, 183, 238
intelligence, 21, 35, 46, 70, 97, 117,
  118, 191
intergroup conflict, 18, 42
internal inhibitation, 20, 161
International Conference on Psychological
  Abuse of Children and Youth, 183
international factors, 10, 40
interpersonal problems, 39, 42, 44, 62,
  95, 104
intervention, 8, 9, 17, 37, 39, 48, 53,
  56, 63, 65, 69, 72, 76, 94, 97, 120,
  127, 139, 140, 147, 148, 149, 155,
  164, 183, 184, 219, 238, 239, 241,
  242, 298, 300, 303, 305, 312
intrapsychic: dynamics, 41, 44, 134,
  136, 151, 153; theory, 15, 37–41, 228
Isaacs, C., 36
isolation, 20, 23, 49, 50, 104, 122, 174,
  182, 184, 190, 191, 195; of child,
  161; of family, 141, 177; social, 18,
  24, 28, 42, 44, 49, 50, 51, 86, 108,
  138, 148, 156, 176, 199
Israeli collective settlement, 122

Jackson, J. W., 247, 248, 250, 251, 253
Jacobsen, J. J., 9, 16, 20
Japan, 65, 111, 130
Jerry, M. B., 158
Jewish upbringing, 158
job loss, 195
Johnston, C., 101
Jones, E. S., 155
Judeo-Christian influences, 3
Justice, B., 68, 53–55, 115, 120, 139
Justice, R., 68, 53–55, 115, 120, 139
juveniles, 93, 244

Kadushin, A., 45
Kalang tribe (Java), 115
Kandel, D., 47
Kant, H. S., 163
Kantsmith, D., 136, 142

Kaplan, M. G., 89
Katan, A., 152
Katz, R., 47, 48
Kaufman, I., 135, 136
Kazdin, A. E., 88
Keller, H. R., 7, 9, 17, 36, 298
Kelly, J. B., 179
Kelly Repertory Grid, 155
Kempe, C. H., 4, 5, 16, 33, 34, 36, 190
Kempe, R., 16, 33
Kennell, J., 112
Keshet, J. H., 48
Kessler, D. R., 72
kibbutz children, 122
killing unfit children, 26. See also
  infanticide
Kinard, E. M., 36, 37
Kitahara, M., 80, 81, 223
Klaus, M., 112
Klein, M., 99
Kluft, R. P., 35
Koers, L., 58, 60, 197
Kohlberg, L., 59, 181, 199
Kohlberg's stages of moral reasoning, 58,
  197
Kokkevi, A., 35
Korbin, J., 92, 223
Krafft-Ebing, R., 154, 155
Kratcoski, P. C., 66, 95, 96
Kroers, A. J., 60
Kryso, J., 124
Kuffman, M., 22
Kurdek, L. A., 179
Kuttner, R. E., 92, 93

labeling of abuse, 36, 45, 74, 83
labor unions, 46
La Greca, A. M., 100, 101, 102, 103
Lana, R. E., 252
Landau, H. R., 181
Langevin, R., 155, 163
Lanyon, R. I., 155
Larrance, D. T., 89
Latin America, 45
learned helplessness, 35
learning: difficulties, 176, 179; processes,
  20, 94, 133, 153
learning/situation paradigm, 13, 26, 27,

94, 228, 265–67, 269, 270, 285, 304, 305, 308, 309

legal: issues/proceedings, 8, 29, 53, 96, 107, 108, 115, 120, 124, 148, 176–178, 224, 235–37, 293, 294, 296, 298; model/perspective, 3, 8, 242, 244; profession, 293–96; system, 14, 16, 17, 43, 45, 63

Lenoski, E. F., 112

Lesnik-Oberstein, M., 58, 60, 197

Lesser, G., 47

Lester, D., 35, 119, 120, 155

Levenson, E. A., 101

Levesley, S., 173

Lévi-Strauss, C., 118, 119

Lewinsohn, P. M., 36

Libet, J. M., 36

Liebert, R. M., 111

life events, 69, 210

Lindzey, G., 95, 97

Lobb, M. L., 48

locus of control, 27, 58, 101, 103, 179, 192

Locus of Control Scales, 101

Loeber, R., 102

Loening, W. E. K., 223

Loevinger, J., 37

loneliness, 42, 190

longitudinal analysis, 6, 9, 79, 84, 149, 245

Lorenz-Tinbergen ethological school, 91, 93

Lourie, M. D., 8

love needs, 125, 180, 203

Lunkanowicz, N., 136

Lustig, N., 22, 129, 134, 135, 136, 137, 138, 153

Lutier, J., 122

Lynch, M. A., 33

Lystad, M. H., 36

MacMurray, V. D., 192

macrosystem, 83, 84, 109, 120, 174, 181, 183, 205, 209, 216

Maden, M. F., 50

Maisch, H., 115, 129, 155, 164

male-accompanied abusers, 169

male-coerced abusers, 168

male-oriented culture, 96. *See also* patriarchal perspective

Malinowski, B., 119

maltreatment domains, 183

Manyard, P. E., 22, 75

marital: characteristics, 60, 67, 77, 78, 97, 120; conflict/discord, 29, 34, 39, 44, 51, 55, 105, 111, 123, 126, 128, 146, 176, 177, 199; relationship, 19, 144; status, 58, 82

marriages, nonconsanguineous, 116

Maroulis, H., 34

Martin, J., 9, 37, 45, 86, 99, 179, 298

Marvasti, J., 170

masculine identity, 18, 23, 74, 135, 156

Mash, E. J., 89, 101

Maslow, A., 125, 180

Massachusetts, 129

mass media, 65, 68, 74, 79, 94, 104, 111, 145, 148, 225, 245

masturbation, 167

material acquisition, 43

maternal perceptions, 78, 82, 83

Mathews, R., 167, 169, 170

Mathias, B., 9, 45

maximum profit theory, 106

May, W. H., 212

Mayes, P., 15, 125, 126, 127

McCarty, D., 170

McCord, J., 6

McCreary, C. P., 155

McDonald, G. W., 107

meaning systems, 204

measurement, 8, 36, 210

medical, 8, 14, 184, 301; history of parents, 61; model, 33, 45, 154, 242

Mehta, M. N., 184

Meiselman, K. C., 155

Melton, G. B., 64

mental: cruelty, 183; health, 8, 76, 244; illness, 21, 34, 44, 54, 70, 168

Merrill, E. J., 112

methodology, 10, 16, 20, 36, 48, 58, 83, 100, 103, 140–43, 148–49, 153, 160, 176, 197, 209, 250, 269, 277, 282, 284, 287–88, 300–304

microsystem, 181, 183, 205, 209, 216, 223, 229

middle class, 46
Middleton, R., 115
mildly abusive family, 29, 178
Milner, J. S., 92, 101
minimax strategy, 62
minitheories, 30, 112
minority elite, 18
Miron, M. S., 212
mismanagement of national resources, 18
mitigating factors, 147
MMPI, 155
modeling, 26, 74, 95, 183, 266
moderately abusive family, 29, 178
Mohr, I. W., 158
Monahan, U., 111
Monroe, R. H., 96
Monroe, R. L., 96
Montageau, A., 26, 93
moral development, 19, 142, 180, 181
Mormons, 115
Morse, C., 111
Moser, C., 88
motivation, 95, 161
motor excess, 102
Mrazek, P. J., 34
Muldoon, L., 138
Mulhern, L., 50
multidimensional interactions, 57
multidisciplinary approaches, 7, 9, 13,
    217, 239, 245, 301
multigenerational view, 137
multilevel theory, 108–12, 228
multiple personality disorder, 35
Munroe, R. L., 65, 96
murder, 74
Murdoch, G., 115
Myers, D. G., 15, 36, 96, 97

national incidence study, 5, 7
natural selection, 24, 90
nature-nurture debate, 93
Neale, J. M., 111
need for power, 146
Neel, A., 252
Neel, J. V., 116, 272
Neff, R. L., 20, 58, 143, 144, 145, 146,
    147, 148, 149, 155, 184, 273
neglect, 3, 4, 5, 6, 25, 35, 44, 70, 298,
    313; children of, 196; paradigm analy-
sis, 280; prevalence of types, 5, 7,
    189; psychosemantic analysis, 231–32
neglectful parents, 196; compared to
    abusing parents, 197; compared to
    non-neglectful parents, 192; education
    of, 193; emotional state of, 191
neighborhood: factors, 29, 104, 144,
    145, 149, 150, 174, 176, 192; levels
    of crime, 29
neighbors, 22, 28, 63, 75, 107, 110
neurosis, 152
Newberger, C., 14, 16, 28, 35, 36, 37,
    104, 105, 153, 184
Newberger, E. H., 14, 16, 28, 35–37,
    45, 99, 104, 105, 153, 184
newborn behavioral assessment, 82, 83
New York State, 112
Niem, T. C., 65, 111
nonabusive families, 29, 177, 197
nonorganic failure to thrive, 60, 81, 200
nonparticipant family members of incest,
    23, 136, 137
nonpathological characteristics of per-
    petrator, 58
nonpsychopathological sexual offenders,
    154
normative theory, 69, 108, 115, 118–21,
    229
norms, 38, 97; family, 68, 74, 108, 129;
    privacy, 99; real man, 63; reciprocal, 62;
    social, 15, 21, 43, 45, 63, 65, 68, 70,
    74, 94, 99, 118, 145, 147, 214, 223
North Brazil, 96
Nurse, S. M., 112
nursing, 8, 112, 217
nurturing activities, 49, 123
Nye, F. I., 28, 106, 107

objective culture, 203, 204, 208, 209,
    218, 223, 229, 231, 299, 312; stress,
    59, 199
observational learning, 94, 95
occupation, 22, 43, 47, 48, 52, 78
Ochiltree, G., 179
oedipal conflicts, 136, 142, 151, 153
offender typologies, 13, 20–22, 69, 164–
    67, 228, 231, 265, 267, 277, 304,
    308, 309
Oliver, A., 35, 36

operant conditioning, 26, 94
operational definitions, 20, 266, 282
Oppong, C., 47
organic brain dysfunction, 33
organization of work and production, 42
Oriental households, 65
Osgood, C. E., 212
Osgood Laboratory for Cross-Cultural
    Research, 10
outer-directedness, 78
outside agencies, 63
Ovaschel, H., 89
overestimation of children's capabilities,
    107

Panton, J. H., 165
paradigm evaluation, 255–81
parent aides, 184
parental: anger-proneness, 53; awareness
    of children's cognitive development,
    105; conflict, 29, 30, 178, 179; expecta-
    tions, 99, 107, 199; feelings, 92; history
    of sexual abuse, 142; incompetence, 21,
    72; inconsistency, 101; investment, 25,
    90, 91; rejection, relation to delinquen-
    cy, 6; relations, 51, 53, 127, 161, 178,
    223; rights, 45; role, 28, 81, 104;
    thinking, 21, 28, 70, 72, 104
parental acceptance-rejection: question-
    naire, 81; theory, 23, 76, 79, 80, 81,
    228
parent-child: attitudes, 61; conflict, 86,
    104; interaction paradigm, 13, 23, 24,
    76, 228, 267, 304, 305, 308, 309;
    interactions, 11, 23, 24, 27, 53, 54,
    57, 76, 84, 88, 90, 100, 103, 110,
    111, 223, 265, 270; perceptions, 174;
    physical contacts, 57; relationship, 24,
    49, 76, 80, 81, 95, 107, 194–97; role
    reversal, 49, 178
parenting, 22; costs vs. rewards, 64;
    group, 184; skills, 27, 34, 46, 57, 58,
    71, 82, 100, 103, 111, 176, 194, 195,
    224
Parents Anonymous, 50, 237
Parke, R., 8, 28, 50, 99, 108, 109, 110,
    111, 112, 155
Parker, H., 92, 93, 121, 122, 123, 132,
    133, 155, 272, 273, 312

Parker, S., 92, 93, 121, 122, 123, 132,
    133, 155, 272, 273, 312
Parsons, T., 119
participatory gerontocracy, 153
passive-dependent type family, 166
passivity, 49
Passman, R. H., 50
paternal energies, 25
pathological profiles, 35, 68, 136, 190,
    193, 195, 301
Patria Protestas, 3
patriarchal perspective, 18, 23, 127–31,
    137, 142, 147, 148, 156
Patterson, G. R., 26, 102
payday effect, 48
payoff of abusive behavior, 38
Peck, A., 22, 135
Pedersen, F. A., 111
pedophiles, 152, 163, 169
Pelton, L. H., 18, 45
penis envy, 153
Pennsylvania, 57
Penrod, S., 94, 95
perceived investment vs. returns, 64
perceptions related to abuse, 19, 29, 49,
    174, 177
Peres, Y., 47, 48
perpetrator, characteristics, 14, 15, 16,
    19, 21, 24, 33, 34, 39, 44, 48, 50,
    53, 54, 65, 81, 151, 169, 176, 301
personalistic theory, 232, 189, 190–93,
    280
personality, 15–16, 20–22, 33–37, 51–
    54, 60, 70, 76, 84, 93, 100, 108, 131,
    151–52, 155, 168, 174, 178, 190–92,
    195, 219
Peru, ancient, 120
phylogenetic factors, 24, 90, 116, 123,
    132
physical abuse, 5, 7, 10, 15, 17, 19, 20,
    21, 22, 23, 24, 25, 27, 28, 29, 35,
    168, 169, 190, 200, 267, 269, 270,
    297, 298, 302, 311; association with
    sexual abuse, 132, 137, 138, 156; dif-
    ferential community rates, 176; evalua-
    tion of theories, 225; psychosemantic
    analysis, 225–29; related to psycholog-
    ical maltreatment, 173; relation to ne-
    glect, 197; typology, 20, 70–74

physical dysfunction, 55, 85, 176
physicalistic conceptions of child, 104
physiological needs, 90, 125, 180
Piaget, J., 181
Pierce, R. L., 148
Pilaga (culture), 97
Planned Parenthood, 53
plasticity of human behavior, 26, 93
Plotkin, R., 89
Polansky, N. A., 190, 191, 192, 193, 197
police, 45, 63, 96, 107, 148
Polish-Finnish study, 97
political factors, 8, 17, 43, 45, 68, 128, 174
Pollock, C., 49, 50
Polynesian cultures, 118
pornography, 18, 148, 156, 159, 182, 183
positive feedback, 74
Post, S., 72, 75
post hoc studies, 36
postnatal development, 59, 61, 78, 199
postseparation families, 178
postulations, 266, 282
poverty, 17, 18, 25, 30, 43, 44, 53, 78, 82, 84, 92, 104, 108, 138, 176, 177, 184, 190, 191
power, 35, 38, 46, 47, 64, 104–5, 146–47
prebirth parental personality, 77, 78
precipitating factors, 22, 194
preconventional cognitive-developmental level of morality, 59, 199
prediction, 83, 300
predisposing factors, 167, 223
pregnancy, 82, 112, 146, 199; unwanted, 30, 44, 52
prejudice, 183
premarital sexual intercourse, 120
prematurity, 19, 20, 25, 61, 64, 85, 91, 99, 111, 112
prenatal care, 20, 30, 59, 83, 100, 112, 199
preschool children/teachers, 78
prestige, 47
Preston, G., 28, 29, 103, 177, 179
prevalence, 4–7, 9, 17, 52, 74, 93, 145, 189, 219; age correlates, 64; aggres-
sion, 145; child sexual abuse, 156, 159, 230; incest, 116, 147, 230; in Japan and China, 111; neglect, 193; stepfamilies vs. biological, 92. See also incident reports
prevention, 4, 8, 9, 13, 17, 37, 40, 43, 53, 63, 64, 71, 83, 84, 93, 97, 98, 124, 149, 176, 179, 180, 183, 184, 200, 239, 241, 244, 245, 300, 303, 304, 308, 312, 314; of incest, 129, 136, 147, 148; of psychological maltreatment, 180, 184; of sexual abuse, 158, 164
principle of distributive justice, 62
private clinics, 299
problem solving, 50, 51
profile characteristics, 35, 242
prognoses of child sexual abusers, 167
programs, 100, 127, 237, 244, 303, 304, 309
projected emotional needs, 20
Project Interact, 57, 58
propertied minority, 42
propertyless majority, 42
prosecutors, 63, 127
prosocial behaviors, 17, 97
prostitution, 183
protection agencies, 110
protective instinct, 93
pseudomaturity, 23, 137, 179
psychiatric: disorder, 8, 29, 30, 33, 36, 179, 219; theory, 15–17, 33–37, 53, 151, 193, 225, 231, 242; theory of physical abuse, 33, 37–41; theory of sexual abuse, 154–56
psychoanalytic: perspective, 15, 21–22, 134, 149, 153, 155, 164, 275; theory, 15, 17, 151–53, 231
psychodynamic, 75; analyses, 51, 54, 75, 140, 190; characteristics of incestuous family, 141–42
psychological, 8, 301; disturbance, 169, 231; factors, 13, 19, 26, 53, 57–58, 140, 156, 167; law, 302; maltreatment, 6, 8, 28–30, 35, 79–80, 97, 173, 183–85, 231–32, 278, 280, 284, 287, 288, 297; needs, 42, 181; neglect,

181; pathology of sexual abuse, 155; resources, 105; testimony, 296; testing of the offenders, 169
psychopathology, 15, 19, 22, 34, 37, 51–52, 60, 72, 151, 154–55, 168, 194, 195, 219, 308
psychosemantic process model, 203–8, 217, 218, 225, 233–42, 245, 298, 299
psychosexual development, 152, 181, 231
psychosocial: development, 180, 181; system model, 53, 54, 56; themes delineated by theories, 219
psychosomatic symptoms, 179, 190
public: agencies, 7, 149, 238, 299; awareness, 148; clinics, 299; service, 147; standards about sexual contact, 130
punishment, 3, 4, 19, 22, 27, 52, 53, 55, 65, 96, 98, 100, 105, 106, 108, 110, 111, 146, 194, 237; corporal, 42, 105, 184; methods, 127, 229; vs. reward, 65

Quay, H. C., 102
question of blame, 56
Quinsey, V. L., 163

racial minorities, 184
Radbill, A., 3
Rahe, R. H., 210, 302
rape, 18, 183
rationalizations for abuse, 16, 35, 38, 136
Redfield, D., 120
regressed child sexual offenders, 21, 165, 167, 169
Reid, J. B., 102
Reidy, T. J., 153
rejection cycle, 80, 182
relative deprivation, 69
relatives, 107, 192
religious factors, 4, 156, 300
remarriage, 18, 156
removal of child from home, debate, 79
replication of findings, 250
repression, 21

reproductive success, 91
research issues, 253, 298, 300–302
resistance by child, 161
Resnick, E. H., 52
resource: base, 19, 25, 26, 42, 46, 92; theory, 46–48, 94, 228
Revised Behavior Problem Checklist, 101
Richardson, C. M., 15, 37
Riemer, S., 138
rights of children, 108, 176
Rigler, D., 35, 36, 300
risk factors, 25, 27, 29, 30, 47, 64, 69, 82, 84, 92, 95, 102, 104; incest, 128, 142, 149, 158; neglect, 191; psychological maltreatment, 176; sexual abuse, 158
Rist, K., 119, 153
Rohner, R. P., 24, 79, 81, 223
Rohrbeck, C. A., 192, 196
role: confusion, 23, 140; expectation, 74; models, 195; reversal, 23, 50, 59, 105, 136, 138, 139, 199
Romans, 3, 26
Rosenberg, M. S., 89, 95, 97
Rovine, M., 76
Rubinstein, B. B., 125
rural background, 158, 163
Rush, F., 128, 129, 148
Russell, B., 3
Russell, D., 9, 18, 20, 37, 138, 156, 158, 159, 160, 165, 166, 167, 169, 170, 312
Rutter, N., 132

safety needs, 125, 180
Sahler, 111
Salter, A. C., 15, 37–39
Sameroff, A. J., 23
sampling errors, 300
Sandgrund, A., 111
Sandler, J., 83
Sanford, E. E., 42, 45, 95
San Francisco, 159
Sardoff, R. L., 179
Scanzoni, J., 47
Schaller, G. B., 92
Scher, M., 159

Schetky, D. H., 20
Schilling, R. G., 88
schizophrenia, 219
Schneewind, K., 52
Schneider, G., 49, 50
school, 21, 70, 77, 176, 179, 183, 184, 244
Schuerman, J. R., 58
Schull, W. J., 116
Schultz, N. W., 136
scientific: methodology, 53, 247–52, 275, 300, 311; theories, 248–53
Sclare, A. B., 52
Seagull, E. A., 192
seductive role, 16, 129
Seeley, J. W., 6, 8, 28, 29, 99, 174, 176, 177, 184, 312
Segall, M. H., 97
Segner, L. L., 116
self-actualization, 42, 125, 127, 180, 184
self-anger, 39
self-centered, 34
self-concept, 29, 36, 74, 100, 125, 126, 190
self-esteem, 15, 16, 24, 35, 36, 46, 48, 50, 51, 77, 78, 81, 85, 125–26, 155, 168, 174, 179, 199
self-identified abusers, 60
selfishness, as positive attribute, 43
self-protective stage of development, 38, 39
self-victimization, 238
Semai of Malaya, 96
semantic differential, 155
service areas, 7, 9, 72, 83, 176, 184, 189, 235, 239, 242
seven service domains, 42, 239, 242–45, 303
severely abusive family, 30, 178
severity of reported cases, 5
sex, 43, 48, 86, 195; education, 147; roles, 68; as valuable commodity, 160; of victims, 52, 153, 166
Sexual: abusers, 20, 132, 133, 154, 155, 163, 165; aggression, 166; arousal,

161, 163–64; avoidance mechanism, 121; compared to nonsexual forms of affection, 158; development, 167; division of labor, 128, 129; drive, 121, 161; harassment, 18; inequality, 63, 65, 145; knowledge, 20; orientation, 158, 219, 155; promiscuity, 34; relations between parents, 23; revolution, 156; seduction, 35
sexual abuse, 5, 8, 10, 16, 17, 18, 19, 21, 23, 58, 71, 75, 86, 90, 93, 183, 231, 237, 276, 277, 278, 288, 297, 298, 301, 302, 313; by boyfriends, 156; counterinhibitors, 161; higher rates by men, 65, 158; related to psychological maltreatment, 173; by stepfathers, 159; as tension-reduction mechanism, 137
sexuality, 18, 156, 158, 168
sexualization of power, 158
Sgroi, S. M., 135, 158
Shay, S., 149
shelters, 148
Shengold, L., 152
Shepher, J., 121, 122
Sherman, D., 149
Sherrod, D., 94, 96
Shull, J. V., 272
shyness, 35, 161
siblings, 84, 96, 179
Sidel, R., 65, 111
sim-pua marriage, 121, 123
situational: abusers, 70; /contextual factors, 21, 24, 27, 36, 52, 53, 68, 70, 71, 86, 105, 133, 161; stress, 42, 51, 52, 54; theory, 98–100, 228, 244
slapping, 37, 80
slavery, 43
small-scale societies, 116
Smith, S. L., 8, 35
social: agencies, 24, 176, 177; class, 18, 29, 43, 52, 53, 110; consequences, 23, 27, 63, 208, 299; control, 19, 63, 64, 75, 96, 107, 159; development, 183; deviance, 55; exchange theory, 27, 62, 100; factors, 17, 20, 44–45, 53, 54–

55, 60, 68, 118, 120, 133, 145, 190, 191; forms of child abuse, 43; habitability, 173, 174; influences of neglect, 191; institutional consequences, 214–16, 224, 225; institutions, 45, 107, 214, 216; interaction model, 193; interaction theory, 19, 56–58, 189, 194–97, 228, 232, 280; learning theory, 26, 94–98, 133, 228, 242; networks, 104; policies, 64; position, 51, 195; processes, 128; programs, 4, 127, 235, 239, 309; psychological perspective, 19, 26, 98, 99, 302; psychological theory, 51–53, 228; redesign, 42, 45; relationships, 112; resources, 47, 174; Security Act, 4; skills, 16, 47, 57, 78, 93, 161, 167, 219; status, 184; stigma of abortion, 53; structure, 42, 63, 177, 223; support, 57, 67, 82, 110, 112, 145, 147, 148, 174, 176, 192, 223; systems, 28, 43, 45–47, 103, 173, 174, 179; systems theory, 17, 41–46, 228; values, 118; work, 4, 23, 74, 127, 217

Social Adjustment Rating Scale, 210

socialization: factors, 18, 28, 42, 51, 67, 72, 77, 93, 96, 97, 107, 108, 110, 132, 194, 195; of male sexuality, 18, 130, 156, 158; theory, 17, 156–60, 231, 276

socially and parentally incompetent abusers, 70

society, 3, 4, 6, 14, 17, 28, 37, 42, 53, 54, 67, 93, 97, 103, 104, 105, 106, 107, 119, 124, 130, 143, 144, 145, 148, 149, 150, 153, 160, 181, 183, 184, 194, 204, 205, 214, 215, 230, 235, 305, 308, 309

Society for the Protection of Cruelty to Animals, 4

Society for the Protection of Cruelty to Children, 4

sociobiological: factors, 116, 120, 265, 270; paradigm, 13, 24, 25, 90, 93, 228, 267, 304, 305, 308, 309; theory, 47, 69, 90–94

sociobiological-sociopsychological continuum, 13

sociocultural: determinants paradigm, 13, 17–19, 41, 115, 118, 127, 156, 228, 229, 230, 231, 265, 267, 269, 271, 272, 274, 275, 277, 304, 305, 308, 309; factors, 3, 17, 18, 19, 22, 23, 27–29, 41, 43, 45, 63, 94, 97, 103, 104, 110, 116, 118, 129, 145, 153, 156, 177, 181, 183, 205, 217, 305

socioeconomic: factors, 44, 145, 192; status, 11, 18, 19, 42, 44, 45, 47, 51, 57, 69, 78, 90, 91, 147, 149, 160, 174, 195, 303

sociological: factors, 8, 19, 26, 36, 40, 41, 46, 52, 53, 58, 140, 156; foundations, 57; paradigm, 44

sociopathic disorders, 195

South Africa, 45

South Venezuela, 96

spanking, 64, 65, 100, 111, 199. *See also* punishment

Specktor, P., 148

Spinetta, J. J., 35, 36, 300

spouse abuse, 65, 75, 105

Sroufe, L. A., 76

Starr, R. H., 89, 153

Steele, B. F., 4, 33, 36, 140, 190

Stefano, L., 8

Steinmetz, S. K., 72, 111

stepfamilies, 25–26, 47–48, 68, 91–94, 96, 120, 122–24, 129, 132, 156, 158–59, 301

stereotyping, 190

Stern, L., 99

Stevens, M., 159

Stevens-Long, J., 112

Stewart, K. V., 184

stimulation deprivation, 183

Storr, A., 152

Strasburg, P. A., 66

Straus, M. A., 7, 22, 27, 45, 47, 64, 68, 72, 74, 75, 302

stress, 20, 26, 27, 29, 50, 51–53, 64, 66, 67, 100, 176, 302; coping, 48, 97;

stress (*continued*)
  experienced, 59, 199; factors, 21, 51, 58, 68, 81, 82, 167, 195; family response capabilities, 67; individual response capabilities, 67; management, 100; psychological, 57, 123, 168; seven components, 66; social, 17, 23, 29, 37, 44, 49, 57, 110, 86, 123; theory, 47, 68, 81, 94; vulnerability, 68
stressors, 17, 29, 50, 54, 57, 242; family, 11, 24, 28, 55, 82, 99, 105, 108, 137, 176, 223; long-term, 153, 208, 210, 215, 224, 242, 299; short-term, 16, 208, 210–13, 215, 224, 299; triggering, 27, 153
Stringer, S. A., 100, 101, 102, 103
subcultural: abusers, 70; factors, 21, 42, 51, 144, 194, 195, 303; groups, 214; male, 129; norms/values, 29, 40, 68, 70, 86, 94; of violence, 19, 21, 52, 71, 145, 184
subjective: culture, 184, 203, 204, 209, 210, 214, 218, 223, 229, 231, 299; speculation, 300
substance abuse, 15, 16, 18, 20, 35, 42, 59, 63, 68, 155, 169, 176, 183, 199
Succop, R. A., 36
suicide, 42, 212
summative-induction form, 248
Summit, R., 124
superego, 147
supporting baseline characteristic, 207, 215
support systems, 22, 24, 28, 29, 42, 46, 104, 109, 111, 127, 176, 191, 232
survival motivations, 25, 90
susceptibility to exposure, 223
Swan, R. W., 120, 139, 158
Swedish culture, 81
symbiosis theory, 19, 53–56, 228
systems: of family, environment and culture, 54; offenders, 236; theory, 22, 23, 55, 72, 74, 75, 139, 140, 228
Szasz, T., 36

Tagiuri, G. E., 22, 135
Taiwan, 65, 111, 122, 123

Taylor, D., 47, 76
teachers, 65. *See also* education factors; school
television, 4, 97
theoretical issues, 8–10, 20, 247–48, 250–53, 255, 259, 266, 282, 284, 287, 298, 300, 310–12
therapists, 45, 74, 127
therapy/therapeutic issues, 37, 53, 75, 79, 129, 139, 167, 301
Thomas, C., 4
three-factor theory, 19, 48–50, 58–62, 189, 193, 197–200, 228, 232, 280
Tisza, V., 136, 142
Toby, J., 63
Toobert, S., 155
transactional theory, 55, 56, 76, 81–84, 142, 228
transfamilial roles, 119
transmission of cultural attitudes to parental behavior, 112
treatment, 4, 8, 9, 13, 14, 17, 21, 38–40, 53, 64, 70, 71, 97, 100, 102, 125, 126, 127, 130, 138–40, 153, 160, 167, 169, 170, 179, 180, 237, 239, 241, 244, 299, 300, 301, 303, 305–8, 312
triad of interactions, 54
Trivers, R. L., 91
trust, in offender, 20, 77
Turner, R. E., 158
Twentyman, C. T., 87, 89, 192, 196, 197
Tzeng, O. S. C., 9, 10, 36, 71, 203, 211, 237, 242, 247, 248, 250, 251, 253, 296, 303, 312

United States, 4, 43, 46, 47, 130
unconscious processes, 15, 17, 22, 75, 136, 151, 153
unemployment, 17, 42, 44, 51, 104, 174, 176, 177, 184, 194, 195
unicausal theories, 300
unknowing abusers, 70
unrealistic expectations, 34, 50, 176
U.S. culture, 4, 43, 46–47, 52, 64–66, 68, 130, 148

U.S. Department of Health and Human Services, 5, 7
Utah state legislature, 115

validity difficulties, 8
Vallois, H. V., 3
value systems, 51, 97, 180
Van den Berghe, P. L., 121
Vander Mey, B. J., 20, 58, 143, 144, 145, 146–49, 155, 184, 273
Van Stolk, M., 111
victim of abuse, 23, 70, 71, 74, 75, 136, 137, 168; characteristics, 19, 21, 23, 24, 38, 40, 49, 53, 54, 57, 58, 72, 81, 86, 97, 105, 109, 133
Vietze, P. M., 23, 82, 83, 92, 312
violence, 18, 22, 26, 29, 35, 37, 41, 42, 43, 45, 46, 49, 51, 63, 92, 93, 95, 97, 107, 178, 183, 195, 212, 215, 229, 303; elicitors of parental, 99; to gain power in family, 48; and mental illness link, 36; perpetrated by abused vs. nonabused youth, 96; and sexual abuse, 169; social, 18, 23, 43, 145; sports, 68; tolerance of, 23, 148
Virkkunen, M., 155
vocational skills, 191
Vondra, J., 176

Wallerstein, J. S., 179
Walters, D. R., 9, 20, 21, 69, 70, 71, 86, 298
war, 93, 183
Ware, R., 9
Waters, D. R., 76, 86
Watkins, H. D., 7, 299

Watts, D. L., 159
Weghorst, S. J., 91
Weiner, I., 129, 164
Weis, K., 159
Welch, G. J., 89
Westermarck, E., 121, 131, 132, 272
Westermarck hypothesis, 121, 123
Western culture, 65, 214
West German families, 52
White, R. B., 58, 119, 120, 181
White House Conference on Children, 4
wife beating, 65. *See also* spouse abuse
Wiggins, J. A., 26, 27, 98, 99, 100
Will, D., 140, 141, 142
Wilson, E. O., 25, 90
Wilson, M., 91, 92
withdrawal, 24, 179, 240
Wolf, A. P., 121, 122, 123, 272
Wolfe, D. A., 5, 170
Wooley, P. V., 34
woozle effect, 300
work, 42, 44, 104, 129, 183. *See also* employment
workshops, 302
world view, 38, 40, 81
Wright, L., 36
Wulkan, D., 120

Yanomamo, 96
Yorukoglu, A., 142
Young, L., 99, 112

Zalba, S., 52
Zecevic, A., 47
Zillmann, D., 159
Zimrin, H., 23, 24, 84, 85, 86

ABOUT THE AUTHORS

OLIVER C. S. TZENG is a professor of psychology at Indiana University–Purdue University at Indianapolis. He is also director of the Osgood Laboratory for Cross-Cultural Research, director of the Graduate Applied Social Psychology program, executive director of the Consortium of Child Abuse and Neglect Resources and Information Services, and director of the Multidisciplinary Graduate Training Program on Child Abuse and Neglect. Tzeng has developed many theories and models for research, training, and service programs and has written over 100 scientific articles, books, and training manuals. His most recently published books include: *Sourcebook for Child Abuse and Neglect; AIDS: Incurable Disease with Curable Epidemics* (in Chinese); *Love's I-Ching and Vectors: Conspiracy, Conflict, Resolution, Harmony and Fraternity* (in Chinese); and *Language, Meaning and Culture* (Praeger, 1990), which he coedited with Professor Charles E. Osgood.

JAY W. JACKSON is a research associate of the Osgood Laboratory for Cross-Cultural Research. As assistant director of the Osgood Laboratory, he has made significant contributions to various research projects involving topics such as the etiology and prevention of child maltreatment; interethnic hostility; interpersonal aggression; family conflict resolution; methodological frameworks for theory construction and evaluation; and prevention of and intervention in child abuse and neglect.

HENRY C. KARLSON, a professor of law at Indiana University School of Law, is chairman of the faculty advisory committee of the Multidisciplinary Graduate Training Program on child maltreatment at Indiana University–Purdue University at Indianapolis. He offered the first law course in Indiana dealing with child abuse and neglect and has been active in legal educational programs relating to that topic. With his interest in and knowledge of comparative law and history at the intercultural and international levels, Professor Karlson has made significant contributions to evaluation of child abuse and neglect issues from legal and historical perspectives.